# The Maxims of Politics

*Making Government Work*

Thomas S. Mullikin

Vox Populi Publishers, LLC
100 North Tryon Street, Suite 4700
Charlotte, NC 28202-4003

10 9 8 7 6 5 4 3 2 1

ISBN    978-0-9790178-8-9
           978-0-9790178-9-6

Copyright © 2009 by Vox Populi Publishers, LLC

All rights reserved. No part of this publication may be reproduced, stored in a retrieval system, or transmitted in any form or by any means, electronic, mechanical, photocopy, recording, or otherwise, without the prior written permission of the publisher.

Printed in the United States of America.

# Contents

**Foreword** — v

**Introduction** — 3

**Maxim 1** — Don't assume a losing position and try to turn it around. Assume the winning position, stay on message and bring them around. — 7

**Maxim 2** — Identifiable tasks with identifiable goals will lead to identifiable progress. — 75

**Maxim 3** — Assume the moral high ground early and make your opponent knock you off. — 125

**Maxim 4** — Exchange fire when fired upon. — 153

**Maxim 5** — Plan your work and work your plan, but remain fluid. — 191

**Maxim 6** — Politics is a game best played on the ground. — 239

**Maxim 7** — Document and demonstrate support to build third-party credibility. — 281

**Maxim 8** — Absolute truth applied absolutely is absolutely persuasive. — 321

**Maxim 9** — The genius is not in the idea; it is in the implementation of the idea. — 367

**Maxim 10**    Politics is like a game of marbles . . . he who has a bigger pile at the end of the game wins.    403

# Foreword

In the late 1970s and early 80s, I had the good fortune of studying political science under two of the sharpest political minds of their generation—one a Democrat and one a Republican. Dr. Don Fowler would lead the Democratic National Committee under President Clinton. Lee Atwater would go on to run the successful campaign of Ronald Reagan and Chair the Republican National Committee under President Reagan.

During my studies at the University of South Carolina, both men impressed on me the need to start any effort with a well-reasoned campaign plan—a plan that enveloped the best science, the best political intelligence and the best methods of organization. Their advice was sound and their tactics were keen. They taught me, as the legendary Chinese master military strategist Sun Tzu once said, that "[t]he general who wins a battle makes many calculations in his temple before the battle is fought."

Reminiscent of Sun Tzu's words, it is critical to work from a very specific and detailed plan of action. Atwater was the master at controlling the dialogue of a campaign. His genius was grounded not just in his well-honed instincts regarding message and timing but also in his dedication to making sure he had a thoroughly developed campaign plan.

In many ways, successful campaigns are designed to control the pace and substance of a campaign. Atwater's insightful design allowed him to choose his battlefields and select issues that would sharply distinguish his candidate from the opponent. (Readers might remember the Willie Horton ad, which created "sharp distinction" in the George H.W. Bush and Dukakis race in 1988.) Lee boasted that he read Machiavelli's pragmatic guide to the exercise of raw political power in *The Prince* at least twice a year, but I see his political paradigm as being closer to that of Sun Tzu's, as laid out in the *Art of War*.

I have had the immense pleasure of working for brilliant lawyers, politicians, campaign managers, engineers and business leaders. These leaders were smart enough to understand that very complex issues are built upon simple foundations. What has been most interesting to me is that even the most complicated applications in mathematics, physics, or natural science are built upon simple formulas. From $E=MC^2$ to deoxyribonucleic acid (DNA), life's mysteries are being solved with the genius of simple formulas.

Not unlike the natural sciences, the social sciences of politics and issue management are also directed by simple formula. Guided by recent examples of simple concepts, such as Bill Clinton's "Its the Economy Stupid" or Ronald Reagan's "Mr. Gorbachev, tear down this wall!", societies have changed and initiatives have been won. So what rules have been used to win these wars and advance the winning initiatives?

While some have advanced complex theories of wedge politics and complex statistical analysis of economic, racial, and demographic cross-tabulations, our work in governmental and public affairs is a little easier to understand if not more difficult to apply. By understanding the basic rules of social engineering and political mechanics—breaking them down into the simple concepts—the more sophisticated statistical theories can be applied with greater ease.

However, no matter how well grounded are one's plans, I have been constantly reminded that there is little genius in an idea "un-applied." The true brilliance of an idea is in its implementation. Was the genius of the non-confrontation strategies employed by Martin Luther King, Jr. and Mahatma Gandhi in the idea or in its execution? Was the enormity of General George S. Patton's success due solely to his plan or was it in his dogged execution? When Moses came down from Mt. Sinai with his rules for life, were the commandments sanctified for their complex and shining brilliance or were they recognized as challenging in their application and execution?

While I would be the first to add my voice to the chorus that recognizes the brilliance of a well-conceived strategy, a glib and timely political retort, or a contemplative and reasoned understanding of acute statistical analysis, I would also be quick to add that success will only result from the implementation of the concept. As the old adage says: "Plan your work, and work your plan."

Many years of experience in countless campaigns across the United States and at various venues around the world have led to the development and testing of my ten maxims of politics. The simple rules expounded upon in this treatise are a collection of the ten maxims that have helped me meet various political and issue management challenges in order to make government work for me and my clients.

I also must credit those who have helped develop these maxims into a coherent statement of my purpose and intent. This work would not have been possible without the tireless efforts of my Government, Policy and Regulatory Affairs team at our law firm, Moore & Van Allen, PLLC. In particular, I would like to thank my friend and colleague Todd Muldrew, whose constant support and encouragement made this work possible. Todd has earned the title "Wizard" on our team as a fountain of knowledge in legal and political affairs. At Todd's side during much of the research and editing for this text was Joel Groves. Joel brought a lifetime of pertinent experiences, which added great weight to our book. Finally, I am eternally grateful to our research team, which included some of the brightest young minds in the country: Ben Carter, Sourav Choudhury, Morgan Dibble, Leslie Pedernales, Ian Qua, Allison Summerville and Judy Ward.

I would also like to thank my good friends and senior editors Bob Johns and Tony Scully. Bob has taught me more about industry and domestic manufacturing than I could have ever hoped to learn in a lifetime. But he has taught me about something much more important - he has taught me about life. His guidance and his example have served as beacon for me. Likewise, in many ways Tony has been much more than editor. He has been my conscience keeping my feet firmly planted with ideas of what is not just effective but what is right and good. He is also been the best friend a man could hope to have. For this guidance and much more I thank these friends and editors.

To my team partners, Nancy Smith and John Saydlowski, thanks for your unyielding support for my wide and varied projects. Your dedication and loyalty is beyond anything that should be expected and is instrumental to our team's success.

And finally, to my partners at Moore & Van Allen, thank you for giving me the latitude to develop and build one of the largest and most successful Government, Policy and Regulatory Affairs teams in the country.

It is my hope that in the pages that follow, I can inspire the reader by sharing with you this collection of maxims and analysis in support of them that are an accumulation of the lessons I have learned, both from the words of others and from my own experiences as I have implemented plan after plan across this great nation of ours.

Tom Mullikin
Camden, South Carolina
October 7, 2008

# The Maxims of Politics

## Making Government Work

Thomas S. Mullikin

# *Introduction*

The purpose of this book is to share with you my experiences from more than twenty-five years of issue and campaign management on how to begin from a winning position, adapt to changing circumstances, and achieve your ultimate objectives—whether in the board room or on the campaign trail. The ideas captured by these maxims are not new; as you will see in the pages that follow, entrepreneurs, generals, politicians, and philosophers have been expounding on the virtues of these principles for centuries.

Civilization as we know it today was sculpted and forged from a highly fluid, continuous stream of guiding principles, moral codes, sworn testaments, rules and regulations, and noble declarations. After all, we have come to understand that, without such rules of conduct, mankind would destroy itself. A community whose strength depends on individual members, each one dedicated to his/her own well-being and satisfaction, defies the concept of "civilization." Not until these individuals unite under a common purpose and conduct themselves according to established parameters can they expect to achieve and then maintain a "civilized community." And, almost paradoxically, it is within this same framework that we as individuals find the support, security, and incentive to contribute to the good of the greater community.

History has repeatedly shown us that formulaic or guiding principles—what I refer to as "maxims"—must exist both in spirit and in reality. To sway majority rule and thus achieve positive results, these guiding principles must simultaneously be all-encompassing and specific. History has also shown us that no one set of maxims survives the inevitable change in the human condition and the human perspective over time and space.

From our earliest history, America has drawn upon one set of guiding principles or another—not all of them stemming from a political or governmental source. Once colonists found their way to the Atlantic coastline, they knew that a new society would not survive without rules, restrictions, or at least general guidelines. After all, for a hodgepodge of nationalities, religions, political interests, outcasts, independent thinkers, criminals, and upstarts to unite effectively to champion a single cause, some form of organizational system had to develop.

Benjamin Franklin, definitely a forefather, realized the colonists' need for common ground and a social measuring stick when he penned *Poor Richard's Almanac*. For over twenty years, Franklin provided weather, household hints, poetry, astrological information, and behavioral maxims in the guise of proverbs and sayings. Typically aimed at issues of courtesy, thrift, time management, and moral values, *Poor Richard's Almanac* and its collection of maxims influenced multitudes of readers whose decisions and actions were determined in part by Franklin's maxims. In fact, his last *Almanac* publication, *The Way to Wealth,* used maxims to advise potential entrepreneurs on how to build and maintain profitable businesses. We hear echoes of these same maxims in the philosophies of our most renowned 21st-century financial advisors and gurus.

As a veteran in America's corporate system, I have seen economic paradigms shift, "hot" business trends rise and fall, "solid" investment tips skyrocket and plummet, and "opportunities of a lifetime" ebb and wane. I have observed these phenomena from various vantages—attorney, political activist, legislative assistant, lobbyist, environmentalist, writer, economic advisor, husband, father, and patriot. The single common thread that all these vantage points revealed to me is that American society today owes its amazing resiliency and ability to cope with major setbacks to those who have steadfastly clung to guiding principles, whose value and effectiveness bring ideas to fruition, promote moral courage, require the best from the best, and establish America as one of the leading nations of the world.

Naturally, I have selected those ideas and beliefs that have guided me effectively throughout my multi-faceted career. Politics—with its intricacies, eccentricities, biases, strategies, and unpredictable twists and turns—has always fascinated me both as a living, breathing entity and as a cold, hard, unpredictable machine. From a political science graduate of the University of South Carolina to the current leader of Moore & Van Allen's Government, Policy, and Regulatory Affairs team, I have had numerous opportunities to observe those proverbial "political wheels" in motion. What I have surmised over time is that, although politics is predominantly a "soft science," certain prescriptive elements within the discipline ("hard-science" applications) still exist at the very core of the political machinery. And if indeed we isolate and name these elements, we can offer more objective, concrete solutions for policymakers to deal effectively with the issues that matter to those of us doing business in America.

What I hope to do in this treatise is demonstrate how these maxims work together to create a formula for successful navigation of the political system that is involved in more and more aspects of our society. Within the confines of this book, I offer a template for success in the guise of simple maxims that I have discovered work well and work consistently among business and industry in the United States. Each chapter reveals the philosophical, historical, and economic roots from which the maxim has been weighed, measured, and found to be effective. And with the foundation of each maxim substantially laid, I will illustrate how that maxim's power and influence can reshape government and politics to be tools that are as resilient, as fluid, and as sound as they have been for America's economy. This template is not touted as a "miracle formula" for issue management; however, the template does have a track record for successful application—a pathway to successful decision-making that has already been charted by those who came generations before us.

# Maxim 1

## *"Don't assume a losing position and try to turn it around. Assume the winning position, stay on message and bring them around."*

The side that knows when to fight and when not will take the victory. There are roadways not to be traveled, armies not to be attacked, walled cities not to be assaulted.

— Sun-Tzu, ancient Chinese military strategist, (c. 544—496 B.C.E.), author *The Art of War*

**Overview: Picking the Proper Time, Place and Method to Ensure Victory**

In the gray, pre-dawn hours of June 22, 1941, colossal blasts of 105-mm German artillery ranged along hundreds of miles of the border with the Soviet Union, signaling the beginning of a massive Nazi assault against Adolph Hitler's most hated enemy—Joseph Stalin and the Communists of Eastern Europe.[1]

The Soviets were taken totally by surprise. And the German "lightning strike" military tactics known as the blitzkrieg made rapid advances, steamrolling the surprised and disorganized Russians, breaking through a shaky defensive line and charging ahead 20 miles or more per day.

A total of 3,050,000 men, 7,184 artillery pieces, 3,350 tanks, 2,770 aircraft, 600,000 vehicles, and 625,000 horses (one quarter of the German Army was horse-drawn) were arrayed in three prongs aimed at the Soviet Union.[2] Code named "Operation Barbarossa," the invasion of the Soviet Union was the largest military operation launched by Germany in World War II.[3]

The Germans advanced at breakneck speed to reach Moscow before the deadly cold Russian winter set in. More than a century earlier, the brutality of the season played a large part in the defeat of Napoleon's assault on Russia. Once again, time and distance were on the Soviets' side. The deeper the Germans advanced into Soviet territory, the more difficult it became to maintain their supply lines. And the more drawn out the operation, the more likely the advance would be stopped in the freezing grip of a Russian winter.[4]

The Russians have long understood that their ultimate winning position is to retreat to their Kremlin, or ancient fortified city. The Kremlin has stood as the Russian equivalent of Pergamon, the ancient Greece fortress city, because Russians took refuge behind its strong walls to resist the attacks of the Mongol hordes.[5]

The Soviets were unwilling to give up Moscow, Stalingrad, or Leningrad, for obvious patriotic and ideological reasons. They drew a line in the snow at Moscow and resolved to make their stand there. Trying to stop the German advance before this point, however, was hopeless. The forces of the Wehrmacht were too well equipped, too quick, too battle-hardened, disciplined, and powerful. The Soviets knew exactly their winning position.

By the time Hitler's troops reached the outskirts of Moscow, more than a 1,000 miles east of Berlin, the Germans were exhausted, malnourished and poorly equipped. As the Soviets had expected, the German army had outrun its supply lines and suffered from shortages of every type of war materiel. Winter had already set in, and the German soldiers were dressed in summer uniforms. Cases of frostbite began to run rampant.

So it was here on the outskirts of Moscow in December 1941 that the Russians began a counterattack that sent the Germans into retreat—a retreat that would not end until April 1945 in Berlin. There, in his underground steel-reinforced bunker, Hitler would avoid checkmate in a deadly chess match with the Russians by taking his own life.[6] (For more information about the Nazi winter campaign in Russia, see Chapter 3.)

The invasion of the Soviet Union is an excellent example of picking the proper time and place to make a stand, and it aptly illustrates the truth of Maxim 1: "Assume the winning position, stay on message and bring the opposition around. Never assume a losing position and attempt to turn it around."

In this chapter, we will examine what constitutes a winning position and the difficulties in selecting one. Using historical examples, we'll see how the most promising position is an approach that unifies rather than divides and appeals to the masses where political power lies.

On the other hand, "What is a losing position?" and how—if it is possible at all—to turn it around into a winnable—and winning—position. We'll examine these concepts from a military, political and governmental affairs perspective.

**What Is a Winning Position?**

Remarkably, choosing a winning position is not as easy as it may seem. It is a complex analytical task that requires a thorough understanding of all the issues and stakeholders affected in the pursuit of a particular objective. Generally, a stakeholder is anyone directly or indirectly affected by an action or activity. Stakeholders comprise a particularly diverse and eclectic group of people. Depending upon a specific point of view, stakeholders may also be constituents, elected officials, customers, competitors, colleagues and peers or simply the public.

Sometimes factors affecting an outcome include non-human influences, such as terrain or weather, as in the German-Soviet example just mentioned. In a less military setting, political impacts may come from various demographic groups, racial or ethnic biases, religious perspectives or special interest organizations.

To win, assume a winning position from the start. To do this, you must incorporate a specific formula for winning: Select your battle, when it's fought, where it's fought, and how it's fought. Assuming the right position is a studied position that requires complex analytics to determine what is a winning position in the face of the myriad of potential impactors and stakeholders. In our day-to-day existence, those stakeholders and impactors are often more familiar as our constituents, our competitors, customers, neighbors, and so on.

> ## *Chapter 1 Synopsis*
> - Success in any endeavor depends to a great degree in picking a winnable position from the start.
> - It is significantly more difficult, however, to assume an unpopular stance and change the mind of the opposition to an alternate point of view than to take into account multiple viewpoints.
> - Choosing the correct position to maintain is not any easy task.
> - Examples from history and politics have shown us that the position that unites rather than divides and takes into account the views of diverse stakeholders is the winning position to choose.

The thrust of this book is about effective politics and issue management. Business and industry must live and die in the global marketplace, and cope with all the competitive pressures such a market brings. Political actions taken in our local, state, and federal legislatures often create additional competitive hurdles that impact the bottom line for these businesses. Taxes, regulations, surcharges, rebates—these all add up to profit and loss, and are often the difference between the failure and success of a particular business model. A successful issue management strategy may not only assist business in reducing these pressures, but also may turn government into an advocate for the goals of business and industry.

For example, when a regulated industry is attempting to obtain a permit extension or modification to allow construction of a new business line or expansion of a current enterprise, this process is seldom a matter of simply filling out the proper forms. However, the fact that a business is adding new jobs or increasing tax revenues in an economically depressed region of a state may be enough to bring about the necessary community and governmental support for the desired change.

However, other potential issues may tilt the scales the other way. The parents of children attending a nearby school may object to the increase in truck traffic from an economic expansion of a local industry, because the parents perceive the traffic as a risk to students walking to school. Perhaps the additional noise may be thought to increase the stress levels of the residents of a nursing home in the area. Or perhaps the industry is in a large minority community that believes it will be affected by increased environmental releases.

These are not business or economic considerations. Nevertheless, they are just as vital to the success or failure of a particular business initiative, because they relate to the welfare of the host community. Issues such as these can generate emotion and tireless, unrelenting opposition from community activists. Issue managers must identify issues affecting the welfare of the community's stakeholders and incorporate these considerations as part of the overall solution. The welfare of children and the elderly—two groups that must be afforded the protection of the community—can generate great emotion, to the point of anger, if not properly identified and accounted for in the decision-making process. Lack of sensitivity in these areas can quickly turn a winnable position into an unwinnable quagmire of politics and in a worst-case scenario, legal action.

Even in electoral politics, mere numbers do not always tell the complete story. Traditionally, candidates and campaign managers look at previous election results and calculate how votes in a particular precinct need to be reapportioned to secure a win. Sometimes winning requires stabilizing the voter turnout and targeting the undecided or swing vote, which can provide the winning margin to one side or the other.

Another important consideration: who is most likely to be affected by the proposed legislative activity? This issue is best managed by strategic communications to draw reference to the broader economic impact. For example, if a tax relief measure for business and industry is considered in a purely narrow fashion as to the direct increase of taxes on working families, it might be an impossible burden. However, if the same measure is considered as an economic stimulus that would generate hundreds of new jobs or millions of dollars of investment in the community, a very different opinion may be formed by the community.

Therefore, there is no formula or calculus that can be applied to every situation to determine a winning position. In an era of rapid change, multi-channel communications and an abundance of credible information, issues and public opinion of the issues flip with the frequency and rapidity of a weather vane. Political knowledge and insight coupled with hands-on election experience is necessary for determining the most pressing issues and responding strongly and appropriately.

In another setting, the military for example, it may be the terrain. Chinese General Sun Tzu recognized the importance of terrain to victory or defeat. Six types of terrain: easy; difficult; neutral; narrow; dangerous; distant. Sun Tzu wrote: "These six types of position terrain must be studied carefully and understood well by all commanders." (For more on Sun Tzu and terrain, see Chapter 6)

In electoral politics, there are other types of terrain to study and analyze. Demographics frequently determine the outcome. In the current electoral scheme, an issue manager may need to change the variables (such as increasing the number of registered voters or encouraging previously apathetic registered voters to vote) to achieve a win. In other cases, it may be a matter of keeping the variables constant and playing upon the message of why consistency is so important in a time where everything seems to be moving so fast. The goal is to assure the potential voter of stability.

## Historical Application of a Winning Position

Consider the example of Indiana's 8th Congressional District. This is an excellent case where micro-targeting voters victimized by the loss of manufacturing jobs completely changed the outcome of politics in that district. A careful analysis of demographics begins the process by which political change may occur.

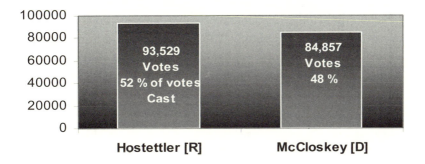

**Challenger John Hostettler Won By Less Than 9,000 Votes to Unseat Incumbent Frank McCloskey in 1994**

In 2002, Representative John Hostettler won election to Congress by a margin of approximately 10,000 votes. While that sounds like a large margin to overcome, in reality, if the total number of votes remains consistent, an opponent would only have to "turn" one vote more than half the margin (or 5,001 votes) to achieve a victory.

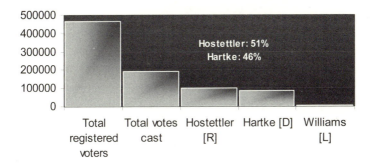

**In 2002, 8th District Congressman John Hostettler Won by Only 10,000 Votes**

In the 2005 American Community Survey, the U.S. Census Bureau estimated that 59,475 people were employed in manufacturing in the 8th District. If we assume that every manufacturing job supports 1.7 voters in a household (employees and spouse or voting-age dependent), then we can calculate that Indiana's 8th District has 101,107 eligible voters who directly depend upon the future of manufacturing. This is a large demographic target to address. It also means a potential candidate would have to change the minds of only about 5 percent of the total registered electorate to reach a 5,001 majority.

One factor that requires consideration is the fact that not everyone in this group will be registered voters. The 8th District has a registration rate of 96.5 percent. Therefore, we can assume that the manufacturing economy has 97,568 registered voters who will be directly affected by and have a direct stake in its health.

Continuing our mathematical analysis, there are obviously more "manufacturing voters" than the margin of victory in the previous Congressional District election—97,568.

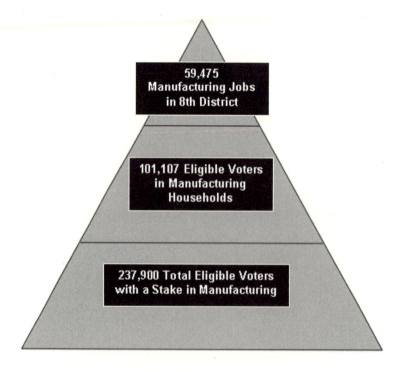

Analysis of Manufacturing Voters in Indiana's
8th Congressional District Race

*Maxim 1: Assume a Winning Position*

The number of manufacturing voters in that district represents almost 10 times the difference in the winning margin in the 2002 election. Therefore, if the losing candidate can make up just one vote over half the losing margin (5,001) votes, then a political challenger can reverse the outcome of that Congressional race. And the good news for the candidate focusing his campaign around manufacturing issues is this: the number of potential voters affected by manufacturing is nearly 20 times the votes need to change the outcome.

From a campaign or issue manager standpoint, here is a strong opportunity to change the district's representative to Congress. More to the point, here is an opportunity to put someone in Congress who is more responsive and proactive to the needs of the constituency.

Now, moving this analysis to reality, the 2006 Democratic candidate Brad Ellsworth did attack incumbent Representative Hostettler's failure to address the needs of the manufacturing workers and spoke repeatedly about saving the jobs of manufacturing workers in Indiana. Ellsworth's focus on an issue deeply affecting voters in his district spurred so much interest that the voter turnout increased by almost 10 percent over the previous election. That's an increase of some 20,000 voters. Ellsworth captured 61 percent of the vote to Hostettler's 39 percent, a crushing defeat for the incumbent.

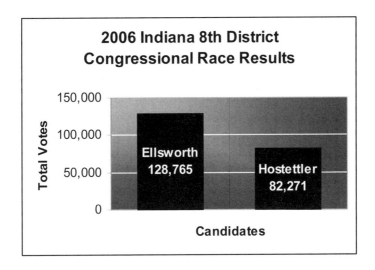

Indiana's 8th District typifies how political experience, combined with insightful analysis, planning, and follow through can produce a winning ticket. As previously noted, picking a winning issue can be tricky and require creative ways of looking at old statistics. Only a skilled political analysis can appreciate some of the subtleties of an issue or issues that result in an electoral change. Only a skilled issue manager can spot the railroad spikes lying on the rail tracks that derail a project moving along smoothly like a freight train.

**Identify the target constituencies that will put you in a winning position and find your mutual interests.**

Even the shrewdest of politicians can make a slip without a deep and thorough understanding of the winning position. President Ronald Reagan, known as an astute politician, made a similar political faux pas on a 1984 campaign stop in Charlotte, North Carolina. A staunch opponent of the forced busing of school children to desegregate public schools, the great communicator President Reagan attempted to make political points by referring to the federal court-ordered busing for schools in the city of Charlotte and surrounding Mecklenburg County as a failed social experiment. Instead of applause, stony, uncomfortable silence greeted President Reagan's remarks.[7]

While President Reagan's conventional wisdom suggested that parents of children who are bused out of their neighborhood to another area of the city to achieve racial balance would welcome his negative views on busing, it turned out that was not the case. The truth was that the community—initially distraught and divided over the racially charged issue—had joined together and ironed out a plan that was working. Parents and school officials were proud of their accomplishment. Jay M. Robinson, the school superintendent from 1976-86 said, "What happened in Charlotte became a matter of community pride."[8]

Defining a winning position, therefore, requires detailed analysis of the local community and target universe. The emphasis on particular points of local interest can be the difference in a politician or business manager winning or losing. The subtle differences in delivery—not a capitulation of meaningful positions—can define a winning position or a hostile reception.

Avoiding such mishaps requires careful research and analysis of positions and actual events. It requires an understanding of people from all walks of life and their relationships to their environment and local community. For example, if someone had mentioned to President Reagan that Charlotte was an area in which busing had brought the community together to find a solution, he had at least two options: avoid the subject altogether or praise the community for its efforts to make a difficult situation work.

**Political Theory Defining a Winning Position**

The initial phase of choosing the winnable position rests in knowing both sides of the situation and selecting the best position to fit stakeholders' needs—or the needs of others. From years past, philosophers, as well as many present day social theorists, have been troubled by questions, such as, how does one determine what is the best position? Which is the winnable one? Is it the one that benefits the most people, or is it a case of helping the most needy or deserving? Not a question with an easy answer, it has been addressed by a number of philosophers and political scientists.

Political philosopher and Harvard professor John Rawls (1921–2002) focused on one aspect of a winnable position—that which helps the most people with the biggest needs. Rawls, who has been described as the most influential philosopher of the 20th century, articulated a theory he called "The Difference Principle," which balances the differences of liberty and equality to claim the highest sense of justice.

Rawls's theory about justice differs from other philosophers in that he focuses more upon the concept of "what is most fair to those most needy" than to "what is an equal distribution for everyone." Traditional philosophers often evaluate the implications of morality and sociology by analyzing their effects upon various class systems and their effects upon socio-economic differences that create a natural divide within the environment.

For many corporations and businesses, this analysis can be particularly insightful as leaders attempt to address the various statutory mandates for public participation both for regulated industries and for various shareholder actions.

Rawls's theory, however, permits inequalities in the distribution of goods only if those inequalities benefit the neediest members of society.[9] This method of distribution seeks to assume a position that favors one class of people over another in an attempt to balance the differences of each class passed down from previous generations. At the same time, this methodology is an attempt to place all classes in a position equivalent to one another. In other words, this is an effort to achieve equality.

This theory is particularly applicable in my experience with economic and environmental justice. Later in Chapters 2 and 5 these topics will be covered in more detail. But basically, industry that is perceived to be the most detrimental to the environment often is found in areas with large minority populations—but because of economic reasons, not racial inequities. For example, an enterprise processing hazardous waste often will locate in sparsely populated, economically deprived areas. These areas are selected because the price of land to build processing facilities and/or store hazardous substances in such areas costs substantially less.

From a legal and justice standpoint, residents of these areas have been treated fairly. They are not victims because of race, but because they are poor. Rawls might take exception to this situation because these people are most in need and are entitled to more.

While treated fairly—as in not victims of discrimination—they are nonetheless victims of poverty. Rawls might suggest that to be fair requires providing more resources: such as assistance to leave the area or education and training to take up a livelihood in a more economically advantaged area. Even though the operator of a hazardous waste facility is not legally bound to do so, it may be appropriate to buy surrounding property as a buffer zone to meet a perceived standard of fairness to residents.

In his book of political and moral philosophy, *A Theory of Justice*, Rawls combined the principles of fairness and liberty to that of greed and [unwillingness to compromise], and journeys to resolve the theory of equal distribution of justice by utilizing a form of the familiar device of the social contract. The idea of social contract is that government exists because the people have ceded certain rights to the government in order to maintain societal order. A *Theory of Justice* deviates from the similar pioneers of the social contract tradition, such as Thomas Hobbes, John Locke, Jean-Jacques Rousseau and Immanuel Kant, in that Rawls challenges readers to remove their personal goals and narrow views from each issue.

This observation separates the individual from all personal beliefs and preconceived notions and challenges him to explore an alternate approach to justice. Rawls's theory allows one to entertain the notion of a solution that likely will not advance any one particular class over another, yet continue to embrace an outcome that treats all people fairly.

Applying this practice would require placing one's self in the "Original Position," a position discussed in *A Theory of Justice*, which enables objective observation of the self behind the veil of ignorance. In arguing for a principled reconciliation of liberty and equality, Rawls states:

> No one knows his place in society, his class position or social status, nor does anyone know his fortune in the distribution of natural assets and abilities, his intelligence, strength, and the like. I shall even assume that the parties do not know their conceptions of the good or their special psychological propensities. The principles of justice are chosen behind a veil of ignorance.[10]

Embracing Rawls's theory of using this blind, unbiased approach to an issue enables one to craft a resolution that is perceived as fair to all concerned. The "fair" position prompts one to seek the position naturally pursued if the given situation was hypothetical and the problem solver personally had nothing to gain from either side of the issue. In an attempt to identify and select the "winnable position," one can see that Rawls's theory helps us step away from the limitations of our own understanding and observe the situation from another person's perspective.

While this theory and matrix may not be the dispositive theory for business decisions, its analytics might aid in the development of a plan involving community issues and concerns. Thus identifying issues that should be addressed early might avoid protracted and costly community and public battle.

**A winning position should give the key stakeholders the perception that they have received a fair resolution.**

Developing a winning position may require more than simply being fair. Seeing a situation from the viewpoint of the economically disadvantaged stakeholder helps gain an understanding of all opposing viewpoints, which leads to win-win scenarios for everyone.

Rawls applies his inquiry into discovering the right thing to do by embracing two "Principles of Justice." Somewhat controversial—and often viewed as extreme—these two principles result in the best outcome for all and are arrived at in a nontraditional way.

First Principle of Justice: Each person is to have an equal right to the most extensive scheme of equal basic liberties compatible with a similar scheme of liberties for others.[11]

The First Principle, according to Rawls, must not be compromised by any means. An absolute solution can not be derived apart from the fairness to all parties involved. A winnable position cannot be obtained without this fairness principle.

Second Principle of Justice: Social and economic inequalities are to be arranged so that: a) they are to be of the greatest benefit to the least-advantaged members of society (the difference principle); and b) offices and positions must be open to everyone under conditions of (fair equality of opportunity).[12]

In other words, Rawls' rationale is that inequalities can be considered just when they benefit the least well off.[13]

Rawls's theories are extreme and seem antithetical to strategies to encourage incentive. However, they do provide a possible matrix through which we can consider all factors and potential outcomes of a particular strategy. Through consideration of these broader analytics, one could gain valuable insight into potential obstacles to a given strategy.

While no one advocates becoming Robin Hood, Rawls's ideas highlight the need for seeing issues from the perspective of the other side. Sometimes the other side is an economically disadvantaged group with little or no power and inadequate legal representation, should the issue come under review by the courts. How this all relates to issue management is simple. By understanding the wants and needs of other stakeholders and making an effort to find common ground with their objectives, it is more likely that an issue manager will be able to attain a winnable middle ground.

Compare Rawls's position with the winnable economic position propounded in President Ronald Reagan's economic policy. Where Rawls believed that by tipping the scale to benefit the less fortunate and removing personal gain from the decision-making process, others believe there are better ways to help the lower economic classes.

Proponents of the "trickle down theory" espoused by President Reagan argue that economic growth flows down from the top economic classes to the bottom, indirectly benefiting all those in between. "Reganomics" is a term used to label the economic theories of President Reagan. The "trickle-down" theory is one of a series of four approaches that were the foundation for policies that were expected to increase employment and thus increase spendable income among Americans. The four pillars of his economic plan were designed to:

1. Reduce the growth of government spending;
2. Reduce marginal tax rates on income from labor and capital;
3. Reduce government regulation of the economy; and
4. Control the money supply to reduce inflation.

Some supporters credit his approach to the so-called Reagan "Boom Years." In an Op-Ed piece published in the New York Times a decade after President Reagan was elected to his first term, Martin Anderson of the Hoover Institution of Stanford University declared that "the seven year period from 1982 to 1989 was the greatest, consistent burst of economic activity ever seen in the U.S. In fact, it was the greatest economic expansion the world has ever seen—in any country, at any time."[14]

To understand the popularity of Reaganomics, one must also recognize the situation that President Reagan inherited from his predecessor, President Jimmy Carter. The Hauenstein Center for Presidential Studies at Grand Valley State University notes:

> ... After Jimmy Carter had been in the White House for four years (1977-1981), the economy 'was in the midst of its worst crisis since the Great Depression. In January 1981 the unemployment rate stood at 7.4 percent, on its way up to 10 percent. Persistent double-digit inflation had pushed interest rates to an unbelievable 21 percent. Real pre-tax income of the average American family had been dropping since 1976, and—thanks to bracket creep—after tax income was falling even faster. The supply of oil and other raw materials seemed precarious. The outgoing president warned of a bleak economic future.[15]

An astute politician, President Reagan took careful note of the mood of the country and knew that most citizens were ready for a dramatic economic change. He addressed job and economic issues with his Reaganomics solution. At the core of the system—reduction in government and taxes—struck a positive chord with almost every taxpayer in upper and middle class America. President Reagan found a popular target upon which to blame the country's economic woes: big government and taxes.

And in making Reaganomics work, President Reagan cut funding for another group of Americans that was unpopular with the public at large at that time: families supported by "welfare" government assistance programs. The differences in approaches by the presidents preceding and following President Reagan are shown in the table below:

## Government Growth by Administration[16]
(Real Average Annual % Change)

|  | Total FYs | Domestic Spending | Defense Spending | Net Spending | Interest |
|---|---|---|---|---|---|
| Kennedy | 1961-64 | 4.0 | 8.5 | 0.4 | 5.1 |
| Johnson | 1964-69 | 5.4 | 6.1 | 4.8 | 5.5 |
| Nixon | 1969-75 | 2.7 | 9.3 | -6.9 | 4.0 |
| Ford | 1975-77 | 3.0 | 5.1 | -2.0 | 5.1 |
| Carter | 1977-81 | 4.0 | 3.3 | 2.9 | 13.1 |
| Reagan | 1981-89 | 2.5 | 0.7 | 4.7 | 7.4 |
| Bush | 1989-93 | 1.5 | 4.2 | -4.7 | 0.5 |
| Clinton | 1993-97E | 1.6 | 3.8 | -5.9 | 1.3 |

The Domestic Spending Column shows the percentage of growth by each administration from Kennedy to nearly the end of the Clinton years. While Kennedy at 8.5 percent and Nixon at 9.3 percent had the greatest increases, President Reagan had the slowest growth at 0.7 percent. The growth of Defense spending, on the other hand, was smallest under Nixon at a negative 6.9 percent, but as expected, highest under President Reagan at 4.7 percent.

Although he was unable to stop completely the growth of spending for domestic programs, the rate of growth on President Reagan's watch was the lowest during the period 1961 to 1997. And as promised, President Reagan strengthened America's defenses against the threat of the "evil" Soviet empire by showing the largest increase in Defense spending over the 36-year period.

Clearly, in 1981 Reaganomics created a winning position for the President because it appealed to the economic concerns of mainstream America. His re-election in 1984 was a landslide and nearly the only shutout in Presidential electoral history, collecting 525 out of 538 electoral votes. It was easily the largest winning margin in electoral votes by any President in history. His Democratic opponent, Walter Mondale, won only 13 electoral votes, including those of his home state of Minnesota.[17]

**President Ronald Reagan's administration effectively employed "trickle-down economics" to create synergy between conservative principles and the economic concerns of the mainstream American voter.
In 1984, Reagan won by a historic landslide.**

While many critics of Reaganomics make strong cases for their argument that poorer classes suffer at the benefit of the wealthy, the founding principles of Reaganomics—less government, reduced taxes—trickled down to every form of state and local government. Michael Mandell, a news analyst for *BusinessWeek*, took a balanced look at the legacy of Reaganomics in a June 2004 article.[18] Mandell found that some notable economists credit President Reagan's economic policies as a major contributing factor to the information technology boom of the 1990s.[19] Even this point is hotly debated:

> Still, there's heated dispute about just how important Reaganomics was to the tech boom. To Milton Friedman, the Nobel prize-winning economist, Reagan's tax cuts—especially the 1986 bill—were "one of the most important factors in the boom of the 1990s." Adds Robert A. Mundell, another Nobel laureate: "[They] made the U.S. economy the motor for the world economy in the 1990s, on which the great revolution in information technology was able to feed."

Other economists, however, are far less willing to give President Reagan credit for the boom. They argue that the big deficits generated by the drop in tax revenues were detrimental to business investment; had the red ink continued, it would have been much harder for companies to fund their spending on info tech in the 1990s.[20]

The theories behind Reaganomics actually have ideological bases in the works of noted scholars and philosophers such as John Locke and Jean-Jacques Rousseau. In correlating the connection between Locke's theories and in selecting the winnable position, Locke's contribution is evident in a review of his treatise "The State of Nature" in *Second Treatise on Civil Government*. Locke often used reason as a way to describe one's approach to evaluating facts and making informed decisions. Locke's belief that reason teaches that "no one ought to harm another in his life, health, liberty or possessions," and that transgressions of this nature may be punished.[21] This theory was supported by others espousing thought in the social contract tradition, such as Thomas Hobbes.

For example, when I was given the task of reaching out to the people of South Central Los Angeles (an example which I discuss more fully in the next chapter), I was faced with a local citizens' group that was ready to fight to a bitter conclusion to prevent a regulated industry from obtaining an extension of the company's operating license. This type of situation clearly demonstrates the need for finding solutions that produce win-win resolutions.

Politically organized residents perceived that there were risks stemming from the presence of the operations, without any tangible benefits to the community. By literally going door-to-door and using effective interviewing techniques, I determined that neighborhood objections to the continued operations of the transfer station for recyclable wastes could be quickly neutralized by creating a job training program that would lead to gainful employment of the community's residents. And by listening to the needs of the community, the company found a more economical way to staff the operations as well as obtaining the critical extension of its operating license.

## A Winning Position Involves a Complex Calculus and Inclusivity

While there are many historical, philosophical, sociological and political science approaches that may be applied in selecting a winnable position, there are at least three rules of thumb that assist in completing this task.

First, a mainstream approach creates the foundation for a winning position. That simply means that tapping into the concerns, hopes and dreams of the individuals in a "targeted universe" and addressing these issues will lead to the discovery of a winning position. Second, winning positions must be inclusive and uniting, not exclusive and dividing. And third, a winning position is one that is active rather than reactive. It examines the strength of a position and relies on the concept of influencing one's destiny. It is better to exert what influence is available rather than waiting for events to happen, which is a position that is more difficult to change. The earlier you can exert influence in a process, the greater the chance of your success in obtaining an objective.

Taken together, these rules mean that a successful political or issue management campaign will seek to involve people in a mass inclusion approach, solidify support by positively addressing issues that keep the working person awake at night and taking consensus building actions that will influence the final resolution of the issue at hand. We'll examine throughout this chapter how these three main themes serve as guiding principles in issue management.

These considerations are not repugnant to the concepts of cost efficiencies and profitable operations. Given the wide range of potential public influences within business and industry, this broader matrix is an effective means to control costs by considering all the potential factors and controlling them at the outset (rather than as a "hurry now and pay more later strategy").

## A Winning Position Includes Study of Human Behavior

An examination of winning positions would not be complete without an examination of how religious issues have interfaced with U.S. electoral politics in recent history. No topic has created more emotion, debate, and conflict than the issue of abortion. Because of the U.S. Supreme Court ruling in *Roe v. Wade*, which has allowed legal abortions since 1973, issues of morality suddenly took the spotlight in U.S. presidential campaigns. The issue galvanized much of the population to protest what conservative religious groups deemed a serious moral offense. In a November 2004 editorial, the evangelical magazine *Christianity Today* stated its opposition to abortion: "We continue to believe the classic Christian teaching that abortion is the wrongful taking of innocent human life and a grave sin."[22] For the Christian Right, pro-life has become a winnable position, one for which they have battled for decades.

Because vacancies on the Supreme Court are filled by the sitting President, presidential politics has steadily taken on a moral imperative. Add to the anti-abortion fervor the resentment in many areas of the country toward another Supreme Court ruling that banned prayer and other organized religious activities in the schools. The Supreme Court ban on prayer in schools came as a ruling in 1963 on two similar cases. One involved the plaintiff, Madalyn Murray O'Hair, an avowed Communist and atheist who was stridently outspoken in her criticism of God and religion.

Mrs. O'Hair perceived a strong connection between Communism and atheism. In 1986, she resigned as president of an atheist organization she helped found—American Atheists—because "Americans no longer equated atheism with Communism." At the time of her resignation, Mrs. O'Hair said the Austin-based group had chapters in 30 states and produced a cable television program that was broadcast in 85 major cities. She also claimed that about 1,000 public college and university libraries subscribed to the organization's magazine.[23]

The fact she was an avowed atheist and Communist, plus her abrasive public manner when appearing on television, further exacerbated the public's feeling that the Supreme Court was upholding two "evils"—Communism and atheism—both vilely antithetical to the "American Way." Once again, many voters looked to the next president, who would appoint Supreme Court justices who were sympathetic to their cause and who, they hoped, would return Christian values to the public schools.

Conservative politicians quickly recognized the political potential in the issues of abortion and prayer in school and embraced them as part of a conservative Christian agenda. Mild-mannered President Jimmy Carter, the nation's 39th President (1977 – 1981) professed his faith as a born-again Baptist, which seemed to heighten voter interest in incorporating religious and moral issues into politics and government. Carter also began his term right after the Nixon administration, whose lapses of integrity in the nation's highest office resulted in the Watergate scandal. Nixon resigned to avoid impeachment, and quite possibly a criminal indictment for obstruction of justice.

A belief in God and a strong support for Christian activities is a historical characteristic of America that may trace its beginnings to the ascetic Puritan settlers in colonial America. In a 2004 Fox News poll, 92 percent of Americans stated they believe in God.[24] Additionally, an Associated Press poll in 2005 found that only 2 percent of Americans do not believe in God and 40 percent believe religious leaders should attempt to influence policy makers. For these Americans, a winnable Christian position should be conveyed to policy makers by clergymen.[25] In stark contrast, 85 percent of survey respondents in France, another country surveyed in the poll, believe the clergy should stay out of political matters.[26]

It is not surprising, therefore, that God and religion would take such a major focus in American politics. The candidate who can convince voters that she has a strong faith is more likely to capture the hearts and minds—and commitment demonstrated through the ballot—of American voters. While President Carter was one of the first presidential candidates to discuss his personal religious beliefs, it has become standard political fare, almost to the point of being a plank in the candidate's platform. Since Carter, we've seen a parade of candidates incorporate religion into their politics.

Start with our 43rd President. Then-Governor George W. Bush, leader in the race for the Republican presidential nomination in 2000, announced that he had "recommitted his life to Christ." In the same presidential race, Vice President Al Gore informed the press, "the purpose of my life is to glorify God." And the Reverend Jesse Jackson, who made an impressive showing in both the 1984 and 1988 Democratic presidential primaries, defended those who openly parade their religious beliefs: "Jesus never performed any miracle at night." All politicians now, to some extent, communicate their personal values and religious viewpoints to the masses to demonstrate their integrity is a solid plank in their winning platform.[27]

In a publication of the Brookings Institution Press, *The Diminishing Divide: Religion's Changing Role in American Politics*, authors Andrew Kohut, John C. Green, Robert C. Toth and Scott Keeter point out that the more recent attempts by organized religious groups to affect actions and events permeate society more extensively than just in areas of electoral politics. Some of the Christian Right activists encourage organized attempts by Christians to directly influence the state and federal legislative process, a trend that began 40 years ago.

Although public acceptance of religion's role in the political process has increased since the 1960s, the issue of how much political power certain religious groups enjoy continues to provoke concern. Gallup polls in the 1960s found that, by a margin of 53 percent to 40 percent, Americans believed that churches should refrain from involvement in politics, and only 22 percent of respondents believed that it was acceptable for clergy to discuss political issues or candidates from the pulpit. By 1996, however, these results had reversed: by a margin of 54 to 43 percent, the public thought that churches should express their views on political and social issues of the day, and 29 percent of respondents supported outright politicking from the pulpit.[28]

The strong religious influence not only supplies a positive political effect, but it also affords another advantage—wrapped in the cloak of godliness, the candidate achieves an almost unassailable position. Who has the audacity to attack God's will? As the Christian apostle Paul writes in Romans 8:31: "What shall we then say to these things? If God be for us, who can be against us?"[29]

Traditionally one can avoid criticism and attack by relating an issue to a higher moral position and charging that the political challenger's position is un-American or un-Christian, for example. A perfect example of this is the idea of war and patriotism. If a war is unpopular and its political reasoning subject to attack from a broad-based, bottom-up approach, then the obvious defense is to link it with patriotism. Anyone who questions the need for the war or wisdom of it is accused of being unpatriotic and a collaborator with the enemy, providing aid and comfort and undermining the security of American troops in harm's way.

This is a winning tactic that dates back to the Vietnam War era. Richard Milhous Nixon, president at the time, saw war protestors as political enemies. Instead of defending or altering his political position, which was apparently unpopular with many Americans, President Nixon attacked war protestors as hurting America and impeding a clear-cut military victory. President Nixon ran for re-election on a law-and-order campaign. He said: "The antiwar movement is a wild orgasm of anarchists sweeping across the country like a prairie fire." It is noteworthy that President Nixon compared war protesters to anarchists and suggested a linkage to sexual deviation with the sexually charged phrase "wild orgasm."[30]

While Christian or patriotic themes are not likely to be used as a winning tactic in issue management, these examples illustrate how issues can be framed in such a way to make them more winnable or at least easier to defend from attack. Wrapping an issue in the flag and declaring God's support can inflict severe divisions among stakeholders.

## Nixon's Southern Strategy . . . Successfully Divisive

President Richard Nixon is significant in political history for a number of reasons, but one of his campaign tactics not only helped him win the presidency in 1968 and again in 1972, but also has influenced Southern politics in such a way that it is still being felt today. President Nixon is known for having developed, used and perfected "The Southern Strategy," which radically reversed the Southern landscape from a solid Democrat majority to a period of unprecedented growth of the Grand Ol' Party.

Although the Southern Strategy proved to be the golden touch for Republican politics in the South, it is an approach that unfortunately was deeply divisive, because it encouraged racist considerations by many in the South and leveraged those strong emotions to produce Republican majorities.

However, to understand how the Southern Strategy was transformed into a winnable political position, it is necessary to first take a look at the history of the South and Southern politics, from the Civil War, through Reconstruction, and into the Civil Rights Movement.

Southern Anti-Republican, pro-Democrat sentiments trace back to the ante bellum days of Southern history and the presidency of Abraham Lincoln. President Lincoln, the first Republican U.S. president, was elected on an anti-slavery platform in November 1860. On December 24, 1860, the state of South Carolina became the first state to vote to secede from the Union. A total of 11 states followed suit and formed the Confederate States of America.

While the issue of secession involved a number of complex sectional and economic issues, the overriding cause of the Civil War is asserted by many to be the issue of slavery. The Southern secessionist states did not view the conflict solely on the basis of the North's opposition to institution of slavery. These states believed that the right of a state or territory to determine its destiny was a principle worth dying for. Therefore, they argued, the federal government should reserve a broad spectrum of authority to each state under the concept of "state's rights."

Pointing to the Declaration of Independence as legal grounds for secession, the Confederate states declared their sovereignty and initially viewed the military action that ensued as a defensive war. The Southern states believed in their right—as a new sovereign nation—to repel an invading army of conscripted "Yankees" attempting to deny them of their inalienable right to secession.

Lincoln's Emancipation Proclamation in 1862, which freed slaves only in Confederate-held states, and General Robert E. Lee's surrender to the Union's leading general and future 18th president Ulysses S. Grant at Appomattox, Virginia, in 1865, ingrained a deep dislike for Lincoln and the Union Reconstruction Republicans. Twelve years of Reconstruction only further augmented a Southern hatred of Republicanism and the federal government. Southerners believed that their interests were best represented by the Democrats, and a massive political migration to the opposing Democratic Party ensued.

The overwhelming advantage by Democrats in the South is clearly evident simply by taking a look at the traditional make up of the Southern delegation in the U.S. House and Senate. In 1950 there were no incumbent Republican senators from the South and only two Republican representatives out of 105 in the Southern House delegation. Such a disproportionate representation by a single party in a massive block vote earned the Southern states the nickname "Solid South," as in solidly, unyieldingly Democratic.[31]

Historians (and brothers) Earl and Merle Black in their examination of the politics of this era, *The Rise of Southern Republicans*, described the politics of the Southern Democrat as a throwback to Reconstruction. While most Southern white voters called themselves Democrats, the term was totally the opposite of how progressive Democrats today would define their party platform.

> The old southern politics was transparently undemocratic and thoroughly racist. "Southern political institutions," as V.O. Key Jr. demonstrated, were deliberately constructed to subordinate "the Negro population and, externally, to block threatened interferences from the outside with these local arrangements." By protecting white supremacy, southern Democrats in Congress institutionalized massive racial injustice for generations. Eventually the civil rights movement challenged the South's racial status quo and inspired a national political climate in which southern Democratic senators could no longer kill civil rights legislation. Led by President Lyndon B. Johnson of Texas, overwhelming majorities of northern Democrats and northern Republicans united to enact the Civil Rights Act of 1964 and the Voting Rights Act of 1965. Landmark federal intervention reformed southern race relations and helped destabilize the traditional one-party system. In the fullness of time the Democratic party's supremacy gave way to genuinely competitive two-party politics.[32]

Within the next 50 years, the shift of the South to Republican would be decisive and dramatic. By 2000 the Republican senators would constitute 13 out of 22 Southern senators and 71 of 125 representatives.[33]

By 1948, however, the landscape of politics and race relations was already changing. Democratic candidates seeking a winnable position running on a blatantly racist "white supremacy" platform generally could not gain a nomination in national elections. The result was the formation of a third political party called the "Dixiecrats," which adjusted its racist platform of "white supremacy" to focus on the more politically acceptable issue of states' rights.

Historian Kari Frederickson, associate professor and director, Summersell Center for the Study of the South at Rutgers University and author of *The Dixiecrat Revolt and End of the Solid South* (1932 – 1968), explains the rise of the Dixiecrats in an article for George Mason University's History News Network:

> The roots of the 1948 Dixiecrat revolt stretch back to the tumultuous New Deal and war years, when Southern conservatives became increasingly uncomfortable with the direction of economic policies that threatened to redefine the region's economic, racial, and political relations. The revolt took definite shape in February of 1948 after Harry Truman delivered his civil rights address to Congress. Practically every white southern leader roundly denounced the civil rights legislation proposed by the president; however, few were receptive to the idea of independent political action that would threaten the Democratic Party's chances for success in the presidential election in November. Greater still, few congressmen and senators were willing to break with the party and threaten their seniority.
> 
> From February until the election in November, the states' rights revolt was piloted by a small group of conservative Democratic state leaders from the Deep South and primarily from Mississippi and Alabama, men who had long opposed the New Deal and had been involved in the 1944 attempt to deny Franklin Roosevelt his fourth nomination. By and large these men --and they included Mississippi Governor Fielding Wright, Mississippi Speaker of the House Walter Sillers, former Alabama governor Frank Dixon, and Louisiana political boss Leander Perez -- represented the conservative agricultural and industrial forces in their respective states. Such men were neither temperamentally suited nor philosophically given to organizing a grassroots campaign. Although they liked to boast that the revolt had emanated from the voters, it was in fact a top-heavy organization dedicated to controlling existing political machinery and in grabbing existing political power. They were less interested, at least initially, in creating a new political party than they were in regaining control of the

old. The Dixiecrats hoped to convince the individual state Democratic Parties to withhold their electoral college votes from President Truman, the nominee of the national Democratic Party. They sought to deny Truman victory and throw the election into the House of Representatives, where they could then barter and trade for a compromise candidate. They would have demonstrated their power and would have recaptured the South's preeminent position within the Democratic Party.

As the Dixiecrat's presidential candidate, Strom Thurmond proved both a blessing and curse for the organization. Thurmond had leapfrogged to the front of the states' rights revolt at the Southern Governors' Conference in mid-February 1948. This meeting came in the wake of Harry Truman's unprecented civil rights address to the United States Congress. Not everyone—especially the Mississippi Dixiecrats—was pleased with Thurmond's assumption of leadership. At the conference of southern governors, Mississippi governor Fielding Wright advocated a hard line against the president. Wright recommended that a "Southern Conference for True Democrats" meet at Jackson, Mississippi, in March to draw up a plan of action. Thurmond recommended a moderate approach, suggesting that the governors meet with the national party forces to seek a compromise on the civil rights issue. Thurmond's suggestion won the support of the governors, much to the irritation of Wright and others. Of course, the administration did not compromise. Although Thurmond stayed within the states' rights camp, Wright and many Alabama and Mississippi Dixiecrats viewed him warily.[34]

Note that in the preceding passage, the Dixiecrats are characterized as being a top-down organization, not created by the masses at the broadest possible organizational level. While the incumbents and politicians who already had power organized the Dixiecrats, the lack of input from the masses most likely accounted for the party's failure to take root and grow. But even if the party had succeeded, it would never have been strong enough to influence the outcome of a national election. In the '48 election, Thurmond won all the electoral votes from Alabama, Mississippi, Louisiana, his home state of South Carolina and one of Tennessee's 12 votes. It was apparent to Southerners that the divisive politics of a third party would not work well enough to stop civil rights legislation from being imposed upon them by the federal government. White supremacy was not a winnable position.

On February 2, 1948, President Harry Truman delivered his "Special Message to the Congress on Civil Rights." In this speech, Truman announced that by executive order he was ending segregation in the military. Truman clearly stated in his address to Congress the intention of the federal government to ensure equal rights for every American citizen. He said: "As a first step, we must strengthen the organization of the Federal Government in order to enforce civil rights legislation more adequately and to watch over the state of our traditional liberties."[35]

Truman also recommended that Congress establish a permanent Commission on Civil Rights reporting to the president. The role of the Commission was to continuously review the country's civil rights policies and practices, study specific problems, and make recommendations to the president at frequent intervals. Truman instructed that it should work with other agencies of the Federal Government, with state and local governments, and with private organizations.[36]

Other requested action from Congress included strengthening federal laws that safeguard the right to vote and the right to safety and security of person and property. These laws, Truman pointed out, provided the basis for the civil rights enforcement programs at that time. Truman also sought to protect persons against conspiracies to deny them their rights, and extended these protections to all inhabitants of the U.S., whether or not they were citizens; to pass a specific federal measure to deal with the crime of lynching; and to enact legislation ending interference—either through official action or intimidation by private groups or individuals—with a citizen's right to vote. And finally, Truman asked Congress to enact fair employment practice legislation prohibiting discrimination in employment based on race, color, religion or national origin. [37]

Truman's strong stance on civil rights attempted to end divisiveness in American society. It also spelled the beginning of the end for the Democratic Solid South. The original 11 Confederate states anticipated more federal involvement in what they viewed as their individual state's local business. Proponents of local governance and state's rights reshaped their positions and this schism opened the door to the federalists within the Republican Party.

There, historical events lead us to the beginnings of the development of Nixon's Southern Strategy. In the 1960s a young conservative political analyst, Kevin Phillips, correctly predicted in 1966 that Republicans would begin to dominate Southern politics within the decade and continue until the beginning of the 21st century. Phillips saw the potential for this happening if the party tapped into the Southern disdain for Northern liberals and leveraged the anti-civil rights tendencies of the populace into a politically correct, winning position. In a nutshell, Phillips based the new Republican strategy on the alleged hostility of the Irish, Italian and Polish, whose ethnic traits are conservative, toward Jews, African-Americans and affluent Yankees, groups who were traditionally liberal.[38]

One of the valuable by-products of Phillips' involvement in conservative politics was the understanding that by concentrating on specific issues that fire the emotions of voters, a campaign can sway the "undecided" into definite political camps. Phillips, contrary to conventional wisdom of the late '60s, was severely critical of Nixon's 1968 campaign because it utilized the glib advertising tactics of Madison Avenue, an unprecedented campaign approach chronicled in *The Selling of the President 1968* by author Joe McGinnis. Phillips provided this visionary commentary on Madison Avenue's involvement in Nixon's 1968 campaign in Boyd's 1970 *Times* article: "It was a catastrophe—millions of dollars spent by Madison Avenue lightweights who converted certain victory into near defeat. The soap salesmen drained all of the issues out of the campaign that would have won it big. McGinnis could have called his book *The Unselling of the President*."[39]

Boyd's subsequent description of Phillips' approach is uncomfortable in current terms and political reality, but it was not far-fetched in America's 1965 racially divided culture:

> Sterilized and scientific as are the terms by which Kevin Phillips plots the emerging Republican majority, its common denominator is hostility to blacks and browns among slipping Democrats and abandonment of the

Democratic party because of its identification with the colored minorities. In the Northeast, the slippage is among blue-collar Catholics who find their jobs threatened and their neighborhoods and political clubhouses overrun by invading Negroes, while their erstwhile party seems to be clucking approval. In the Outer South, the national Democratic party has begun to replace the G.O.P. as the symbol of alien causes—the Negro politicians and Federal interference with local autonomy. Hence, the shift to Republicanism, a trend which for the same reasons has engulfed the milder border states and will, Phillips insists, capture the perfervid Deep South when events force the abandonment of the more extreme (George) Wallace alternative.[40]

If Phillips developed the seed for the Southern Strategy, Harry S. Dent, Sr., an aide to South Carolina Senator Strom Thurmond, sprouted the seed and nurtured its growth. Thurmond, a former lifelong Democrat turned Republican, campaigned for his new party's presidential candidate, Barry Goldwater, in 1964. Goldwater was beaten overwhelmingly by Johnson, but he did carry five states in the Deep South. He had campaigned in part on "states' rights," and Goldwater had voted against civil rights legislation, facts not lost on vote-counters in either party.[41]

Four years later in 1968, Thurmond helped hold much of the South for Nixon by reassuring Southerners that, as President, Nixon would not be too aggressive on civil rights issues. Segregationist Governor George C. Wallace of Alabama won five states in the Deep South, but Nixon's strength elsewhere in the region was crucial to his narrow victory over Vice President Hubert H. Humphrey. Dent has been described as having helped articulate the Southern strategy.[42]

Even Nixon gave much credit to The Southern Strategy for his 1968 victory, and Nixon rewarded Dent with a post as special counsel and political strategist. Dent worked in the White House for four years, also finding time to rehabilitate the image of his former boss Senator Thurmond. "We're going to get him on the high ground of fairness on the race question," Dent was quoted as saying in 1971. By that time

Thurmond was genuinely trying to change by beginning to hire black people for his staff and steering federal grants to rural black areas.[43]

**The effectiveness of the Southern Strategy derived from determining a core of issues which were of mutual interest to the target constituencies. By appealing to those mutual interests, the Republicans captured support from voters in key regions.**

Nixon's winning Southern Strategy did not die with the Nixon Presidency. As Phillips predicted a decade earlier, Republican dominance began to grow, which culminated nationally in the 1980 election of President Ronald Reagan to the White House. A former Hollywood actor and radio broadcaster, President Reagan leveraged his substantive communications skill to build a vision of a great awakening of America, a nation once again riding high and proud and a beacon of light to the rest of the world. This contrasted sharply with the seemingly inept, feckless nation associated with the Presidency of Jimmy Carter. President Reagan appealed to voters with political positions that called for a great reduction in the power and scope of the federal government, deep cuts in taxes, a hard line against Communism, peace through military superiority and a *laissez faire* economic policy that stressed deregulation in business in industry.

While race is the easiest fashion to explain the profound differences in deeply held views of many in the South from those in the Northeast and other parts of the country, the differences are much more complex and deeply held. For generations, those who inhabited the largely agrarian South emigrated from parts of the world with long-standing contempt for a central authority (such as the Scots-Irish disdain for the King). Their passion for local rule was handed down from generation to generation and formed deeply rooted preferences for state and local governance.

This fiercely independent preference is particularly antithetical when juxtaposed to those views of a large block of African-American voters who ascribed to more national control and needed desperately the intervention of the federal government. Reagan was keenly aware of these differences in exploiting the states' rights and pro-military views of many white Southerners.

It should not have come as any surprise, then, that Reagan kicked off his 1980 Presidential campaign in Philadelphia, Mississippi, of all places. Why in Neshoba County, population 20,000? For one thing, it was the site of one of the nation's worst hate crimes in national history. William Raspberry, African-American columnist for the Washington Post remembered the moment in a column shortly after former President Reagan's death in 2004:

> Philadelphia, county seat of Mississippi's Neshoba County, is famous for a couple of things. That is where three civil rights workers -- Michael Schwerner, James Chaney and Andrew Goodman – were murdered in 1964. And that is where, in 1980, Republican presidential candidate Ronald Reagan chose to launch his election campaign, with a ringing endorsement of "states' rights."
> It was bitter symbolism for black Americans (though surely not just for black Americans). Countless observers have noted that Reagan took the Republican Party from virtual irrelevance to the ascendancy it now enjoys. The essence of that transformation, we shouldn't forget, is the party's successful wooing of the race-exploiting Southern Democrats formerly known as Dixiecrats. And Reagan's Philadelphia appearance was an important bouquet in that courtship.[44]

The shift toward Republican power was obvious from 1968 onward. In 1967, the U.S. Senate comprised 64 Democrats and 36 Republicans; the House 248 Democrats and 187 Republicans. By the Reagan presidency in 1981, the numbers had shifted to 46 Senate Democrats, 53 Republicans and one independent. Democrats still controlled the House 242 to 192. By 1995, the Republicans controlled both House and Senate. In the Senate the Republican edge was 52 – 48; in the House 230 – 204 with one independent. In the current 110th Congress, the Senate count is even at 49 to 49 with two independents. In the House, Democrats once again control by a count of 233 to 198 with four vacant seats.

While the Republican strategy once turned the tables on the Democrats, the advantage seems to switch back and forth as race slowly becomes less of an issue for many Americans. More volatile issues include oil and energy supplies, global climate change, greenhouse gas emissions and tough economic issues such as fair trade, the loss of manufacturing jobs and the implementation of potentially costly environmental regulations on business and industry.

With no current dominating party, achieving results in Congress may be a more difficult task because increasing numbers of legislators take more independent positions on issues that previously were either conservative or liberal. This means, for example, that a legislator cannot be assumed to be a global climate change skeptic because of his political leanings. Some Democrats vote like Republicans and vice versa depending upon the issues.

For example, Utah's 2nd District Congressman Jim Matheson is a Democrat, voting to ban oil exploration and production in the Arctic National Wildlife Reserve, a typical Democratic position. On the other hand, he has voted against keeping a moratorium on drilling for oil offshore and against raising the Corporate Average Fuel Economy standards. (Note: Corporate Average Fuel Economy (CAFE) is the sales weighted average fuel economy, expressed in miles per gallon (mpg), of a manufacturer's fleet of passenger cars or light trucks with a gross vehicle weight rating (GVWR) of 8,500 lbs. or less, manufactured for sale in the United States, for any given model year. Fuel economy is defined as the average mileage traveled by an automobile per gallon of gasoline (or equivalent amount of other fuel) consumed as measured in accordance with the testing and evaluation protocol set forth by the Environmental Protection Agency (EPA).)[45]

Recently, however, Matheson joined Republicans in opposing HR 6124, also known as the Second Farm, Nutrition, and Bioenergy Act of 2007 (Farm Bill). This bill proposed to increase spending on certain forms of agricultural assistance, extend selected agricultural assistance programs until 2012, provide funding for the purchase of certain foods for domestic nutrition programs, lower income tax credits for ethanol producers, and make other agriculture-related changes. The bill passed, but was vetoed by the President. On June 18, 2008, Congress voted to override the President's veto. Matheson opposed the bill and the override of the President's veto, as did most Republicans.[46]

Matheson's votes highlight the difficulty in predicting how a House member or Senator will vote. Making this type of prognostication is becoming more and more difficult and complex. Ideological fights are becoming more about bread and butter issues, such as jobs, fair trade and support for working families. A winning position is not an easily determinable issue. There are many subtleties intertwined among equally complex issues, such as the environment, oil and energy supplies (or lack thereof) and a rational tax structure. Selecting a winning approach to a complex issue requires—now more than ever—accurate information augmented by insightful analysis that only comes from extensive legwork and experience.

For example, if you analyze Matheson's positions, it makes sense that he would break with traditional party lines on the farm bill vote. First, he is a member of the Blue Dog Coalition in Congress. Quoting from the caucus' web site:

> The fiscally conservative Democratic Blue Dog Coalition was formed in 1995 with the goal of representing the center of the House of Representatives and appealing to the mainstream values of the American public. The Blue Dogs are dedicated to a core set of beliefs that transcend partisan politics, including a deep commitment to the financial stability and national security of the United States. Currently there are 49 members of the Blue Dog Coalition.[47]

Second, Matheson is the only Democrat in a five-member House and Senate delegation from Utah. Politically, Matheson may be sensitive to looking out of step with the other legislators of his state. Combining a fiscally conservative outlook with the predominantly conservative nature of one's state may result in surprising bipartisan outcomes on a number of issues. Representative Matheson has likely determined that a winning position for him requires his support for this type of legislation.

Approaching a Congressman with these political leanings, then, would require a strong justification for any legislative initiative that results in additional government spending. Even with a well-founded justification, the lobbyist or issue manager will need to demonstrate how the initiative will improve the legislator's winning position.

## Winning the Iowa Caucus

Nowhere is assuming a winning position more important than in primary elections and caucus votes. In states such as Iowa, voters cluster in public schools, church basements, fire stations—and even private homes. During the bitter Midwestern winter of each presidential election cycle, the nation eventually focuses its attention on the voters of the 99 counties in the rural state of Iowa who participate in a curiously genuine American event called the Iowa Caucus.

The Iowa caucuses—actually two of them, one for the Democratic candidates, another for the Republican hopefuls—have existed in some form or another since the early 1800s, even before Iowa became a state in 1846. The state experimented with a voting primary in 1916, but abandoned it immediately when voter turnout dropped to only 25 percent.[48]

The word caucus is a North American Indian word—probably of Algonquin origin—meaning "a gathering of ruling tribal chiefs." The modern use of the word is defined more accurately as a process by which political party members gather to make policy decisions and to select candidates.[49]

The Iowa Caucus, which has come to be nicknamed "First in the Nation," recognizes the Iowa Caucus as the first opportunity for presidential candidates to gain national public attention and create early momentum. While it is possible—and highly advantageous—for candidates to win an outright majority of votes, winning in a pre-political convention caucus or primary is not always measured solely on votes cast. The success or failure of candidates in these events is based upon the concept of expectations—simply beating expectations or overcoming the daunting hurdle of actually performing up to expectations are both considered a win.

For example, a candidate expected to smash through the field of presidential contenders with a lead of 15 to 20 percentage points may actually be considered to have "lost" if the margin of victory is less than the expected two digit percentages. While many political analysts scoff at the importance of Iowa—not truly representative of a cross-section of

American voters, critics say—no serious candidate for the presidency can afford to perform poorly in the race. Historically, remaining as a serious candidate means finishing at least in the top three.

Take the 1988 Democratic presidential primary races, for instance. A field of multiple candidates jockeyed for the front-runner position with each primary. Those who witnessed the various state primaries could not determine who won simply by the final vote count. Political analysts defined winners and losers by those who had the edge and lived up to expectations or those who were underdogs but far exceeded their expected mediocre showing (winners) versus those who were expected to win by large margins and didn't (losers).

The field of candidates that year included: Massachusetts Governor Michael Dukakis, the eventual Democratic nominee; civil rights activist the Reverend Jesse Jackson; Tennessee Senator Al Gore, Jr.; Missouri Congressman Richard Gephardt; and Illinois Senator Paul Simon. The pack of presidential hopefuls traded primary wins on a routine basis as the candidates bolted at the opening bell onto the primary campaign trail. [50]

Dukakis and Simon were viewed as the most liberal of the candidates. Gore and Gephardt defined themselves as moderates. Although his voting record had been more liberal than that of most Southern Democrats, Gore had positioned himself as a moderate who believed in deficit reduction, free trade, and a strong defense. Gephardt's protectionist message had a certain appeal to many Southern Democrats, particularly blue-collar voters in hard-pressed regions. Arthur H. Miller, a political scientist at the University of Iowa who analyzed the Missouri Congressman's primary win there said: "Gephardt isn't just selling protectionism; he's selling patriotism. That may be bad economics, but it's good politics in Iowa and in the South."[51]

However, even before the primary season had begun, two surprises had occurred. Early in the campaign, two Democratic candidates thought to have some centrist appeal with voters—former Colorado Senator Gary Hart and Delaware Senator Joseph R. Biden Jr.—both dropped out of the race early. Hart quit after allegations of an extramarital affair; Biden when he was accused of plagiarizing a speech that was caught on video. [52]

The all-important Iowa caucus on February 8—as expected—set the stage for what was to come. Gephardt surprisingly won the Iowa Caucus, but with an unconvincing 31 percent, as compared to 27 percent for

Simon, and 22 percent for a third-place Dukakis. Because Dukakis had already achieved a quasi-frontrunner status, the New Hampshire primary was a must-win state for Dukakis—the son of a Greek immigrant whose family had first settled in Manchester, New Hampshire. As a two-term governor of Massachusetts, a next-door-neighbor state to New Hampshire, Dukakis also had scored much-needed political points with antinuclear activists by opposing licensing of the Seabrook Nuclear Power Station, a controversial project owned by Public Service Company of New Hampshire.[53]

Dukakis regained his momentum by beating Gephardt by a nearly two-to-one margin, 44,112 votes to 24,513. Simon was not far behind in third place with 21,094. As expected, Dukakis was elated with the win: "A terrific boost; we went for the gold and we won it," Dukakis said of his victory during an Olympic year. Gephardt considered his second-place showing a type of win, telling reporters, "A week ago, they said I couldn't compete in New Hampshire." [54] Nevertheless, Gephardt was already starting to drift behind the pack.

New Hampshire set the stage for the nation's first Super Tuesday, 16 states, 14 in the South or bordering it, holding primaries in both parties on the same day. The total turnout was estimated at 14.4 million voters—9.6 million in the Democratic primaries and 4.8 in the Republican contests.[55] The first Super Tuesday, in 1988, was designed to give Southern states a bigger role in picking presidential nominees. But both parties quickly grew accustomed to the idea of multi-state primaries and caucuses as a way to settle nominating contests early, end intraparty bickering, and save cash for the big battle in the fall.[56]

In an interview March 9, 1988, on the MacNeil-Lehrer News Hour, then former-Virginia Governor Chuck Robb, who later served in the United States Senate, explained the concept for Super Tuesday and its advantages in determining candidates' views on broad issues and how the candidate would perform in a large regional race. Robb said:

> Super Tuesday was designed to test candidates' skills in a general election. We're not terribly concerned, those of us who were part of the formation of the Super Tuesday concept, about how many states are in it, and there may be a few less in it the next time around, but what we wanted to do is to move away from the individual

approach, the so-called retail approach, and see if a candidate could talk about issues and priorities and presidential terms, and that requires an emphasis on organization, on money, on the ability to motivate on a broad scale, without doing it on the basis of one on one approaches to an individual ward healer or somebody else in a state that may encourage them to bring out all these friends on a cold February night. We wanted them to talk about the broad issues that are facing the country and there is a certain amount of tarmac campaigning in a presidential election.[57]

The Super Tuesday concept—if it can be considered successful, an issue that undergoes constant debate—forced candidates to take on winning positions that are on a national scale, not just single issue, local politics. In support of Super Tuesday, appearing in the glare of a national political spotlight quickly reveals whether a candidate can appeal to a broad spectrum of voters and appear presidential on important matters of national and world interest, such as defense, foreign affairs, world trade, and environmental issues.

In 1988, Dukakis won six primaries, Jackson and Gore each winning five states, and Gephardt one. Jackson, who gathered a large share of African-American voters carried Alabama, Georgia, Louisiana, Mississippi and Virginia. Gore won his home state of Tennessee and also led the field in Arkansas, Kentucky, North Carolina, and Oklahoma, but it was far from the sweeping regional victory he needed to sustain his campaign.[58]

Dukakis, meanwhile, scored a couple of Southern victories himself, in Florida and Texas, easily outran Jackson in Maryland, and dominated Massachusetts and Rhode Island on his New England home turf. The next election event, the South Carolina Caucus, saw Dukakis and Gore attempting to gain momentum that would enable one or the other to break away from the pack.

In South Carolina, Jackson, a native of Greenville, S.C., won 54 percent of the caucus votes; Gore, 18 percent, just behind 19 percent uncommitted; Dukakis, 7 percent; Gephardt, 2 percent; and Paul Simon, who had asked that his delegates remain uncommitted, 1 percent.[59]

Analysts viewed the results as a resounding victory for Gore. Party insiders had long given the race to Jackson, the hometown candidate, and the race was largely seen as one between Gephardt—who had the support of most of the parties' leading officials—and Gore, who energized a new base of young and more moderate voters. Gore's 18 percent to Gephardt's 2 percent shot Gore to the top of the moderate party base and pushed Gephardt's leading candidacy out of national contention.

Illinois favorite son Paul Simon was big in his state, gathering 42 percent of the vote; Jackson, 32 percent; Dukakis, 17 percent; Gore, 5 percent; and Gephardt, 2 percent. Dukakis went on to sweep the remaining 14 primaries—his only loss to Jackson coming May 3 in the District of Columbia contest.

When Gore suspended his campaign in April 1988, the Columbia *State* newspaper interviewed me, as one of South Carolina's delegates from Camden, and because I was also serving as Gore's state campaign manager. Even at that early point in the campaign, I questioned whether Dukakis' liberal politics would present a winnable position for Democrats. I said, "As an individual delegate, I have no intention of switching to anyone right now. I still think Governor Dukakis will do nothing to help South Carolina Democrats. He's too liberal."[60]

While candidates in Super Tuesday races are more obligated to develop consistent, national policies, the 2008 Presidential race has witnessed primary candidates who took the extremely risky political tactic of changing their stance on issues vital to Iowa voters solely to reinforce their "winning position" in this all-important Midwestern state.

For example, according to the Iowa Caucus 2008 Web site, Iowa is first in the nation in ethanol production, much of which comes from Iowa grown corn. Corn is the United States' largest crop, in terms of both volume and value. The states of Iowa, Illinois, Nebraska, and Minnesota account for more than 50 percent of U.S. corn production. The United States also grew 42 percent of the world's corn during fiscal year 2006.[61]

Democratic primary candidate, Illinois Senator Barack Obama expressed a long-standing support for ethanol as a fuel and for agriculture in general. While his number one message was "Change," he also campaigned in support of one of his major constituencies: corn. The New York Times reported in June 2008 that when VeraSun Energy launched a new ethanol processing plant last summer in Charles City,

Iowa, prominent attendees at the ribbon-cutting included boosters for the ethanol industry, corn growers, renewable fuels, and . . . Obama.[62]

Then running far behind Senator Hillary Rodham Clinton in name recognition and in the polls, Obama was in the midst of a campaign swing through the state where he would eventually register his first caucus victory. And as befits a senator from Illinois, the country's second largest corn-producing state, he delivered a ringing endorsement of ethanol as an alternative fuel.[63]

Obama also supported farm subsidies to corn growers and opposed importing Brazilian-produced ethanol from sugar cane. He argued that America needs to create its own ethanol industry. There's no point in replacing imported oil with imported ethanol in terms of ending this country's dependence on imported fuels.[64]

In contrast, Arizona Senator John McCain was a strong advocate for eliminating the multibillion-dollar annual government subsidies that domestic ethanol has long enjoyed. As a free trade advocate, he has also opposed the 54-cent-a-gallon tariff that the United States slaps on imports of ethanol made from sugar cane, which packs more of an energy punch than corn-based ethanol and is cheaper to produce.[65]

Not surprisingly, Obama kicked off his presidential bid with a significant win in Iowa with 38 percent of the votes cast by Democrats. Former North Carolina Senator John Edwards and Hillary Clinton finished in a virtual tie for second. Largely as a result of statements about ethanol, McCain finished a distant fourth in the Republican primary with 13.1 percent of the vote behind the winner, former Arkansas Governor Mike Huckabee with 34.4 percent; former Massachusetts Governor Mitt Romney with 25.2 percent; and former Tennessee Senator Fred Thompson with 13.4 percent. McCain was able to recover from Iowa, but few candidates have gone from a fourth place finish in Iowa to regain a lead.

The Iowa Caucus was not always regarded as a "must-win, place or show" election—not until political and major cultural events of 1968 prompted changes in the Democratic party's nominating process. The disastrous 1968 Democratic Convention held August 26-29 in Chicago that year bore witness to divisive politics, violent demonstrations and massive police riots brought about by antithetical positions by delegates on the stalemated Vietnam war. These upheavals—never before seen as part of the country's orderly democratic process—prompted the national

Democratic party to completely overhaul its rules for selecting presidential delegates—opening up the political process to millions of new political participants.[66]

Dramatic events began with the 1968 New Hampshire Democratic primary. Political experts expected incumbent President Lyndon B. Johnson, architect of the increasingly unpopular Vietnam War, to be a likely nominee. No major Democratic candidates were willing to take on the President and his political machine. No one tried except Minnesota Senator Eugene McCarthy, who originally intended to bypass New Hampshire and concentrate on the Massachusetts primary a week later. McCarthy didn't even begin campaigning in New Hampshire until January 25, just six weeks before the primary. A Gallup Poll projected that McCarthy would receive about 12 percent of the vote, some of it from people who confused him with the 1950s, anti-Communist witch hunter Republican Senator Joseph McCarthy of Wisconsin.[67] In this election year, the winning position began to shift toward broad based issues.

Political writer Al Eisele, who covered the 1968 Presidential campaign as a young reporter, recalls the mood of the country and New Hampshire:

> It was the first primary I covered as a young Washington correspondent for Minnesota newspapers, but I could see that something special was happening in the snowy landscape of New Hampshire. Despite press criticism of his low-key, pedantic style and his refusal to attack Johnson, McCarthy deftly exploited a growing disenchantment with the escalating war.[68]

The 1968 New Hampshire primary is a perfect example of a candidate's choosing a winning position and skillfully incorporating the hot-button issue as part of a campaign platform. While most Americans were essentially untouched by the Vietnam War, the draft and increasing number of war dead began to affect citizens in every small town and city in America. Visual media also contributed to the growing awareness of the Vietnam issue. Photographs and film footage of caskets coming home from battlefields have always been a stark reminder for Americans of the toll of savage warfare. During the Vietnam War, the image of caskets arriving at Dover became a staple of the nightly news. The phrase "Dover

Test" later came to signify public tolerance, or lack of it, for mounting war casualties.[69]

The Vietnam War issue grew slowly, as did America's involvement, escalating from only a limited scale engagement that was practically invisible to the public in the early 1960s to a build up of more than a half million combat troops at the peak of the war. The United States had been involved in Vietnam for six years before total fatalities surpassed 500 in 1965, the year President Lyndon B. Johnson ordered a massive buildup of forces. There were 20,000 troops in Vietnam by the end of 1964. There were more than 200,000 a year later.[70]

By the end of 1966, U.S. combat deaths in Vietnam had reached 3,910. By 1968, the peak of U.S. involvement, there were more than 500,000 troops in the country. During the first 15-day period of April that year, 752 U.S. soldiers died, according to a search of records kept by the National Archives.[71] The failure of President Johnson to develop a strategy for effectively dealing with escalating casualties in war with no end in sight created an unwinnable position for his administration.

For Johnson, the end was near. On January 31, 1968, the first day of the Vietnamese New Year, an important holiday called Tet, the Viet Cong launched a widespread major attack on South Vietnam that many historians have called the turning point of the war. Although the U.S. forces eventually overcame the setback from a military perspective, it spelled political doom for President Johnson. His public approval rating of his handling of the Vietnam war slowly plummeted from a high of 57 percent in January 1966 to a low of 32 percent in 1968 after the Tet Offensive.[72]

Johnson's sinking Vietnam approval ratings, the mood of the country, and the near victory of relatively unknown candidate Eugene McCarthy in the New Hampshire Primary in March apparently convinced the President that he could not win in November. On March 31, 1968, Johnson made the shocking announcement to the nation that he would not seek another term as President.

Eugene McCarthy's strong finish in the Democratic primary in New Hampshire demonstrated convincingly that a mainstream presidential campaign opposing the Vietnam War was viable. Robert F. Kennedy, brother of the late President Kennedy and a U.S. Senator from New York, threw his hat into the ring, winning both the Indiana and Nebraska primaries. Just when it appeared Kennedy might take the Democratic nomination in Chicago, he was shot by an assassin a few minutes past midnight on June 5, only moments after his victory speech at the Ambassador Hotel in Los Angeles, following his win in the June 4 California Democratic primary.[73] He died the day after the shooting.

In contrast to McCarthy and Kennedy, who were winning primaries on anti-war, anti-Lyndon Johnson platforms, Vice President Hubert H. Humphrey assumed a very different position entering the race in the absence of the incumbent President. A native Minnesotan, like McCarthy, and the number two man in the Johnson Administration, Humphrey was duty bound to run in support of Johnson's failing Vietnam policies. If Humphrey had any notion he was assuming an unwinnable position, then his eternally optimistic and effervescent spirit must have convinced him he could turn things around by hitting voters with a consistent message and staying there with his bulldog-like determination.

What might seem to be political suicide today for a candidate seeking the nomination for president worked out differently for Humphrey, because of the manner in which candidates were chosen in 1968 by the Democratic Party system. Unlike 2008, votes cast in the 1968 primaries did not always equate to delegate votes at the national party convention. For example, Senator McCarthy received 75 percent of the votes cast for Democrats in the Pennsylvania primary, but Humphrey was the candidate who received 80 percent of the state's convention delegate votes in Chicago.[74]

How could this happen? Under the rules of 1968 electoral politics, candidates for president were selected by party officials. The system was not directly responsive to the wishes of the electorate. Primaries and caucuses were for the sole purpose of convincing high-ranking Democrats about the so called "electability" of any given candidate. The party looked to party bosses to decide who would be the candidate and deliver the needed votes in each precinct. Thus, in the old political tradition of Tammany Hall and similar sources of local political clout, Humphrey was nominated behind closed doors by party bosses in the dark, proverbial "smoke-filled room." [75]

Following the Chicago convention debacle, the chairman of the Democratic party created the McGovern-Fraser Commission, which was charged with revising party rules to eliminate some of the unfairness and injustices of 1968. During his campaign, Senator Kennedy voiced his support for the emergence of a new type of politics that were tapping into the power of "mass citizen involvement." Speaking on May 22, 1968, the New York Senator acknowledged that this "new politics" could not dominate the Democratic National Convention, but warned "to disregard it would be a great mistake for the Democratic Party." Kennedy described himself and McCarthy as the two chief exponents of participatory democracy, and pointed to their combined victories in New Hampshire, Wisconsin, Washington, D.C., Indiana, and Nebraska.[76]

The new-found political power unleashed by widespread citizen involvement in the election process changed politics in a way that is felt even today. Just as the winner in politics must appeal to the masses, so does any position proposed by an issue manager. Cell phones, text messaging, and the Internet have removed the veil on processes that traditionally have been shielded from public scrutiny. In addition to political activities, open meetings laws or sunshine laws, as they are commonly known, have opened up many decisions of government to public review. Thus, it is incumbent upon an issue manager to take into account all stakeholders involved in an issue and conduct business above board. The public will be watching.

Forty years ago secrecy still held a tenuous grip on the decision-making process of many public endeavors. While McCarthy and Kennedy traversed the country gathering votes, Humphrey knew he could win the nomination by staying home and soliciting support from party leaders. Of the 13 Democratic primaries held in 1968, McCarthy won six, Kennedy four, Johnson one (New Hampshire), Democratic Senator Stephen M. Young of Ohio won his state's primary, as did Florida Senator George A. Smathers in Florida.[77] Humphrey did not enter or win any primaries.

Based upon popular vote in the primaries, McCarthy was the big winner with 2,914,933 votes or 38.7 percent cast in the Democratic primaries. Kennedy collected 2,305,148 votes or 30.6 percent. Humphrey, the eventual nominee received only 166,463 Democratic votes or 2.2 percent because he did not enter any primaries. Ultimately, none of these votes would matter to the outcome of the 1968 presidential race.

Then came the Chicago convention. Haynes Johnson, a Pulitzer Prize-winning author, historian and commentator, recalls the horror, sadness and disappointment of that epochal event. Writing in the August 2008 issue of The *Smithsonian*:

The 1968 Chicago convention became a lacerating event, a distillation of a year of heartbreak, assassinations, riots and a breakdown in law and order that made it seem as if the country were coming apart. In its psychic impact, and its long-term political consequences, it eclipsed any other such convention in American history, destroying faith in politicians, in the political system, in the country and in its institutions. No one who was there, or who watched it on television, could escape the memory of what took place before their eyes. [78]

Johnson goes on to describe the red-faced rage and shouting matches among delegates inside the convention hall, confrontations lasting until 3:00 a.m. He relates the violence instigated by Chicago police, who removed their badges, charged into throngs of chanting protesters, and clubbed the demonstrators to the ground. Johnson ably expresses the feelings of betrayal and loss of American democracy felt by convention delegates: "The eventual nomination of Humphrey, perceived heir to Johnson's war policies, compounded the sense of betrayal among those who opposed the war. The bosses, not the people who voted in the primaries, had won."[79]

**Democrats who did not benefit from the party boss system saw an opportunity to marry their objective—to obtain power within the party—with the interests of voters, who were left feeling disenfranchised after the 1968 nominating convention and would support a more open nomination process.**

National Democratic Party Chairman Fred Harris, a U.S. Senator from Oklahoma, appointed a commission, chaired initially by South

*Maxim 1: Assume a Winning Position* 53

Dakota Senator George McGovern and later Congressman Donald Fraser of Minnesota, to make changes to party rules that increased participation by more people and minority groups who felt left out of the party affairs. Some of the new rules adopted by Democrats required that adequate notice be given about meetings and that party members be given ample time to discuss platform resolutions. To abide by these directives and still hold their state convention in June, state Democratic leaders decided to hold their caucuses in late January.[80]

One of the first candidates to benefit from these changes was none other than George McGovern. In 1972, a young campaign manager named Gary Hart, working for then obscure presidential candidate Senator George McGovern was seeking a way to get attention and gain momentum for the upcoming New Hampshire primary. He reasoned that the Iowa caucus might provide that opportunity. McGovern campaigned extensively in Iowa and surprised political reporters by collecting 22.6 percent of the Democratic vote. Maine Senator Edmund Muskie—and running mate of Presidential candidate Humphrey in 1968—received 35.5 percent, finishing second to "Uncommitted" delegates at 35.8 percent.[81] The stage was set for the March 7 New Hampshire Primary, where official ballots were cast at regular polling places.

Unfortunately, Muskie had more to contend with than simply McGovern's momentum, as remembered by *Congressional Quarterly Politics* Editor, Bob Benenson:

> Muskie then had a bumpy New Hampshire campaign, best remembered for his emotional reaction to negative stories about him and his wife published in the Manchester *Union Leader*, which then was a strongly conservative voice in state politics. Muskie held a press event on a snowy day to denounce the stories (some of which, it later turned out, were dirty tricks waged by operatives in the campaign of incumbent President Nixon). Muskie appeared to some observers to be crying during the event, though he said the water running down his face was melted snow. The outcome of the contest was similar to that in Iowa: Muskie won, but his 46 percent to 37 percent lead over McGovern was treated as

a poor performance for the resident of neighboring Maine. Muskie soon faded from the race . . . [82]

In the 1976 Democratic nominating process, another Presidential unknown, a peanut farmer and former Georgia Governor Jimmy Carter, would campaign extensively and seemingly come from nowhere to win the Iowa Caucus with 27.6 percent of the caucus votes to Indiana Senator Birch Bayh's 13.2 percent, the only other close contender. After being elected president, Carter attributed some of his success to his favorable finish in Iowa, a strategy quickly adopted by future presidential candidates.

**Issues Are Human Needs**

When setting out to define a winning position in the minds of the targeted universe and multi-various stakeholders, it involves a complex understanding of psychology, sociology and political science. Consider, for example, the Hierarchy of Human Needs developed by American psychologist Abraham Maslow.[83] Maslow's theory stated in its most simple form is that human beings focus on the most basic needs until those are met before they are able to focus on higher-level needs.

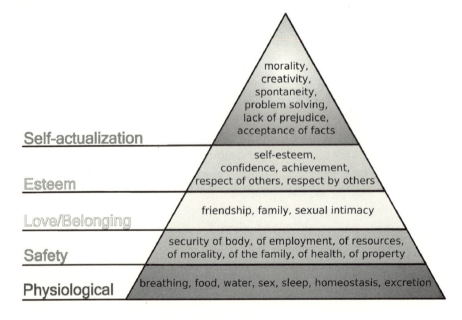

For example, the most basic necessities are oxygen, food, water, sex, sleep, homeostasis and excretion. Once these most basic needs are met, the individual then focuses on a higher level of need, such as safety of the body and security of employment, financial resources, moral issues, family well-being, health, and property matters. Love and belonging (friendship, family, sexual intimacy) is the next level, followed by matters of self-esteem (self-esteem, confidence, achievement, respect of others, respect by others). At the top of the pyramid in terms of human needs are issues of self-actualization. These include morality, creativity, spontaneity, problem solving, lack of prejudice and acceptance of facts.

This theory helps explain why the major issues of one election may be around moral and patriotic issues, such as prayer in schools, respect for the American flag or morning recitation of the American Pledge of Allegiance in public schools. According to Maslow's theory, only voters who have a pretty good situation—plenty of food, shelter, a secure job, a safe family environment, and opportunities for self-actualization—would have the ability to focus on topics such as whether or not school children recite a pledge of allegiance each morning. On the other hand, voters who are facing unemployment or feel threatened by terrorists or foreign governments will direct their attention to those issues and be compelled to vote for candidates who they believe identify with them on those needs.

Issue managers can almost certainly equate lifestyle with money concerns because the availability of income generally drives lifestyle choices. Money matters—income tax, property tax, additional sales tax, value-added tax, capital gains tax, price of gasoline, food costs, housing values, interest rates—anything that directly affects money coming into or out of a household will receive top priority. Future money matters—healthcare costs and insurance, retirement savings and investment, paying for a child's education—also rank high with voters.

## International Failure to Define a Winning Position

In other parts of the world, race issues continue to produce strife and tragic events. In the summer of 2008, 50-year-old Dereck Gurupira, 50, was bathing in the river near his home in Zimbabwe's Manicaland Province late one afternoon. He was surprised to see a woman on the opposite bank begin to remove her clothes. Normally men and women bathe at different parts of the river, and he wondered if it was possible she did not see him.[84]

But the woman called him by name and invited him to sit by her. When he complied, Gurupira was startled by a man wielding an ax emerging from the brush. The seemingly irate husband accused him of having a sexual relationship with his wife. The case was settled in the traditional Zimbabwe court. Gurupira was fined two cows and a goat for the "illicit relationship," which the woman falsely attested to.[85]

Incidents such as these are on the rise in Zimbabwe where severe and chronic hunger is forcing residents to lower their personal codes of conduct and ethical behavior just to get an adequate amount of nutrition, according to Integrated Regional Information Networks (IRIN), the humanitarian news and analysis service of the United Nations Office for the Coordination of Humanitarian Affairs. For decades Zimbabwe was a nation rich in at least 40 different commercial minerals, including gold, copper, nickel, iron coal and chrome. The backbone of its economy has been agriculture, and the country once served as a breadbasket for other countries in the sub-Saharan region, raising corn, cotton, tobacco, wheat, coffee, tea, sugarcane, peanuts, cattle, sheep, goats and pigs.[86]

But in 2008, the country is beset by a combination of economic woes. In August of this year, the government revalued its dollar by dropping 10 zeros from the dollar exchange rate. Prior to the revision in exchange rate, an American dollar equaled 10 billion (10,000,000,000) Zimbabwe dollars. The monetary action became necessary when the nation's treasury was forced to print a 100 billion dollar note to cover the smallest purchases. Bank computers faltered, unable to process so many transactions involving billions of trillions of dollars. Tragically, even the 100 billion dollar note was not enough to buy a simple item such as a loaf of bread.[87] The monetary chaos was the result of a hyperinflation rate officially stated at 2.2 million percent a year. But other economists suggest it is closer to 12 to 15 million percent. Unemployment is at 80 percent.[88]

Famine is a serious threat to survival in Zimbabwe. In testimony submitted July 30, 2008, to the U.S. House of Representatives Committee on the Budget by Josette Sheeran, Executive Director of the United Nations World Food Programme, stated that Zimbabwe is one of 17 countries in the world facing urgent food needs that will be helped by a supplemental appropriations bill, which was signed by President George

W. Bush on June 30, 2008. The act supplies $850 million to address new emergency needs in countries such as Darfur, Somalia, Ethiopia, Afghanistan and Myanmar as well as Zimbabwe.[89]

Westerners may look on in puzzlement and disbelief at why such a once prosperous African nation can arrive at such a regrettable state of ruin. The evolution of Zimbabwe as a modern nation presents a vivid case study in the foolhardiness of choosing a position that is untenable and the tragedy that may ensue.

To understand the current situation in Zimbabwe, it is necessary to first examine the history and geography of this beautiful land, home to Victoria Falls, one of the natural wonders of the world. Located in southeastern Africa, Zimbabwe is slightly larger at 150,873 square miles than the state of Montana. It is bordered by Mozambique on the east; by Zambia on the northwest side; Botswana on the southwestern border and South Africa due south. Ethnically, the country's estimated 8 to 9 million people are 71 percent Shona, Ndebele 16 percent, other African 11percent, white 1 percent, mixed and Asian 1 percent.[90]

Zimbabwe is a confusing mix of contradictions. It is 75 percent Christian, and offshoot Christian sects, animist (primitive spiritual belief) and Muslim converts compose the rest. The official language is English, and surprisingly, the literacy rate is 90.5 percent. On the other hand, the health situation is not as impressive. The life expectancy, according to the

World Health Organization, for males is 37 and women 34.[91] That is a decline over the past two decades from an average life expectancy of 62. The dramatic drop in life expectancy is blamed on the Human Immunodeficiency Virus (HIV), which is the cause of Acquired Immune Deficiency Syndrome (AIDS). HIV infects approximately one in five citizens of Zimbabwe. The country's 1.8 million estimated cases in 2001 make it the fourth highest HIV-infected country in the world.[92] The infant mortality rate per 1,000 live births is 55, comparable to South Africa at 56, but much better than neighbors Mozambique (138), Zambia (102) and Botswana (90).[93]

Historically Zimbabwe has been home to a proud and industrious people. Archaeologists who discovered Stone Age implements and pebble tools in several areas of the country believe that the human history of Zimbabwe began centuries ago. Stone ruins also indicate that early inhabitants were organized into a primitive civilization. Scientists estimate the early inhabitants built the structures between the 9th and 13th centuries C.E. Bantu peoples from equatorial regions supplanted the original inhabitants and are the ancestors of the region's Africans today.[94]

Not until the 16th century did the Portuguese become the first Europeans attempt to colonize south-central Africa. Otherwise, the area was generally untouched by whites until the arrival of explorers, missionaries, ivory hunters, and traders some 300 years later. [95]

Then in 1888, Zimbabwe received great attention from the United Kingdom after gold was discovered in the area of what is now South Africa. In 1888, Cecil Rhodes, an English-born South African statesman, founder of the DeBeers Mining Company, and philanthropist, who left his fortune to create Oxford University's Rhodes Scholarships, obtained a concession for mineral rights to the land of the Ndebele (Matabele) Kingdom. Rhodes further assumed authority to take whatever steps necessary to exploit the minerals of the region, even if that action required taking over control of the kingdom itself. Rhodes chartered the British South Africa Company in 1889, and established the settlement of Salisbury (now Harare, the capital) in 1890. In 1895, the territory was formally named Rhodesia in honor of Rhodes. Rhode's mining enterprise, the British South Africa Company, took over administration of Rhodesia.[96]

In 1923 the United Kingdom annexed the Rhodesian territory from the British South Africa Company, calling it the British Colony of Southern Rhodesia. Not until after World War II did more than half of white Zimbabweans, primarily of English origin, arrive in Zimbabwe. Until the mid-1970s, there were about 1,000 white immigrants to South Rhodesia per year, but from 1976 to 1985 a steady emigration resulted in a loss of more than 150,000, leaving about 100,000 in 1992.[97]

Despite the small number of white settlers, the country has been ruled and dominated by whites. A 1961 constitution was formulated that favored the whites already in power. Unfortunately, the ruling white minority did not realize that by this point in history, the sweeping tide of independence by a host of other African nations would eventually help determine the fate of Rhodesia, either in a positive or negative way.

Between 1958 and 1964, 26 African nations gained their freedom from colonial rule. A new group of empowered visionary men were leading the way—among them, Dr. Kwame Nkrumah in Ghana, Ahmed Sckou Toure in Guinea, and Patrice Lumumba in the Belgian Congo.[98] In the ensuing struggles for independence and majority rule, a tragic pattern began to emerge—a black majority attempts to assume its share of power from a European white minority; the whites resist; a military struggle ensues ultimately resulting in widespread death and destruction; finally the whites lose power or are forced to share it as the cost of resistance becomes too great.

Instead of avoiding this pattern, Rhodesia blindly followed its treacherous path. In 1964, Ian Smith—born of Scottish parents in Rhodesia and who ultimately renounced his British citizenship—gained political power among South Rhodesian whites by adamantly opposing black rule. When the British government under Prime Minister Harold Wilson pressured Smith to share power and grant more civil rights to Africans, Smith on behalf of his fellow Rhodesians unilaterally declared independence from the Commonwealth on Dec. 22, 1966. The U.K. refused to recognize Rhodesia as an independent country under white minority rule and demanded more complete voting rights for the black African majority in the country.

Britain, which supported a policy of independence only for colonies that practice true majority rule, tried to negotiate, offering Smith terms that would have delayed black majority rule until after 2000. The stubborn prime minister rejected the deal outright. Using discriminatory voting requirements, blacks were essentially barred from voting in Rhodesian elections. Rhodesia never won international recognition as an independent nation and faced United Nations sanctions for 14 years. The only supporter Smith could turn to was South Africa, which practiced another racist policy called apartheid.[99] Slowly taking on all characteristics of a despot, Smith banned opposition parties and jailed political opponents, such as Robert Mugabe, who would spend 10 years in prison, but eventually become a national hero and the nation's first black leader.

Smith's African nationalist opponents fled government persecution to neighboring countries, where they recruited and trained guerrilla fighters. Tragically, the African leaders such as Mugabe were exposed to Marxist and Communist political theories and practices. Both China and the Soviet Union offered assistance, which lent a Cold War aspect to the struggle for independence among former African colonies. Guerillas launched a war in 1972 to oust the Smith regime and take back the land from whites. In the long, bloody struggle, 30,000 to 40,000 people died. South Africa initially sent combat police to help defend Rhodesia but tired of the war that was destabilizing its northern border and withdrew financial support.

With great reluctance Smith accepted a peace plan proposed in 1976 by a U.S.-led diplomatic delegation headed by Secretary of State Henry Kissinger to introduce black majority rule to the country within two years. Smith begrudgingly accepted the terms. Smith won re-election in 1977 by an overwhelming margin, the last year a white minority would be voted into power. Under the 1977 electoral system, only 85,000 whites elected 50 white Members of Parliament (MPs) while eight MPs were elected to represent 6 million blacks. According to the electoral system at the time, such a small number of blacks were elected because only 7,000 black voters were eligible to vote.[100]

Ninety years of white minority rule finally ended in June 1979. A moderate black, Bishop Abel Muzorewa, was named interim prime minister and the name of the country changed to Rhodesia-Zimbabwe. Muzorewa served only six months until the country reverted to a British colony under a British governor Lord Soames, as a part of the process moving the country toward independence.

Mugabe returned in triumph from exile on January 27, 1980, and declared: "We will not seize land from anyone who has a use for it." He also said that there would be no more injustice based on race and color. But even as Mugabe made a speech to an estimated gathering of 200,000 rejoicing supporters, a man suspected of being a supporter of outgoing Prime Minister Muzorewa was seized by the crowd and accused of carrying a gun. He was carried to the front of the podium where Mugabe was speaking, punched, kicked, his clothes torn off and thrown under the stand.[101] Was this a foreshadowing of things to come?

Mugabe eventually won election in 1980 and has served as the country's only black prime minister until 1987 when he became president. The country became independent under the name Zimbabwe on April 18, 1980. Unfortunately, disturbing events began to occur under the Mugabe reign. In March 1983, political opponent Joshua Nkomo fled the country under death threats.[102] Mugabe accused him of plotting to overthrow the government.

*Frontline* journalist Stephen Talbot, who interviewed Mugabe as an idealist guerilla leader in exile in Tanzania in 1977, is troubled by the change in Mugabe. He described the change he had observed in an article in 2006:

> Yet even as early as the 1980s, there was an ominous turn of events. Mugabe had formed a coalition "Patriotic Front" government with a rival guerrilla leader, Joshua Nkomo, but it soon fell apart when Mugabe accused Nkomo of plotting a coup against him. Mugabe shocked many of his international supporters by unleashing his North Korean-trained Fifth Brigade against Nkomo's minority Ndebele tribe in southern Zimbabwe. Thousands were killed. *Frontline* was one of the few media outlets in the United States to sound the alarm, in the 1983 documentary Crisis in Zimbabwe, reported by Charlie Cobb, an African-American journalist, who, like me, was dismayed to see Mugabe acting as brutally and repressively as the white-minority rulers he had replaced.[103]

Despite a promise not to seize land, Mugabe also declared in 1976 as he battled for majority rule, "Half the land is in the hands of 250,000 settlers."[104] And according to 2002 government figures, some 4, 400 whites owned 32% of Zimbabwe's agricultural land—around 10 million hectares—while about one million black peasant families farmed only 16m hectares or 38%.[105]

In 2000, Mugabe announced at a rally that all white-owned farms could be seized and given to landless blacks. Despite Zimbabwe court rulings that land seizures are illegal, the government in 2001 announced it would confiscate 5,000 white-owned farms. A serious economic crisis and serious food shortages developed, yet farmers were banned from cultivating fields. Most Western donors cut aid because of the land seizure program.

Talbot pointed out in his story for the Public Broadcasting Service (PBS) that Mugabe's confiscation of white-owned farms in the last six years has been highly political. Zimbabwe inherited an inequitable agricultural system from colonial Rhodesia. A quarter of a million whites owned most of the fertile, productive farmland in a nation of what was then 7 million blacks. The farms were efficient and bountiful, producing tobacco as a cash crop and more than enough corn to feed the country and to export. African demand for land reform was strong, but Mugabe did not want to jeopardize the economy, and despite some militant talk, he did almost nothing to redistribute land until he was challenged in the polls.[106]

Then, Talbot noted, Mugabe suddenly played the race card when his popularity waned. He urged "war veterans"— unemployed, demobilized guerrilla soldiers—to occupy white farms. Also, ownership of many farms was simply transferred to Mugabe's cronies, who proved to be either incapable of farming or totally disinterested in it. Most whites have left the country, sometimes invited to start over in neighboring Zambia or Mozambique. Thousands of black farm workers have lost their jobs, and agriculture has collapsed. Malnutrition is now widespread.[107]

"The whole country, now some 12 million people, has closed in upon itself, cut off from the rest of the world, trapped in its own private torment," Talbot reported.[108]

But much of the white-owned land is in more fertile areas with better rainfall, while the black farming areas are often in drought-prone regions. So in terms of prime farming land, whites still own a disproportionate share.[109]

Mugabe's own native Africans, not whites, are the worst victims of Mugabe's policies. In 2005, Mugabe launched Operation Murambatsvina, a "cleanup" program that destroyed tens of thousands of shanty dwellings. More than 700,000 Zimbabwean were left homeless.[110] Opponents of Mugabe say the slum clearance was aimed at scattering potential political opposition. Ordinary Zimbabweans believe Mugabe had the dwellings destroyed to clear the way for occupation by businesses from China, a country that recently has begun strengthening ties with the Mugabe government.[111]

"Overnight, Zimbabwe has been turned into a massive internal refugee center with between 1 million and 1.5 million people displaced in Harare alone," Morgan Tsvangirai, the opposition leader who ran for president on the Movement for Democratic Change (MDC) ticket, said at a news conference in 2005 following the destruction of shanties. "Property worth millions of dollars has gone up in flames. Families are out in the open without jobs, without shelter."[112]

Now as an octogenarian, Mugabe continues to hold on to power as he begins his sixth term in public office. The British Broadcasting Corporation (BBC) says of Mugabe, he "belongs to the African liberationists tradition of the 1960s—strong and ruthless leadership, anti-Western, suspicious of capitalism and deeply intolerant of dissent and opposition."[113]

Today, Mugabe is one of Africa's longest-reigning dictators, routinely denounced by Amnesty International and Human Rights Watch for abusing his people. "A disgrace to Africa," says Wole Soyinka, Nigeria's Nobel Prize-winning author. "A caricature of an African dictator," says Desmond Tutu, South Africa's Nobel laureate. And Pius Ncube, the Catholic archbishop of Bulawayo, Zimbabwe, says he prays for "a popular uprising" to topple Mugabe's regime.[114]

Mugabe's despotic activities have continued even during the most recent Zimbabwe presidential election held in March 2008. His main opponent, MDC's Tsvangirai claimed victory but did not win enough votes for an outright election. Tsvangirai pulled out of a planned June runoff election because of state-sponsored violence that killed more than 150 opposition supporters, injured thousands and left tens of thousands homeless during the election cycle. Mugabe went ahead with a one-man presidential runoff widely dismissed by the international community as a sham.[115]

Talks began in South Africa shortly after Mugabe's uncontested election between representatives of Tsvangirai and Mugabe to discuss the creation of some form of power-sharing agreement. President George W. Bush applied pressure to reach a compromise by issuing an executive order on July 25, 2008, to step up sanctions against what the President called the "illegitimate" regime of Zimbabwe's President Robert Mugabe and his supporters. Bush added the further incentive of economic assistance.[116]

"Should ongoing talks in South Africa between Mugabe's regime and the Movement for Democratic Change result in a new government that reflects the will of the Zimbabwean people, the United States stands ready to provide a substantial assistance package, development aid, and normalization with international financial institutions," Bush said.[117]

U.S. Senator Russ Feingold, a Democrat from Wisconsin and chairman of the Senate Foreign Relations subcommittee on African affairs, also called upon the international community to bring an end to what he termed the "staggering" reports of killings, torture and sexual violence.[118]

**Staking out an intractable position that puts you in direct conflict with motivated stakeholders is a recipe for spectacular failure.**

After more than 40 years, Zimbabwe is no longer the strong, prosperous African nation it was in the earlier part of the 20th century. While many will say history has affirmed the apocalyptic prophesies of former Rhodesian Prime Minister Ian Smith, the opportunity for a peaceful transition to a government that more equitably represents its citizens was lost under Smith's leadership for all time. Had Smith and other white minority leaders accepted the inevitability of power sharing with blacks and embraced a more inclusive form of governance, more moderate black leaders would have emerged. By taking a position that drove black political leaders from the country and forcing them to wage guerilla war for freedom, the best and brightest leadership came under the influence of the Soviet Union, China and other governments promulgating Marxist doctrines.

Had the Smith government accepted the fact that the government would be made up of both blacks and whites and then prepared individuals to take on leadership positions, the government could have gone on without the destructive turmoil of guerilla war and unnecessary deaths of men, women and children. By ruthlessly resisting the inevitability of power sharing, the white government diffused hatred throughout the land. Forcing black leaders into exile created a power vacuum filled by those bold and unscrupulous enough to seize authority by force.

Speaking at a U.S. State Department conference in June 2008 on African trade, Secretary of State Condoleeza Rice perhaps best summed up what has now become the inevitable course of history for the Mugabe government: "In the Mugabe regime, we see the page of history that Africa must turn—a leader for independence, which inherited a nation full of promise, but which has devolved into a tyranny that values nothing but power," she said. "It is hard to imagine how Africa will ever reach its full potential until all of its leaders are accountable to and respectful of the will of its people."[119]

Age and the changing times may soon bring the Mugabe regime to a peaceful end. Like the white minority rule before him, Mugabe embarked upon an unwinnable position.

## St. Paul—Tracing a Winning Position that Reshaped World History

While citizens of Zimbabwe struggle to survive more than 40 years after ruling whites tragically rejected a winning position, in another millennium, the Christian Apostle Paul rejected the idea that a religion was exclusive, and thereby changed the course of world history.

The basis for Paul's actions is evident in his letter to the Galatians in the New Testament of the Bible. His letter begins with a startling and harsh tone—Paul is angry. His words are blunt and to the point. To paraphrase what he says, "I thought we had all of this worked out, and then you do this." He accuses Peter and James (the brother of Jesus), two of the primary pillars of Christianity, with hypocrisy. And the precipitating event that becomes the object of Paul's scorn is the fact that Peter, James, and other brothers of the faith refused to eat with non-Jews, commonly referred to in New Testament times as Gentiles.

Paul writes:

> **2:11.** "But when Cephas [referring to Peter] came to Antioch, I opposed him to his face, because he had clearly done wrong.
> **2:12.** Until certain people came from James, he had been eating with the Gentiles. But when they arrived, he stopped doing this and separated himself because he was afraid of those who were pro-circumcision
> **2:13.** And the rest of the Jews also joined with him in this hypocrisy, so that even Barnabas was led astray with them by their hypocrisy.
> **2:14.** But when I saw that they were not behaving consistently with the truth of the gospel, I said to Cephas in front of them all, "If you, although you are a Jew, live like a Gentile and not like a Jew, how can you try to force the Gentiles to live like Jews?"[120]

While this incident seems minor in the overall 2,000-year history of Christianity, it actually represents a major turning point in the development of the world's most popular religion, in terms of numbers of followers (2.1 billion, or one-third of all the people in the world, practice Christianity; 1.3 billion, or one in five, are Muslim; and there are 851 million Hindu).[121] It also marks the moment at which Paul selects his "winning position," and rejects a divisive, exclusive doctrine that in the course of the ages, most likely would have relegated Christianity to a minor Jewish cult, possibly abandoned, and all but forgotten by modern times.

To analyze how Paul's decisions in picking the proper fight helped ensure the survival of Christianity, we first must place his actions in the proper context of events occurring in the first 40 years following the narrative of the death and resurrection of the proclaimed Messiah, Jesus of Nazareth.

The pre-Christian Paul—who was first a Jew and a Pharisee—saw the world composed of two groups: Jews and everyone else.[122] Jews saw themselves as a special selected group apart from the rest of the world. "Christianity is so easily imagined as somehow the opposite of Judaism, because that's how Christianity has presented Judaism to itself in the centuries long after Paul," says Paula Fredriksen, William Goodwin Aurelio Professor of the Appreciation of Scripture at Boston University. Fredriksen specializes in the social and intellectual history of ancient Christianity, from the late Second Temple period to the fall of the Western Roman Empire. "In Paul's lifetime, Christianity is only understandable as an extreme form of Judaism. And Paul thinks of himself as a Jew."[123]

Scholars such as Fredriksen and others paint a smoothly homogenous picture of society and culture of the New Testament times in Jerusalem and other areas mentioned in Christian literature. The common language was Greek, but the political and military organization was Roman. Some inhabitants were Jews, and Judaism incorporated the early forms of Christianity into its beliefs. Jews and Romans mingled, each with their God or gods, respectively. Neither side took it upon themselves to offend the other. Jews who chose to believe in Jesus were still Jews. They still obeyed dietary restrictions, and Jewish men continued the practice of circumcision. But Jews and the Christian Jews still worshipped the same God of Israel.[124]

When Saul of Tarsus, the Pharisee who eventually became Paul, was struck blind by the appearance of Jesus on the road to Damascus, contrary to many Christians' beliefs, Saul did not suddenly become Christian and a non-Jew. In a 2005 interview, James D. Tabor, chair of the Department of Religious Studies at the University of North Carolina at Charlotte points out that not even Paul could be considered a Christian in the early days of the faith. Tabor, who specializes in biblical studies, with an emphasis on Christian origins and ancient Judaism, spoke with *Vision.org* publisher David Hulme:

> If anyone could be labeled as a Christian, you might think it is Paul, until you back off a bit and look. I often point out to my students that he is preaching the Hebrew God, Yahweh or Jehovah. He is telling the gentiles about the Hebrew Bible. It is translated into Greek, but it is essentially Abraham, Isaac, Jacob. So instead of reading about Zeus, Apollo and the pantheon, they are going to hear Jewish stories. If you look at Paul's letters, he refers to the stories as if they either know them or should know them: "our father Abraham," "consider Isaac." He

expects these gentiles to be very Judaized. He is giving them a very Jewish form of morality, a Jewish view of time and the future (eschatology)—they are very apocalyptic. So when you add up all of that, what would you call them? It's clear to me that the movement for the first hundred years should be seen as part of Judaism.[125]

The miracle—as well as considerable irony—associated with Paul is that he was one of the most zealous persecutors of the early Christians, and yet he became the second most important figure in Christianity next to Jesus himself. As a Pharisee, Paul was a strict enforcer of the Jewish laws in both written and oral forms. In the book of Acts, Paul, then called Saul, observes no boundary to the degree of violence to which he would go to punish Christians for professing their belief in Jesus. Saul participates in the martyrdom of Stephen—looking after the cloaks of those who stoned Christianity's first martyr in 34 C.E.—and according to Acts 8:1-3, becomes a sworn, bitter enemy of the early Christians:

> **8:1.** Now on that day a great persecution began against the church in Jerusalem, and all except the apostles were forced to scatter throughout the regions of Judea and Samaria.
> **8:2.** Some devout men buried Stephen and made loud lamentation over him.
> **8:3.** But Saul was trying to destroy the church; entering one house after another, he dragged off both men and women and put them in prison.[126]

Following Saul's religious experience on the road to Damascus and subsequent changing of his name to Paul, he went to Jerusalem and then to Antioch. Scholars, such as L. Michael White, Professor of Classics and Director of the Religious Studies Program, University of Texas at Austin, believe that Paul began preaching to Gentiles apparently out of his own revelatory experience that this was the mission that had been given him by God, when God called him to function as a prophet for this new Jesus movement.[127]

It was during Paul's early preaching that he went to Antioch to create a sort of base of operations, where he began to come into conflict with other members of the new Jesus movement. It is here that the issue arises, primarily out of work converting Gentiles to a belief in Jesus: Does one first have to become a Jew to become a Christian? [128]

For Paul, the answer is "No." He perceived the winning position to be that Christianity should be inclusive and should appeal to a large, popular base of support. Jews traditionally saw themselves as separate from the rest of the population. Christianity, for them, was a matter of teaching Jews about Jesus. If a Greek or Roman subject were not Jewish, then from the Jewish viewpoint, they were required to become a Jew and uphold all Jewish laws pertaining to circumcision for men, food restrictions, and other laws for men and women in every area of daily life.[129]

As a Roman citizen steeped in rich Greek culture, Paul could anticipate the difficulties in converting a Gentile to a Jew and then to a Christian. For one thing, the Greek culture, which stressed physical fitness and the beauty of the body, would have resisted circumcision as a requirement for conversion. Because males exercised nude in the Greek gymnasiums, some scholars are convinced this would have been a major hurdle in bringing Greeks and others into the fold.[130]

So when some Jewish believers arrived in Antioch where Paul was building a foundation for his missionary work, they insisted that Gentiles brought to Christ should be circumcised and keep all the Jewish customs based on the Laws of Moses.[131] The tensions resulting from this theological conflict led to the Jerusalem Council, where Paul met with the apostles Peter, John, Jesus's brother James, and other leaders of the Jerusalem Church. Paul apparently made a convincing case for his point of view based upon his results in preaching a "Law-Free" Gospel among the Gentiles.

The decision made by the Jerusalem Church leaders set the stage for the growth and history changing success of Christianity. Paul received approval to take Jesus's message to the Gentiles. Peter and the others would concentrate upon converting Jews to Christianity.[132]

For Paul, this was a great victory, and it reinforced his message of equality and inclusiveness among all peoples. Paul's authority for preaching the Law-Free Gospel was based upon his interpretation of Jesus's mission to bring God to all peoples on earth, regardless of sex, race or previous religious belief.

It is in this context in which Paul becomes irate with Peter for shunning contact with Gentiles during a meal in Antioch. At this point, Paul changes his mission to focus upon Gentiles, which enhanced Christianity's opportunity for success by appealing to a much greater population of non-Jews than Jews. His targeted audience was now the masses, not just a limited number of people within Judaism.

With Peter's blessing, Paul began his far-reaching missionary work. An article authored by *Christianity Today International* points out that Paul was ideally equipped to serve as a missionary for the fledgling Christian movement.

> In him three great cultures merged. A Roman citizen, he had entree to the entire Roman world. Steeped in Greek culture, he could convey his ideas across the Hellenized world. A Pharisee, strictest of the Jews, he carried in himself the Mosaic law and had points of contact in the synagogues of the empire. . . . In addition to his Christology, Paul pioneered the missionary tactics of the early church, brought the gospel to the Gentiles and came as close as any apostolic writer to creating a systematic theology.[133]

University of Texas Professor L. Michael White comments on a similar advantage Paul had in blending Jewish and Greek culture:

> Paul's an interesting case because he is so able to blend a thoroughly Jewish self consciousness and a thoroughly Jewish interpretation of scripture with a great deal of knowledge of Greek rhetoric and philosophy of standard letter writing and other aspects of Greek culture. Paul really is a blend of all of those things and it's precisely that blending that seems to provide a lot of the dynamic quality of his understanding of early Christianity.[134]

Following the break with Peter, Paul chose another winning tactic by taking the Christian message to all peoples through a series of successful crusades. He left Antioch, which Paul initially had selected as a base of operations because of a substantial Jewish community among the half-million residents. Antioch would also become the third largest city in the Roman Empire by the 1st century C.E., and it was here that residents coined the term "Christian," 10 to 15 years after Jesus's crucifixion.[135]

**Achieving sustainable success will require thinking outside the box for ways to bring other stakeholders around to support your cause.**

Paul also wisely selected major population areas along busy trade routes and near bustling ports. For example, Corinth, whose Christians were the recipient of Paul's two epistles to the Corinthians, was a major commercial city with a diverse population of 475,000. Inhabitants included Romans, Greeks, Jews, Syrians, Egyptians and a host of sailors, traders and slaves.[136] Or, for example, Thessalonica, the chief city of Macedonia, situated around a harbor at the head of the Aegean Sea and on the great Roman thoroughfare enabled it to become a great commercial city, with a mixed population of Greeks, Romans and Jews, the first being the most numerous.[137]

Paul would not live to see his life's mission fulfilled or to witness the power of Christianity as a major world religion. While no one knows for sure what happened to Paul, he ended his Aegean career and traveled to Rome to garner support to start a Gentile mission in Spain where no one had heard the message of Jesus. Tradition holds that Paul was martyred in Rome without ever reaching Spain.[138]

Nevertheless, in his lifetime Paul had made several decisions that created winning positions in the battle to establish the early Christian church. He chose unity over divisiveness; he took a position that appealed to the masses as opposed to a few righteous zealots as Paul had once been; and embarked upon a path that allowed him to influence the message he was preaching and the audience to which it was addressed. Paul successfully blended the three main elements of his world—Judaism, Rome and Greek cultures—to help create a religion and set of moral values that most successfully fulfilled the spiritual needs of the New Testament times.

## Conclusion

As history has so aptly illustrated, starting from a winning position, is a basic strategy that, if followed, will help shape a direction and action plan that leads to long-term success.

First, solutions to challenges facing our nation and world should be inclusive and benefit the greatest amount of people. Divisive tactics that play upon irrational fears, may prove initially successful but will not withstand assaults by principled opposition.

Solutions should unite rather than divide. The viewpoints of all stakeholders must be taken into account and made part of the problem-solving process. Solutions should also appeal to the core values of the masses that create the foundation for a community, state or nation.

And finally, those seeking to create and manage change should take every opportunity to positively influence the outcome of an issue using best resources available in a proactive rather than reactive manner. For example, if a state legislature is considering the enactment of more stringent environmental regulations on an industry, then stakeholders in the business should proactively seek to influence the final legislation before it becomes law. An industry often does not have the political backing or popular support to stop environmental legislation in its tracks. That is no reason to give up. There may be a way to mitigate the effects of the proposed legislation upon business.

Sometimes it is possible to obtain present cost concessions or exemptions based upon a past record of effective environmental protection efforts. There may be a way to alleviate burdensome costs if the information is accurate and supports a reasonable business conclusion. The most important point, though, is that for a business to claim to be environmentally responsible, it must first be responsible and able to document such a claim.

Working within the framework of a state legislative system, these activities depend upon careful analysis of issues and facts, a thorough understanding of the political and legislative process and an impeccable sense of timing. Politics is not for amateurs. However, the business willing to acquire the necessary talent and expertise to effect change in politics, public issues, and regulator matters will undoubtedly craft a winning position that serves corporate shareholders, employees, and executives well.

# Maxim 2
## "Identifiable tasks with identifiable goals will lead to identifiable progress."

*A journey of a thousand miles begins with a single step.*

— Lao-tzu, Chinese philosopher (604–531 B.C.E.), author, *The Way of Lao-tzu*

## Overview

While traveling the country in the company of his dog Charley, Nobel Prize winning American author John Steinbeck considered the daunting task of writing a full novel from start to finish. He said:

> When I face the desolate impossibility of writing five hundred pages a sick sense of failure falls on me and I know I can never do it. This happens every time. Then gradually I write one page and then another. One day's work is all I can permit myself to contemplate.

As Steinbeck explains, the thought of having to tackle a complicated objective can be paralyzing. Instead, it is better to set incremental goals that make it possible to focus on one thing at a time and to make progressive movement toward the larger, cumulative objective. Because of their complexities, many situations seem inapproachable at first. Even the initial steps seem unclear.

That is the message and goal of Maxim 2: "Set tasks and goals that lead to identifiable progress." This chapter will delve into the concept of accomplishing the difficult, achieving goals such as the passage of a particular bill in the U.S. Congress or a state legislature, obtaining an operating license from a state regulatory agency, or even winning an election. These are projects that all have definite, measurable outcomes, but many people have no idea where to begin. It requires finding the steps in between the start and finish.

One of the great challenges in undertaking a complex task is in framing an overall goal in a way that it can be embraced and broken down into specific, measurable tasks. For example, a tangible project such as building a house is easier to think about in terms of decomposing the job into specific steps.

In such a situation, a project manager is working with real objects that have a heft and a feel. When the project is half finished, an observer can see half of a house. When it is finished, there is no doubt about it. A house with doors and windows that work, a roof, individual rooms with electrical wiring and plumbing, heating and air conditioning, and so on will be standing for the world to see, touch, and use.

Much of the world runs on projects that are not so tangible. Writing the Declaration of Independence resulted in a paper document containing ideas for a new form of government. The work in that situation involved capturing lofty ideas of justice and equality and stating them in a way that could serve as the basis to start a new country. Completing such a noble task requires the ability to apply achievable, measurable steps to a "soft" subject. Such soft subjects involve disciplines such as social science, political science, psychology and even marketing.

## *Chapter 2 Synopsis*

- Complicated, challenging tasks are overwhelming in their nature and can defeat a project manager before he is barely able to begin.
- Major projects should be viewed as a series of small steps with individual goals that are attainable and lead to each of the next steps.
- A series of tasks also serve as a roadmap showing the project manager and team the progress they are making and how far they have come.
- Achieving the goals of each step eventually leads to overall success of the greater objective.

As will be explored throughout this chapter, history teaches us that humans constantly strive to define our existence and control our destiny. In so doing, we attempt to make sense of our interactions with each other and the natural world. As opposed to natural science, in which a technician measures the temperature of a boiling substance or the pressure of a quantity of gas, "human science" attempts, in a sense, to measure the immeasurable.

For it is necessary to first define data, create measures, and then use these measures to predict outcomes of the irrational events encompassing human behavior. Just as a scientist knows that raising water to the temperature of 212 degrees Fahrenheit will cause it to boil and turn to vapor as steam, scientists studying human nature attempt to perfect a science that will lead to accurate predictions about how an individual will vote, or even what soft drink she will buy.

Through the centuries, one of the most enduring intellectual pursuits has been to create systematic frameworks to observe, classify, and quantify day-to-day experience. Although the emphasis was initially on defining the hard sciences, such as mathematics and physics, the contemporary focus has shifted to the importance of quantifying soft science disciplines such as psychology and sociology.

In any discipline, it is necessary to plan and set incremental goals, to set forth a comprehensive framework to an otherwise unapproachable problem, so that the completion of each task builds upon the progress of the tasks that preceded it. Because we measure progress by the continuing completion of these tasks, we are, in essence, creating quantifiable measures for intangible situations.

In issue management, setting identifiable tasks and goals enables the issue manager to change a complex issue by starting small and working forward. This concept has been proven effective long before the need for issue management arose, and on much larger international stages. Events of world history have illustrated that the ambitious and sometimes barbaric figures, such as Genghis Khan and Russia's Peter the Great, employed this technique on a grand scale to create a world empire.

## Genghis Khan, Boy Conqueror, Achieves Power Incrementally

Stories of Genghis Khan's accumulation of lands, resources, and military power have transcended the expanse of geography and generations, securing his reputation as one of the most successful and tough barbaric rulers in world history. During his reign, the Khan gained possession of his enemies' property and members of their tribes through the careful plotting and execution of identifiable tasks and goals.

Although scholars have focused on his international and intercontinental conquests, Genghis Khan embarked upon what would become a quest for world domination by starting on a much smaller stage. His blood-thirsty ambition ignited at the tribal level where, lacking the powerful armies he would eventually assemble, the future Khan achieved gradual, incremental increases in military might. Initially named Temujin, in honor of a bitter enemy his father admired, the young barbarian patiently gathered his conquests around him to build a major empire.

Born about 1162 C.E., Temujin was the son of the chief of the Yakka Mongols near the modern capital of Mongolia. When he was only nine years old, one of the tribe's enemies poisoned his father. Although Temujin was the rightful heir to the tribe's leadership, his own clan refused to recognize such a young child as their leader.

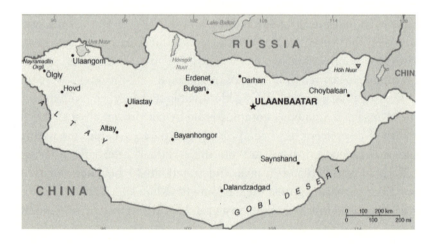

Instead, they ordered Temujin and the rest of his family into exile. Abandoned and left to fend for themselves, he and his mother, sister, three brothers, and two half-brothers, experienced the hardship of a nomadic people: traveling across harsh terrain, enduring extreme weather and relying on small game and wild fruits for a bare sustenance.

Several early experiences helped to shape Temujin as a fearless warrior and ruthless leader. When Temujin was 13 years old, he and one of his half-brothers were engaged in an impassioned quarrel over the spoils of a hunting expedition. In a territorial rage, young Temujin bludgeoned his brother to death.[139] This incident of early violence set the stage for the unbridled violence to come and solidified Temujin's place as the family's leader.

Sometime later, a rival tribe captured Temujin. His fortitude in withstanding torture and eventually in escaping from the shackles that held him furthered Tumujin's reputation as a resourceful leader. Stories of his exploits and bravery eventually enabled his family to end their exile and return to their tribe.

Even before the age of 20, Temujin had already begun to build on his burgeoning reputation as an unwavering, untamed fighter. Once restored to his native tribe, Temujin set out to achieve world domination.

Many ambitious leaders fail because of an unclear vision and strategy for arriving there. By the time Temujin had become Genghis Khan, he had learned his lessons in leadership quickly and thoroughly. Though no record exists of Temujin's step-by-step plan, one can presume—based on his tactics—that he sought to increase his might through strategic alliance and by dominating and destroying resistance along the way.

Operating under the military principle that there is strength in numbers, Temujin's first task would have required that additional tribes be assimilated into his increasing numbers. Presumably, Temujin's interaction with neighboring tribes enabled him to identify those clans with which he could likely align and those that he would have to contend with at a later time. Using a common project management approach to pick the low-hanging fruit that required less effort first, and save the more difficult out of reach tasks for later, Temujin built the easy alliances first.

Temujin began his campaign by setting his sights on the centrally located region of Mongolia. From a strategic standpoint, Mongolia represented the center of the wheel, where the spokes spread out to each of the outer reaches of Asia. It was here that Temujin began to forge relationships with small, neighboring tribes. Many of these tribes were no bigger than extended families, yet each new allegiance increased the group's overall numbers, and in turn, its strength as a united body.[140] With a specific goal of combining his growing clan with an influential neighboring tribe, Temujin attempted to form one of his alliances through marriage to his first wife Bortei. When an enemy tribe later kidnapped his bride, Temujin further increased his ranks of warriors, defeated the enemy and safely rescued his wife—a successful military campaign that drew additional families to his protection and power.

The strategic acquisition of "swing" clans placed a moderately sized tribe under Temujin's control and enabled him to apply various offensive strategies. Based upon their strength in combined manpower and resources, Temujin was able to attack tribes that could not have been peacefully absorbed.

After several more successful military campaigns, Temujin had organized the entire Mongol kingdom under his control by the young age of 25. By the ripe old age of 41, he was thenceforth known as Genghis Khan, which is translated, "Universal Lord."

Decades of shrewd alliance building and strategic military campaigns had gradually increased the sphere of Genghis Khan's influence, placing him in a position to control an abundance of land, wealth and military might. The Khan did stop there but continued to set make gains on a much larger scale than before. Genghis Khan began to organize his military into groups of 10, where 10 of each subset formed the larger set until they composed a "tumen" of 10,000 soldiers.[141]

Vowing to keep trusted leaders in charge, Genghis Khan placed family and close friends in positions of authority. In terms of weaponry, he placed nearly all of his army on horseback and improvised ways to keep his army mobile. For example, one such tactic was to use spare horses to carry extra supplies. He gathered enemy intelligence through spies and reconnaissance missions, attacking weaknesses aggressively and constantly evolving his military to adapt to different cultures, weapons and terrain.

In addition to innovative military strategies, Genghis Khan employed effective social strategies to reinforce his control over his subjects. He put local languages into writing, which allowed him to keep official records and to further record and continuously develop his Yasa, a code of laws that often alleviated a particular situation or hardship that he experienced earlier in life. For instance, The Khan prohibited the kidnapping of women because of the unpleasant experience of his own wife. He also banned the sale of women into arranged marriage, the theft of animals, and the hunting of game during certain seasons.[142]

Genghis Khan displayed the wisdom of setting tasks early on that would help him achieve his overall goal. His approach to success enabled him to survive when living in exile; to fight furiously—and deadly—when battling as a young warrior; to form strategic and family alliances with tribes to build his army's strength; to control the tribesmen and the culture of the peoples he had conquered. These represent a series of accomplishments on his way to becoming the Universal Lord, Genghis Khan.

**Genghis Khan did not become a world leader in one master stroke. He built his empire step-by-step, focusing on the specific tasks required to accomplish his immediate goals, while keeping his larger vision in sight.**

As he successfully accomplished each of these tasks, Genghis Khan took yet another discrete step in his progress to unmatched power. In the process he grew from a warrior to a leader, from a nomad who wanders the land to a ruler who controls it. His successful progress set the stage for the Khan to march his way across the world stage, and into history.

Many of his later successes are well-documented in the pages of history. The Khan and his organized Mongol army targeted and seized, in order: China, Iraq, Iran, western Turkestan, northern India, Pakistan, and Russia. As viewed on a current map, Khan's empire in 1226 stretched west to east from Poland to Korea, and north to south from Russia to Vietnam.

Even after the death of Genghis Khan in August 1227 following a fall from his horse, his well-organized army continued to fight and expand the Mongolian empire. One of their last conquests took place in Russia, where in 1237, the Mongol legions entered Moscow and destroyed the

Kremlin, a fortress erected to protect Russian nobility and to shut out enemy invaders.[143] The longevity of both the army and the empire is a testament to the skilled planning and execution of Genghis Khan.

## Peter the Great Westernizes Russia

Jumping ahead more than four centuries to Western Europe, a mysterious Russian ruler was attempting to travel the continent incognito. Nevertheless, standing nearly seven feet tall, with a disproportionately small head, small hands and feet, and a facial tic that sent one side of his face into uncontrollable seizures, Russia's Peter I, later known as Peter the Great, probably stood out like a sore thumb, despite his disguises of wigs and peasant costumes. Unlike Genghis Khan, who had not been allowed to rule his clan at the age of nine, Peter I was only 10 years old when he was appointed joint-czar of Russia.[144]

Even as a young man, however, Peter I had a vision for westernizing Russia in a way that would make it competitive with its European neighbors. To accomplish this goal, he began a series of tasks that, when completed, would boost Russia into the 18th century.

Born Pyotr Alexeyevich Romanov, Peter I ascended to the throne in May 1682. In the early 18th century, while Peter's Russian forces engaged in combat with Sweden seized an area of marshland that was not good for human habitation, but Peter recognized its strategic importance. On May 16, 1703 (May 27 by the modern calendar) Peter ordered a fortress constructed there, which he named the Fortress of St. Peter and St. Paul. Residents called the land around the fortress St. Petersburg.

Eventually St. Petersburg became the capital of the country and Peter was determined to make the city a model for the rest of Russia, what he termed a "window to the West." In Peter's mind, St. Petersburg would become a living model of the modernization that Peter hoped to impose upon the country in its entirety.

His ambition to "Westernize" Russia was a challenge made particularly difficult because the population, spread over great expanses of land, still lived in a medieval state. Peter realized that he would need a detailed, step-by-step plan that laid out a series of goals achieving the ultimate objective of modernizing the military, business, social and scientific institutions that would be critical to making Russia competitive among the European powers.

A major part of Peter's research required traveling across Europe, observing and absorbing the best of business, culture, and science that each country had to offer. Peter often traveled incognito or in costume. At one time, for example, he dressed as a common sailor while touring the English shipyards. Although he was often recognized or discovered, one can imagine the possibilities of Peter's attempted disguises: wigs, masks, exotic clothing, and any number of diversions to publicly obscure or conceal his identity as the Czar of Russia. Most likely, all to no avail.

One such incident involving the German emperor illustrates Peter's difficulty in going about Europe unnoticed. Nearing the end of his stay in Vienna, the German emperor threw a masquerade ball in Peter's honor. Peter attended the formal affair dressed as a peasant from West Friesland, a territory in Northern Holland. Throughout the course of the evening, the emperor—also in costume—poured glasses of expensive drink and offered them to Peter, publicly toasting 'to the peasant of West Friesland and his undying love for the Czar of Russia.'[145] The joke was not wasted on the other attendees of the ball, who were quite aware that the peasant was actually the Czar of Russia.

In response, to the toasts, Peter drank to the wellbeing of his host and to his host's unyielding affection for the Emperor of Germany. The audience was also aware that the host was the Emperor of Germany in masquerade costume. The revelers sent up a roar of applause in appreciation of the clever, role-playing toasts by Peter and the German Emperor.

Throughout 1697 and 1698, Peter traveled, often under a pseudonym, to a broad cross-section of Western European countries, such as England, Switzerland, Holland, Italy, and Prussia. Along his journey, he visited military and civilian schools, factories, and museums, in addition to military arsenals facilities. Having educated himself in all aspects of Western European culture and military knowledge, Peter returned to Russia with Western philosophers, educators, businessmen, and military personnel in tow to serve as advisers.[146]

Although Peter was building a city from the ground up, he recognized the value in implementing programs and policies that other countries had already ironed out through the earlier course of their development. Peter used available knowledge as a means for identifying a path forward.

Despite his enlightened attitude toward Western ideas and progress, Peter was known for his ruthlessness and cruelty in quelling political opposition to his plans. He sent spies throughout Russia to ascertain exactly who had articulated negative viewpoints toward his program. Armed with this knowledge, he conducted purges to quash any chance of rebellion.

As a visionary with a talent for strategic thinking and detailed planning, Peter knew early on that access to the Baltic Sea through Sweden would enable St. Petersburg to increase trade with Europe. However, he also recognized that before Russia could attack Sweden successfully, the Russian army needed to undergo considerable modernization. Using what he had learned about Western European tactics and weaponry, Peter established a military school in which generations of young men learned the art of warfare and built nearby shipyards to bolster the presence of his navy.

In business, Peter encouraged St. Petersburg's role as a center of commerce by offering trade incentives to foreign ships. According to historian Evgenii V. Anisimov, author of *The Reforms of Peter the Great: Progress Through Coercion in Russia*, by 1825 Peter had fostered the growth of over 200 new businesses through the use of state economic intervention.[147] As part of social modernization, he relocated hundreds of bourgeoisie (middle class) families from Moscow to St. Petersburg. Peter even went so far as to import European plants and animals.

While historians are quick to point out that rulers preceding Peter had introduced their own plans for reformation, Peter succeeded in organizing the broader goal into achievable tasks. He then carried the reformation forward through the completion of these tasks in St. Petersburg's military, economic, and social sectors. According to historian and biographer Lindsey Hughes:

> There is no doubt that Peter's reign was a turning point [for Russia], though it was less abrupt than many historians have thought for a time. Westernizing reforms were introduced for the first time by Ivan the Terrible, but Peter's grandfather and father also looked to [Western Culture], especially for reforming the backward Russian army. But it was Peter who came to believe that Russia needed more than partial reforms to become a great power in its own right. And it was Peter who conceived of step-by-step plans to accomplish just that.

To become an equal of other European powers, Russia should reform as soon as possible, and after his accession, Peter started to force Russia to Westernize and reform [at] a breath-taking pace. During his entire personal rule – from about 1694 to his death in 1725 – Peter would not stop issuing proclamations, edicts, and laws in an attempt to replace Russian traditions with Western culture. Despite what the majority of Peter's critics say, it was a remarkable event in a calculated and carefully manipulated chain of events; Peter had thrown away the Orthodox tradition that had existed for centuries.[148]

The success of Peter the Great's planning has lasted for centuries. Having served as the Russian capital for nearly 200 years, St. Petersburg today is the second largest city in the country with more than six million inhabitants living in the immediate vicinity.[149] Steeped in history and culture, the world recognizes St. Petersburg to this day as the Russian city most closely reminiscent of Western Europe. Thanks to Peter's ability to see such a great effort in terms of a series of tasks and goals, St. Petersburg remains a world-renowned city.

**Peter the Great succeeded where previous czars failed by carefully breaking up his reformation plan into a series of discreet tasks that would combine to be greater than the sum of its parts.**

Whereas Genghis Khan and Peter the Great used unfettered power and vast resources to implement large-scale change in their respective worlds, leaders in a democratic arena must implement change by operating within a framework of constitutional constraints: written law, the will of their constituents, the political climate, and other hurdles of popular sentiment. Perhaps the most notable instance of a modern leader implementing vast change occurred during the unprecedented administration of United States President Franklin D. Roosevelt from 1933 until his death during the last year of his unprecedented fourth term in 1945.

**America Got a New Deal**

Following his inauguration, President Roosevelt inherited the complex and dire economic situation that America faced following the 1929 stock market crash. Roosevelt immediately assessed those areas of society most in need of assistance and began to implement a planned series of self-help programs and government sponsored initiatives to speed economic recovery.

In the United States during the early 1930s, the miserable poverty of the Great Depression was widespread and touched nearly all aspects of every day life. In the cities, desperate men crowded around unemployment bureaus seeking work, while their less hopeful brethren loitered in the streets. Together, they ate meals at soup kitchens and lived in dingy seas of tents and lean-tos, shantytowns with families displaced by hardship.

Drought turned once fertile farmland covered by amber waves of grain into dust bowls, wracked by drought and buried in the gritty precipitation of unrelenting dust storms. Americans of all origins and livelihoods shared in the devastation, victims to a problem that crossed social and economic boundaries and permeated the very fiber of the country's collective identity.

A host of economic woes greeted newly inaugurated President Roosevelt when he assumed office in 1933. These conditions were caused in great part by the disastrous October 1929 stock market crash, in which stocks lost almost $16 billion during the month. Roosevelt understood that the desperate conditions were of such a magnitude that the situation would require a multifaceted solution, one containing distinct tasks and goals that would lead to observable economic progress. The proposed solution was the New Deal, a series of legislative acts intended to aid in the ultimate goal of social and economic recovery, a framework by which the country could rise above its plight.

Using the radio as a forum, Roosevelt broadcast a series of proposals to the public in a folksy format the President called "Fireside Chats." The intimacy of being addressed by the president in one's own living room

## Maxim 2: Identifiable Goals Lead to Identifiable Progress

proved effective, as Roosevelt was able to gain support and push many of his reforms through Congress.

During a period known as the First Hundred Days, Roosevelt and the Congress passed acts that affected nearly every sector of industry. Among these initiatives was the National Industrial Recovery Act, which established industry wide codes of regulation.

Other legislation included the Tennessee Valley Authority Act, which allowed for the introduction of electricity in a particularly poor and rural region of the country. The Agricultural Adjustment Act set production limits and subsidies for farmers. The Works Progress Administration created jobs for federal projects such as construction of roadways and bridges. And the Banking Act created the Federal Deposit Insurance Corporation and removed American currency from the gold standard.[150]

These organizations and the tasks they undertook facilitated change and gave explicit directions to improve a complex economic situation. The men who had once crowded through the doors of unemployment bureaus were able to take pride in going to work daily to complete public improvement projects, such as the construction of buildings, roads, and infrastructure. These men no longer loitered in the streets but instead earned wages and regained self-respect.

According to biographer Jean Edward Smith, Roosevelt's presidency "... brought the United States through the Great Depression and World War II to a prosperous future. He lifted himself from a wheelchair to lift the nation from its knees."[151] Although it would be a simplification to credit Roosevelt with the entirety of America's eventual economic recovery, it is not a stretch to recognize his New Deal package as a political defibrillator applied to re-start the heart of the nation's industry and enterprise.

The programs were effective in mediating the aftermath of the Great Depression within the United States. In addition, Roosevelt's leadership helped our country secure its role as a superpower on the world stage. America became the primary arms supplier for the Allies and played a central role in the creation of the United Nations.

Although he faced many critics, Roosevelt was doggedly determined in completing the tasks he set out as the plan for America's recovery. He was reelected four times, for two terms more than any other president (term limits were enacted after Roosevelt), and several of his programs, such as Social Security, remain in effect today. In surveys among historians, Roosevelt ranks among the three greatest presidents in American history, the other two being Abraham Lincoln and George Washington.[152]

**Roosevelt accomplished the herculean task of restarting America's economic engine by identifying key pressure points where the federal government could exert the most effect, setting concrete goals for implementing these stimuli, and pushing timetables for each task.**

Roosevelt's legacy is a testament to the success of his reforms, and evidence that solutions to complex problems can be achieved by breaking the ultimate goal into sub-goals and then breaking them further into tasks, the completion of which will result in incremental progress toward a larger accomplishment.

The wide-ranging social upheaval created by the Great Depression further spawned social and political movements that would prompt political scientists to develop new approaches to the study of human political behavior. The need for a similar, new approach to the soft sciences was becoming increasingly apparent.

The idea that the intangible—such as political or product preferences—can be quantified has been in the development states for centuries. In examining how the idea was developed, we will begin with historical philosophers and then observe how quantifying the intangible is valuable in science, business and politics alike.

## Descartes and Comte Attempt to Bring Objectivity to "Soft" Sciences

Rene Descartes, the 17th century philosopher, discounted many of the musings developed by his predecessors as hollow and contradictory assertions that lacked substantial backing in terms of measurable truths.

He decried other philosophers' ignorance of the hard sciences, ridiculing their inability to reach incontrovertible conclusions, and asserting that philosophy has been studied for centuries by some of the greatest minds in history without ever having been distilled into measurable or inarguable truths.

Falling back upon his mathematical genius, Descartes proposed that the ambiguity of soft sciences could be eradicated using mathematics. He believed that an absolute truth could be divined only through mathematics. Descartes wisely shied away from the abstract in favor of the concrete, focusing only on those things that could be measured. It is often the case in issue and political management that the difference in a victory or loss is the ability of a party to define and meet clear quantifiable terms. By examining Descartes' life and philosophy, we can see how his passion for applying mathematics to soft sciences began to take root in the 17th century scientific community.

Even as a student, Descartes became disenchanted with the teachings of his school and of the church and developed a high level of skepticism for what he felt were confusing ideas, unsubstantiated claims and religious dogmas.[153] At a young age he had already become dissatisfied with concepts that were not rooted in, or explained by, a quantifiable or proven truth.

While traveling with the army of the Prince of Nassau as a volunteer, Descartes was able to study music and mathematics. His immersion in these studies further developed his interest in those things that are ordered and structured under a systematic framework.

Remarkably, a journal entry was discovered, still essentially intact from the year 1619, which allows a glimpse into Descartes mind: "I was filled with enthusiasm, discovered the foundations of a marvelous science, and at the same time my vocation was revealed to me."[154] His life's driving question was this: Can the certainty and truth found in mathematics be extended and applied to other forms of knowledge (for example, philosophy or the study of social behavior)?

Descartes' ambition was to create a science that would incorporate philosophy and other soft sciences with the mathematical sciences. The qualitative would be measured quantitatively and the normative would become empirical, so that mathematics could be employed toward reaching an ultimate truth in new fields of study.

After Descartes death, other renowned scientists and philosophers deliberated on the supposition that absolute truth could be extracted from the soft sciences by applying quantifiable methods similar to those used in studying the natural sciences. In the middle of the 19th century, philosopher and sociologist Auguste Comte developed a theory that purported to show that the only true knowledge is scientific knowledge, or knowledge that can be positively affirmed using the scientific method. The scientific method, already in its early stages of development in Comte's era, is a process by which evidence gathered through empirical observation confirms the veracity of a hypothesis .

Comte's scientific mission was to complete the intellectual journey upon which Descartes embarked before him. He gave extensive lectures on philosophy, which eventually became a six-volume work *The Course of Positive Philosophy*. In setting the stage for an explanation of positive philosophy, or positivism, Comte outlined the progressive course of the human mind. The mind, he asserted, passes through three successive theoretical conditions:

- Beginning with a theological state, the human mind attributes the origin of the universe to the will and power of supernatural beings.
- The metaphysical state flows away from a supernatural explanation and instead credits abstract forces with the creation and existence of the universe.
- Finally, in the positive state, the mind no longer seeks absolute notions about the origin of the universe but instead studies the laws that govern the universe.[155]

Through the observation of patterns in his interaction with the universe, man is able to predict consequences and act accordingly. The study of these laws through observation and reason make up the hard science disciplines. As Comte said in *Course of Positive Philosophy*, "We have only to complete the positive philosophy by bringing social phenomena within its comprehension."[156] In other words, we must observe social sciences as we would observe hard sciences by applying systematic steps for observation. Thus, by qualifying specific objectives and meeting measured goals, this process can provide a formula for obtaining desired and predictable results. At last the early scientists began to view what may have been considered non-scientific in a scientific way: observable, measurable and consistently repeatable.

**The basis of Western science and thought is the isolation and understanding of the individual concept or principle. When each element of an interaction is understood, the full process is revealed. So, too, can the performance of individual tasks result in the fulfillment of the overall goal of the plan.**

The term sociology is widely-thought to have been coined by Comte as a replacement for the phrase commonly used at the time, "social physics." He believed that when sociology entered its final, positive state it would ultimately bring all the sciences together by uncovering the progress of human thinking and reveal the logic of the mind.

In the political arena, Comte felt that the development of sociology as a science would create a more stable political environment because, viewed logically, people would be less likely to fight over their ideological and religious differences. Rather optimistically, Comte believed that sociology as a science would create a rational society. Because the scientific method is central to the theory of positivism, it may be more clearly understood by the following thumbnail description of the scientific method.

**The Scientific Method—A Tool for Defining Tasks and Goals**

> Science is best defined as a careful, disciplined, logical search for knowledge about any and all aspects of the universe, obtained by examination of the best available evidence and always subject to correction and improvement upon discovery of better evidence. What's left is magic. And it doesn't work.[157]

— James Randi, Founder of the James Randi Educational Foundation

Although a bit tongue-in-cheek, Randi's description of the science disciplines is quite accurate. What is not science is magic; or, whatever cannot be subjected to the scientific method is fanciful and illusory . . . or more bluntly, phony. The purpose of the scientific method is, in essence, to describe occurrences in the world around us. It follows a basic structure or, if you will, a set of identifiable tasks:

- Observe a specific phenomenon;
- Create a tentative description, or hypothesis, based on initial observations;
- Using the hypothesis as a basis, make predictions about what will happen;
- Conduct experiments and engage in further observations to test the predictions and modify the hypothesis in light of test results;
- Repeat steps three and four until there are no discrepancies between theory and experiment and/or observation.[158]

Completion of these tasks leads to identifiable progress in the form of data. Once an experiment consistently generates the same data, the hypothesis gains the status of a theory, thereby containing fundamental propositions that explain the observed phenomena and allowing a basis for further predictions. Because science approaches the unknown systematically, the scientific method is invaluable when applied to situations that can be observed but resist understanding.

**Einstein and Hawking**

It has not always been easy or even acceptable to assign rational or scientific based definitions to phenomena, which, having no visible origin, had previously been explained by superstition or faith. Science can be especially troublesome when its definitions conflict with the community's widespread or commonly held religious beliefs. In earlier centuries persons with mental illnesses were thought to be possessed by demons or were confined to inhumane asylums and ill-treated.

Perhaps the most well-known example of a commonly held superstition or faith-based understanding undermining an objective, hard science knowledge involves the Italian astronomer Galileo Gallilei and the Roman Catholic Church. In the spring of 1633, Galileo's discovery that the Earth, among other planets, revolved around the Sun, and not the other way around, ran contrary to the teachings of the Church. At the time, the Church deemed it necessary to maintain the myth that the Earth, God's chosen planet, was indeed the center of the universe.

Accepting the science that the Earth was merely one of several planets in rotation around the sun was an unacceptable truth, therefore, the Church suppressed Galileo's discovery (the Church did not reverse itself until 1992). Because he would not recant his scientific evidence, Galileo was tried on charges of heresy and denounced, according to a formal statement, "for holding as true the false doctrine . . . that the sun is the center of the world, and immovable, and that the earth moves!"[159]

The proclamation went on to state that "the proposition that the sun is the center of the world and does not move from its place is absurd and . . . heretical, because it is expressly contrary to the Holy Scripture!" The Church convicted Galileo of heresy, and, after being forced to renounce his views, he was sentenced to a life of perpetual imprisonment and penance.

Galileo's example likely gave caution to those philosopher-scientists who came afterward, though by the 20th century, some emboldened scientists were ready to present their theories—strengthened by the support of scientific research—to the world at large. One scientist who opened new doors of understanding in the first half of the 20th century was Albert Einstein. Another scientist, building on Einstein work in the latter part of the century was England's Stephen Hawking.

These two physicists recognized that certain invisible forces are at work within our universe, and they set out to identify the forces through systematic observation. Using mathematics, they were able to set benchmarks as a measure of the success or failure of their hypotheses. Much in the same way, we approach issue management by breaking the ultimate goal into smaller, incremental tasks and measuring success through the completion of these.

As a child, German born Albert Einstein had an experience that made "a deep and lasting impression."[160] Upon viewing his father's pocket compass, Einstein understood that the compass' needle was being moved by an external force that could not be seen. As an adult, he would dedicate his life's work to studying these external forces, ultimately generating his theories of relativity and gravitation, as well as countless other contributions to physics.

His contributions to the sciences were so prolific that Einstein became a household name, despite the subject or the complexity of his theories. He began his studies in his teen years, won the Nobel Prize in Physics in 1921, and continued to work until his death in 1955.[161] Einstein was successful because of the way he approached his subjects—by breaking a complex ideas into mathematical truths, through universally applicable equations.

Stephen Hawking, born 300 years after Galileo in Oxford, England, has completed extensive research on the laws of the universe, and has made great strides in developing an understanding of the theory of general relativity, gravity, black holes, and other workings of the universe. In several essays and books, Hawking tries to explain these seeming mysteries of the universe through a set of scientific laws.

In his book, *The Universe in a Nutshell*, Hawking explains the concept of quantifying the dimension of time:

> If one takes the positivist position, as I do, one cannot say what time actually is. All one can do is describe what has been found to be a very good mathematical model for time and say what predictions it makes.[162]

Hawking's explanation is closely reminiscent of Comte's quote "from science comes prediction; from prediction comes action."[163] In setting identifiable tasks and goals, we can make predictions and then take action based on the accuracy of our predictions. In other words, the study of these hard sciences relies on the identifiable steps of the scientific method. Without the concrete progress points of the scientific method, there would not be a way to measure correlations between theory and experiment and thus there would not be a basis for a sound theory.

For the moment let us examine a specific subset of science, the study of medicine, specifically mental illness. Because the problem lies in the firing of the brains synapses, it requires a different method of observation. Just as voters' beliefs and preferences can be measured through their voting behavior, patient's suffering from mental illnesses can be diagnosed based upon observations of their behavior. In measuring these behaviors, scientists and doctors can set tasks toward the goal of producing a remedy.

## Identifying the Invisible by Observing Behavior

Several industries make predictions about the physical behaviors of humans. For instance, actuaries and insurance companies try to predict a person's lifespan based on evidence gathered and conclusions drawn from the observation of lifestyle choices. Nutritionists and biologists determine health risks by calculating physical fitness habits, body weight, body mass index and other factors. In the same way these observations help make predictions about a person's length and quality of life, the goal in issue management is to form theories about likely behaviors in humans based on previous behaviors of voters. For example, learning about the decision making process in humans is done through study of observable outcomes, just as observable lifestyle choices predict future health issues.

Because human behavior is a palpable event linked to the unobservable process of decision making, we can observe and quantify human behaviors to predict future actions. How the human thought process works is related to the tangible, quantifiable result of psychological issues. Just as there are tools used to measure the results of scientific observation, there are several mechanisms, such as legislative voting records, opinion polls, and demographic databases, for gathering data from social phenomena. Information based upon the observations of human nature can then be used to form strategies for issue management.

For instance, behaviors as "symptoms" are the basis for classifying and diagnosing conditions in the field of psychology. By classifying an observable set of symptoms, psychiatrists can diagnose a psychological syndrome that constructs a framework from which to predict future behavior as well as a basis for alleviating extreme cases, whether through medication or other regimens.

The *Diagnostic and Statistical Manual of Mental Disorders* handbook for Mental Health Professionals provides a uniform list of the categories of mental disorders and the criteria for diagnosing them as set forth by the American Psychiatric Association. The *Diagnostic and Statistical Manual* is used worldwide by clinicians and researchers as well as insurance companies, pharmaceutical companies, and policy makers.[164] Such well-documented scientific and uniform criterion for classifying mental behaviors is essential for the diagnosis and treatment of psychological disorders.

By now it is apparent that defining the intangible is necessary to begin defining a complex problem and to set tasks toward completing a broad goal. The same tactics used in the hard sciences can be employed in the soft sciences. Just as the science of psychology uncovers invisible mental activity through observation of visible human behavior, success in politics has increasingly relied on the observation of voter behaviors and preferences.

**Identifying Voter Behavior**

In the case of the Great Depression, the problem areas of American society were fairly obvious. Jobs, social initiatives, and government regulation were all needed to save and encourage businesses and thereby create jobs and boost morale. Human activities observed during the depths of the Great Depression provided a clear case study for political scientists. In studying the conditions and consequences of the Great Depression, political scientists began viewing politics in a way that favored quantification of the intangible, such as measurable voting results.

As the economic crisis of the Great Depression drove the extensive reforms of President Franklin Roosevelt's New Deal, it also pushed along social and political transformations on a broader level. Desperate citizens, struggling economies, interventionist governments, radical reforms, and compelling ideologies were each a product of the times. The study of politics and of sociology warranted the development of a new approach, an approach that caused political scientists to analyze societal changes empirically.

Socially, there was an upcroppring of movements among segments of the population such as factory workers, the elderly, and the unemployed.[165] In terms of government and elections, political scientists began to veer away from a normative approach to politics and instead toward realism.[166] In this way they attempted to make sense of the transition from the prevailing big-business, limited government ideology of the 1920s, to the government regulation and social provision-laden reforms of the New Deal.[167]

The new approach required that political scientists assess the influence of business, social movements, and political structure, as well as the more subjective influences stemming from race, gender, geography, and other demographic factors. As a result, divergent philosophies evolved. Two of these ways of thought were behavioralism and the rational choice method. Both of these theories focused on observable and quantifiable political behavior surrounding voting and ideology, and they heralded a move toward greater scientific analysis of political activity.

Behavioralism, popular during the 1950's and 60's, is based on the premise that political institutions are reflective of a dynamic undercurrent of social forces, and that the study of behavioral sciences, with a focus on observable phenomena, is the first step toward understanding politics.[168] Conversely, the rational choice theory, which operates on a set of assumptions about how people make decisions, concludes that humans are purposive, that they have sets of ordered preferences, and that they make rational cost-benefit calculations.

According to Jonathan Turner, in *The Structure of Sociological Theory*, rational choice theory assumes that social phenomena emerge as a result of choices made by individuals and that the social phenomena affect subsequent choices of individuals because they determine distribution of resources, obligations, and opportunities.[169] Operating under the broad principle that humans make rational choices, it is possible, therefore, to make predictions about future behaviors.

Both of these theories attempt to rationalize or explain the thought processes behind a voter's political decision-making process, even if the process is not a conscious deliberation between available choices. In other words, the theories attempt, in some way, to quantify or predict the subjective nature of voter preferences through observation.

Modern candidates vie for control of this limited electoral resource much as the conquerors throughout history fought for control over land or riches. Those who wish to seek political power are restrained by one of the main components of democracy—the requirement that one win votes through elections. There are only a certain number of votes that can be cast—the maximum being 100 percent of all eligible voters who are also registered to vote—making votes cast on election day a limited resource. A candidate can gain power only by winning the majority of the vote. To do this, the politician must have a grasp of the major issues that affect his constituents to the greatest degree and that will mobilize them to vote on election day. How well a candidate can identify issues, align them with the preferences of a majority of voters, and communicate the candidate's stand on those issues will determine who wins or loses.

**Politicians win elections by identifying the specific constituencies that they need to target and laying out a step-by-step plan to mobilize each voting block on election day.**

For instance, in a U.S. presidential election, an early front-runner must maintain momentum by winning in the initial primaries while an underdog candidate may strive to gain momentum by faring better than expected (see Maxim 1). In any event, each presidential primary candidate will aim to generate as much publicity, name recognition, and support as possible within the primary election state. Campaign efforts must target the swing vote of "undecideds" and pursue the districts and regions from which an investment of time and effort will yield the largest return in the number of votes. Micro-targeting the swing vote is a vivid example of setting an identifiable task that if accomplished leads to success measured through an election win.

Voters clearly express their preferences for candidates through the act of voting. Therefore, empirical evidence of voting behavior enables us to view issue management in quantifiable terms, to make political predictions and to take action by applying a goal-oriented formula to any given scenario. One of the most effective ways of gauging voter behavior, aside from past voting records, is the use of political polling.

## Quantifying Public Opinion through Use of Political Polling

Polls are a means to an end. Yes, sample polling helps measure public opinion. But its purpose is not simply to satisfy an intellectual curiosity about what the electorate is thinking. Public opinion research indicates the extent to which a campaign has succeeded or failed in defining issues and shaping public opinion. Successful issue management, particularly in politics, requires that one must identify public opinion trends so that tasks can be set toward adjusting or reinforcingthe trajectory of those opinions.

Public opinion polls have become a staple of modern politics in quantifying subjective preferences. Polling is not a new tool, but it has improved to become more accurate over time. In addition to measuring public response to political candidates and issues, polling has long played a role in fields such as healthcare, marketing, and the social sciences. Known formally as statistical surveying, polling allows a unique set of data to be gathered; it is not merely a body of observation and analysis, but a set of direct responses by individuals addressing specific questions.

Polls are an effective means for data collection for a number of reasons. They enable researchers to cover a broad range of topics and to obtain information from a large segment of the population. Also, the standardization of questions, answers, and administrative practices minimizes error and provides direct responses to specific questions producing substantive, non-tangential feedback.

Applying science to human preferences is a process subject to change as humanity changes. The critical point is that we recognize new trends and adapt accordingly. This is also true in the practice of issue management where it is just as important to stay abreast of subtle changes that may occur so that identifiable goals can be re-set, and revised, if necessary (see Maxim 5). Polling has become an indispensable way to apply science to an intangible phenomenon based on personal preferences. Political polls in the United States date back as far as 1824. The presidential contest that year is considered to have been the first instance of—or at least the most noteworthy early attempt at—political polling. The election was a heated race in which candidates who had splintered from the same party ran against each other. Of the four office seekers, the two most notable contenders were Andrew Jackson and John Quincy Adams. In an attempt to gauge the public's opinion of each of the candidates, The Harrisburg *Pennsylvanian* conducted a local straw poll.

The polls results indicated that Andrew Jackson was leading the pack with 355 votes, far ahead of John Quincy Adams, who came in second place with 169 votes.[170] In the actual election, Jackson won the most votes nationally, ahead of Adams, his closest opponent, by 77,000 votes. Although the straw poll was statistically unsound, it became the primary semi-scientific way to gauge local public opinion for more than a century.[171] It was obvious to most political observers and journalists that the public was hungry for a measurement of the political outlook.

Early in the twentieth century, a general interest magazine called *The Literary Digest* began conducting another type of random political survey to predict election results. The purpose was simply to increase the *Digest's* circulation. Merely by counting the returns from a direct mailing of several million postcards, *The Literary Digest* was able to correctly predict the outcome of five consecutive presidential elections:

- 1916, Woodrow Wilson over Charles Evans Hughes
- 1920, Warren G. Harding over James M. Cox
- 1924, Calvin Coolidge over John W. Davis
- 1928, Herbert Hoover over Al Smith
- 1932, Franklin D. Roosevelt over Herbert Hoover

This remarkable streak of accuracy came to an end in 1936 when *The Literary Digest*, a week before election day, claimed that public support was heavily behind candidate Alf Landon, as opposed to Franklin D. Roosevelt.[172] Although *The Literary Digest's* streak of accurate predictions came to an end in 1936 (likely due to a deficiency in sampling methods) the science of polling continued to develop and to gain popularity.

At the same time as *The Literary Digest's* debacle, a smaller, more scientific poll was being conducted by George Gallop. Gallop's poll was designed so that those polled comprised a demographically representative sample. The Gallop poll predicted a Roosevelt win, which was confirmed in a landside victory on election day.[173]

The win created recognition for Gallup and his polling methods. Gallup's early career began in the New York advertising firm of Young & Rubicam, where he headed the marketing and copy research departments. Gallop persisted in statistical research in several fields, originating his own methods for their measurement. Coincidentally, his polling method was used to measure nationwide radio audiences. Afterwards, he created the impact method, still used today to measure the efficacy of print and television advertising. Over the years he worked with Walt Disney and Samuel Goldwyn, among other studio heads, to create a research program that measured celebrity and movie appeal. This data formed the foundation for predicting a film's future box office success.[174]

After Gallup's extensive work in the fields of marketing and entertainment—and partly out of a desire to assist his mother-in-law in her campaigns to become the first woman elected as Iowa's secretary of state—Gallup made his first foray into the discipline of public opinion, especially in regard to election predictions.

In 1935, Gallup founded the American Institute of Public Opinion, which later became The Gallup Organization.[175] Long after the 1936 election, Gallup continued to make accurate predictions in election forecasts and public opinion. Its United Kingdom subsidiary accurately predicted the outcome of the 1945 election in which the Labour party defied expectations that Winston Churchill's Conservative party would enjoy a handy victory.[176] More recently, Gallup polls were used in Iraq to measure Iraqi opinion on Saddam Hussein and U.S. occupation.

Throughout his career, Gallup was seemingly dedicated to remaining unaffiliated, and therefore unbiased, when gauging public opinion in various sectors of society. Because of this, he claims to have rejected thousands of job requests from interests groups and political parties form all ideologies. Gallup, Inc. stakes its character on that of its namesake, who was known for "delivering relevant, timely, and visionary research on what people around the world think and feel is the cornerstone of the organization."[177] In other words, he was successful in adeptly analyzing and quantifying thoughts and feelings, which in themselves are intangible.

**The Power of the Scientific Model**

Polling experts say the Gallup Organization remains successful because of its use of scientific models. Admittedly, much care and consideration goes into the creation of a truly scientific poll, also known as a statistical survey. Pollsters conduct surveys in one of two ways. First, a researcher can administer the survey, or the respondent can self-administer it. Self-administered surveys are often called a questionnaire, and it is the form most frequently used in daily life, probably because it is easier and less expensive to conduct. Customer service providers frequently ask consumers to complete short questionnaires or customer satisfaction surveys to document their experience and the quality of the service they received. This type of data helps businesses identify needed areas for improvement and adjust services accordingly.

Polls lauded as most accurately indicative of actual public opinion achieve a high level of accuracy because they are designed to reduce bias to the fullest extent possible. The key to success is in creating survey samples that most closely resemble the actual population. The next essential step is in selecting a statistically random survey from the available sample. There are a number of additional factors involved, however, in the creation of an accurate survey, even before a sample has been selected.

For instance, the questions must be worded in a way that does not, however subtly, influence the respondent toward one answer over another. Similarly, the sequence of questions should not lead the respondent towards a conclusion, but should stand independently of separate, distinct questions. For the sake of consistency all participants should be asked the same questions, in the same order, and at the most reasonable extent possible, under similar conditions.

Once the inquirer formulates questions and structures the survey in an objective way, she must collect a sample. Although the survey may employ a non-probability sample, it is not an accurate representation of the population as a whole because it only includes those who are available and willing to complete a survey.[178]

On the other hand, a probability sampling approach uses statistical methods such as stratified random sampling or simple random sampling. A stratified random sample classifies the overall population into subcategories and draws random samples from each. A simple random sample draws from the population as a whole. Each of these is a more precise representation, and therefore more accurate results than a non-probability sample.

Both the structuring of questions and the selection of a random sample are important because they are the guidelines for categorizing the subjective (answers from survey respondents based on their personal set of opinions and beliefs) and turning it into the objective (a quantifiable tally or set of data based on the opinions and beliefs of individuals within a whole population).

There are many possibilities for failure if a survey is shoddily constructed. However, even the best polls, those most carefully structured and administered may suffer disadvantages that reflect bias in the results. There are several potential causes for data bias. Some respondents may not provide accurate answers, whether from inability, unwillingness or in rare cases, deception. They may not remember how or why they feel the way they do or may not hold an opinion on the subject at all.

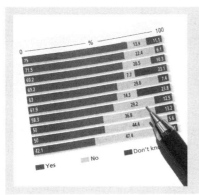

**When identifying goals and setting out concrete tasks, it is critical to have the information available to assess which tasks, undertaken in which order, will achieve the results you desire.**

The advent of improved technology has enhanced polling methods significantly and continues to do so. Advanced communications technology offers a quick, inexpensive way to reach a large sample of respondents. On the other hand, the use of technology in polling has implanted an inherent bias. Technologically advanced households, those with Internet access, for instance, may belong to a distinct socioeconomic class and therefore, may hold markedly different opinions than those homes without the same middle-class amenities.

Just as the use of advanced forms of technology might generate bias in the administration of polls—namely those conducted via e-mail or Internet survey—there has recently been an opposite trend with a similar effect. In this case, it is not the use of new technology that is causing data bias, but instead, the phasing out of old technology.

A recent poll by the Center for Disease Control and Prevention's National Center for Health Statistics found that nearly 8 percent of the nation's adults use cell phones as a substitute for landline phones, a trend that has developed at a steady pace of about 2 percent a year—and shows no sign of slowing down.[179] The group of people switching to the singular use of cell phones make up a very specific demographic. According to an AP-AOL-Pew study, the "cell phone only" group is "typically younger, less affluent, more likely to be single, and more liberal on many political issues from those who can be reached by landline."[180]

This unique demographic disrupts the polling process because pollsters have traditionally used landline phone numbers to contact households that fall within the randomly collected sample. As an increasing number of adults divest themselves from the use of household phones in favor of cell phones, polling companies fear that current practices will fail to capture and measure the preferences and opinions of a specific segment of the population, thus skewing the overall data.

Trusted polls, such as those run by the Gallop Organization and Rasmussen Reports, are powerful indicators of public opinion. Used to measure favor for a candidate or an issue, these polls deliver data that is concise and easily digested. In some instances, poll results can actually reinforce or shape a voter's opinion of a candidate or issue. Although anyone can read a poll, it takes the expertise gained through experience to analyze those results and understand the actual implications for the overall objective. Polls produce only numbers. Political and issue experts must analyze the collected data and correctly interpret the results. Here the richness and depth of the political experience of the expert will enhance the accuracy of the results based on a thorough understanding of human behavior.

Poll results also must be followed by a plan of action expressed as a set of identifiable tasks and goals that serve as milestones toward progress in gaining voter support.

Quality scientific polling coupled with surgical, quantifiable work in the field lend to successful planning and execution.

In measuring voting patterns and past predictable outcomes, it is possible to design a campaign that can overcome even an unfavorable political climate, as illustrated by the following example of a successful re-election bid of a prominent United States Senator.

## Setting Identifiable Tasks and Goals in Modern Political Campaign Management: A Case Study

In 1992, I managed the re-election campaign for long-time United States Democratic Senator Ernest "Fritz" Hollings of South Carolina. The political atmosphere crackled with the electricity of "change," and Republican incumbent President George Herbert Walker Bush would win South Carolina overwhelmingly 48.02 percent to 39.8 percent over former Arkansas Governor and Democrat William Jefferson Clinton. Texas billionaire H. Ross Perot, running as an Independent, received 11.55 percent. Nationally, Clinton was elected president with 43.01 percent of the vote, Bush 37.45 percent, and Perot 18.91 percent.

After careful analysis, it became evident to me that to win this election, the Hollings campaign would need to establish a close connection between the incumbent Senator and a voting constituency largely identifying with the party of his opponent or by the desire for change. I've learned that anytime a candidate must identify with an opponent, it spells potential re-election trouble.

At that time, the state had 1,867 precincts, and the job of the campaign manager was to gain a greater number of collective votes across these precincts. Given the difficult circumstances in which the Hollings' camp was running, the campaign constructed a plan (or rather a series of plans) that would require the re-election team to identify a specific number of votes required in each precinct/ward and a specific plan for reaching this number. By micromanaging each precinct, campaign organizers called upon relationships built over many decades and diffused Hollings' opponents' significant war chest.

In 1992, the state had 1,537,140 registered voters from about 2.6 million eligible voters. And of this number of registered voters, records show 1,237,467 voted in the 1992 statewide elections. Therefore, in establishing micro-campaign plans, I knew the Hollings workers would have to identify a specific number of eligible voters to register and of the new total, establish a plan to get-out-the-vote (GOTV), targeting a specific number based upon the predictable voting patterns for each precinct. These plans enabled the campaign to begin with a quantifiable number of voters who—given past predictable outcomes—would provide Hollings with a margin of victory.

This plan also cut against conventional wisdom that says a candidate should not concentrate in organizing voters in an area with demonstrable and strong vote margins for the opposing party. Hollings' plans would require his opponent to engage his campaign in every precinct, including those where historical results would predict a Republican victory.

Hollings' teams implemented 52-week-long campaign plans in every precinct. The campaigning went largely undetected until late in the campaign, which made a counter-strike of similar planning by Hollings' opponent virtually impossible (given the length of time necessary for meaningful mass organization campaigning).

Hollings' multi-faceted campaign plan, which established a series of identifiable tasks with identifiable and measurable outcomes, resulted in a victorious campaign for Hollings in the same year that President Bush (although losing his re-election bid) won South Carolina by an 8.22 percent margin.

The key to prevailing in any issue or political campaign effort is to plan the necessary work day-to-day for as long as possible (for example, covering 52 weeks if feasible) with specific macro-goals and daily/weekly micro-deliverables/goals. By micro-targeting key neighborhoods within each precinct and establishing registration and ultimate voter-turn-out goals, the Hollings' campaign increased his margin of victory in historically favorable precincts, reduced the margins of loses in historic opposition precincts, and successfully captured a number of swing precincts.

For example, a quick look at the results of an historically opposing precinct provides support of this systematic, surgical goal-setting. Ward 6 in Richland County, South Carolina, is a historically strong Republican Precinct. In the 1988 presidential vote in Richland County Ward 6, Bush/Quayle received 548 votes to 263 for Dukakis/Bentsen, a ratio of about 2 to 1. Hollings was a life-long Democrat with an extensive record for left-of-center voting.

By quantifying the necessary votes to result in an election victory and micro-targeting eligible and disenfranchised potential voters accordingly, the Hollings campaign surgically knitted together a constituency sufficient to win in this traditional stronghold for the opponent's party.

Neverthelesss, in Ward 6 where President Bush beat Michael Dukakis 68 - 32% in 1988, and Bush/Quayle beat Clinton/Gore 61 – 39% in 1992, Senator Hollings beat (former) Congressman Tommy Hartnett 51 – 49% Statewide, Hollings barely eked out a win, collecting 50.1 percent of the vote to 46.9 by the Republican challenger.

Whether the campaign is a political campaign or an issue management campaign, the key to victory is in creating a clear campaign plan with identifiable long-term and short-term goals that ensure measurable progress along the way. As did the successful Hollings' campaign, politicians and successful people in other spheres attempt to identify public behavior or opinion.

In doing so, agents of change are able to identify areas of opportunity and present strong, mass citizen supported alternatives. Once a course of action is known, then it becomes simply a matter of developing a step-by-step, task-oriented plan.

Similar to politics, the identification and quantification of consumer preferences are critical to setting goals and tasks in a business marketing setting. That is because once buying habits are determined, marketers can manipulate those habits to favor one product over another.

The ability to target consumer preferences has become the crux of a successful business model and therefore, has resulted in the proliferation of methods toward that end. The following examples show that the knowledge resulting from observation of consumer preferences allows businesses to set and achieve further quantifiable goals and, in turn, measure progress toward success.

**Setting Identifiable Tasks and Goals in Business**

With the continued advance of technology, marketing organizations have developed innovative methods for tracking personal preferences. These tools create marketing and demographic databases by collecting information about consumers. We have seen this trend manifest itself in many different ways, namely because empirical evidence of the subjective choices of consumers is of high-dollar valuable to those companies who wish to shape consumer preferences in their favor. Successful issue management and politics are two disciplines that operate in much the same way—both use voter turnout and affiliation data to micromanage and set goals toward success.

Social utilities such as the popular MySpace and Facebook websites allow users to voluntarily display personal information such as age, gender, location, occupation, and preferences for books, music, movies, and more. The sites glean demographic and other information from this voluntarily offered info. Armed with this information, the social utility websites become attractive to companies who wish to place strategically targeted advertisements. These companies are keenly aware that their money is better spent planting a few seeds in fertile ground than throwing handfuls of seed on barren ground, to borrow a parable from the New Testament. In turn, the social utility websites are able to generate more revenue through advertisement sales.

Recently, Facebook CEO Mark Zuckerburg announced plans for an even more sophisticated advertising approach in which members could rate and review products they have used or purchased. Ads for the product—along with the member's picture and personal review—would then be displayed to the member's "Facebook friends."[181]

Similar to a mass organizational strategy in issue management, the idea behind the new Facebook advertising approach is that people are more receptive to word-of-mouth or personal endorsements from friends and acquaintances than they are to blanket, broad-side advertising. It is the difference between a top-down method for disseminating information and a bottom-up approach, and thus, is a new way to target potential consumers.

Grocery store chains have their own methods for tracking the purchasing preferences of their customers. Nearly every major chain offers frequent shoppers the option of participating in a bonus card program, which provides incentives in the form of discounts and sales.

The store gives a customer a plastic card with a magnetic strip that is swiped before each purchase is made. After each shopping trip, the store logs details about the purchases and stores the information in a database along with information about the customer's previous purchases. Based on this information, retail sales organizations can make predictions about what consumers like and what sizes, brands and types of products they may be willing to buy in the future.

The targeted electronic marketing wave started as early as the late 1980s but began to pick up speed in the early '90s. Grocery store owners realized that, although scanning capabilities allowed them to track the products that were sold, they were unable to attach the data to any particular demographic because they could not connect customers with their specific purchases.

By identifying who is making which purchase, manufacturers can target certain customers and attempt to sway their decision-making process with the aid of incentive coupons. A *New York Times* article on the subject of grocery chain micro-targeting describes an example of how the Catalina Marketing Corporation targets customers using this type of strategy.[182] Basically, when a purchase is made, a coupon for a similar item manufactured by a different brand is printed at the cash register. For instance, if the customer bought a bottle of Coke, a Pepsi coupon would print out, redeemable at a future date.

Measures for tracking and quantifying preferences continue to develop and appear in new ways. For instance, Google's e-mail server, known as Gmail, displays advertising that corresponds in some way to a word or phrase used within an e-mail or chain of correspondence.

For instance, someone e-mails a message to a friend requesting to meet for a cup of coffee, the sponsored ads on the page will all pertain to coffee. In a real-life situation, the following advertisement headlines would all be displayed: Free Coffee For a Year, Premium Daily Roasted Coffee, ColoradoCoffeeMerchants.com, Coffee Beans Online, Fresh Roasted Bulk Specialty Coffee At Wholesale Prices, Pure Hawaiian Kona Coffee and more. Based on the content of an e-mail, marketers attempt to detect a preference and then infer what products the correspondent may be interested in purchasing.

**Identifiable goals must be built upon a winnable position. Tasks should bring key stakeholders on board with your mission by emphasizing your mutual interests, whether you're selling products—or a message.**

Another example of quantifying personal preferences is illustrated by the proliferation of companies that compensate participants who complete surveys and participate in focus groups. The surveys and focus group opportunities are offered to participants based on some combination of demographic information submitted upon registration.

Depending upon which product is being evaluated, the data-gathering organization will form a focus group or administer a survey to those registrants who fit the target audience, no matter whether the audience is based on age, gender, or some other specific piece of demographic information. The data-gathering organization shares the opinions of those surveyed with paying clients who use the data to formulate marketing strategies. This process is similar to the research methods of political or issue management campaigns, methods which involve speaking with citizens and local leaders to gain an understanding of the dynamics of an issue within a community as a necessary step in formulating a solution for positive change.

The behavior of Internet users is tracked constantly. Browsers, such as Mozilla Firefox and Microsoft's Internet Explorer, track individual user history through the use of "cookies." Cookies are short pieces of data sent by a web server to an individual web browser on an individual computer when that browser visits the server's site. The bits of information captured by the web server include the user's internet protocol (I.P.) address, browser type, as well as the type of operating system upon which the individual browser is running.

Cookies are a way to count how many visitors a website attracts and record the browsing preferences of those users. This process has become a quantifiable way to measure the extent to which people "surf" the Internet and identify what they are most interested in. Other commercial uses for cookies involve the tracking of items placed in a user's online shopping cart, while customizable home pages also use cookies to display set preferences, such as local weather and news feed data.

These preferences help website developers gauge the style and content that will have the most appeal for the company's target audience. Each of these corporate enterprises—Facebook, Myspace, grocery chains, Google, and Internet browser developers—have used tools to gather subjective, preferential information in a way that is both transparent to the user, but quantifiable to the data gatherers. Whether in science, business, or politics, once the intangible factors have been identified and quantified, then an issue manager, marketer, or change agent can begin to set tasks and to approach a given set of stakeholders in terms they are most familiar with.

**Finding the Best Approach for the Issue at Hand**

The specific pathway to achieve success will vary from issue to issue. But each issue will require some common steps. First, an ultimate objective must be established. While the actual desired result is situation-based an overall objective remains: to achieve the ends in a mutually beneficial way. Success is possible by framing the debate in such a way that all parties' interests are served. The key is to turn ideas into something tangible, whether electorally or legislatively. Next, quantify how legislators, voters, and other stakeholders form opinions. And finally, calculate what efforts will be required to influence those opinions in favor of the ultimate goal. This process helps identify and quantify the effort necessary for success, which would otherwise be simply a vague ambition.

In issue management projects, an important, tangible part of the endeavor is a written charter. A comprehensive charter should outline the roles and responsibilities of all major parties involved, from the project manager to individual stakeholders. The charter provides a basic explanation of why the project is being commenced and a clear statement of objectives and constraints. Overall, the charter serves as a mission statement that defines the scope of the project's ambitions and acts as a reference point for measuring progress and accountability throughout the project's duration.

Goals in the charter should be clear and well-defined statements of purpose that contain not only a beginning but also a definite conclusion. Goals should be measureable increments of performance and not merely open-ended or relative moves toward the ultimate objective. Lastly, goals should be achievable and paced in a way that uses time and resources in the most effective way. It is important that each step remains strategically focused on the single, immediate goal and not scattered to points and goals further down the line of progress.

> **From Propaganda to Partnerships: A Case Study in Issue Management**
>
> A wise, ancient Chinese proverb states: "Tell me and I forget. Show me and I remember. Involve me and I understand." Therefore, to make the principles we just covered in issue management more tangible and concrete, I'd like to cover a real life example.
>
> South Central Los Angeles 1998. I was working there as an issues manager for Safety-Kleen, Inc., one of the world's largest cleaning and environmental services company. We were attempting to extend an operating permit for Safety-Kleen's hazardous waste treatment, storage and disposal facility operating in the South Central area.
>
> South Central was still haunted by painful memories of violent citizen uprisings such as occurred in Watts in

1965 and in 1992 when L.A. police officers were acquitted of the video-taped brutal beating of drunk driving suspect Rodney King.

Today the area is known simply as South Los Angeles. In 2003, the Los Angeles City Council dropped "Central" from the name in an attempt to improve the neighborhood's image by removing reminders of its stormy past.

But in 1998, Safety-Kleen's facility resembled a gray-walled prison. It was encircled by a foreboding chain-link fence topped by shiny concertina razor-wire. The precautions may have had the positive effect of making a few employees feel a little less threatened. The overall ambiance, however, was that of a fort under siege.

And the community lived with the daily burden of another kind of fear . . . the fear of chemical solvents from a facility they didn't understand. Regardless of the reality of the precautions the company was taking with the materials it recycled, the public perception of "hazardous waste" is that the danger posed by the materials earned the name.

Additionally, residents had no reason to see the facility as a benefit to the community. Despite the low income of many residents and high unemployment rates in the area, Safety-Kleen hired few—if any—workers from the local community. Well-paying jobs were filled by outsiders supplied by temporary agencies.

My job was to assist with the extension of the plant's operating credentials. Based on the mood of the neighborhood, I knew it would not be easy. We anticipated a fight—a vicious fight. And for good reason. Within recent memory, residents had united to successfully oppose and shut down a waste incinerator that had been operating only a few blocks away from the Safety-Kleen facility.

Based upon my past experience, I was well aware that the costs associated with extending a license in such an adversarial situation could run as high as $12 million to $15 million in fees for lawyers, engineers, environmentalists, and an assortment of scientists and expert witnesses. These witnesses most certainly would have to be called to testify in any regulatory hearings or civil court actions.

I believed we could find a process by which we could avoid this battle. Quoting Sun Tzu, a Chinese general from around 500 B.C.E., who is still known to the modern world for his classic treatise on military strategy *The Art of War:* "For to win one hundred victories in one hundred battles is not the acme of skill. To subdue the enemy without fighting is the acme of skill."

I wanted the same type of victory—to achieve positive results without a protracted, contentious administrative or legal battle. Working with my trusted friend and outstanding environmental engineer Billy Ray Ross, we sought to create a novel, innovative approach for regulated industry, an approach that would bring industry and communities together, rather than drive them apart.

Wanting to avoid a fight may seem a paradoxical quality in a lawyer and former soldier, such as myself. Our objective, however, was to extend operations at the facility in the most cost effective manner. But that was only half of our mission.

The other half was to win the hearts and minds of the host community, so that they would accept—even welcome—the presence of this facility. And that certainly did not involve treating residents of the neighborhood as an "enemy." So we began looking for ways to "win the war" without engaging in a time-consuming, senseless court battle.

We proposed to Safety-Kleen that the situation called for a new calculus—the technique I had used in political situations, called "micro-targeting."

While managing political and issues campaigns, I had found that in every election there are typically those strongly in favor of a candidate and those strongly against. You won't likely change the minds of either group. It is the swing vote—those undecided or most likely to waiver or change sides—that you must micro-target.

To successfully micro-target swing voters means discovering the nature of these voters' hot issues and adequately addressing their concerns. Assuming all else is equal, if 100 swing votes are up for grabs, then winning the election does not require capturing all 100 votes. Changing the minds of only 51 of 100 swing voters can secure a victory.

I began my work in South Central conducting "boots on the ground" research—by walking around the neighborhood and talking with the local political leaders and opinion makers. Eventually, it became apparent to me that the employment issue was a major source of irritation for area residents.

Neighbors of the facility frequently expressed a common conviction that the potential chemical hazards far outweighed any known benefit to the community. And because few people from the neighborhood were employed there, the community commonly believed none of the local residents were directly benefiting from the operation of the Safety-Kleen facility.

The residents' concerns were easy to understand. South Central was an inner city flirting with economic collapse. While national unemployment rates were below 5 percent, in South Central the unemployment rate topped 52 percent. The area desperately needed jobs and steady wages.

It was also apparent that the toughest resistance to the waste recycling plant would come from a group called Concerned Citizens of South Central Los Angeles. Concerned Citizens is California's oldest environmental justice organization. It had led the successful fight earlier to remove the industrial waste incinerator from the neighborhood.

Going head to head with Concerned Citizens would minimize our chances for success. And even if we did succeed, such a battle would ensure we would have to repeat the process every time a new permit or extension was needed. Considering the company's considerable investment in the facility, Safety-Kleen saw no other path before it aside from hiring lawyers and environmental engineers to lead the fight. The company began mustering its forces for a tough, protracted legal and administrative struggle.

A tough fight was exactly what we did not need. We convinced executives that the company could save millions of dollars and greatly increase our chances for success if we abandoned the idea of trying to gain this license extension through a contentious process. We proposed, instead, that we actively engage the community in the process. They agreed . . . if somewhat reluctantly at first.

But once negotiations between Safety-Kleen and the neighborhood began, something remarkable happened. *Instead of focusing on the differences in their positions, the company and citizens' group concentrated on the common interests that bound them together.*

On one hand, the company needed trained workers and the goodwill of the community. On the other, the community was desperate for jobs that paid well, but many members of the community lacked the training and education that would make them viable employees. In 1998, 46 percent of the area had less than a high school education.

Taking into account the needs of all parties, the solution was obvious: train workers to fill jobs at the Safety-Kleen plant. But could we accomplish our goals in the prevailing atmosphere of fear and resentment?

Yes, we could . . . and did. By 1999, 72 workers had proudly graduated from an environmental services training program sponsored by the newly formed "Partnership for Environmental Training" (PET). PET enabled Safety-Kleen and Concerned Citizens to work together to reach their common goals.

PET provided 80-hours of training paid by Safety-Kleen. The program prepared the new graduates to take well-paying, high-tech jobs at Safety-Kleen or at any similarly operated environmental services company.

In addition to the training costs, Safety-Kleen underwrote the cost of pre-employment medical exams and drug screenings and paid for respirators, safety boots, work clothes, bus fares and all training materials.

These were significant costs for Safety-Kleen, but as an added bonus, the firm was able to recover its initial investment through reduced hourly labor costs. While the workers supplied by a technical temporary agency received approximately $12 per hour of the $25 per hour paid to the agency, the new graduates started work at $15 an hour, a great-paying job for such an impoverished neighbor-hood.

Safety-Kleen recovered their costs for training and job placement through the reduction in wages paid to the hourly contract employees versus the $25 per hour paid to the technical temporary employment agency.

Here the employee was compensated at a higher wage and Safety-Kleen still saved $10 an hour by hiring directly rather than hiring through the agency. The savings per hour more than paid for the entire program.

What made the difference between success and failure? How did this seemingly certain stalemate reach a satisfactory conclusion for all sides and avoid a costly, embittered battle in the courts?

*The Collaboration Compact Model* made PET a success. *The Collaboration Compact Model* is a methodology I have developed and applied over years of management work in politics, corporate communications, public affairs and issues management.

The success of *The Model* is deeply rooted in the principle that *the most effective way to resolve community differences is by creating a binding corporate-*

*community partnership. The Model* unites basic theories of receiver-centered communications with the win-win objectives of negotiated rule making.

In simple terms, get everyone who has a stake in what's going on involved in the problem-solving process (collaboration).

Together, reach a solution and ensure that everyone sticks to the agreed upon terms (compact).

PET was successful because it was created through a partnership among all stakeholders in the community. A seven-member volunteer advisory council managed PET. Four of the seven seats were appointed by Concerned Citizens.

A representative of Safety-Kleen occupied one seat, and the remaining seats were filled by representatives from La Esperanza, a Hispanic housing project that bordered an adjacent side of the facility.

PET created a win-win situation for everyone. In addition to the community and the corporation, the graduates of the training program were the real winners. Some were able to move immediately into jobs with Safety-Kleen.

Still others were placed in jobs with similar environmental services companies, including competitors of Safety-Kleen. The ultimate goal was to ensure that the trainees had a new set of technical skills as well as the opportunity to put those skills to work in relevant, real-world situations. Most importantly, PET inspired hope.

Another winning stakeholder was the City of Los Angeles. PET provided citizens with the necessary skills to assist in household hazardous waste cleanups throughout the city. By helping to rid neighborhoods of dangerous materials, these residents were able to use their new technical expertise to assist in creating the safest community possible for their children and families.

### Another Case Study: The Collaboration Compact Model Replaces Traditional Methods of Issue Management

Issue management. Crisis management. Media relations. Community affairs. Strategic communications. Public relations. All of these disciplines have been used in the past to manage difficult issues. *The Collaboration Compact Model* is about one thing: getting what you want. And that's done through active negotiation, not glib public relations rhetoric.

Forget "spin." Stretching or distorting the truth is just a more sophisticated form of propaganda. The widespread use of electronic databases, electronic recordkeeping and the Internet has made information easily and readily available for anyone who cares to fact-check a set of talking points. When a company is dealing with parties with a vested interest in an outcome, rest assured that they will find the weaknesses in one's position. Attempts to stretch the truth in today's information-rich environment will often lead to embarrassing—if not disastrous outcomes.

Forget empty "messages." Actions create genuine messages. "Walking the talk" shouts truth 10 times louder that anything that emanates from a corporate communications spokesperson. And the truth is readily available. It shows through relationships between company and customer, management and employees, parents and children. The truth shines through the camouflage of slogans, brand images and plain old deception. Typical public relations tactics are no way to forge partnerships with a group of stakeholders. The task is much more complex and requires consistent and sincere effort.

Productivity guru Stephen R. Covey, author of *Seven Habits of Highly Effective People*, writes about the difficulty of forming and maintaining good relationships. Close relationships, he says, take effort in the form of closeness, togetherness and caring. Treating a friend or loved one with kindness and caring, Covey says, creates a deposit to an "emotional bank account."[183]

Those who are unkind, thoughtless and uncaring, make an emotional withdrawal, Covey says. If withdrawals begin to outnumber deposits, then the strength of the relationship becomes fragile.

Therefore, corporations that want to be thought of as a friend of the community must first BE a friend of the community. A CEO seeking acceptance and support for corporate actions from customers or neighbors should demonstrate these same qualities to the host community. And most importantly, corporate actions must be worthy of public support.

A friend of mine who was attending a weekend MBA program at a major university in the Southeast said her professor stressed that every action in a corporation should have a direct payback—even charitable activities. Regrettably, the business community typically accepts the idea of payback in the most superficial of terms. The application of this principle is most often more sophisticated and the payback is the product of *mutually* beneficial activities.

A friend who is kind and supportive only when it serves her purpose would soon create distrust and cynicism. Those on the receiving end of this type of friendship quickly feel used.

The same is true in corporate/community relations. Which is more effective, then: for a corporation to see a way to make life better for employees, customers and residents of the community and provide the leadership and capital to make it happen? Or does it send a more comforting message when the company performs a grandiose gesture of charity as an act of penance for committing an unconscionable act of selfishness against the community?

Wise executives become friends to the communities that are hosting their business because life—for everyone involved—is better that way. That corporate citizen—for better or worse—may some day have to call upon the host community to be a friend of the corporation.

Visionary executives seek to build mutually beneficial relationships and to create constructive opportunities for filling the coffers of the community's "emotional bank account." The prudent CEO scrupulously avoids fights that could potentially evolve into destructive and costly battles. A company that side-steps a fight now by communicating openly and honestly about its operations may avoid many future skirmishes with the watchful denizens of a politically active community.

If there is a presumption of honesty and trust, citizens of a host community can more easily accept corporate actions that are less than perfect. The organization that treats a community with dignity and respect will be generously repaid the same courtesy and offered the benefit of a doubt. This type of relationship for a regulated industry will result in tangible, demonstrable cost savings or costs avoided.

Unless there is evidence to the contrary, the host community will believe their corporate neighbor did all that could be done to avoid the bad news they are receiving. This is one of the most common ways an enterprise makes a withdrawal from an "emotional bank account." And it's always good to have a well-maintained account to fall back on.

Always looking for ways to help others and making regular deposits to the emotional bank account create constantly evolving win-win opportunities. By offering a win-win solution, one is able to seek a common ground upon which differences can be successfully and amicably reconciled.

This is a completely different calculus to apply in business. At the crux of *The Model* is the desire to avoid costly legal battles and replace them with cooperative relationships. It is a way of extending corporate earning

> opportunities in a more cost-effective—and neighborly—manner.
>
> Many less sophisticated business entities do not even bother to investigate win-win relationships. They assume there are always legal costs and significant risks associated with expanding—sometimes simply continuing—operations within a host community. They rationalize, "It's just the cost of doing business." Resistance from a community arises because residents of an area may feel threatened by corporate actions. They fear change, and most of all: they fear the future.
>
> Many in business do not stop to consider it, but tremendous costs are associated with human emotions, particularly fear. Concerned residents will band together and fight tooth and nail to protect their community, their homes and neighborhood schools. The fear may come not from a real threat to their way of life but only a perceived danger.
>
> *The Model* seeks to avoid this fight as well as take the emotion out of the decision-making process. In the case of South Central L.A.'s PET project, Safety-Kleen's estimated that the costs associated with its license extension efforts would range between $12 million and $15 million.
>
> If that is the case, then one might consider even half that amount spent proactively on community improvement efforts to achieve the same objectives quite a bargain. And there are no losers . . . or victims.

## Creating Action Out of Chaos

Legendary military strategist and *Art of War* author Sun Tzu once said, "The difficulty of tactical maneuvering consists in turning the devious into the direct, and misfortune into gain."[184] In other words, the difficulty lies in turning mystifyingly complex issues into direct action plans that lead to tangible success. To the extent that you can create quantified goals, then you can make identifiable gains.

Covered in this chapter, the methodology for exploring social sciences has become increasingly quantitative and objective, mimicking those methods used in the hard science disciplines and obscuring the dichotomy between the two.

In their application to issue management, such methods are effective in marking identifiable progress and thereby turning vague ideas into tangible success. In identifying the opinion making processes of political leaders, voters and businesses and targeting key issues within communities, we are able to strategically shape the issue in question, and hopefully, see its resolution play out in our favor. This formula has shown repeatedly that setting identifiable tasks with identifiable goals will certainly lead to identifiable progress.

# Maxim 3
## "Assume the moral high ground early and make your opponent knock you off."

*O philosophy, our guide through life! Investigator of virtues and expeller of vices. One day spent well and in accordance with your precepts is to be preferred to a sinful mortality.*

— **Marcus Tullius Cicero, Roman orator, lawyer, politician and philosopher, (106—43 B.C.E.),** *Tusculan Disputations* **5.2.5.**

### Overview

One way to demonstrate morality to an audience is through persuasive communication. Speakers who are capable of aligning their platforms to the values held by a given audience are much more capable of winning support and approval than those who profess an objective platform. An important distinction should be made, however, between making mere promises of doing right and actually complying with pledges through actions. Moreover, of even greater significance is the falseness and hypocrisy that results from creating rationalizations for unpopular actions and boldly proclaiming that the perpetrator has assumed the moral high ground.

Maxim 3: "Assume the moral high ground early and make your opponent knock you off," is not about "messages" or "spin" or other artificial constructs of language. Dealing in semantics sometimes help obfuscate the actual motives and objectives of actions—whether by individuals, organizations, legislative bodies, or political candidates—that have real-life effects and consequences for the public. Usually double-talk is exposed for what it is.

Assuming the moral high ground also does not mean scrambling for a moral imperative in explaining questionable actions when an issue hits the proverbial public relations fan. Grasping at straws when drowning in public scorn and humiliation is damaging enough to a public image. However, claiming that the straw is the Holy Grail is simply ludicrous.

## *Chapter 3 Synopsis*

- Many campaign managers or issue managers attempt to seize the moral high ground by distorting their viewpoint to appear to be morally superior.
- The best way to appear moral and ethical is to find a way to act morally and ethically in all dealings.
- One who has acted in conjunction with the best interests of a third-party constituency or through shared motives is difficult to assail from a moral standpoint.
- Assume the moral high ground by building it through consistently fair and forthright actions.

**Defining a Moral High Ground**

Before continuing our inquiry, it will be useful to define just what constitutes the *moral high ground*. More than likely, the term "*high ground*" has its literal origin in military strategy. It is no coincidence that historically a great number of fortresses, bastions, and strongholds were located at the highest point in the terrain. By establishing an elevated position, campaigns were able to obtain the advantages of vantage point and gravity.

Vantage point refers to the ability to see great distances fostered by superior altitude. Depending on the elevation of the viewpoint, an outfit would not be hindered by the obstacles that traditionally inhibit long range vision (i.e. hills, trees, buildings, etc.). The advent of optical equipment like telescopes and binoculars increased the advantage of an elevated position significantly.

On the contrary, an adversary's advancement is inhibited by an inferior vantage point because its line of vision extends only as far as the man in front of it. Imagine the inverse of a theatre or stadium where the seats are such that the view is impeded by the immediate obstacles and then imagine trying to fight a battle under these circumstances.

The second advantage of establishing an elevated position relates to the endurance enabled by gravity. Soldiers traveling downhill expend much less energy than their counterparts. The opposition, hindered by a limited view, must counter the forces of gravity as they literally fight "an uphill battle." If this is difficult for a solider, imagine the strain on horses, elephants and more recently, tanks. The law of gravity also allows the campaign with the superior position an advantage with projectiles. Firing a rifle or cannon, or more traditionally, throwing a spear, is much easier from an elevated position.

Add to this the mysticism that is associated with higher elevations, such as the idea that deities tend to reside above the clouds or the metaphorical respect that accompanies "looking up to someone," and it is not difficult to see how the term *"high ground"* came to imply superiority.

The term *high ground*, when combined with the term *moral* changes significantly the concept of high ground. When used in terms of issue management, politics, or diplomacy, moral high ground focuses upon the use of persuasive power, not military.

> Parties seeking the moral high ground simply refuse to act in ways which are not viewed as legitimate and morally defensible by the larger the society. The most common example is people who refuse to use violence against an opponent. Nonviolent actors generate an enormous amount of sympathy among outsiders, as they clearly are not threatening their opponents (at least not physically). Therefore, any physical force used against them appears to be highly illegitimate and immoral. In addition to generating outside sympathy, by taking the moral high ground, disputants can generate a sense of

guilt among their opponents, which will greatly lessen their opponents' effectiveness.[185]

Another pragmatic reason for assuming the moral high ground is that it enables the candidate or participants in an issue campaign to protect themselves from their opponent's efforts to use moral arguments to mobilize opposition. Finally, when one side of an issue faithfully remains on the moral high ground, it encourages all parties involved to do "the right thing." This, of course, assumes all parties are acting in a legitimately moral way and not acting immorally and claiming moral superiority. Such a tactic is indefensible.[186]

By taking the initiative and situating a campaign on the metaphorical *high ground*, the campaign benefits from many of the advantages analogous to those listed in the military application of high ground discussed earlier. The vantage point becomes the opportunity to foresee adversarial attacks on the ethics of campaign policies and practices. By being able to view these potential attacks on the proverbial horizon, the campaign is able preclude opposition from the beginning by aligning issues with the obvious proper ethical position. Thus, the campaign is less likely to be caught off guard by accusations of amoral action or inaction.

**Credibility and Persuasion Establish the High Ground**

As previously illustrated, two of the key concepts in developing a moral high ground for a base of operation are persuasion and credibility. A campaign or issue management initiative claiming the moral high ground must have credibility and the ability to present a persuasive argument.

Persuasive communication is not a modern construct. Since human beings developed the unique ability of speech, they have spent great amounts of time obtaining increased effectiveness at using verbal communication. During the second half of the 5th century B.C.E., a group of Athenian teachers know as the *sophists* (from the Greek *sophos* for "knowledge") began to advocate the power of rhetoric as an effective means of persuasive communication. This idea was adopted by Socrates and passed down through Plato to Aristotle.

In Book II of his treatise, *Rhetoric*, Aristotle outlines the importance of *ethos* as a persuasive rhetorical technique. Though modern thought tends to define "ethos" as the general sociological characteristics of a given people, Aristotle discusses *ethos* as the ability to establish credibility with an audience by demonstrating an understanding of the qualities esteemed by a particular society (in his case, the Athenians). *Ethos*, in other words, is the ability to prove to a people that you possess the traits considered to be requisites of a true leader in order to earn their trust.

Aristotle's ethos is broken down into three components: *phronesis* (knowledge), *eunoia* (goodwill), and *arête* (virtue).

Phronesis, or knowledge, is Aristotle's first component in creating a convincing argument. Because most individuals recognize that one person's knowledge is not infinite, speakers who are capable of providing expert instruction or imparting knowledge in another matter will immediately create a listening audience. And if listeners believe that a speaker has the adequate intellect to make informed decisions, they are likely to trust his judgment. On the contrary, if an audience believes that the knowledge of the person speaking is insufficient, they are unlikely to consider him credible.

For example, an engineer attempting to instruct a dentist on the merits of oral hygiene may be greeted by a cordial listener, but he will unlikely change the mind of the dentist. The dentist views the speaker as having a level of knowledge that is inferior to her own on the subject. On the other hand, patients are more likely to adhere to almost any advice given by a medical professional, because of the extensive amount of knowledge associated with that particular line of work that is unknown by the lay person.

After considering the above analogy, the importance of knowledge in issue management is obvious. It would be difficult to promote a platform or agenda without a genuine understanding of the issue. Abraham Lincoln once said: "You can fool all the people some of the time and some of the people all the time, but you cannot fool all the people all the time."

The scrutiny accompanying today's issue management techniques renders the convincing pretense of wisdom impossible and makes a true understanding of the matter at hand imperative. For this reason, even if an issue manager's professional expertise lies with political advocacy, he must first become an expert on the issue at hand. Only then can the issue management team assume the responsibility for educating the public. Maxim 8 "Absolute Truth Applied Absolutely is Absolutely Persuasive" will delineate the role that factual information has in supporting an issue.

In addition to purely academic or "textbook" knowledge or *phronesis*, Aristotle would likely add to the list the wisdom that comes from experience. In the same way that job applicants present a lengthy résumé or curriculum vitae citing their employment history, candidates for office list credentials to prove that they are viable leaders. Those who have been through challenges and proved resilient are certainly more likely to garner public trust than the neophytes who have merely studied adversity.

How often does one hear political candidates referring to their history of public service when vying for a coveted elected seat? Candidates who claim that they "know Washington" are not simply suggesting that they are familiar with the geography of our nation's capital—or even political theory—but that they have spent time on The Hill, as our nation's seat of government is frequently called, and know what it takes to get the job done.

While Aristotle suggests that *phronesis* is only as effective as the end to which one directs knowledge, he argues that use of knowledge for the self-interested goals of the speaker is far less convincing than the demonstration of goodwill, or *eunoia*, toward the community at large. The idea of *eunoia*, Aristotle's second component of *ethos*, focuses less on the tangible outcomes of a relationship than it does on the importance of genuine amity between the speaker and audience. The concept of goodwill is discussed at length in Chapter 8 of Aristotle's *Nicomachean Ethics*, where he classifies relationships into three classes: those based on utility, those based on pleasure, and those based on what is beneficial to all (mutual well-being). Aristotle contends that a sincere concern for the happiness of others—that is, genuine friendship—is much more valuable than those acquaintances based purely on usefulness or satisfaction. He says, "In the case of each object there is a corresponding mutual affection that does not go unrecognized, and those who love each other wish good things to each other in respect in which they love one another."

At this point, the reader may say "Stop right there! This book is not about loving one another . . . it is about advocating policy." And to a degree that is true. The business world is not at all about making friends out of everyone. There are, however, advantages to establishing rapport with the public through the demonstration of care and concern.

For example, in commerce, "goodwill" is defined in terms of customer relationship management. Customer loyalty to a brand or product is an intangible quality that may still be considered an asset with a real dollar value in terms of the favorable reputation of a business and the positive relationship it maintains with its customers. Such qualities result in customer loyalty and continuing future business.

Good relationships between business and the community translate into increased business. That is because communities tend to respond more favorably to companies who take the best interest of the host community into consideration in all business dealings. As a result, the business is more like to engage citizens of the community in commerce.

On the other hand, if a company acts with complete disregard for the well-being of its consumers or the people that its operation affects, such callous behavior is likely to discourage purchases or participation by the community, regardless of the company's low prices or the high quality of its goods. One may state, then, with confidence that good corporate citizenship eventually translates into better customer relationships and ultimately higher profits.

**We can take from Aristotle a lesson in positioning yourself on the moral high ground. Trust can be built with stakeholders by demonstrating that you hold qualities esteemed by our society.**

The third component of Aristotle's *ethos* is *arête*, or virtue. While a simple translation of this concept would be "virtue," a single word does not do justice to this metaphysical concept. Ancient Greeks considered arête to be the realization of the ideal form of an object in its function as well as its character. The arête of an athlete would be his physical prowess while the arête of a bridge may refer to its durability or longevity. Applied to man, the ideal of "excellence" would translate more accurately to the realization of virtue.

Aristotle made it painstakingly clear that his concept of virtue was never the extreme of a quality. Rather, it is a delicate balance between two poles (his so called "golden mean," the midpoint between two vices). In Chapter 6 of *Nichomachean Ethics* he writes:

> Virtue, then, is a state involving rational choice, consisting in a mean relative to us and determined by reason—the reason, that is, by reference to which the practically wise person would determine it. It is a mean between two vices, one of excess, the other of deficiency.

This Aristotelian idea of moderation or median virtue may be best understood through the use of examples. Courage, Aristotle would suggest, is a delicate balance between foolishness and diffidence. Soldiers who act rashly will not last long, while their timid counterparts will be completely useless on the field of battle.

Financial liberality is the ability to manage our accounts without being too prodigal or too parsimonious. Certainly we should not spend our money on ephemeral pleasures but we must also be willing to take the occasional risk in order to increase our health or prosperity.

Wit is the balance between cunning and ignorance. Those who use knowledge to manipulate the opposition are malicious while those who are completely without a clue are not deemed adequate to handle the situation.

Like Aristotle, Prussian military strategist Karl von Clausewitz echoed the necessity for temperance in the *esprit de corps* of a military force. He notes the great distinction between military virtue and mere bravery or enthusiasm: "In the soldier the tendency for unbridled action and outbursts of violence must be subordinated to demands of a higher kind: obedience, order, rule, and method." Clausewitz, having seen many battles in his lifetime, realized that passion and virtue were not synonymous. Virtue, Clausewitz concluded, often requires a concerted effort of refinement.

While morality may be culturally relative, as Aristotle continues in his logical thought, there is something akin to a universal standard of right and wrong. Generally speaking, he said:

> . . . we approve of traits such as being just, truthful, humane, altruistic, cooperative—all these traits please our sentiment of benevolence and are useful to us or to others. By contrast, we feel disapproval universally of traits contrary to the sentiment of benevolence: unjust, lying, deceitful, murderous, or viciously antisocial traits."[187]

Aristotle sought to attach this feeling of benevolence to the speaker in order to obtain the support of the audience.

## Historical Analysis of Moral High Ground

Because mass publication was not possible in ancient Greece and Rome, nearly all communications were through the spoken word. Therefore, Aristotle's ethos was concerned primarily with oration or rhetoric. Even today, we see the role that oration has in campaigning, whether it is via radio, television, or Internet streaming video. Today's speakers, often in the roles of corporate executives, public officials, and candidates for office, attempt to convince audiences that their knowledge is extensive and they seek good for the community by spearheading initiatives for positive changes. *While their promises for action may be sincere, there is great divide, however, between assurances and actions.*

Niccolo Machiavelli, an instrumental figure in the development of political realism, wrote extensively about the occasional necessity of immoral actions to obtain favorable results in his seminal work *The Prince*. Machiavelli argued that it was certainly important for a prince to be well-liked by his subjects, but it was more important that they fear his ability to quell any dissidence. The use of shrewd measures to obtain stability made Machiavelli notorious for his "the ends justify the means" approach. In *The Prince*, "Chapter XVIII: In What Way Princes Should Keep their Word," Machiavelli claims that it is sometimes necessary to feign virtuousness through speech. He writes:

> Therefore a prince will not actually need to have all the qualities previously mentioned [clemency, faithfulness, frankness, humanity, and religion], but he must surely seem to have them. Indeed, I would go so far as to say that having them all and always conforming to them would be harmful, while appearing to have them would seem useful.

This seems to reflect the traditional public relations approach, expecting a measurable, expected payback for every charitable act. The idea here is that as long as a campaign (political, corporate, or otherwise) has used the appropriate rhetoric, and effectively convinced an audience that they have pure—or at least unselfish—intentions, they have effectively fulfilled their corporate citizenship obligations.

If the campaign wishes to indulge the public, they may even demonstrate a few token acts of benevolence—broadcasting a public service announcement, posing for a photo shoot, making a few random contributions to local charities—to establish a favorable public image. In this way, a campaign or communications agenda achieves its goal in disseminating carefully considered and crafted "messages" of virtuous behavior while conducting business as usual. Hypothetically, traditional public relations firms believe this is an effective way to accomplish a communications "plan." They believe, quite erroneously, that an effective and thorough communications campaign does not require the heavy toll of "doing the right thing."

If there was ever an age in which the perception of service to the community enjoyed the luxury of empty promises, that time is slowly waning. In the 21st century, the public is demanding that organizations be transparent, transmitting open and honest information expediently. There is no point in altering or retarding the diffusion of information because the public will aggressively pursue the truth anyway. It is difficult for a public figure to hide in reeds of a swamp and claim to be on the moral high ground. The clearest "messages" are delivered by action, not glib statements, sound bites, slogans and platitudes.

Former U.S. President Bill Clinton, delivering an address to the 2008 Democratic National Convention in Denver, pointed out the power of the example and walking the talk. Referring to the image of the United States in the world, Clinton stated: "People the world over have always been more impressed by the power of our example than by the example of our power."[188] Even as Clinton understands, it seems easier to defeat an enemy than to win them over by demonstrating and extolling the virtue of their opponent's position.

Not only do citizens insist on an accurate transmission of the facts, they demand that speakers be accountable to what they promise. The general population has achieved an unprecedented role in punishing representatives who do not live up to promised actions.

In politics punishment is administered through elections. Incumbents who do not comply with their promises have a greater chance for defeat in either a primary or a general election. In the business world, active shareholders hold board members and executives accountable for profits and reasonable business growth. To the point: the degree to which a leader adheres to his commitments may directly affect the tenure of that leadership, for good or bad, depending upon one's point of view.

Machiavelli was not naïve. He realized that there will always be spectators close enough to the source of the illusion to see past the smoke and mirrors. To this, Machiavelli prescribed countering dissidence with force:

> Generally, men judge by the eye rather than the hand, for all men can see a thing, but few come close enough to touch it. All men will see what you seem to be; only a few will know what you are and those few will not dare to oppose the many that have the majesty of the state on their side.

Machiavelli's concept ties closely with the familiar children's tale about the Emperor's new clothes. (See Maxim 8: Absolute truth applied absolutely is absolutely convincing.) An emperor was tricked into thinking his new clothes were invisible to himself, but visible to everyone else. No one would go against the emperor's opinion and authority and tell him he was naked. The king foolishly strutted about naked in his ignorance until an irrepressible child blurted out that the emperor had no clothes.

Machiavelli envisions the use of brute force as an authoritarian form of peer pressure. Citizens are kept in check—not by the fear of going against the majority—by the fear of royally administered retribution. The use of brute force may seem appalling to the reader but it is important to realize the context of Machiavelli's Florence. The exiled Italian statesman wrote from this father's farm in Casciano that the enslaved state of Italy was "leaderless, disordered, beaten, despoiled, bruised, trampled, subjected to every kind of injury."[189]

Furthermore, Machiavelli saw few limits to what might be considered necessary to the Medici's to restore order. Machiavelli wrote: "Hence it is necessary that a prince who is interested in his survival learn to be other than good, making use of this capacity or refraining from it according to need."[190]

Today, however, those few dissidents that traditional tyranny would have subverted with might are now protected in most of Western civilization by democratic societies that ensure the freedom of expression. Monarchs who enjoyed the security of drawbridges and private armies are now held accountable to a technologically savvy public today that disseminates information at an alarming rate. The few that were close enough to recognize the deception has been replaced by an audience that extends to the most remote parts of the globe.

There is still the possibility of quieting criticism by non-violent means. Companies could invest extensively in cover-up campaigns that promote an image of *ethos* but this begs the bigger question: is the deception worth the trouble?

Book II of Plato's *Republic* involves a dialogue between Socrates and Glaucon on what is more valuable to the individual: to be just or to be unjust. Glaucon argues that acting unjustly is much more beneficial to the individual, and that those who act justly do so for the merits that accompany a reputation of justice. The only reason that we do not always act unjustly, he suggests, is that it is extremely difficult, if not impossible, to be perfectly devious:

> We must allow that, while doing the greatest injustice, he has to nonetheless provide himself with the greatest reputation for justice. If he happens to make a slip, he must be able to put it right. If any of his unjust activities should be discovered, he must be able to speak persuasively or to use force.[191]

Thus, even in Plato's era, men attempted to seize the moral high ground as an after thought when caught in the act of "unjust activities." Then it becomes a matter of credibility. If one can explain embarrassing circumstances with a believable explanation, then a moral high ground has been reached. But what is a better and faster way to form an exculpatory statement than to be able to speak the truth. If one is doing what he says he is doing, then many perception problems damaging to personal and professional reputations evaporate.

And while, certainly, the unjust man incurs advantages that are not offered to the just—such as freedom from the worked required for success—Glaucon's point is that these advantages come at a price. The unjust man is constantly looking over his shoulder to make sure that his spot-free perception is in tact. If he is not worried about public approval, he is haunted by the fines—or even imprisonment—that may be imposed on him by regulatory bodies and enforcement agencies. What value do we attach to the peace of mind that comes with acting ethically and not having to worry about attempting to whitewash a muddied image? The truth is that deception quickly becomes more costly than doing the right thing at the outset.

While Glaucon's arguments for the just as well as unjust are thought provoking, bear in mind that his arguments are purely hypothetical. The ideals of being perfectly just and perfectly unjust are impractical in real life.

In the field of issue management, it is impossible to act unjustly with impunity. Rather than expend money and other resources on public relations campaigns that place a thin veneer on a less than ideal image, why not do the right thing in the first place? Why not launch a project, campaign or initiative from the moral high ground and dedicate a portion of the effort to staying there? As the colloquial quip goes, "Telling the truth is easier because it's not necessary to remember the details of a story." And an individual conducts his social, economic, and political practices ethically, he will not have to worry about covering his trail.

Aristotle and Machiavelli both agree that it is important for a figurehead to be perceived as moral, or at a minimum ethical. The point of contention is whether or not the leader should actually adopt this polity in all actions. Plato, in his narrative of Glaucon's debate with Socrates, presents the difficulties of acting unjustly without getting caught and suggests that this type of policy might be futile. Let us illustrate their thoughts by adding them to a very pertinent contemporary issue.

Though virtually non-existent in Aristotle's Athens, the price of gasoline, the effects of global climate change, and the conflicts arising from a dependence on foreign fuels have highlighted the importance of environmental consciousness. As a result, businesses and politicians alike are going to unprecedented efforts to incorporate the value of "going green" into their political and marketing campaigns.

It may come as a surprise that some of the largest investors in the green movement are the producers of traditional fossil fuels themselves. British Petroleum, for example, has changed its name to Beyond Petroleum in an effort to demonstrate that it is among the pioneers in alternative energy suppliers. BP claims, however, it is also making considerable investment in the development of solar and wind-generated power to demonstrate a significant commitment to research and development in renewable energy sources.

Service industry sectors have begun constructing new work environments (or re-outfitting old ones) with more energy efficient facilities to reduce energy consumption. Installing fluorescent light bulbs, encouraging employees to wear cooler clothing to reduce air conditioning costs, and providing passes to increase use of public transit to reduce single-commuter traffic are just some examples of the ways in which the service industry is catering toward the public's concern for the environment.

Corporations are not the only ones ramping up their environmentally friendly platform. Anyone who has witnessed a political campaign during the last few years has probably heard the term "green collar jobs." Politicians emphasize the demand for jobs rooted in the American economy that lead to the development of alternative energy sources. In this way, candidates are not only recognizing the public's demand for employment opportunities but aligning green jobs with another public value.

The corporations and politicians have recognized the value that the public places on the environment and have made a concerted effort to incorporate this sentiment into their policies. Earlier in the chapter it was suggested how assurances and actions are not at all synonymous. In this same vein, there is a difference between the mere "green washing," which is little more than changes in language, and actual measures implemented by various parties to benefit the environment. Machiavellian rhetorical skills involve presenting a company as environmentally conscious while keeping many of the same practices. And while it is possible for companies or politicians to hide behind an environmentally conscious facade that bears no real concern for the ecosystem they affect, they constantly face the fear of detection by the environmental watchdogs who avidly seek to call their bluff.

Real ethos takes into consideration the people's true concern for their ambience and makes an effort to operate ethically. After all, while the focus on the environment is relatively recent, it is really only a synthesis of other long-established moral values: good health, natural resource conservation and stewardship, the future education and development of the young, protection for the old, and many more.

In the three scenarios mentioned above, the individuals or organizations that assume a position of environmental consciousness not only appeal to constituents who take the morally responsible position but receive advantages of their own: energy companies invest in a source of future capital, the service sector saves on energy costs and politicians attempt to alleviate economic woes. Before discussing the ways in which we can reconcile morality and money-making, we should first explain just what it means to take the moral high ground.

It may sound a bit pedantic to suggest that companies should have a "sense of shame" but it would be difficult to deny the role that acting ethically has in enhancing a corporation's *ethos*. In recent years, the business world has welcomed the introduction of the term "corporate social responsibility." This idea implies a company's *voluntary* decision to take action to improve the quality of those directly and indirectly affected by their decisions. A corporation, it is suggested, is no longer accountable only to its share holders but to its employees, their families, the surrounding community and society in general.

C.S. Lewis, the famous children's author and moral theologian, likened morality to other natural laws, such as gravity, genetics, and thermodynamics. Unlike those scientific laws that are compulsory, that is, those that operate regardless of the will of the individual, we have the ability to decide whether we want to act ethically or not. An excerpt from his *Mere Christianity* reads:

> Every man is at every moment subjected to several different sets of laws but there is only one of these which he is free to disobey . . . That is, he cannot disobey those laws which he shares with other things; but the law which is peculiar to his human nature, the law he does not share with animals or vegetables or inorganic things, is the one he can disobey if he chooses.[192]

Lewis believed that rather than dictate human conduct, a higher being instilled in us the free will to choose between right and wrong. Moral empiricists like David Hume believe that we act morally because we derive from it a physical sense of pleasure. Aristotle and Socrates believed that reason alone was enough for us to be able to make the right decision.

Whether we are acting right because of reason or because it feels correct the important thing is that we are able to decide how we act.

## Moral High Ground Defined U.S. History

When faced with a highly contested issue, it may be our moral position that gives us the edge over our opponents. If you ask Americans today what the cause of the Civil War was, a great many of them are likely to answer "slavery."

The truth is, President Abraham Lincoln declared from the beginning that the institution of bondage would not be the justification for declaring war on the Confederacy. America was built on the foundation of property and for the government to meddle in the affairs of its citizens' private property would be the closest thing to tyranny that the nation had seen. Instead, Lincoln claimed that he was declaring war in order to demonstrate that the Union was capable of suppressing a rebellion that would jeopardize the unity of the *United States*. In 1862, he delivered a speech, declaring:

> My paramount object in this struggle is to save the Union and is not either to save or destroy slavery.

Before Lincoln ever entered office, South Carolina, Mississippi, Georgia, Texas, Alabama, Florida and Louisiana had seceded from the

Union in order to protest the prohibition of slavery in the new states. By June of 1861 they would be joined by North Carolina, Virginia, Arkansas and Tennessee. The *Anaconda Plan* sought to reduce casualties by cutting off supplies to the South and forcing an eventual surrender.

Unfortunately, however, losses for the Union and Confederacy reached unprecedented levels. On September 17, 1862, at the Battle of Antietam, nearly 23,000 troops lost their lives, marking the single deadliest day of the entire struggle. The battle was considered a Union victory because it pushed back Confederate troops long enough for President Lincoln to give the now timeless Emancipation Proclamation speech.

While some may contest that the Battle at Gettysburg (1863) was the turning point in the war, the declared motivation for the conflict changed on September 22, 1862, when Lincoln issued the first Emancipation Proclamation. The edict asserted the freedom of all slaves in Confederate states that did not re-claim allegiance to the Union by January 1, 1863.

Certainly the idea of abolition had been an undercurrent from the incipiency but this declaration made the issue of slavery the crux of the Civil War. While Federal troops were moderately enthusiastic about preserving the Union, the idea of ensuring freedom provided an insurmountable moral impetus.

America was founded on the grounds of freedom from religious prosecution; her declaration of independence had abolished the tyranny of British mercantilism; the wide expanses of America represented an unlimited ability to make your living and your future as *you* saw fit. Young Northern males realized that fighting for the freedom of their black brethren was not only natural but their obligation and men began to enlist in record numbers.

The writ was difficult to enforce because it applied to slaves living in States that had seceded from Union control but this was really only a matter of semantics. African-Americans throughout the South realized the implications of even a nominal declaration of freedom. Whereas before the initial sense of apathy at the idea that there was no promised end in sight, blacks were not engaged initially in the war effort.

The possibility of abolition established a legitimate reason for support. Blacks "laid miles and miles of military roads; dug innumerable rifle-pits, raised forts, felled forests. They built bridges, drained marshes, filled sandbags, unloaded vessels, threw up entrenchments, dragged cannon to the front." It is estimated that nearly 200,000 black troops enlisted in the Union army, constituting approximately one-eighth of Federal troops. In the South, slaves tried harder than ever to break away from their plantations with the hope that liberty might soon be theirs. Often times the refugees would help captured Union soldiers (at great peril) en route to their Northern refuge.

Lincoln's political brilliance came from his ability to align the war with the causes of democracy, freedom, and equality. As bad as he wanted to respect the institution of private property, however, he knew that an appeal to ethics, and more specifically to freedom, was necessary to lead the Union to victory. This does not mean to suggest that Lincoln was manipulating the Northern public by misleading them with promises of utopia—he really did believe that the abolition of slavery was in accordance with the ideals of the forefathers. Southerners could cite their financial woes due to an economy based almost exclusively on agriculture cultivated using slave labor, but the bottom line was that morality trumped any economic concerns.

## Moral High Ground Compatible with Capitalism

There is a prevalent idea in contemporary society that making money and acting morally are mutually exclusive. On one extreme are the greedy capitalists willing to do whatever it takes, no matter how cruel, in order to improve their bottom line. On the other end of the spectrum are the morally conscious who believe that any capital gain is necessarily dependent on callous exploitation. If virtue and goodwill are the pure and transparent water, then capitalism is a toxic oil spill, contaminating and irreconcilable.

There is no reason to believe in this myth of ethical polarization. Maxim 1: "Assume a Winnable Position" focused on the ability to find mutual interests between parties with seemingly divergent objectives. By engaging the interests of both parties, the maxim demonstrates how compromise does not necessarily lead to concession. Following a similar line of strategy, this chapter aims to demonstrate how acting morally does not equate to a diminishing bottom line. In fact, the ability to align a platform with positive moral sentiment often reduces costly obstacles and garners public support which leads to positive economic gains.

The principles underlying capitalism are perhaps best examined by the Scottish philosopher Adam Smith. In his seminal work, *The Wealth of Nations*, Smith advocated the concept of *laissez-faire* or "let-do" economics, which relegated economic decisions to market forces, as opposed to the traditional regime regulated system. The theory was centered on the idea that man is motivated by self-interest, which fosters competition, leading to efficiency and eventually resulting in prosperity. A widely quoted passage from this text reads:

> It is not from the benevolence of the butcher, the brewer, or the baker that we expect our dinner, but from their regard to their own interest. We address ourselves, not to their humanity but to their self-love, and never talk to them of our own necessities but of their advantages.[193]

Read alone, *The Wealth of Nations*, and this passage in particular, seem to suggest that man is selfish and unsympathetic. Man's actions appear to be guided solely by the desire to improve himself without thinking twice about the consequences of his actions on his counterparts. If this were the case, the skeptical moral watchdogs mentioned above would have a legitimate argument against the ethics of capitalism.

*The Wealth of Nations*, however, was not Smith's only examination of the motives of people in a societal system. In 1759, nearly twenty years prior to his economic treatise, Smith produced a work on the emotional psychology of man titled *The Theory of Moral Sentiments*. The objective of this work was to demonstrate the existence of an intrinsic characteristic in man that sought to relate to others. Out of this desire to understand the sentiments of others arose a feeling of sympathy. Smith writes:

> How selfish soever man may be supposed, there are evidently some principles in his nature, which interest him in the fortunes of others, and render their happiness necessary to him, though he derives nothing from it, except the pleasure of seeing it.[194]

The subsequent text goes on to explain just how we might understand our fellow man. Because we cannot sense exactly what he senses, we must imagine ourselves in his position and infer what sentiments he is experiencing. From this we are presented with a sense of propriety. Actions that would make us feel bad are inappropriate, while those that make us feel good are appropriate.

**Adam Smith posits that the competitive forces of self-interest are the key drivers of prosperity. Positioning ourselves to fulfill our self-interests, including the innate pleasure we derive from doing right by other people, will give us a competitive advantage.**

Because we have no immediate experience regarding what other men feel, we can form no idea of the manner in which they are affected, but by conceiving what we ourselves should feel in the like situation.[195]

When a dispute arises, emotions are often charged and neither of parties is entirely without bias. To this Smith prescribes the "impartial spectator," who is capable of judging whether an action is right or wrong based on the sentiments he is imagining without the interference of personal interest. The resulting sentiment acts as a scale for justice: "If a spectator sympathizes with a recipient's resentment at the agent's act then he judges the act demeritorious and the agent worthy of punishment."[196]

This profound philosophical explanation is a circuitous way of saying that we should take into consideration the concerns of the opposition by imaging how we might feel when faced with similar circumstances. The idea of sympathy does not preclude competition or *laissez-faire* economics, but it does suggest that we cannot act with total disregard for others. The market is contingent on justice, and justice, itself, is contingent on the system of prosperity engendered by our sympathy.

Smith was not the first to reconcile the idea of economic competition with moral obligation. In the last year of his life, the great Roman orator Cicero wrote a treatise to his son, who he saw as a debaucherous soldier in need of guidance. *De Officiis*, translated as "On Duties," is a treatise on appropriate conduct, particularly balancing that which is "right" with that which is "advantageous." Echoing Smith's idea that consideration for the sentiments of our fellow men is essential to civil society, Cicero writes:

> For if we each of us propose to rob or injure one another for our personal gain, then we are clearly going to demolish what is more emphatically nature's creation than anything else in the whole world: namely, the link that unites every human being with every other.

The question of moral sympathy is not one of conservative or liberal politics. Cicero suggests that fellow feeling lies at the very foundation of civilization. When we engage in cutthroat activities that rob our opposition (figuratively or literally), we deteriorate that bond which enables our societies to function.

Does this mean that Cicero was an early communist? Certainly not. The Roman orator would probably agree with Smith that competition is the most effective means of progress as long as there is some regard for others:

> Granted that there is nothing unnatural in a man preferring to earn a living for himself rather than for someone else, what nature forbids is that we should increase our own means, property, and resources by plundering others.

The needs of others might not always be readily apparent. For this reason we must find out what the fundamental interests are before we can attempt to find common ground with them. For example, the Tylenol poisoning cases in the 1980s illustrate the correct process for ensuring the right steps are taken.

## Case Study of Application of Moral High Ground

The Tylenol product tampering slayings and resulting recall by Johnson & Johnson have set the standard in America for a high moral ground response. This 1982 crisis, in which seven people died, brought the leading pain killer in America face-to-face with possible extinction.

According to a U.S. Department of Defense crisis communications analysis of the Tylenol case, before the crisis, Tylenol was the most successful over-the-counter product in the United States with over 100 million users. Tylenol was responsible for 19 percent of Johnson & Johnson's corporate profits during the first three quarters of 1982. Tylenol accounted for 13 percent of Johnson & Johnson's year-to-year sales growth and 33 percent of the company's year-to-year profit growth. Tylenol was the absolute leader in the painkiller field, accounting for a 37 percent market share, outselling the next four leading painkillers combined, including Anacin, Bayer, Bufferin, and Excedrin. Had Tylenol been a corporate entity unto itself, profits would have placed it in the top half of the Fortune 500[197]

The crisis began September 29, 1982, when seven people died in the Chicago area after taking Tylenol extra strength capsules. Initially, the fear was that the medication had been contaminated in the manufacturing process, and that millions of consumers might be at risk.

Johnson & Johnson chairman, James Burke, reacted to the negative media coverage by forming a seven-member strategy team. The team's strategy guidance from Burke was first, "How do we protect the people?" and second "How do we save this product?" The company's first actions were to immediately alert consumers across the nation, via the media, not to consume any type of Tylenol product. They told consumers not to resume using the product until the extent of the tampering could be determined. Johnson & Johnson, along with stopping the production and advertising of Tylenol, withdrew all Tylenol capsules from the store shelves in Chicago and the surrounding area.

After finding two more contaminated bottles, Tylenol realized the vulnerability of the product and ordered a nationwide withdrawal of every capsule. By withdrawing all Tylenol, even though there was little chance of discovering more cyanide laced tablets, Johnson & Johnson demonstrated that they were not willing to take a risk with the public's safety, even if it cost the company millions of dollars.

The result was that the public did not blame Johnson & Johnson for the contamination of the product. The public and media viewed Tylenol in the more favorable light as an unfortunate victim of a malicious crime.

Johnson & Johnson also used the media, both PR and paid advertising, to communicate their strategy during the crisis.

> Johnson & Johnson used the media to issue a national alert to tell the public not to use the Tylenol product. In the first week of the crisis Johnson & Johnson established a 1-800 hot line for consumers to call. The company used the 1-800 number to respond to inquires from customers concerning safety of Tylenol. They also established a toll-free line for news organizations to call and receive pre-taped daily messages with updated statements about the crisis. [198]

The decisive action in seizing the moral high ground was costly for Johnson & Johnson. The company spent an estimated $100 million or more for the 1982 recall and re-launch of Tylenol. While marketers predicted that the Tylenol brand would never recover from the sabotage, only two months later, Tylenol was headed back to the market, this time in tamper-proof packaging and promoted by an extensive media campaign. A year later, Tylenol's share of the $1.2 billion analgesic market, which had plunged to 7 percent from 37 percent following the poisoning, had climbed back to 30 percent.[199]

**Johnson & Johnson took an immediate and aggressive stance to stake out the moral high ground, despite the short-term losses it would incur. Customers rewarded the company by returning Tylenol to its position as the market leader.**

Many corporate executives, even today, would be hesitant to absorb the type of losses incurred by Johnson & Johnson. In this situation, there was something more at stake than $100 million worth of product on store shelves. It was the reputation and credibility of the company. Consumers use drugs and other over-the-counter products only through a high-level of trust that they are ingesting a pure, uncorrupted substance. Had Tylenol not pulled all existing product and replaced it with a protected, tamper-proof version, consumers would have always been nagged by a lingering doubt. Is it really safe?

Tylenol's remarkable recovery and return to its previously secure position of market share proves that the company handled the situation correctly. Some corporate executives are torn between the choice between doing the right thing and protecting the profit sheet. The Tylenol case clearly demonstrates that in most instances, doing the right thing from a moral high ground perspective is also doing the right thing from a business standpoint.

It is becoming more and more common for opposing viewpoints to attempt to seize the moral high ground to add credibility and support to their position. To illustrate this idea we should consider the contemporary example of the Iraq War. The stated motivation for the occupation of Iraq was the possibility that the nation possessed weapons of mass destruction that could jeopardize American security. This, however, did not prevent both sides from attaching the war to two very different moral sentiments. Opponents of the war shouted chants of "blood for oil" in an attempt to paint the efforts of the administration of President George W. Bush as a war with to make money by seizing foreign fossil fuels. This argument cast those who were in favor of the war as greedy insensitive capitalists who did not care about disrupting a sovereign state.

Supporters of the war aligned the occupation of Iraq with the ideals of liberty and democracy. In their rhetoric, those who opposed the Iraq War were essentially opposed to the quintessential American value of freedom. Some even accused those who questioned the war as creating danger for American troops.

This may seem like two oversimplified, emotionally charged views of a very complex issue—and they certainly are. The point is not whether either of these paradigms is correct. What these two perspectives illustrate is that both sides believed that they could best advance their positions by utilizing communications that appealed less to the merits of an invasion and more to the respective moral virtue of their positions. How much stronger are the feelings associated with "fairness" and "freedom" than complex policy explanations of a balance of power in a volatile region, the legacy of the U.S.-Iraqi relationship, the history of Jewish-Arab conflicts and so on.

The controversy associated with this war is illustrative because both sides use a moral sentiment to support their arguments. While right and wrong are sometimes difficult positions to defend where warfare is concerned, those who appear to be doing the right thing definitely have the advantage from a public opinion and electoral viewpoint.

In both of the above examples, the entities that supported their platform using morality did so voluntarily. The reason this maxim is titled "assume a *moral high ground*" and not "if all else fails, use morality" is because it requires some initiative on the behalf of the actors involved to proactively pursue that which is moral or fair. In other words, when a campaign decides to act ethically, it should be doing so because it genuine feels like it is motivated by integrity and not by the fear of appearing unpopular.

> **An Environmental Example: Factors Impacting Moral High Ground**
>
> One way to curb unwanted behaviors is to establish rigid guidelines and ensure their compliance by associating them with a corresponding punishment. For decades, this has been the government's approach toward the issue of environmental regulation. Command and control policies set universal emissions standards and held polluters accountable to meeting those standards.
>
> Recently, however, a policy of economic incentives has gained prominence. This policy model grants a pollution-source flexibility in dealing with emissions, and then either punishes them or rewards them based on their adherence to the aforementioned guidelines.
>
> The problem with the older command and control system is that it incurs significant administrative costs as regulators are constantly monitoring the compliance of the industries. Furthermore, because there is a fixed limit to the amount of pollution tolerated, there is no motivation to reduce pollution beyond the mandatory

limit. For example, if a company has reduced its contamination to the required one hundred megatons, there is no reason for that company to aim for eighty. Due to this lack of justification for further reduction of emissions, the research and development of new technology is limited to only that which reduces the cost of production.

Economic incentives are capable of providing a more effective approach, which sees companies decrease their emissions by whatever means possible in order to uphold their commitment to keeping the environment clean. Unlike traditional command and control practices that allow regulatory bodies to determine what must be done to curb environmental degradation, economic incentives allow a pollution source to determine the most cost-effective way to handle their pollution problem.

Often companies are rewarded for exceeding Industry standards and are able to sell negative credits to competing companies to offset their pollution excesses. This is commonly proposed as part of a cap-and-trade system. This means a source of pollution is allowed a certain leeway in emissions and then the option to buy additional "credits" from another source that does not need them.

This continual incentive to reduce pollution fosters the development of new technologies and tends to favor cleaner, more efficient industry.

The difference in these two approaches is that command and control practices are reactive, while economic incentive based programs are proactive. Reactive policies change their targets to coincide with government regulations while proactive policies act positively in the first place and preclude government pressure.

Certainly the rules and regulations imposed on us may be sufficient to force us to act morally, but this is not the point. Rather than conform to the hard guide-

> lines imposed by regulatory bodies or the soft persuasion of public opinion out of necessity, we are able to preclude this by incorporating ethics into our policies from the start. The idea that we should be guided by the virtue of integrity and not be the fear of repercussion was outlined by a great Chinese sage over two millennia ago.
>
> Sixth century B.C.E. Chinese philosopher Confucius suggested the importance of being proactive when he told leaders that the most effective means of leading a people was to instill in them a sense of morality from which they could proactively direct their behavior. He wrote: "Guide them by edicts, keep them in line with punishments, and the common people will stay out of trouble but will have no sense of shame. Guide them by virtue, keep them in line with the rites, and they will, besides having a sense of shame, reform themselves."

The above example demonstrates how it is advantageous for companies to take a proactive approach to environmental regulation. Confucius makes this a precept more universally applicable when he says that we should not do only that which is sufficient in avoiding legal castigation, but also should actually act in accordance with morals. Such a precept implies going beyond what is the minimum requirement for compliance.

In issue management, the regulatory bodies listed above are analogous to the public. Companies can avoid the public's scorn by meeting the absolute minimum requirements, but they cannot necessarily win their approval. People are, with the help of the media, generally perceptive enough to realize when a corporation is acting in their own interests solely because it is required by the law and not out of a pursuit of well-being. The process of nagging corporations to comply with public standards is taxing on both parties involved.

On the other hand, politicians and executives who act ethically without being prompted to do so are much more likely to garner public support for taking the initiative. Just as in the above example of economic incentives, the companies allow themselves the ability to exceed minimum responsibilities

Regulations require an element of public participation to ensure that the people that they affect have a voice in decisions. For this reason, it is imperative that companies do that which is perceived as moral in their host communities. Rather than face the volatility of future animosity with the affected community, it is advantageous for the company to act virtuously in the first place.

In order to do this, we must understand the values of the target audience and then find where our platform can dovetail with theirs. Find out where the opposition comes from and what their main concerns are, and then develop a strategy to find areas of mutual interest. Demonstrate that there is a mutuality of benefit or concern. This is very similar to the concepts we explored in the first chapter on finding a mutually beneficial scenario. The ethics behind the issue are one of these keys to finding common ground.

**Summary**

Morality cannot be faked. It is a losing battle, therefore, to attempt to seize the moral high ground through a public relations coup and appear in the right when it is simply not true. An easier position is to build an issue or political campaign on moral high ground from the very start. A candidate who genuinely cares about the electorate and has the welfare of his county, district, or state as his main concern does not have the problem of appearing disingenuous.

Appearances are of great concern anytime public issues, political campaigns, or community projects are undertaken. The code of ethics of many professional organizations state that an ethical violation occurs when there is even an appearance of impropriety. The best rule of thumb for successful public relations: people who want to appear moral and ethical must first be so. To ensure that a public service project or endeavor is for the good of the community, first make sure that true. By incorporating all stakeholders into the problem definition and design of a solution, projects generally do not have difficulty in assuming the moral high ground . . . they already have solid footing on this hallowed ground.

# Maxim 4

## "Exchange fire when fired upon. Protect your reputation—vigilantly guard against being defined by your opponent."

*Nemo me impune lacessit!*
("No one harms me with impunity!")

— **Latin motto on the Royal Coat of Arms of Scotland**

*A sudden powerful transition to the offense—the flashing sword of revenge is the greatest moment to the defense.*

— **Carl von Clausewitz (1780–1831), Prussian general and military strategist, author of *On War*, a classic treatise on military theory.**

### Overview

Few who witnessed the television images can forget the pictures of Democratic presidential candidate Michael Dukakis's head protruding from a U.S. Army Abrams M-1 tank. Wearing huge headphones that resembled cartoon-character ears, Dukakis looked more like Mickey Mouse than a serious candidate for president of the United States of America, the most powerful country on earth. Dukakis had hoped that by demonstrating his interest and familiarity with heavy combat weapons, he could dispel political attacks that he was "soft" on national defense. He seemed to be symbolically taking refuge in a tank so he could metaphorically "exchange fire" with his aggressive and vocal detractors.

Dukakis's opponents seized upon the moment and turned the tank's guns upon him, so to speak. It was they who used the footage on television, not Dukakis. The candidate's photo opportunity blew up in his face and probably contributed heavily to his campaign's second half loss of a double-digit lead over George H. W. Bush. While other attacks also inflicted political damage, the war would not have been lost had Dukakis reacted swiftly and decisively. But his failure to respond appropriately shifted momentum in Bush's favor. The former two-term vice president under President Reagan won handily in November.

The Dukakis debacle is a perfect example of the truth of Maxim 4: Exchange fire when fired upon. This means vigilantly guarding against being defined by an opponent—in other words, having one's position framed by those most opposed to it. This aspect of the maxim, including a closer look at the Dukakis example, will be covered later in the chapter.

## Chapter 4 Synopsis

- Dating back to the earliest civilizations, humankind has believed in "an eye for an eye," vigorously retaliating in response to an attack.
- Modern culture tends to discourage such actions of retribution as uncivilized.
- In the arena of politics and public opinion, an unfair attack based on untruths or half-truths must be countered with a measured, well-calculated response.
- Always guard against allowing your opponent to define your character, platform, or position on issues in their terms.

**Historical Analysis of Exchanging Fire**

The idea of *exchanging fire when fired upon* is not the product of modern issue management. Since the beginning of our existence, mankind has used retaliation as a self-defense technique necessary for survival. Whether the propensity for reciprocating aggression arose due to genetic or behavioral traits, "norms of reciprocity and retaliation stand as universal principles in virtually every human society, both historical and contemporary."[200]

It is important to realize that response to attacks, particularly in the forum of public opinion, must be made immediately and forcefully. Look at it in terms of killing an unfair and unwarranted attack. Nevertheless, the response should be thoughtful, swift and well grounded. It should reestablish credibility for the victim and perhaps inflict a quantifiable public opinion win, or at least a cost that might dissuade further assaults.

While reciprocal violence seems to be a human biological imperative, with the rise of civilization, cultures adopted social and legal rules that regulated reciprocation to ensure greater stability. One way to mitigate unconstrained retaliation against real or imagined slights was to codify the acceptable punishment for particular acts.

Ancient artifacts suggest that thousands of years ago humanity was concerned with setting guidelines to limit transgressions among inhabitants of primitive societies. For example, when archeologists unearthed a massive engraving in Iran in 1901, they found far more than just a relic of civilizations past. There, etched in cuneiform script on a giant basalt stone, site excavators discovered the Code of Hammurabi, evidence of one the earliest developments of legal codification.

The eight-foot stele displaying 282 laws engraved on its surface was created by the King Hammurabi about 1,800 B.C.E. Hammurabi claimed he had been in contact with the gods, who commanded him to construct the code to bring righteousness to the land. Hammurabi, then, directed his people:

> Let the oppressed man who has a cause
> Come into the presence of my statue
> And read carefully my inscribed stele

The significance of Hammurabi's Code is not in the fact that it represents an entirely new set of rules introduced into the region. The rules, most of which regarded family, property, and commerce, had been common law in Mesopotamia for centuries. What is genuinely significant about the Code is that during Hammurabi's reign, it removed discretionary justice from rulers and their subjects and limited the appropriate retaliation for a catalog of offenses to a uniform set of guidelines.

The fact that the Code was written into stone emphasizes its intended permanency. When the stele was found more than 3,000 years after its construction, much of its material integrity was still preserved. More important than its physical legacy, however, was the influence that the text exerted on the codification of laws in subsequent civilizations.

Perhaps the most notable of Hammurabi's immediate successors were the ancient Judean people who descended from Abraham. Their story begins in the Old Testament book of *Genesis* which explains the material and spiritual creation of the earth dating back more than 2,000 years ago. According to the *Genesis* version of creation, mankind is given paradise on earth, but after giving in to temptation, his race becomes permeated with sin.

Even the God of the Old Testament has a temper and could be provoked to violence. God exacted almost total annihilation upon the human race with a great flood brought on by his disappointment in humanity. Only Noah and his family were left to repopulate the earth. Of this lineage, God deems Abraham the heir to his kingdom, the one to whom he will provide a Redeemer. But before that occurs, God must ameliorate man's behavior by first delivering a set of laws to live by.

The second book of the Bible, *Exodus*, provides the required moral instruction. *Exodus* chronicles the nation of Israel as the Jews attempt to flee the slavery inflicted upon them by the new Pharaoh of Egypt. After Moses condemns Egypt to a series of 10 plagues, the people are released from captivity, cross the Red Sea and find their deliverance. The rest of the book deals with the principles of living righteously as dictated by God through Moses.

But at Mount Sinai an event occurs that would serve to shape the course of Western civilization. God descends the mountain and delivers to his faithful servant Moses a pair of stone tablets (reminiscent of the Code of Hammurabi) inscribed with a set of 10 broad rules—commandments—by which the people of Israel are to live by.

If the Ten Commandments (*Exodus* 19-20) represent the guidelines of healthy individual living, the subsequent verses represent a series of civil and ceremonial codes. In one of the most often quoted passages from the Old Testament, *Exodus* chapter 21, Moses declares that:

> [I]f there is any further injury, then you shall appoint as a penalty life for life, eye for eye, tooth for tooth, hand for hand, foot for foot, burn for burn, wound for wound, bruise for bruise. (Exodus 21: 23-25).

This call for retribution as a way to "exchange fire" was to serve as a justification for retaliation for nearly 1,400 years, until rejected by Jesus of Nazareth in his Sermon on the Mount, which provides a "user's guide" for Christian behavior.

**The effectiveness of an equitable and aggressive response to injurious action has been recognized throughout history, across numerous civilizations.**

Although the just cited Old Testament passage seems to be a literal interpretation of retributive justice, a more figurative interpretation of God's directive suggests imposing punitive measures comparable in nature to those suffered initially. This concept is commonly referred to as *lex talonis* (*lex*, the Latin for "law;" and *talonis*, Latin for "in kind") and constructs a system of one-to-one ratio of retaliation, limiting the upper and lower bounds of the acceptable in redressing an offense.[201]

Judaism was not the only world religion to incorporate a system of equitable retribution. The Muslim concept of *qisas*, or "equality," directly parallels the Western idea of *lex talonis*. An English translation of Sura 2, Verse 178 of the Quran warns the reader:

> O believers! Retaliation is prescribed for you in the cases of murder: a free man for a free man, a slave for a slave, and a female for a female. But if anyone is pardoned by his aggrieved brother, then bloodwit (a ransom for manslaughter) should be decided according to the common law and payment should be made with gratitude. This is a concession and a mercy from your Lord. Now, whoever exceeds the limits after this, shall have a painful punishment.[178] O men of understanding! There is security of life for you in the law of retaliation, so that you may learn self-restraint. [179] 2:[178-179] [202]

This Islamic holy text also promotes forgiveness in lieu of retaliation but leaves the decision at the discretion of the victim's kin. Established over a millennium ago, the practice of *qisas* is still carried out in countries that follow Sharia law (e.g. Saudi Arabia, Iran, and Pakistan).

*Qisas* marked a critical step in the mitigation of retaliation. Early legal statutes like the Code of Hammurabi and the Mosaic Code established the principle that individuals were no longer able to exercise justice as they deemed appropriate. They were confined, instead, to the limitations set forth by the community. In the case of *qisas*, the aggrieved victims were not executing "eye for an eye" retaliation but demanding its execution from the appropriate authorities. As noted by Vincy Fon and Francesco Parisi, in their essay on revenge and retaliation:

> [the] injured party, who was originally allowed to carry out the execution himself (subject to a constraint of proportionality), later was only allowed to do so under the supervision of authority, and eventually was only permitted to attend the execution.[203]

If mutilation and murder appear to be extreme forms of justice, these acts of violence at least provide insight into the intrinsic need for fairness in human nature. Though contemporary society has certainly attached a negative connotation to the term "vengeance," reciprocating injustices were understood to be a fundamental part of the human ethos and as a result were incorporated into early legal statutes.

Many great literary classics hinge on the theme of man's need for taking vengeance against those who have wronged him. William Shakespeare's tragedy *Hamlet*, perhaps one of the greatest literary works in the English language, is about the melancholy Dane's efforts to avenge his father's death at the hands of his father's treacherous brother and unfaithful wife. But note that all the main characters die at the end of the play, which should serve as a warning about the risks of hasty action and the potential price for getting even.

Another great literary treatment of revenge, Edgar Allen Poe's classic short story "The Cask of Amontillado," is the epitome of a calculated reprisal. The aggrieved narrator, Montresor, demands revenge on his contemporary, Fortunato, for a series of undisclosed insults. Acting under the guise of esteem for Fortunato's ability to discern exotic wines,

## Maxim 4: Exchange Fire When Fired Upon

Montresor leads his inebriated transgressor away from a costume party through a labyrinth of the estate's catacombs to a secluded wine cellar deep underground. Once sufficiently removed from the threat of detection, Montresor chains his foe Fortunato to a wall and immures him alive, the bells on his jester's costume jingles as he continues to cough and gasp from the dampness of the cell.

In contrast to Hamlet, what is remarkable about Montresor's revenge is the meticulous planning borne of his cold and calculating—yet fastidious—deliberation. In the opening paragraph, the narrator himself tells us:

> At length I would be avenged; this was a point definitively settled—but the very definitiveness with which it was resolved precluded the idea of risk.

Whether it is giving his servants the evening off or burying the trowel and mortar used to brick up the wall to dispose of all incriminating evidence, Montresor takes every precaution necessary to avoid detection. And he is successful. In the final paragraph the narrator reveals that the act was committed 50 years prior.

**Poe's Montresor implements a calculated plan to silence Fortunato, who had impugned his reputation. Although Montresor ensures his defamer will no longer define his character, he does not specifically counter the particular insults in question—a key part of any response.**

Quite appropriately, Montresor's family crest is "[a] huge human foot d'or, in a field azure; the foot crushes a serpent rampant whose fangs are imbedded in the heel." The crest displays the Latin phrase: "Nemo me impune lacessit" or translated, "No one strikes me with impunity." If this short story had to be summarized in a single adage, this would be it. Montresor vows revenge for an insult against his name, and he is willing to take the necessary risks. Like the image of the snake on the family crest, anyone who attempts to do him harm will be assured of mutual harm.

**Contemporary Application of Exchanging Fire**

Traditionally perceived as the model environment for politeness, political correctness, and perfectly professional behavior, the standard response to rudeness and bullying in the office has been, "Just ignore it." White collar workers have always been advised never to get personal or show emotion, even to the point of creating a phony office culture. More recent advice by career counselors and psychologists, however, strongly emphasize the opposite: "Exchange fire when fired upon."

Today's experts in personal and professional development are quick to point out the dangers of bullies in the workplace and instruct others in how to appropriately respond to insulting verbal attacks.

Dr. Ben Leichtling, Phd, a Colorado-based personal life coach and author of *How to Stop Bullies in Their Tracks*, counsels and coaches professionals and others who are the victims of unwarranted, aggressive attacks in the business place. Dr. Leichtling vigorously disagrees with conventional wisdom, which has been to ignore bullies or not make waves in the office.

"Many of us have been taught to ignore put-downs," said Dr. Leichtling. "It's considered morally superior to rise above them. That's a big mistake. Respond quickly when someone attacks you."

Dr. Leichtling advises the victims of office bullies to stop taking attacks personally, but also emphasizes that they must respond in kind. He also suggests that victims respond to the nature of the comment, not the content.

Dr. Leichtling not only recommends a swift and forceful response, but also that the bully's victim escalate the response in proportion to further attacks. If the bully becomes more vicious, then the response should be equally vitriolic.

It should be pointed out that an exchange of fire should be between peers, not with persons within different levels of the organization. In that case, more serious issues may arise.

## Human Behavior and the Evolution of Exchanging Fire

While the ancients displayed a moral imperative to strike back and right wrongs with in-kind violence, naturalist Charles Darwin may have provided support for the argument that such a notion may have its genesis in the human genome.

The son of an English physician, Darwin's interest in science first led him to follow in his father's footsteps and become a surgeon. While fascinated by the science of biology, Darwin found surgery too gruesome. He turned to the mysteries of natural history, instead.

While still in his early twenties, Darwin spent five years aboard the HMS Beagle, meticulously collecting and cataloging new species located throughout the Pacific. It was on this expedition that Darwin noticed something that would change the scientific view of biology forever.

Darwin's discovery was that an undocumented bird specimen in the Galapagos varied from island to island. This variation suggested to Darwin that an individual species had actually adapted to accommodate the specific environment in which they lived, prompting the idea of the transmutation of species.

From his early ideas about transmutation, Darwin surmised his "Theory of Natural Selection." Darwin's idea, which became known as his Theory of Evolution, propounded that heritable traits that endow a species with greater survivability persist, while those that weaken a species are phased out.

Since reciprocating aggression seems to be a common characteristic of all humans, Darwin concluded that reciprocating aggression was not only a learned behavior, but likely passed down through succeeding generations.

Darwin's theory, therefore, lends credibility to the idea that exchanging fire is not strictly a conscious decision but a reaction ingrained into man's genetic code. While this does not in any way encourage or even condone violence, it does suggest that humans may have a biological predisposition to respond to aggression in kind. Perhaps human beings are somehow programmed to know that a swift, aggressive response well-placed against an aggressor has the definite effect of deterring future aggression.

If we recognize that retaliation was a fundamental principle to even the earliest of mankind, we can only imagine how it was manifested in the beginning. Initially, humans probably reciprocated in the most animalist manner imaginable, using teeth, nails, and fists as their only available weapons.

Not until the advent of primitive technologies were tools such as spears, knives, and swords incorporated into the retaliatory repertoire. "Modern" weaponry, such as firearms and explosives, would not arrive for another several millennia.

The concept of retaliation can be traced through the hunter-gatherers, who—competing for nourishment amid limited resources—were willing to do whatever necessary for survival. And although we use the maxim "exchange fire when fired upon" predominantly in the figurative sense, it is likely that fire did have a literal application in the earliest manifestations of retaliation. Conflagration, man's greatest destructive tool at the time, was one of the most effective ways in which to raze the establishments of rival tribes. It is no wonder that the Age of Reason philosopher Thomas Hobbes considered this life to be "solitary, poore, nasty, brutish, and short."

## Toward Defining "Reasonable" Revenge

If it is man's nature to seek retribution and revenge why is the world not more brutal and savage that it is? To understand the natural behavior of man, one may turn to Thomas Hobbes. Born in Malmesbury, England, in 1588, Hobbes embarked upon a life of thought and pursuit of intellectual excellence through early studies at Oxford between 1603 and 1608. Becoming an academician by profession, Hobbes spent the early part of his life as the tutor of the son of a nobleman in Devonshire.

Hobbes's initial scholastic pursuits focused primarily on the classics, but in 1628, Hobbes produced the first English translation of Thucydides' *The Peloponnesian War*. Through these classical studies, by the time the English Civil War erupted in 1642, the scholar realized that conflict was not just a topic in the study of the antiquities. Whether it was warfare between the Athenians and the Spartans, or war between Charles I and Parliament, Hobbes was determined to understand the true essence of mankind so he could explain the human propensity for conflict and violence.

In his seminal work, *Leviathan*, Thomas Hobbes postulated that the state of nature is an existence motivated by the constant fear of a violent death and characterized by the chaotic struggle for self-preservation. This "dissolute condition of masterlesse men, without subjugation to Lawes, and a coercive Power to tye their hands from rapine and revenge." Hobbes grew to understand the need for primitive man to use any means necessary to survive. Since virtually every violent and aggressive action could be justified as necessary for self-preservation, the limits to human action were unrestricted, Hobbes concluded.

**In the absence of a strong central authority to which all in a society have submitted, Hobbes asserts that there exists a state of perpetual war among men—the "state of nature." In such a condition, attacks require a response. The world of public perception may be closer to Hobbes's state of nature than we would like to believe.**

Hobbes noted, nonetheless, that one strategy in particular was successful in buttressing survival—and that was the reciprocation of aggression in kind. As Vincy Fon and Francesco Parisi of the George Mason School of Law noted in their essay, "Revenge and Retaliation":

> When conflicts arise in the absence of a commonly recognized rule of conduct, interaction between individuals is governed by the most elementary law of nature: what one party can do to another, the other can do as well.

Long before the recognition of a formal code of conduct, early peoples acknowledged that if they returned hostility with hostility, they were much more likely to survive than if they were submissive.

In such a brutal, force ruled environment, retaliation, however, did not necessarily ensure dominance or survival. Its antithesis—tolerance in the face of unilateral aggression—was certain to lead to extinction. Reciprocating aggression was at least in part a conscious decision learned by oral tradition and handed down between generations of early human beings.

## Group Protection under a Social Contract

Returning for a moment to Hobbes, to say that the Age of Reason brought about the concept of a "social contract" would be an error. Long before the emergence of 17th century philosophical thought, civilizations such as the Egyptians, Romans, and Huns thrived.

Uniting for mutually beneficial reasons, a practice that would allow the development of early civilization, also brought about a profound analysis of the cohesive forces that bring people together. This idea is of particular merit as a model for social behavior because it suggests the concession of retaliatory rights to the majority of individuals in exchange for group protection of property and self.

Hobbes believed that the chaos triggered by individualistic self-preservation would lead to a "war of all against all (bellum omnium contra omnes)," a world of total anarchy, cruelty and abject failure. To escape their dismal existence of blood and steel, men form a society to which they concede many of their individual liberties in return for stability. One of these liberties is the right to exact revenge at will. The collective power is then consolidated and transferred to a single point of cohesive power (Hobbes suggested an absolute monarch, for example) which presides over society.

## Further Movement Away from Socially Acceptable Violence

Another English philosopher John Locke (1632-1704) disagreed with Hobbes regarding man's natural state. Gripped with the idea that man is born with a "tabula rasa" or "blank slate," Locke believed that men do not have a propensity for aggression and in the natural state ought to:

[P]reserve the rest of mankind, and may not, unless it be to do justice to an offender, take away, or impair the life, the liberty, health, limb or goods of another.

The idea that health, liberty, and goods (also known as "life, liberty and the pursuit of happiness") are guaranteed to all became extremely influential during the 18th century, and influenced two monumental philosophical undertakings: the American Declaration of Independence and the French Revolution.

Locke's resistance to the sovereign was fostered in part by his patron, the Earl of Shaftsbury, who wished to prevent the Duke of York from ascending to the English throne. Locke's rebellious stance was clearly defined in Two Treatises of Government. The second treatise, which received much more acclaim and is considered to be the root of liberal political thought, used the concepts of natural rights and social contract to provide a theory for a civil society.

In this latter publication, Locke suggests that a government is not a product of force—as was the case in earlier societies—but a concept welcomed by the people to ensure the aforementioned protection of health liberty and goods. Unlike Hobbes, who suggested that the concession of power to the government was absolute and could not be retracted, Locke believed that because the people formed a government willingly, they had a right to dissolve it if it was not serving the people. Chapter XIII: Of the Subordination of the Powers of the Commonwealth reads:

> And thus the community perpetually retains a supreme power of saving themselves from the attempts and designs of any body, even of their legislators whenever they shall be so foolish, or so wicked, as to lay and carry on designs against the liberties and properties of the subject... and to rid themselves of those, who invade this fundamental, sacred and unalterable law of self-preservation, for which they entered into society.

French Enlightenment thinker Jean Jacques Rousseau (1712 – 1778) further expounded upon the idea of social cohesion in his 1762 publication of Du Contrat Social (On Social Contract). According to Rousseau:

> Each of us puts his person and all his power in common under the supreme direction of the general will, and, in our corporate capacity, we retrieve each member as an indivisible part of the whole.[204]

Thus, Rousseau reasoned, we concede our individual power to the general will, administered by an entity we call "government" and expect that the social contract will serve as mutually beneficial. As can be imagined, however, the formation of a collective society in which the interests of the general population are met is not an easy task. Rousseau noted:

> The problem is to find a form of association which will defend and protect with the while common force of the person and goods of each associate, and in which each, while uniting himself with all, may still obey himself alone, and remain as free as before.[205]

This last statement provides insight into the role of retaliation under a social contract. If we hypothetically concede our right to retaliation (a right that history has taught us is intrinsically acceptable) to a society and that society is incapable our protecting us, what are we to do?

Unfortunately, despite the authority that accompanies social contracts, many discretionary injustices remain unpunished. According to these contracts, the concession of natural rights is made to the general will, which often conflicts with the position of individuals or minority groups. In other words, it is the will of the majority that rules. Often those subjugated (either by force or volition) find themselves in need of change.

Adherence to Locke's call to arms, however, may appear to be a paradox: how does one reconcile the use of retaliation towards a government to which it has conceded its rights of aggression?

The response to this dilemma is a history-making idea: non-violent resistance. It also follows then, that *exchanging fire when fired upon* is often most effective when there is no fire at all. In fact, to exchange fire does not entail violence or a physical response at all. To explain this concept, it is helpful to turn to the 19th century transcendentalist Henry David Thoreau.

## Civilized Retaliation

In 1849, Thoreau published his now renowned essay *Civil Disobedience*. Inspired by an impassioned contempt of slavery and the Mexican-American War, Thoreau, echoing Locke, suggested that defiance towards a state that promotes injustice was the obligation of a responsible citizen:

> All men recognize the right of revolution; that is, the right to refuse allegiance to, and to resist, the government, when its tyranny or its inefficiency are great and unendurable.[206]

As per the means of such change, the one-time denizen of Walden Pond detested those men who relied solely on democracy, waiting idly to persuade the majority to right the wrongs of society. Thoreau must have certainly envisioned embattled citizens being "fired upon" by the unjust and inhumane policies of government. Although totally opposed to violence, Thoreau still invoked aggrieved citizens to more assertively demand retribution for their grievances: ". . . cast your whole vote, not a strip of paper merely, but your whole influence."[207]

Thoreau's call for reform is nothing innovative, for human history is replete with revolution. What is unique about the transcendentalist's "return fire" is the non-violent means in which he aspires to effectuate change. His call for reform did not include a call to arms.

Thoreau's non-violent attempts at change may have been forced upon him by circumstance. As a slight figure, he may not have been adequately equipped in size to do conventional battle. A biographical sketch of Thoreau would suggest that he was not a very intimidating figure. The one time pencil-maker was of a limited stature due to his diet of bread and potatoes, which he preferred to meat.

Nineteenth century American author, Nathaniel Hawthorne was quoted as saying "[Thoreau] is as ugly as sin, long-nosed, queer-mouthed, and with uncouth and rustic, though courteous manners, corresponding very well with his exterior." Unlike many of the stronger, more virile men of his generation, Thoreau abstained from the consumption of alcohol and was celibate throughout his entire life.

Physically under-qualified for traditional retaliation, this resourceful revolutionary knew that he must exact revenge with the power he had available. In his case, retaliation meant refusing to pay six years' worth of poll taxes to demonstrate his disapproval. The incident cost Thoreau a night in jail, a small price when compared to the gravity of slavery and the Mexican-American War.

It is unrealistic to assume that Thoreau's obstinacy alone was successful in the eventual abolition of slavery and the end of the Mexican-American War. It is likely, however, that the author's unwillingness to cooperate with a belligerent government was critical in raising awareness about social injustices.

Perhaps Thoreau's greatest impact was his influence on two future revolutionaries, Mahatma Gandhi and Martin Luther King, Jr., both of whom would build upon Thoreau's principles to overcome seemingly insurmountable obstacles in the twentieth century.

**Thoreau's Disciples Learn How to Exchange Fire Non-violently**

Twenty years after Thoreau published his *Essay on Civil Disobedience*, a pupil was born halfway around the world. Mahatma Gandhi, the son of the Prime Minister of Porbander, India, was reared according to traditional Indian culture, carrying out his business under the tenets of non-violence, maintaining a life-long abstinence (from both meat and alcohol), and cultivating the practice of universal tolerance.

Gandhi never divorced himself from the real world, however, obtaining a law degree in the imperial capital of London and working briefly as a barrister in India. Gandhi eventually accepted a position with the British Armed Services in South Africa, hardly an obvious path to peaceful change, where he attained the rank of major.

Ironically, it was in Natal, South Africa, and not in India, where Gandhi experienced the true humiliation inflicted by discrimination against non-whites. Major M. K. Gandhi was on multiple occasions beaten, kicked off trains, and forced to remove his turban, a symbol of spirituality and holiness in Sikhism, Gandhi's faith.

It was under these conditions that Gandhi challenged the inferior status of Indians in South Africa, first by opposing a bill that would deny Indians the right to vote, and then later protesting mandatory registration of his people. In addition to a host of religious texts, Gandhi had spent time reading Thoreau's *Essay on Disobedience.*

Like Thoreau, Gandhi was challenged to stand on firm principles and resist powerful forces even though he also certainly not physically up to it. As frail as Thoreau appeared, he would have been a colossus alongside Gandhi.

While emaciated from habitual fasting (for both protest and purification), Gandhi often dressed in nothing more than the traditional, homespun Indian diaper-like dhoti, which further emphasized his appearance of frailty. Gandhi's physical appearance, however, did not weaken his iron-willed determination to take on and defeat British imperialism.

**Even Gandhi Fights Back**

But rather than attempting to surmount a hostile resistance—the Indians in South Africa numbering in the tens of thousands—Gandhi denounced violence and began his campaign of Satyagraha—a combination of Sanskrit words "truth" and "persistence"—as a means of retaliation.

Upon his return to India, Gandhi continued to "exchange fire" with authorities through his practice of non-violent resistance. This time his efforts were aimed at attaining more agricultural autonomy for the peasants in Kheda and Chamaparan. Through a series of strikes and protests, "Mahatma," or "the Great Soul," was able to improve living conditions and decrease the revenue demands of the imperial system.

During a later incident, Gandhi proved his dedication to the cause by marching more than 200 miles in protest of a British tax on salt, only to further express his contempt for the tax by making his own salt upon arrival.

Gandhi's success, demonstrated by the increasing concessions from London, suggested that non-violent non-cooperation was becoming a viable means of "exchanging fire" without employing reciprocal violence. The brilliance of this strategy was the complex analysis involved in determining the most appropriate path. Non-violent fire was the most effective mechanism and clearly involved assuming the moral high ground. By using the scant tools available him, Mohatma Gandhi struck a decisive blow against an empire.

These prior movements, significant in their own right, served as a precursor for Gandhi's overall objective of Swaraj—a combination of Sanskrit words for self rule—but to Gandhi meaning specifically complete political, social, and spiritual freedom.

Britain's involvement in World War II provided the perfect opportunity for Gandhi to demonstrate the hypocrisy of the Empire. While tens of thousands of British soldiers were fighting (and dying) for the sake of democracy, the sub-continent continued to be subjugated.

Gandhi's "Quit India" campaign launched in 1942 marked the culmination of the Indian independence movement. He refused to support the British war effort without their commitment to sovereignty. Indians were united in their opposition to the war effort, which seemed to offer them little personal incentive. The movement did not receive immediate success, but by the end of the war, it was clear that steps for India's independence were in motion.

In addition to the obvious subversive efforts by the British Empire, Gandhi faced a host of obstacles in his lifetime, extending from constant schisms in Parliament to the Muslim-Hindu divide. Under normal circumstances, one might have given in to the pressure and resorted to the natural reaction of violent retaliation. Gandhi, however, adhered closely to the tenets of Satyagraha.

Though the reforms sought by Mahatma were far ranging— encompassing broad issues such as eradicating the sordid, abject poverty and implementing sweeping agricultural reforms—Gandhi never strayed from his policy of peaceful non-cooperation to exchange violent, physical fire with his adversaries. No, his fire was more calculated and injurious to an empire that need3ed cooperation from its subjects.

In response to the idea of retaliatory violence, Gandhi has been quoted as saying "An eye for an eye makes the whole world blind." By resisting the temptation to retaliate in kind, Gandhi was able to the open the world's eyes to the injustice suffered by Indians.

This is not to say, however, that Gandhi did not exchange fire. In fact, his exchange was swift, thoughtful, and used the strengths that his position afforded. His followers, numbering in the tens of thousands, provided a force that made his non-violent strategy more effective than meeting force with force.

**Gandhi demonstrates that an effective response does not have to be a destructive response. You can create public sympathy for your position, and wield that sympathy as a weapon of retaliation against attacks on you and your reputation.**

While Gandhi's legendary status as a leader of peaceful, non-violent resistance reaches mythical proportions, Gandhi's Satyagraha is *not* synonymous with tolerance—quite the contrary. Gandhi sought to change injustice in the world, but when he met resistance he did not shrink from conflict for the sake of peace.

Gandhi simply exchanged fire in a way that could not be answered by continued violence or incarceration. Just because Gandhi did not form an army of Indians (whose population in India grossly outnumbered the British colonialists) does not mean that he was passive. Instead, Gandhi used his Satyagraha policy of "truth and persistence" to achieve remarkable goals.

**Non-Violence Fit for a King**

Another famous Gandhi adage is "Be the change you wish to see in the world." His message is that rather than merely talking about change, one should go out and initiate change. But turning a dream into reality may not be as easy as it seems. That is exactly what a young African-American minister sought to do, employing Gandhi's principles of Satyagraha in the 1950's and 60's.

In 1947, in rural Claredon County, South Carolina, the state chapter of the National Association for the Advancement of Colored People (NAACP) first attempted, with a single plaintiff, to sue the school board over inferior conditions African-American students experienced under the state's racially segregated school system. By 1951, community activist Reverend J.A. DeLaine convinced African-American parents to join the NAACP efforts to file a class action suit in U.S. District Court. The court found that the schools designated for African-Americans were grossly inadequate in terms of buildings, transportation, and teacher's salaries, when compared to the schools provided for whites. The court issued an order to equalize the facilities, but the order was unsuccessful because school officials virtually ignored it. The schools were never made equal.

By 1955, the American South was primed with racial tension, ready to explode. The U.S. Supreme Court had ruled in *Brown v. Board of Education* a year prior that the segregation of public schools was unconstitutional.

But many Southern institutions maintained a position of racial discrimination. Rosa Parks, a 41-year-old African-American department store clerk, refused to give up her seat on a Montgomery bus to make room for white passengers. She was arrested for her efforts. Although the fine was only $10, the symbolic action caused an outrage about the injustice among local African-Americans that quickly materialized into a citywide boycott.

Emerging from this movement was Martin Luther King, Jr., an eloquent 26-year-old Baptist minister. Named after another celebrated reformist of centuries past and armed with a doctorate in theology from Boston University, King would combine his Christian upbringing with his understanding of Gandhi's Satyagraha to fight racial discrimination throughout the United States. He would indeed *"exchange fire when fired upon."*

White Southern racial policies presented a number of challenges to African-American citizens. Only a fraction of Southern schools had begun desegregation initiatives, and while African-Americans had technically held the right to vote since the 19th century, many Southern communities used literacy tests, registration delays, and even physical violence and intimidation to disenfranchise minority voters.

The Southern Christian Leadership Conference, chaired by King, chose Birmingham, Alabama, to deploy a non-violent strategy upon a Southern political battlefield. It was here that King chose to "exchange fire."

Protestors walked the streets echoing chants of "We Shall Overcome" and "Woke Up This Morning with My Mind Stayed on Freedom," attracting considerable media attention to their cause and creating one of the opening volleys in King's "exchange of fire."

The most obvious retaliatory option provided to the opposition was imprisonment. But local businessmen soon realized that incarcerating the city's entire African-American population was counter-productive, to put it mildly, and that white businessmen and elected leaders would have to concede on some of the contentious issues.

Dr. King elevated his campaign to a national level in the fall of 1963 when he led a 200,000 member "March on Washington for Jobs and Freedom." It was during this march, on the steps of the Lincoln Memorial, that King gave his legendary "I Have a Dream Speech," his eloquent appeal for equality galvanized public opinion against segregation. The speech received national attention and the question of "civil rights" could no longer be ignored.

King's "return fire" brought about more change than ever possible through violent troop assaults. Inspired by King, then President Lyndon B. Johnson championed the cause of social equality by leading legislative efforts to strengthen the Civil Rights Act of 1957 and to establish organizations such as the Civil Relations Service and the Equal Opportunity Commission to help lead change.

While progress was by no means immediate, it is estimated that "nearly 250,000 new black voters were registered before the end of 1965. And in the years that followed, the South continued to register itself in numbers proportional to its strength."[208]

In 1965, King also became the youngest person ever to receive a Nobel Peace Prize. At just 36 years old, he had demonstrated to the world that it was indeed possible to "exchange fire" without ever raising a fist.

Mahatma Gandhi and Martin Luther King Jr. understood that it was possible to retaliate without resorting to violence. Unfortunately, their adversaries did not. Gandhi and King, two men that had fostered their dreams out of truth and compassion, demonstrated the power of truth and justice—two abstract, intangible concepts—to change the world. Those who had no way to overcome truth, gunned down Gandhi and King down before they were able to see the results of their difficult struggles. But because their methods were accepted and effective, their life's work lives on even today.

Sun Tzu, in his treatise *The Art of War*, stressed that thus one is able to gain a victory my modifying his tactics in accordance with the enemy's situation. The success of Gandhi and King speaks to a very important underlying tenet embodied in this maxim. The response must be thoughtful, well grounded, and effective. An ineffective response will only serve to further create a disadvantage for one's position. To quote Sun Tzu:

> There are roads which must not be followed, armies which must be not attacked, towns which must not be besieged, positions which must not be contested, commands of the sovereign which must not be obeyed.[209]

For the general who thoroughly understands the advantages of varying tactics will know how to handle his troops, Sun Tzu concluded.

## Freedom of Expression: A Blessing . . . and a Burden

The experiences of Gandhi and King proved that members of a well-governed society could suffer from unfavorable treatment despite so-called protection of government.

In issue management, there are few rules to protect a group of stakeholders rallied around a common cause from the disparaging and politically wounding remarks made by opposing parties. Stakeholders are once again thrust into a dilemma. They cannot afford to allow false statements to be accepted as truths, but they also cannot react with violence to stop the spread of falsehood and protect against future transgressions—there is no modern day Montresor of issue management to brick up our political adversaries.

Thus it is imperative that issue managers develop an effective retaliatory strategy that operates within the confines of acceptable behavior within our society. Naturally, the need for an effective strategy to counteract and repair damage inflicted by the opening shots of an opponent stems from our right to the freedom of expression.

Though we may find it impossible to imagine a society without the freedom of expression, the opportunity to express oneself without fear of prosecution is a relatively recent development in human history.

Historically, tyrannical rulers restricted the free exchange of ideas among their subjects to more easily maintain authority and suppress attempts to seize power through organized rebellion.

Historically, dissidents were treated to imprisonment, physical harm, and sometimes death. Not until the Age of Enlightenment and the Lockean notion of "inalienable rights" did the concept of a universal right to "freedom of expression" begin to circulate. Without the right of free expression, avenues for socially acceptable ways of exchanging fire become limited. And this is a condition sought by totalitarian states in which criticism, no matter how valid, is prohibited.

The effectiveness of European despotism in stifling intellectual, social, and political progress did not go unnoticed by America's founding fathers. James Madison, Thomas Jefferson, John Adams, and Thomas Paine, men who contributed greatly to the framework of the American Constitution, wisely sought to ensure the freedom of expression by making "freedom of expression" one of the cornerstones of our nation's constitution. The First Amendment in America's Bill of Rights reads:

> Congress shall make no law respecting an establishment of religion or prohibiting the free exercise thereof; or *abridging the freedom of speech, or of the press*; or the right of the people to peaceable assemble, and to petition the government for a redress of grievances.

This fundamental right to free speech guaranteed by the U.S. Constitution ensured citizens the freedom to vigorously criticize their elected leaders and their actions—as well as those of their fellow countrymen—unfettered by the fear of political persecution and imprisonment.

While the First Amendment permits an unprecedented amount of free discourse—often leading to improvements and progress—it also fosters the ability for one to speak negatively about opponents (albeit within the boundaries of the legal restrictions on defamation, libel, and slander). Therefore, does it not seem logical that one has an obligation to "exchange fire" with an opponent for no other reason than to disable falsehoods and correct errors.

Nineteenth century Scottish philosopher John Stuart Mill would agree. He lent credibility to the idea of "freedom of expression" when he proffered his essay, *On Liberty*. According to Mills:

> [T]he peculiar evil of silencing the expression of an opinion is that it is robbing the human race ; posterity as well as the existing generation ; those who dissent from the opinion, still more than those who hold it. If the opinion is right, they are deprived of the opportunity of exchanging error for truth : if wrong, they lose, what is almost as great a benefit, the clearer perception and livelier impression of truth, produced by its collision with error.[210]

Mill believed that suppressing one's right to express a truth was wrong because it precluded the ability to replace an incorrect notion with a correct one. To stifle the opportunity for revelation was, he believed, to impede the progress of humanity. Therefore, it is of vital concern that those who are fired upon exchange fire if for no other reason that to set the record straight.

It may seem conclusive that Mill would advocate the freedom of expression for only truths, but the Scottish philosopher also encouraged the expression of that which is not necessarily true. Note that later in the passage quoted earlier on the utterance of untruths Mill suggests:

> [I]f wrong, they lose, what is almost as great a benefit, the clearer perception and livelier impression of truth, produced by its collision with error.[211]

Unchallenged, a truth may lie dormant and thus remain unacknowledged. The declaration with falsities is necessary because it is only through their juxtaposition with the truth that we may determine what is real.

The freedom of expression thus becomes a double-edged sword: while we enjoy the ability to champion our opinions without fear of prosecution, we must anticipate the ability of our opponents to challenge our claims, regardless of their veracity. Our only option is to fire back in defense and retaliation, particularly in the case of negative campaigning.

The effectiveness of the counterclaim will be driven by timeliness and skillfulness of the response.

Negative campaigning involves deprecating an opponent to gain relative success rather than advocating the virtues of one's own platform, which might provide absolute success. The need to take opinions to a significant level of viciousness may be fueled by the innate human fear that potential conspirators are much more menacing than potential cooperators are promising. According to Vicent Fon and Teresa Parisi:

> [P]eople are in many ways better solving problems that require cheater detection (deciding whether a social contract had been violated), relative to problems that require detecting cooperatives.[212]

In politics we often see campaigns make use of this phenomenon by disparaging their opponents with smear ads. It has been my experience (and one that has proven to be statistically verified through voter exit polls) that voters—particularly those in the undecided category—are generally less likely to make their final candidate selection based on positive attributes than they are to vote against negative ones.

In other words, in contemporary American electoral politics, the undecided voter is much more likely to head for the voting booth because of something negative communicated about a candidate than to go inspired by a positive message.

The bottom line: Undecided voters tend to vote for the "lesser of two evils," not necessarily a candidate who seems to share the voter's own visions and values.

**Campaign Smears: When Ignoring an Attack Is Not an Option**

While the human psyche has a natural tendency to fire back when slighted and may even be controlled by a biological imperative, there are some situations where simply turning the other cheek is not an option. Such is the case in attacks upon one's character and reputation.

Even philosopher John Locke recognized that defending our reputation is inherent to human nature. Locke wrote in his journal:

> The principal spring from which the actions of men take their rise, the rule they conduct them by, and the end to which they direct them, seems to be credit and reputation, and that which at any rate they avoid is in the greatest part shame and disgrace.[213]

Nowhere is this truer than in politics and issue management. Certainly the maintenance of a favorable reputation is desirable for a number of inherent reasons, one of the primary motivations being to satisfy the demand for fairness in human beings.

More important than this personal recognition of credit, however, is the role that public opinion plays in modern issue management. The reason that we cannot simply dismiss false allegations geared at our position is simple: If they are not denounced immediately and adamantly, the public will begin to believe them.

Dictators throughout history have made use of the Big Lie—a lie so incredible and fabulous that the public believes it must be true. No one could make up something that incredible, they reason. But like a winestain on a fresh carpet, the longer the stain of false accusations set unchallenged, the more difficult they will be to wash away.

Imagine also the analogy of character assault to the hardening of concrete. Political candidates will try to pin their opponents in an unfavorable position by launching assaults upon their character and reputation.

Initially the victim of the verbal assault retains some maneuverability. But the longer the accusations persist, the more fixed they become until the victims finally must concede their adversary's slights as one of the major planks in the foundation of their platform.

If one concedes that the freedom of expression is not only an inalienable right but also recognizes that character assassination cannot be tolerated, the result puts one at a confusing crossroads. Human psychological and physiological predispositions suggest swift retaliation. But as part of a civilized society, one has conceded the right to traditional retaliation to the general will and common welfare of the group.

Fortunately, it is possible to retaliate without resorting to violence. The shields of primeval ancestors are hammered into sound ideological positions that are capable of withstanding enemy verbal attacks.

## Maxim 4: Exchange Fire When Fired Upon

Primitive spears are transformed into a political onslaught of facts and accusations that return fire on hostile opponents.

In politics and issue management, an impenetrable defense may really constitute the best offense and serve as a prerequisite to any successful counterattack. Carl von Clausewitz, the Prussian military strategist who saw his share of combat during the Rhine Campaigns (1793-1794) and the Napoleonic Wars (1806-1815) suggested that a proper defense allows an entity the advantages of waiting and position.

By "waiting," Clausewitz is not referring a reluctance to strike back once an assault has been made. What he means is that when one allows the enemy to make the first move—in political parlance, when we leave the decision to engage in negative campaigning to our opponent—we force them to make the first move and have the advantage of responding appropriately from a morally superior position.

By position, Clausewitz was referring to the benefit that comes from forcing our adversaries to operate on our terrain. In military combat, a defensive position allows leaders of the campaign a better understanding of the battle field, since it is being fought on their home turf. Being first to take a defensive position also provides the opportunity to establish protective fortifications. These conditions being met, Clausewitz assures us that there is no need to fear an onslaught by the opposition:

> [I]f we are to conceive of a defence as it should be, it is this. All means are prepared to the utmost; the army is fit for war and familiar with it; the general will let the enemy come on, not from confused indecision and fear, but by his own choice, coolly and deliberately; fortresses are undaunted by the prospect of a siege; and finally a stout-hearted populace is no more afraid of the enemy than he it [the population].[214]

Thus defenders are ready for their aggressors. Their defense is implacable, and they do not fear potential enemy aggression. Clausewitz's emphasis on defense was not limited to the European theater of operations. More than 2,000 years before Clausewitz, when "Prussia" was still a snowy terrain roamed by barbarians, the Chinese philosopher and military strategist Sun Tzu was propounding a similar idea:

> The art of war teaches us to rely not on the likelihood of the enemy's not coming, but on our own readiness to receive him; not on the chance of his not attacking but rather on the fact that we have made our own position unassailable.[215]

Clausewitz suggests that the objective of defense more than simply blocking an attack but involves the parrying of a blow. That being said, the objective of any military conquest is more than merely the ability to sustain an attack. Once the aggressor has fired an opening barrage—in issue management parlance, negative campaigning by the opposition—the attack must be confuted with vigor. Again, no one better to articulate this idea than Clausewitz himself:

> In other words, a war in which victories were used only defensively without the intention of counter attacking would be as absurd as a battle in which the principle of absolute defence—passivity, that is—were to dictate every action.[216]

And once attacked, the recipients of the attack unleash their fury—Clausewitz again:

> A sudden powerful transition to the offense—the flashing sword of vengeance—is the greatest moment for the defence. If it is not in the commander's mind from the start, or rather if it is not an integral part of his idea of defence, he will never be persuaded of the superiority of the defensive form; all he will see is how much of the enemy's resources he can destroy or capture.[217]

## The Best Defense—Threat of Massive Retaliation

In the best case scenario, a sufficient defense—or the threat of untenable retaliation—may preclude enemy aggression all together. If the adversary believes that the damage they will incur is greater than they are willing to bear, they will avoid the attack. American foreign policy in the decades following World War II provides a real-life example of the use of negative reciprocity as a disincentive for aggression.

During the 1950's, the President Dwight D. Eisenhower and his Secretary of State John Foster Dulles implemented a policy commonly understood as "massive retaliation." Though never stated explicitly, the idea was that any enemy aggression (such as from the Soviet Union) would be met with an unthinkable reprisal.

And this seemingly insane position has, so far, proved successful. In spite of the massive armament that characterized post U.S.-Soviet relations, the Cold War was kept "cold" due to the understanding that a nuclear attack by either nation was likely to lead to the annihilation of both—and possibly the end of Western civilization.

Though both nations came close to combat on multiple occasions (perhaps most notably the Cuban Missile Crisis in 1962), the realization that the devastation would be mutual kept both parties at bay. In fact, since the bombing of Hiroshima and Nagasaki in August of 1945, no nation has been willing to gamble with a nuclear strike on their enemy, fearing the potential, world-annihilating repercussions.

Modern campaigns are the political equivalent of zero-sum warfare: candidates who gain ground by assaulting the campaign of their opponents often lose any advantage they have achieved when their opponents strike back. Parties who perceive their opponents to be apprehensive or feeble are likely to attack relentlessly, undaunted by the meager responses they may incur, if the opponent response at all. If, however, a party feels that a verbal onslaught may be met with equal or greater pugnacity, it will be much more reluctant to fire off accusations.

**Being prepared with and having demonstrated a forceful response to attacks on you and your position may discourage further such attacks.**

Despite the bipolar nature of the Cold War, many periphery nations began to acquire nuclear arms. American technology helped the Allied powers France and the United Kingdom achieve armament in the 1950's.

At the same time, Russia established an atomic allegiance with a fellow Communist nation, The People's Republic of China.

India's successful detonation of "Smiling Buddha" in 1974 was seen as a direct response to the armament of its northern neighbor. Ironically, the Indian nuclear weapons initiative encouraged rival Pakistan to develop a retaliatory nuclear weapons program of its own. In the volatile Middle East, Israeli's precarious position was bolstered by the possible menace of nuclear mass destruction it could impose on potential transgressors.

The 21st century continues to witness a parade of developing nations aspiring to membership into the nuclear elite, believing it will serve as a warning against the intrusive influence of outsiders.

Whether the artillery consists of atomic warheads or condemnatory criticism, an effective retaliatory defense is contingent upon the acquisition and maintenance of a menacing arsenal. Since the issue here is public opinion, not physical destruction, how does one assemble a defensive arsenal?

The answer lies in the mobilization of additional tools provided by the maxims. For example: using absolute truth to convince others; building credibility through third-party support; seizing the moral high ground when the situation presents itself. An opponent may be able to dismiss emotional rejoinders as mere capricious rationalizations. But pragmatic, well-documented attacks will not be eluded as easily.

**No One Strikes Me with Impunity**

Unlike the policy of Mutual Assured Destruction (MAD) described earlier, sometimes the threat of retaliation is insufficient in deterring enemy aggression. When opponents dismiss the ongoing risk of reciprocity and attack anyway, their hostilities should not be suffered with impunity.

History has proven time and time again that aggressors must be met with resistance or they will press their advantage until it is imperative they be stopped. Witness German Chancellor Adolph Hitler's early grabs of eastern European territory just prior to World War II. The Western European nations miscalculated their abilities to bring about a peaceful settlement to these territorial conflicts. The result was an inadequate response interpreted by Nazi Germany as weakness, and the planet suffered a second world war as a consequence of inaction by the Western European powers.

## The Apocalyptic Price of Inaction

If retaliation in the face of aggression serves as a viable deterrent, then forbearance as a response has the inverse effect. One of the more recent examples of this principle brings to mind British Prime Minister Neville Chamberlain and the Munich Conference of 1938.

In the spring of that year, Hitler met with the leader of the Sudeten Germany Party to discuss a plot to annex the territory from Czechoslovakia. The Sudentenland's 11,000 square miles in western Czechoslovakia once belonged to Germany and was home to more than three million German-speaking residents.

Hitler announced he would invade Czechoslovakia to regain the territory taken from Germany. Britain and France threatened intervention through military action. But painful memories of the brutal carnage and property devastation of World War I were still too vivid in the minds of Europe's leaders. The two European powers reneged on their threat of military action, justifying the reversal of their position on the premise that this *minor* concession was relatively insignificant compared to another full scale war. They sought a peaceful settlement to the Czech crisis.

Hitler had marched into Austria in March of that year, but he pledged to Chamberlain that Germany would make no more territorial demands. Believing that he was securing "peace in our time," Chamberlain convinced the Czechs to cede the territory to Germany, which was formally agreed upon on September 29, 1938, with the signing of the Munich Agreement.

Germany's annexation of the Sudetenland would not have been so disastrous if it had stopped there. Emboldened by his unchecked aggression, Hitler began making claims to areas home to German ethic populations in Poland and Hungary as well. The German expansion was bolstered in large part by the conversion of well-developed civilian industry in the Sudetenland to fuel the Nazi war machine.

It is unnecessary to explain what transpired next. In less than a year after the Munich Agreement, Germany invaded Poland, forcing Britain and France to declare war, officially beginning World War II. In less than a decade, the fighting would spread from Europe to Asia to Africa and leave over 60 million dead.

It would be only idle speculation to assume that Britain and France could have averted World War II by stopping Hitler's troops at the Czechoslovakian border. But there have been serious questions raised about their reluctance to retaliate. By allowing German expansion to go unchecked—and despite strong opposition by the Czechoslovakian people—the Western European powers suggested that they would do anything to avoid conflict. Ironically, the advantages that were gained from the acquisition of Sudeten manufacturing capabilities made stopping the Germans extremely difficult once the inevitable war had begun.

Just as an aggressive nation is encouraged by lack of intervention by other countries, in issue management, allowing opponents to attack without a significant response instills in them a confidence that their inappropriate behavior will be tolerated. If adversaries are not met with reprisals after the first transgression, it is highly likely they will try to gain an unfair advantage again. Because of their boldness, the Nazis were able to isolate the Sudeten industrial capability for their exclusive use, greatly enhancing their ability to conduct war.

**Many historians contend that Chamberlain's failure to respond to Hitler's aggression merely encouraged Hitler to expand further. If you do not respond to an attack on your position, you will encourage additional attacks.**

By allowing opponents to control the hearts and minds of large cross-sections of the population, they will be able to manipulate these population groups to their advantage and strengthen their own efforts. In politics, the examples of Democratic presidential candidate Michael Dukakis and Republican vice presidential candidate Dan Quayle say volumes about the differences between forceful rebuttals and half-hearted counterattacks.

**Exchanging Fire in Elective Politics**

Having handily defeated his Democratic competition and having won the party's nomination, Michael Dukakis in 1988 was faced with a series of sensitive issues that he would have to overcome if he were to succeed in the November elections.

One topic of contention involved a furlough program endorsed by Governor Dukakis, which permitted the unsupervised release of Massachusetts inmates. The move may have been successful in its goal of gradual reintroduction, but there was at least one glaring exception—the case of Willie Horton, an inmate who raped a woman and brutally assaulted her husband upon release from the Concord Correctional Facility.

Another controversial issue was Dukakis's adamant opposition to capital punishment. Conservatives saw his opposition to the death penalty and his support of abortion rights as a direct contradiction.

A third criticism questioned the patriotism of Dukakis, who, as governor of Massachusetts, had vetoed a bill that would have made the recitation of the Pledge of Allegiance compulsory in the state's public schools.

In 1988 there were 15 states without a death penalty statute. The mandatory recitation of the U.S. "Pledge of Allegiance" had been found unconstitutional by the U.S. Supreme.[218] And the furlough program, though extended to include those serving life without parole, was not established by Dukakis himself but adopted as policy from a previous administration.

This did not stop George H. W. Bush and Lee Atwater, however, from portraying their opponent as what they termed a "bleeding heart liberal" who was far too soft to be the next Commander-in-Chief. Riding on the coattails of a two-term administration that was markedly conservative in its approach to economics and defense, the Republicans suggested that "liberalism" was not merely another approach to governance but the very epitome of evil.

According to Stephen J. Ducat, author of the book *Wimp Factor*, the 1988 Unabridged Republican Dictionary defined a liberal as:

someone who had an abiding affection for violent criminals, was in favor of completely disarming the military and surrendering American sovereignty to the whims of any number of rapacious tyrants, wanted public schools not only to require classes in homosexuality but to mandate flag burning as a substitute for the Pledge of Allegiance, and believed the government should raise taxes on the middle class to pay for programs designed to give every drug-addicted Welfare mother a second Cadillac.[219]

Dukakis's competition across the aisle wasted no time in attaching this description to their opponent. In September of 1988 the "nonaffiliated" National Security Political Action Committee released an ad criticizing Dukakis policy of "Weekend Passes," which showed the remorseless mug shot of Willie Horton.

Bush and Atwater furthered the derision with a staged prison ad, which suggested that Massachusetts prisons were guarded by a "revolving door." Though never convicted of a crime, Bush insinuated that Dukakis himself was a criminal during the Illinois Republican Convention when he claimed that the Governor had released Horton to "terrorize innocent people."

During the October 13, 1988 presidential debate, moderator Bernard Shaw boldly asked the Democratic candidate "If Kitty Dukakis were raped and murdered, would you favor an irrecoverable death penalty for the killer?" Dukakis responded rather stoically, "No, I don't, and I think you know that I've opposed the death penalty during all of my life."

The Bush team could not have asked for a better response . . . or lack of one. Republicans seized the opportunity to brand their opponent as incompetent and cowardly. While they promoted a military hard line based on heavy rearmament, the Democrats, they suggested, were not even able to stand up for their wives.

Dukakis was issued no reprieve for his stance on the Pledge of Allegiance. On the steps on the California state senate, Bush told an audience, "This may seem very hard for you to even believe, but my opponent vetoed a bill that required the teachers in Massachusetts schools to lead their kids in the Pledge of Allegiance."[220] Bush presented the veto not as a mere defense of constitutional rights but as a symbolic act of indifference towards America.

As debilitating as they may seem, the criticisms launched at Dukakis were not entirely insurmountable. Negative campaign tactics are an element of politics that cannot be avoided. What separates the winners from the losers, as suggested before, is a candidate's ability to contest the accusations and paint his or her own portrait. Dukakis's failure stemmed from his reticent response to the criticisms from his conservative counterparts, which many interpreted as an acceptance.

The situation with Willie Horton could not have been predicted by Dukakis. In any case, the response to a fervid criticism by his Republican opponents should have been contested more effectively. For example, he might have responded that the furlough program was established by a Republican governor.

As per his position on capital punishment, Dukakis seemed to lack the intensity most American's would find commensurate with the murder and rape of one's wife.

A more suitable response would have condemned the acts of rape and murder as heinous. A campaign advisor had even prepared material to combat a predicted hypothetical situation by citing the assault of Dukakis's father and the hit and run death of his brother. The advice, however, was not heeded.

Finally, in the case of the Pledge of Allegiance, Dukakis could have reasserted his patriotism with ardor, showing appreciation for the nation that welcomed his Greek parents and provided him with so much opportunity. Instead, the criticism was met with an esoteric explanation of judicial precedence that did little to convince the "regular" American who cares less about legal jargon than just old-fashioned patriotism.

Instead of clarifying his position on the actual issues, Dukakis chose to run as far as he could by deeming himself a "moderate conservative."

As if this distancing strategy were not enough, Dukakis sought to prove himself as a military man by posing in M1 Abrams tank at the General Dynamics manufacturing plant in Michigan. The Democrat's awkwardness was evident and the publicity stunt backfired. The Bush campaign used footage from the commercial to show the juxtaposition of the Democrat looking uncomfortable riding in a machine of death and destruction.

By passively allowing his adversaries to identify him as a "bleeding heart liberal," Dukakis capitulated his image and, with that, the Presidential election. The Democratic party lost by a landslide in terms of electoral college votes.

Dukakis squandered what was once a 17-point lead. Had Dukakis been more aggressive in responding to the opposition and asserting his own identity, he may actually have succeeded.

**Summary**

Beginning at an early age, many Americans are trained in the ways of Christianity through the principles preached by Jesus in his Sermon on the Mount as recorded in the New Testament. Of particular importance is the concept of tolerance, patience, and forgiveness preached by Jesus: "If someone strikes you on the right cheek, turn to him the other also."

This repudiation of earlier teachings, particularly the concept of "an eye for an eye," replaces the traditional tenet of retaliation with pacifism and non-resistance as the new moral standard. While this edict may be fitting, and even attainable, in the Kingdom of God, one usually learns that a polity of tolerance is far less a propos in the Kingdom of Caesar.

In the realm of issue management, there is no merit in martyrdom. Taking the moral high ground by accepting an adversary's false or mischaracterizing statements can be detrimental to the fate of a campaign. The play-ground taunt of "sticks and stones may break my bones" holds little bearing in the world of sensitive public opinion. In this magnified and electronically distorted world, where opponents and undecided voters are seeking any seed of truth or half-truth upon which to base a reasonable opinion, a few careless words can literally destroy a public figure.

Instead of turning the other cheek to derisive attacks by an opponent, whether subtle or overt, such attacks should be countered with celerity and fervor. *Exchanging fire when fired upon* will allow a campaign to denounce false accusations and clarify position with conviction.

The desire to exchange fire when fired upon is a natural human response to an attack, whether physical or verbal. *Exchanging fire* is not a product of modern politics, but is a concept that has existed since the beginning of mankind. Though the retaliation used by our ancestors was manifested distinctly from tactics of retaliation employed today, it served a vital role in the evolution of the species. There is some evidence, in fact, that supports a belief that humans have a genetic predisposition to seek retribution for those who have inflicted hurt. But with the passage of time, civilizations began to realize that legal codes limiting the extent of appropriate retaliation were necessary to establish social equilibrium.

The $17^{th}$ and $18^{th}$ centuries hosted the development of the "Social Contract" theory, which concedes retaliatory rights to society for even greater equanimity. Unfortunately, the will of the majority was not always in agreement with that of the minority. Oppressed peoples were forced to return fire against social injustices. The $19^{th}$ and $20^{th}$ centuries witnessed visionaries' use of revolutionary retaliatory methods to promote their social agendas.

In contemporary society, the necessity for retaliation is a reflection of the importance of public opinion. Because the lines between perception and reality are often blurred, a campaign must retaliate against the accusations of its adversaries to maintain a positive reputation. In issue management, as in politics, the need for public approval is not motivated by pride but the role that the general opinion plays in deciding outcomes.

The concept of "exchanging fire when fired upon" does not have a singular application—rather, the degree of severity must be commensurate with the particular scenario. By closely examining historical incidents, it is possible to identify a variety of retaliatory scenarios that served their unique circumstances very well.

# Maxim 5
## "Plan your work and work your plan, but remain fluid."

*Just keep stirring the pot, you never know what will come up.*

— Former political consultant Lee Atwater, quoted by Peggy Noonan, *Wall Street Journal* columnist and former special assistant to the late President Ronald Reagan.

## Overview

Former political consultant and chairman of the National Republican Party, the late Lee Atwater was known as one of the best political organizers in the business. He was obsessive about organizing to the infinite detail. His plans were both deep and far reaching. Atwater was skilled at keeping the political pot stirred and turning, which continuously presents political opportunities.

As a campaign manager, Atwater planned a year in advance what the weekly topics of the campaign would be; what the candidate's communications would say about them; and how the campaign would disseminate the messages. He practiced a work ethic documented in a 1989 New York *Times* article:

> "THE DIFFERENCE between Lee Atwater and the rest of us," observes Charles R. Black, Atwater's former business partner and Jack Kemp's 1988 campaign manager, is that "Lee is simply more relentless." That relentlessness is evident in the 12 to 15 hours Atwater puts in each day. After being driven to his office by a Republican National Committee-supplied Lincoln Town Car, Atwater meets with senior staff every morning at 7. The meeting is followed by a steady stream of staff talks,

recruitment calls, press briefings, campaign strategy discussions with members of Congress and, more often than not, evening speaking engagements and fundraising appearances. A typical Atwater week is likely to include five public appearances, at least two flights to local Republican gatherings around the country and no fewer than four telephone calls from President (G.H.W.) Bush. In addition, Atwater talks with White House Chief of Staff John Sununu virtually every day.[221]

Atwater's model is enveloped into Maxim 5: "Plan your work and work your plan, but remain fluid." While his intricate planning and straightforward hard work was the key to much of his political success, particularly in field operations, Atwater kept his plans fluid and flexible enough to address issues as they arose. He always took a balanced, objective look at the tasks at hand, whether political or personal.

Even when Atwater discovered in 1990 that he was terminally ill with a malignant brain tumor, he approached his fight to survive as though it were a bare knuckles political brawl with everything to win and everything to lose. He guided his final days with a list taped to the wall of his bedroom: Faith, Superior Attitude, Courage, Strength, Purpose, Determination. Later, when he consulted a spiritual counselor to help him cope with his eminent death, he asked dispassionately, "What is your technical plan?"[222]

Ed Rogers, deputy to President George H.W. Bush's Chief of Staff John Sununu and an Atwater protege, said in 1989 that Atwater "knows the field" better than anyone who has ever sat in the party head's chair. Jack Kemp, the Secretary of Housing and Urban Development in the same Bush administration concurred. Atwater's "mechanical abilities, his nuts and-bolts political sense," are his greatest strength, Kemp said.[223]

When he smelled blood, he was a shark. Atwater is credited with the Willie Horton ad that essentially sunk the 1988 Democratic candidate Michael Dukakis. In one of his deathbed confessions, Atwater admitted that he said he would "would strip the bark off the little bastard (Dukakis)" and "make Willie Horton his running mate." He eventually apologized for both statements.

Despite his no-holds-barred style of campaigning, Atwater was analytic to the point of being scientific in his planning a winning election strategy. Another of his great strengths was in identifying the "swing" voters, usually middle-class "populist" families earning between $25,000 and $35,000 a year, stated in 1989 dollars. In the South, these families are white Protestants, in the North, often ethnic Catholics. Atwater's battleground was contested on the right-leaning populists' cultural turf. The values issues were usually about gun control, school prayer, national defense, taxes and welfare reform. The key, Atwater said, is fashioning an "Us" (the voter) versus "Them" (the arrogant liberal elitists) appeal.[224]

Successful planning methodology approaches each week of the campaign anticipating every possible contingency. Plans are focused on a certain voter base or district. As the weeks progress, the plan should address other specific districts and issues in a methodical, tactical fashion. The tactics for a specific campaign vary based on the issues and targeted voters, but the central idea of pushing the candidate's agenda remains on the forefront.

As the plan unfolds, it puts the opponent on the defensive, forcing the other candidate to keep up with the issues being addressed rather than allowing the opposition to dictate the dialogue. For instance, focusing on taxes one week and then immediately switching to education and then to health care allows Candidate A to push the campaign to her best interests. Speaking on taxes at a time when the opponent, Candidate B, was planning to communicate about education, forces the other side to address tax issue well before he is prepared to do so. By the time Candidate B has finally addressed Candidate A's position on taxes, Candidate A has already moved on to another issue. As the process continues, B is consistently behind A on the issues and their campaign is forced to continually struggle to make up lost ground.

The obvious question follows, then: why wouldn't B do the same plan and attack A first? Though a common idea, it seems that few take advantage of this technique. Taking a firm stance on a topic before a candidate needs to may not allow them to be fluid if there is a need to change that stance. A candidate might want to remain at center as much as possible to avoid alienating any group before the election crunch time.

Atwater well understood that waiting for the issues to develop or curtailing them for the sake of not losing voters does not help a candidate win an election. Atwater's track record for victories as the political head of Republican campaigns is absolutely persuasive to the truth of his victories.

No complex scientific or technical undertaking has ever succeeded without careful planning and tenacity in implementing the plans, that is, plans that are working. When a plan proves to be ineffective or a change in events makes the plan outdated, then it is necessary for the campaign, project, or other undertaking to adapt to the situation. Similarly, success in a military operation is often the result of one side in the conflict being better able to improvise, adapt, and overcome.

> ## *Chapter 5 Synopsis*
>
> - Effective managers always develop work plans to achieve an objective.
> - Always plan to the greatest detail possible.
> - Because life is constantly full of surprises, ensure all plans are flexible enough to accommodate unforeseen events.

No where is this maxim better illustrated than in the United States Apollo Space Program, particularly in the mission of Apollo 13.

**A Space Age Example of Fluidity in Planning**

On April 11, 1970, Apollo 13—the third of the manned lunar landing missions—set off to explore the surface of the moon. After the excitement generated by Neil Armstrong and Buzz Aldrin's historic walk on the moon during the Apollo 11 mission in 1969 and follow-up successful Apollo 12 mission, many Americans had come to think of the Apollo missions as somewhat routine—an attitude that would soon change.

The press coverage of the mission was significantly less impressive than the previous two missions, most likely as a result of a certain "been there, done that" public attitude. All of that changed, however, 55 hours, 55 minutes and 55 seconds into the mission, when on April 13, the spaceship was crippled by an explosion in an oxygen tank that severely damaged the service module, its oxygen supply, and source of electrical power. What many had viewed as a routine mission to the moon was now a national emergency. The nation crowded around televisions anxiously awaiting the fate of the three astronauts—Jim Lovell, Jack Swigert, and Fred Haise—now nearly stranded 200,000 miles from Earth.

While Americans watched, waited, and many prayed, the Apollo ground crew went to work on inventing solutions to a series of very real problems that threatened the survival of the astronauts. The original plan—to transport Americans into lunar orbit, land on the moon, return to the command module, and travel back to Earth—was now downscaled into a simple mission to survive and return home.

Fortunately for the crew, endless drills and space flight simulations prior to the Apollo missions had trained the crew and team members on the ground to plan for every contingency but remain fluid enough to handle the unforeseen. The Apollo 13 mission would require more ingenuity and adaptability than any mission before or since.

The first order of business was to transport the crewmembers from the command module to the lunar landing module, which would act as a space lifeboat. Powering up a space vehicle, though, required specific steps in an exact order. Flipping the switch to one system in an improper sequence could have damaged other vital systems. Ironically, in preparing for Apollo 10, the flight crew was thrown a curve during flight simulations in which it was necessary to use the lunar module as a lifeboat. The lunar module controllers failed in the test scenario and the make believe crew "died." While most said it was an inconceivable scenario, not likely to happen, the controllers doggedly pursued a solution until they produced a set of procedures that would work.[225]

NASA Flight Director Gene Kranz approached the rescue as a planning task. He appointed three key lieutenants to oversee three critical areas of the return flight. One was to assemble the master checklist for powering the command module as well as re-entry procedures. Kranz assigned another flight controller to make sure the lunar module survival resources lasted long enough for the crew to use the lunar landing vehicle as a lifeboat back to Earth. Finally, a controller took on the assignment to deal with powering up the command module prior to re-entry in such a way that it retained enough battery-supplied electricity for successful re-entry.[226]

The ultimate goal was to get the Apollo crew back to Earth before using up life-support resources, such as air to breathe and electricity to power flight computers and other module systems. Following the original plans, the flight controllers decided to put the astronauts into a fly-around the moon, which would use the gravity of the moon as a slingshot putting the spacecraft in a trajectory back to Earth.

But this process required an engine burn to adjust the trajectory of the space vehicle using the engine of the lunar module for the power, a procedure never done before. The fact that the lunar module and command module would still be docked together was another unknown variable. And yet another unknown was that the lunar module guidance system would have to be used to plot the return course, not the command module system.

To overcome these variables, computer programs were loaded into a massive IBM mainframe on the ground that would figure out the angles, time of engine burn, and other variables that would get the crew close enough to Earth for a safe re-entry. All of these procedures were new territory for the flight controllers. Nonetheless, the eventual re-entry and splashdown were more accurate that any previous flight, owing in part to the successful, improvised engine burn.

Controllers took command of the situation and relied on all their technical skills and experience in previous missions to find the best procedures for the rest of the return trip. They did not cling stubbornly to a plan that was now outdated after the explosion on board the command module. They truly exhibited fluidity in trying things that had never been done before and thinking in ways that sometimes seemed in contradiction to conventional wisdom.

> Integrating the power-up sequence with other tasks that would have to be done before entry into a set of procedures that could be read up to the crew was Aldrich's (Arnie Aldrich, Command/Service Module branch chief) job. The result, for a time the most precious document in the U.S. space program, started out as a typewritten document, but as it was revised over and over, it was "updated in pen and pencil . . . It was five pages long," says Aldrich, who still has the final checklist in his possession. [227]

The original typewritten plan scribbled all over with updated, penciled-in plans is a powerful visual image symbolic of this fifth maxim. One of the greatest and most successful technical programs in the history of mankind began the mission working the plan, but ultimately making life-and-death decisions on the fly to cope with a life-endangering situation.

One such life-or-death challenge occurred when the carbon dioxide levels in the lunar module began elevating to dangerous levels. Devices using lithium hydroxide canisters captured the carbon dioxide waste from respiration in both the lunar and command modules. The canister in the lunar module was being overwhelmed by the extra requirements of three astronauts instead of two normally aboard.

There was a plentiful supply of canisters on the command module, but these canisters were square. The canisters on the lunar module were round. So to make the command modules work, flight controllers had to figure out literally how to put a square peg in a round hole.

Again, the anticipation and fluidity of the flight crew saved the day. When one of the engineers who developed and tested life support systems learned the astronauts would be moving into the lunar module, he immediately anticipated the problem. He and other ground engineers had a two-day head start on inventing a solution.

> For two days straight since then, his (engineer Ed Smylie) team had worked on how to jury rig the Odyssey's canisters to the Aquarius's life support system. Now, using materials known to be available onboard the spacecraft—a sock, a plastic bag, the cover of a flight manual, lots of duct tape, and so on—the crew assembled Smylie's strange contraption and taped it into place. Carbon dioxide levels immediately began to fall into the safe range. Mission control had served up another miracle. [228]

While history refers to the "miracle" of Apollo 13, much of the miracle was the result of detailed planning and fluidity in adapting to constantly shifting challenges and priorities. The situation called for persons with a level head, quick and accurate decision-making capabilities and the ability to live with the results of those decisions. Creating these seasoned, confident flight controllers from recent engineering school graduates was a challenge to NASA and key to the success of the space program.

The principal problem NASA had with these neophytes was "one of self-confidence," explains Kranz. "We really worked to develop the confidence of the controllers so they could stand up and make these real-time decisions. Some people, no matter how hard we worked, never developed the confidence necessary for the job." Those not suited for mission control were generally washed out within a year.[229]

Ultimately the crew returned to Earth orbit, jettisoned the lunar module and successfully restarted systems on the command module to make a successful re-entry. Apollo 13 is listed by NASA as a "successful failure." Any success in the mission was possible primarily because the operations team had done the groundwork in putting together the original plan to land a man on the moon, yet remained flexible enough to change directions and come up with alternate solutions following the accident.

**NASA saved the Apollo 13 crew by having a plan—and a plan for modifying that plan when the unexpected happened. Instead of dissolving into panic, the team adapted to circumstances.**

The exemplary actions of the operations team gives meaning to the maxim, plan your work but remain fluid. This approach has worked for the architects of the NASA space program, and it has application for most all other areas of science, business, and even political success. The ability to remain adaptable to change can make the difference between success and failure, survival and extinction. President Richard M. Nixon awarded the operations team the Presidential Medal of Freedom on April 18, 1970, in recognition of their ability to produce "miracles." In making the award at the White House, President Nixon said:

We often speak of scientific "miracles"—forgetting that these are not miraculous happenings at all, but rather the product of hard work, long hours and disciplined intelligence. The men and women of the Apollo 13 mission operations team performed such a miracle, transforming potential tragedy into one of the most dramatic rescues of all time. Years of intense preparation made this rescue possible. The skill, coordination and performance under pressure of the mission operations team made it happen. Three brave astronauts are alive and on Earth because of their dedication, and because at the critical moments the people of that team were wise enough and self-possessed enough to make the right decisions. Their extraordinary feat is a tribute to man's ingenuity, to his resourcefulness and to his courage.[230]

## The Origins of Plans

Charles Darwin (1809-1882), English naturalist and author of the theory of evolution by natural selection recognized the importance of fluidity and adaptability in the survival of mankind and other life forms. Darwin said: "It is not the strongest of the species that survive, nor the most intelligent that survives. It is the one that is the most adaptable to change."

Darwin reached this history-making scientific conclusion on an expedition halfway around the world from his home in England after looking out across the sea to a most exotic location. Off the coast of Ecuador, his boat, the *HMS Beagle,* had landed on an island that would eventually gain international scientific fame as the birthplace of many of Darwin's earth shattering ideas about evolution and natural selection. At first sight, the remote Galapagos Islands seemed similar to many of the other tropical islands Charles Darwin had been charting for the last three years off the coast of South America, but the unique world he would observe on the Galapagos—and the theories he would test there—would revolutionize the world. Darwin would later go on to record some of his first impressions of unchartered ecosystem in his journal.

> The black rocks heated by the rays of the vertical sun like a stove, give to the air a close & sultry feeling. The plants also smell unpleasantly. The country [can be] compared to what we might imagine the cultivated parts of the Infernal regions to be.[231]

Despite his aversion to the particular topography of the island itself, Darwin observed and collected extensive scientific evidence of the creatures that lived there and hypothesized on how they came to be. Though eventually known for the giant Galapagos tortoises (some growing over 660 pounds with a life expectancy over 150 years) the island Darwin encountered in 1831 intrigued him because of its seemingly infinite variety of birds and other creatures.

The finches, for example, looked to be similar to those Darwin had encountered elsewhere with the exception of a few small, subtle differences including the size and style of its beak. Initially, Darwin believed that he had found several different families of birds, however, he later theorized through observation, that these Galapagos finches were actually of the same family of finches found in other areas of the world.[232] The finches on the island, however, had adapted to their environment by developing different traits that allowed them to better survive in this unique habitat. Later, Darwin would develop his theory of natural selection based on these very observations long with other taxonomical data.

Darwin theorized that life forms could become more complex through a series of gradual changes brought on as a result of environmental conditions. Within the scientific community today, natural selection is still considered the most reasonable explanation for the evolution of life. New scientific discoveries also have been used to support Darwin's conclusion that natural selection comes from a change in DNA and genes. Although DNA was first isolated during Darwin's lifetime by the Swiss in 1869, it wasn't until 1953 that, based on X-ray diffraction images, Nobel Prize winning American scientists Francis Crick and James Watson were able to identify that the information in the strands were paired and develop the three-dimensional model for the DNA structure.[233]

Their model, first announced in a scientific paper in *Nature* in 1953, makes it possible to understand the function of genes (mutation, carrying hereditary information that directs the synthesis of proteins, and replication) at a molecular level, and makes a convincing argument that genetic information is carried by DNA, not protein. Watson and Crick proposed that the molecular structure of DNA representing genes consists of two strings of nucleotides connected across like a ladder. Each step contains either a G-C pair of letters or an A-T pair, accounting for Chargaff's observation (see 1952) that there is an A for every T and a G for every C in DNA.[234]

"It has not escaped our notice that the specific pairing we have postulated immediately suggests a possible copying mechanism for the genetic material," Crick and Watson stated in their landmark scientific paper.[235]

Since then, scientists have been able to discern that all living beings require DNA, which provides the biological plan through which organisms grow. Here is how DNA works as a plan for life:

> Sequences of DNA are arranged into genes that contain expressions of an organism's traits. Genes give an organism its uniqueness and biological function. Each gene has a different responsibility for an organism. Hypothetically, one gene may "tell" a bird to grow short wings while another gene may "tell" the bird to grow a yellow beak. Even the slightest changes to the DNA strand can result in a gene expressing itself differently. If DNA is an organism's biological plan, then it follows that the evolving genes are the expression of that organism's remaining fluid to changes.
>
> Scientists have determined that small changes in DNA can cause a gene to express itself differently. Through alterations and mutations of the A, C, T, G nucleotides (the four building blocks of DNA: adenine, cytosine, thymine and guanine), individual or entire segments of the DNA strand can rearrange or drop entirely. Though a mutation or alteration may not change the overall plan of an organism (a bird is still a bird even with a genetic mutation) changes can develop in an organism's behavior or specific traits (a bird might

become faster than other birds to cope with an environmental change). [236]

Over time, a species that adapts and multiplies will successfully control its niche in the environment. However, if a species fails to adapt, it will fade away as other species dominate its niche. Therefore, the surviving species will be those that contain the genetic blue prints that allow for a superior organism for its given niche. That organism must also adapt quickly to its environment to retain the advantage nature has provided for it.

**Adaptation is the key to survival in any environment. Keep the parts of your plan that still work, and add new elements that allow you to succeed and excel in the changed circumstances.**

The basis for planning and adapting is inherent in all living things. While the concept of purposefully manipulating genetic code to change people or ideas is somewhat controversial and likely better suited to discussions between governments and scientists, what can be gained by the discussion is an understanding that the biological imperatives of planning and fluidity reside within each organism's genetic code and thus form the basis of all life. If it is true that all life begins with a rudimentary plan that adapts to the situations around it to survive, then it likely follows that humans can use this knowledge and therefore adapt this process for use in their own lives.

### Abraham Lincoln Successfully Adapts to Change

Studying great success stories, as well as some monumental failures, can provide an overview of how remaining fluid through small, pivotal adaptations in planning can radically change the outcome of history. Sixteenth President Abraham Lincoln was just one of many leaders who successfully managed to execute their plans while remaining fluid.

## Maxim 5: Work Your Plan, but Remain Fluid

Lincoln is venerated as one of our nation's most important and successful leaders, placed in the ranks of George Washington, Thomas Jefferson, and Franklin Delano Roosevelt. While he is credited with ending slavery and salvaging the Union, Lincoln did not accomplish these feats without struggle and without adaptation in the face of obstacles and loss. Success did not come easily, nor did Lincoln's plan for salvaging the Union flow smoothly forth in a series of previously plotted actions.

Had Lincoln been inflexible, we may likely have had an entirely different outcome to the Civil War. Instead, he had an ultimate plan—to sustain the Union—and successfully carried out that plan by constantly fine-tuning the policies he enforced, the issues he championed, and the colleagues he employed to carry out his orders as commander in chief.

In his early career, Lincoln was hesitant to reveal any anti-slavery sentiment in his political actions. He believed that the nature of the controversy was so divisive that he should avoid it while perpetuation of the Union was at stake. In fact, he negotiated with leaders of Border States (Delaware, Maryland, Kentucky, and Missouri), four states that had slavery but did not secede with the South, promising not to interfere with slavery within those states. When Lincoln found that the slavery issue could not be ignored, and that it had evolved into the central pressing issue in the war, he showed flexibility.

He allowed Congress to pass the Second Confiscation Act in 1862, which became law with his Emancipation Proclamation, and nominally freed the slaves in the Confederate states. Even further, Lincoln maneuvered in a way that allowed him to hold as much political ground as possible between both Union slave owners and abolitionists, all in the name of his plan to preserve the union. In a letter to Horace Greeley, editor of the New York Tribune, Lincoln said:

> My paramount object in this struggle is to save the Union, and is not either to save or to destroy slavery. If I could save the Union without freeing any slave I would do it, and if I could save it by freeing all the slaves I would do it; and if I could save it by freeing some and leaving others alone I would also do that...I shall do less whenever I shall believe what I am doing hurts the cause, and I shall do more whenever I shall believe doing more will help the cause. I shall try to correct errors when

shown to be errors and I shall adopt new views so fast as they shall appear to be true view.[237]

This quote shows Lincoln's willingness to adapt his methods where necessary. He remains focused on the ultimate goal, while remaining flexible in his approach. Beyond the specific issue of slavery, Lincoln used the resources at his disposal to adapt to the wartime situation as conditions fluctuated over four years, including powers reserved to the commander in chief that had never been used before. As a part of these powers, Lincoln suspended several civil liberties, thereby claiming the power to jail dissidents and shut down some newspapers. He ordered a blockade of Confederate ports, spent money without first gaining approval by Congress, held 18,000 Confederate soldiers without trial, and suspended the writ of habeas corpus

In terms of military leadership, Lincoln remained extremely fluid. In instances where his appointed generals did not follow presidential orders, he quickly replaced them with a general he thought would do a better job. Lincoln knew his plan would succeed with the right man and he remained fluid in his choices, as each successive general before General Ulysses Grant proved himself maladroit. Lincoln was able to recognize the plan could not move forward if he remained fixed to only one or two options, so he continued to revise and adapt through alternative plans while still pursuing his ultimate agenda.

Lincoln appointed a string of generals: George McClellan, Ambrose Burnside, Joseph Hooker, and then finally, westerner Ulysses S. Grant. The Union generals that preceded Grant did not have the will and focus to achieve the final victory. As each faltered and failed in battle, Lincoln did not remain stubbornly loyal to his top commanders, but instead remained fluid by replacing them with a new option. Finally with Grant, Lincoln was able to settle on an aggressive approach and successfully see it through to help the Union win the Civil War, and begin the process of healing his fractured nation. By remaining fluid in his execution, Lincoln was successful in his plan to save the Union at all costs, even "until every drop of blood drawn with the lash, shall be paid by another drawn with the sword" if necessary.[238]

Abraham Lincoln was just one of many leaders who successfully managed to execute their plans while remaining fluid. Studying great success stories, as well as some monumental failures, can provide an overview of how pivotal small adaptations in both planning and fluidity can radically change the outcome of history.

## Ruling the Ancient World from the Plan Up

The conscious ability of the human race to assess the past, analyzing the successes and failures of those who came before, is one of the unique traits making humanity able to appreciate the nuisances of planning and fluidity. The excellence of civilization can be characterized within the beauty of its art, science, music, and war. War has been a mainstay of human interaction from the beginning of civilization and can be a microcosm of human ingenuity. Battles breed specific tactics and ideals that can be translated to the non-violent tactics similarly employed in advertising, business management, and politics. One leader who was able to succeed in war using his ingenuity to capitalize on his war plans—and conquer most of the known world of the ancient Greeks—was Alexander the Great.

Alexander, also known as Alexander III of Macedon, inherited the kingdom from his father King Phillip II, which occupied present day Greece and the surrounding areas. Alexander would go on to conquer much of the territory from Egypt to India. Alexander could not have achieved these gains merely by great strategy and war plans. Though his overall military plan was to systematically push eastward, he was able to remain fluid and develop new options along the way to augment his great plan.

A shining example of this type ingenuity was Alexander's capture of the Phoenician city of Tyre in 332 B.C.E., which served as a naval base to the Persians. As he moved to invade Egypt, Alexander passed through Tyre and issued a test to their loyalty. The city failed Alexander's test by engaging in battle. Ultimately, they incurred Alexander's wrath by killing his envoys. Alexander decided to destroy Tyre, but was obstructed by a geographic challenge—Tyre was an island city. Alexander did not have adequate naval forces to use strategically in the anticipated siege.

Confronted with a perplexing situation, Alexander needed to devise a way to get his mighty army past the walls of this island city. Using the stone remnants of an abandoned city found on the mainland, his army began to build a causeway to reach Tyre. At the time, confused people believed Alexander was building a bridge on top of the water but later it was discovered that he had been using an existing sandbar as a foundation.

With his superior catapults and land forces, the Greek army could use the causeway to reach the island city. This feat was one of the first plans conceived by a military leader to take an island city.[239] Alexander was able to use his ingenuity to develop an alternate option to his original plan. By utilizing his new option, Alexander forced the Tyrians to react to his maneuvers and conform to his agenda.

Another obstacle to the conquest of Tyre was the Tyrian defensive strategy to keep the length of the causeway just short of the city island so Alexander's catapults could inflict no substantive damage. Again Alexander remained fluid. He called upon the naval forces of his allies. Through a feat of innovation and engineering genius, the Greeks were able to outfit the naval vessels with battering rams, a tactic that never been seen before in Greek history. With the combined might of the navy and the causeway, which enabled catapults to fire within range and provide foot soldier access to the island city, Alexander was finally able to reach Tyre and destroy it.

With every new obstacle, Alexander was able to adapt to a more powerful position and eventually succeed. Conquest of Tyre would have been virtually impossible using only land forces. By employing new strategies and actively pressing his opponent into new situations Alexander was able to dictate the course of the battle. In issue management, there are few fierce armies with which to do battle, but the opposition is always attempting to maximize their gains.

**Alexander assessed the resources he had at hand and maximized the effectiveness of those tools. Had he relied solely on traditional strategies, the city of Tyre would have remained defiant behind their island fortress.**

An effective leader who utilizes his plans but remains fluid in his implementation can change other people's strategies for success.

Alexander was able to demonstrate this idea in his invasion of Tyre, but it was also employed to keep his great empire intact. In ancient times, global communication was non-existent. Overseeing a province was not as easy as it is today with cell phones and e-mail. As the Greeks moved east toward India, Alexander's empire was extended much farther than ever before.

With each new region he conquered, Alexander left behind soldiers to keep control of the newly conquered area. Eventually, there came a time when Alexander realized that he had stretched his army too thin and was in danger of losing to a large opposing force. Alexander's only option was to retreat and regroup forces with the armies he left behind. However, to do so would certainly incite the opposing force to pursue him and very possibly capture or defeat his now smaller army.

Alexander knew that if he could intimidate the opposing force they would be reluctant to follow his army. With this end in mind, Alexander instructed his craftsmen to make several oversized armor breastplates and helmets that would fit "giants," men seven to eight feet tall. As Alexander and his forces withdrew during the night they left behind the oversized armor. As expected, the opposing force found the oversized armor at daybreak and was convinced they had come close to annihilation by engaging in a battle with giants. The oversized armor coupled with the stories related by travelers about the savagery of Alexander's army caused enough doubt and fear that they elected not to pursue Alexander's army.

Alexander could have simply fled and given up the conquered territory or continued to march on his enemies. However, he again realized that to achieve the goals he needed to adapt to the circumstances around him. By changing the strategies of his enemies he was able to regroup his forces and maintain his empire. If he had simply remained fixed in his plan, he may have seen his empire crumble around him. Instead, Alexander adapted to the changing landscape. From his victory at Tyre, through to the periodic reinforcement of his empire along the way, Alexander was able to incorporate all the vital aspects of planning and fluidity: proactive planning and execution along with a meaningful evaluation of alternative options and opponents' strategies.

On the battlefield, adhering to the precepts of planning and fluidity has been shown to result in victory and success. Failure to address these strategies can lead to utter failure and disaster. Examining a case study in which rigid strategies were pursued blindly can serve as a model for exploring what can go wrong and how a successful leader can avoid the pitfalls.

**The Great Rigid Plan and a Flexible Response**

World War II provided a case study in almost all manner of human interaction. In assessing the atrocities and strategic flaws of the German Army under Adolph Hitler, a leader can see vivid examples of great failures in war and humanity. For example, a look at Hitler's engagement of Britain and Russia shows the devastating effect of deficiencies in both planning and fluidity, and how these deficiencies can destroy a goal.

After Hitler's blitzkrieg ended in 1941 he controlled the entire mainland of Europe, stretching from Poland up to the Scandinavian countries and down to France. His plan was for a lightning quick strike on the countries that were least prepared to repel the German army. By executing a quick and decisive plan, Hitler was able to dictate the pace and progress of his objectives and force the rest of Europe to react to his plans. However, as quickly as he gained territories, he would lose much more as he remained vastly rigid and unmoving in his plans.

While a great leader can craft a brilliant plan, the chaotic nature of the world leads to quick changes in such a plan. If a leader cannot remain fluid to those changes then disaster will surely lie ahead. With the capitulation of the mainland, Hitler turned his attention to the island of Britain. The might of the Royal Navy made any sea attempt on Britain a certain failure. The decision was made to commence with a continual bombardment of England by air. By striking Britain's air force and other military installations, the Luftwaffe (the German air force) could establish superior air dominance and control of the skies, which would allow Germany to continually pound away at the military-industrial complex, stifling any progressive war effort on England's behalf. Secondary to those objectives would be the destruction of political or cultural targets like London and the surrounding cities.

The speed and ferocity of the German military resulted in victory after victory against the Royal Air Force (RAF), and it seemed as Hitler's plan was working. Churchill wrote "The scales . . . had tilted against Fighter Command . . . There was much anxiety."[240] A few more weeks of the bombings and Britain's air defenses would have been crippled.[241]

However, a small mission (almost insignificant from the English standpoint) would be the pebble in the pond that would send ripples through Hitler's plan and create a second chance for Britain. A small RAF strike force was able to reach the mainland and bomb Berlin. Although the danger to Germany was minimal from a military perspective, the cultural damage was significant. Embarrassed and annoyed, Hitler, who asserted the invulnerability of the Reich capital, ordered a change in targets from military and economic targets to targets aimed at creating the symbolic submission of London and other major cities. In hindsight, it seems inconceivable that such an insignificant attack would cause far-reaching changes in Hitler's strategic plans. Had he stuck with the original plan, even Churchill agreed that Hitler could have bombed Britain into submission and out of the war. However, little changes like these separate the ineffectual leaders from the successful ones. The German High Commander would make another blunder that would eventually cost him the war because he could not create a plan with viable alternatives and could not remain fluid to new circumstances.

The attack on London would take a toll on Hitler's bombers, never allowing him to regain the advantage of his air forces.[242] Stymied on his western front, Hitler turned his attention east toward the Soviet Union. A non-aggression pact was signed before the war began, but Hitler had an extreme hatred for Communism,[243] and even the Soviets believed an attack was inevitable.[244] Frequently, he spoke of using the vast oilfields and land mass for German industry and for German Lebensraum (living space). Operation Barbarossa was developed, which involved the systematic invasion of the Soviet Union, which the German high command hoped would end before the winter hit. Most of the plans were drawn in response to the failed invasion of Russia by aspiring conquerors throughout history.

Much as he had in previous attempts, Hitler hoped now to conquer the Soviet Union before the winter set in and hindered his military operation. The planned invasion would need to be completed in six months to ensure taking the U.S.S.R. before the arctic freeze. The plan was skillfully designed and took advantage of the quick moving panzer units the Germans employed. With a direct timetable to completion the necessary components of a great plan were in place to succeed. Again, Hitler failed to properly respond and remain fluid to circumstances around him.

The Italians suffered a major defeat on the Southern front, and Hitler sent divisions that would be needed for the invasion of the Soviet Union to assist his Italian allies. Despite quickly turning the tide in the south, Hitler gave the orders to extend the battle into Yugoslavia and Greece. Crushing the resistance in those respective countries secured the Southern front, but did not help the expected invasion of the Soviet Union. Most of the German generals wanted the invasion underway so they could capture Stalingrad before the winter. Hitler could have moved his troops back earlier, but his decision to pursue this southern gambit resulted in a costly four-week delay.[245] He could not remain fluid at a pivotal point of his plan to take the Soviet Union. Also, he did not have any viable alternatives to the invasion if a costly delay occurred. Historians speculate that certain German generals believed the objectives of a Soviet invasion could be obtained by pushing southeast into Turkey and the Middle East. The rich oil reserves could have served the Reich's industrial needs as much as the Balkans.

The severe Russian winter was just one reason for the failure of the invasion. The plan to invade revolved around a swift attack with the quick moving tank units of the German army. However, faulty logistical planning (resource management in military operations) hindered the transportation and supply of the army. These obstacles should have been assessed and practical substitutes devised. The lack of options severely hindered the progress of the plan. Leaders perform poorly when they cannot turn to other options have to rigidly stick to a specific plan. Even great plans require a measure of change that shapes the eventual course and direction. At one of the greatest junctures of human history, the ineptness of a fascist leader to properly implement a plan while remaining fluid helped lead to an end of a horrific war.

In contrast, the Allied forces would use the mistakes of Hitler to their advantage and launch their offensive against the German's Western front. Like the last few moves of the end game in chess, Germany was close to checkmate and the end to the horrific war was on the horizon. Final offensive for the Allied forces was the push into the depths of the German Reich.

An invasion through Italy was projected to take too long, and the Allies would likely suffer massive casualties. Other considered invasion points would limit damage to Germany but hinder the support from other Allied positions.[246] In May of 1944, Dwight Eisenhower, Supreme

Allied Commander of the Allied Expeditionary Force (SHAEF) had decided on the date of June 4, 1944, to launch Operation Overlord, landing on the beaches of Normandy in Northern France.

This operation had been discussed and formulated years in advance. Allied generals had spent months discussing each contingency. Dozens of launch sites were contemplated and various troop formations were devised that would maximize the efficiency of the invasion. The Allied forces spent months transporting troops to strategic positions and setting up the attack without giving any hint to the Axis command of the intended invasion site.

Intelligence operations leaked false information to Nazi spies to cover the Allies' real plans. Despite increased defensive fortifications engineered by famed German General Erwin Rommel, the Allied command ordered the plan to proceed. However, just as quickly as Germany swept Europe in the early years of the war, the plan to attack would be hit by unforeseen circumstances and force the leaders of the Allied command to adapt quickly to the changes.

The date of June 5 was set initially as the date for the invasion because it coincided with a full moon, which would provide better night visibility, favorable tides, and the weather forecast called for relatively clear weather. Instead, a spring squall with gale force winds swept the French coast. Eisenhower met with his staff on Sunday, June 4 and made the decision to postpone the invasion 24 hours until June 6.

Because of the foul weather, the Germans believed they could relax. Many German officers participated in a military exercise. Others went on leave including Rommel, who drove to Berlin to visit his wife on her birthday. He also hoped to meet with Hitler to obtain control of panzer groups stationed near Calais north of Normandy, where Hitler stubbornly believed the Allied invasion would occur.

Eisenhower's meteorologists predicted that a break in the weather on June 5 would provide a small window for the invasion to take place on June 6. Early Monday morning, the consensus was to proceed before the massive operation could be discovered by the Germans.

> A great invasion force stood off the Normandy coast of France as dawn broke on June 6, 1944: 9 battleships, 23 cruisers, 104 destroyers, and 71 large landing craft of various descriptions as well as troop transports,

> minesweepers, and merchantmen—in all, nearly 5,000 ships of every type, the largest armada ever assembled. The naval bombardment that began at 0550 that morning detonated large minefields along the shoreline and destroyed a number of the enemy's defensive positions. To one correspondent, reporting from the deck of the cruiser HMS Hillary, it sounded like "the rhythmic beating of a gigantic drum" all along the coast. In the hours following the bombardment, more than 100,000 fighting men swept ashore to begin one of the epic assaults of history, a "mighty endeavor," as President Franklin D. Roosevelt described it to the American people, "to preserve . . . our civilization and to set free a suffering humanity."[247]

While the assembly of armament was impressive on the day of the invasion, the buildup began years before, as England turned the southern part of the country into a huge military camp in preparation for the buildup. An operation code-named BOLERO began the complicated logistics of preparing for a million troops supplied with all necessary weapons, ammunition, war machines, medical facilities, clothing, food, sanitation supplies, and other material. The initial planning called for a 1943 invasion, but the date was pushed back to 1944.

Logistical planning was a major effort in detailed analysis and follow through.

> As planning continued, the BOLERO buildup in Britain, begun in 1942 to arm and provision the invasion, took on new momentum. With 39 divisions slated to participate in the invasion—20 American, 14 British, 3 Canadian, 1 French, and 1 Polish, along with hundreds of thousands of service troops—there was little time to waste. The number of U.S. fighting men based in Great Britain alone would double in the first six months of 1944, rising from 774,000 at the beginning of the year to 1,537,000 in the week preceding the final assault. More than 16 million tons of supplies would be needed to feed and supply those men and their allies: six and one-quarter pounds

of rations per day per man; 137,000 jeeps, trucks, and half-tracks; 4,217 tanks and fully tracked vehicles; 3,500 artillery pieces; 12,000 aircraft; and huge stores of sundries—everything from dental amalgam for fillings to chewing gum and candy bars.[248]

The invasion attacked five predetermined beaches with a thorough deployment of air, ground, and sea forces. The beginning of the invasion hit an early snag when many of the paratroopers dropped well out of location behind enemy lines. Tragically some drown when they landed in Rommel's flooded plains. Despite the chaos and confusion, many of the Rangers were able to regroup and accomplish their tactical objectives.

With the initial landings, most of the Allied forces were pinned down by German bombardment, and there was little room to advance, prompting some in the high command to call the invasion at Omaha a failure. The infantrymen on the beach knew they could not accomplish their objectives and realized that little cover support was available. Staying fluid but within the overall plan to capture the beachhead, many of the commissioned and non-commissioned officers organized small pockets of troops who slowly secured small portions of the beachhead for the arrival of more reinforcements. Eventually, Army Rangers were able to scale the bluffs surrounding the beach and neutralize the bombarding artillery.

Within a matter of weeks, the Normandy forces broke out of their beachhead and began moving inland. There fighting intensified as the Germans took advantage of the natural terrain made up of a checkerboard of fields and dense hedgerows that provided concealment for German troopers.

Ever flexible and innovative, the American soldiers soon began learning how to fight in conditions they had not anticipated.

> (American General Omar) Bradley's forces were nonetheless gradually learning how to fight in the *bocage* (French hedgerows). Tank and infantry units began to support each other. The tanks supplied the heavy firepower needed to eliminate the enemy's well-sited firing positions while the infantry kept enemy soldiers with antitank weapons at bay. The tankers also

found a way to cross the hedgerows without exposing their vehicles' vulnerable undersides to enemy fire. With huge iron teeth salvaged from German beach obstacles welded to the fronts of hundreds of tanks, they began to bull their way through the hedgerows, taking hours to advance through obstacles that would earlier have required days of fighting to overcome. From then on, the Rhinos, as the men named them, became an invaluable asset to Bradley. They allowed American armor to move across country at will while German tanks had to continue to make do with the roads.[249]

By sundown, the Allied Forces had secured a foothold in France marking the beginning of the end for Nazi Germany. The invasion was the largest amphibious attack in history and would become one of the greatest battles of World War II. When observing the situation from a leadership perspective, it is apparent that many of the successes of World War II can be attributed to the intense planning of the Allied officers and their ability to remain fluid as the circumstances of war manipulated those plans. These skills were not new to the world and these great military leaders of the twentieth century likely benefitted from the teachings of the ancient Greeks in remaining fluid and adaptable to changes in their plans.

## Ancient Wisdom, Modern Planning

Long before the Greek philosophers Socrates and Aristotle were challenging their leaders to seek morality and truth, other philosophers were seeking for answers through critical observation and testing of theories. Heraclitus was one of these scholars who pondered the existence of the universe and would become one of the first who explored the idea of fluidity that would later be applied to science and technology.

Believed to have lived from 535 B.C.E.–475 B.C.E., Heraclitus was born to an aristocratic family in present day Efes, Turkey. Wealthy from birth, Heraclitus was able to spend his time pondering the mysteries of the universe. Among those believing that the world was made from fire, Heraclitus speculated that the universe was constantly in flux.[250] He surmised that the universal flux was analogous to a river that ran through time.

Heraclitus believed that, as a human, one traverses this river one step at a time. With each step, however, the river adjusts to the footprint. Therefore, with each step the river changes and adapts requiring one to adapt as well. A person may have an initial plan to wade into the water, but if the water changes with the initial entry then adjustments must be made with each step. In modern terms, Heraclitus was referring to a new trend or competitive move that can change a macro environmental scenario and result in a paradigm shift of an initial plan. By understanding these shifts, a person can amend his first plan with an updated plan incorporating the new information.

Taking the ideas of Heraclitus a step further, Socrates and Plato focused on the truth of remaining fluid, of not settling for the observed world but seeking to find more. In Plato's dialogues, one of Socrates friends asks the Oracle of Delphi if Socrates is the wisest man in the land. The oracle promptly proclaims that there is no man wiser than Socrates. Unconvinced, Socrates goes into Athens to find those who are wiser than he (though it was tough to argue with an oracle who could theoretically predict the future). Socrates believed he had no real knowledge and that there must be another person who had greater knowledge than he. He went out into city to question the leaders of Athens to disprove the Oracle. Constantly questioning the leaders of the city about their specific expertise, Socrates determined that most people do not know as much as they claim.

**Every step into Heraclitus's river causes the river to change course, and requires an adjustment by the wader. The actions you take pursuant to your plan will necessarily cause a shift in the context in which you are acting.**

Socrates' method of questioning has become what is now known as the Socratic Method, a form of reasoning in which a person suggests a hypothesis and then through a series of questions determines whether the hypothesis can be contradicted. This form of questioning, frequently used in modern law schools, teaches students the importance in honing their knowledge of a subject. The professor will generally pick a student from the class and ask her to express one of the arguments of the court.

The professor will systematically question the premise of the argument through a series of probing questions (many times embarrassing the student by highlighting their lack of reasoning on a certain subject). The focus of the questioning allows the students to follow the reasoning of the court and, in turn, sharpen their critical thinking skills. Like the professors in today's law school, Socrates employed his method to determine whether the political and cultural elite of Athens knew as much about any subject as they claimed to know.

Socrates used his form of questions as his "plan" for discovering the truth of the universe. He had always speculated that his knowledge was insufficient compared to those in the greater world. By using his method of questioning, he was implementing a plan to discover both knowledge and other's ignorance to knowledge. This represented one of the first instances of deep intellectual planning to get to the root of understanding the depth and breath of knowledge. From Heraclitus to Socrates the concepts of planning and fluidity were finding a concrete discipline in philosophy that could be discussed and expounded upon. While this style of thinking was emerging in a relatively peaceful setting of friendly philosophical discussions on the streets of Athens, there was a similar train of thought emerging thousands of miles away in a different time, on a different continent.

Travelling along the path of what would become known as the Silk Road, an explorer would meet with the ancient warring states that comprised the Chinese empire. Despite being technologically and culturally advanced for its time, China was in the midst of a period where over 100 different principalities had been reduced to 40 due to constant warfare. Much like an oversaturated market, the feuding principalities languished in a constant state of warfare. From the cradle of despair, a young man named Sun Tzu would become one of China's greatest military strategists.[251] Purportedly coming from a long line of military advisors, Sun Tzu's teachings would later be compiled into *The Art of*

*War*. This text has been studied and analyzed by military leaders throughout the centuries. The tactics and strategies he set forth are just as applicable to business, political, and economic situations.

Although some believe that the teachings of Sun Tzu are specific to fighting a war, there is great value to be found in the analysis of strategies that do not require actual combat. His machinations emphasize winning a battle before it's fought through a variety of techniques, notably, through rigorous planning and fluidity. When interpreting his philosophy from this perspective, it is much easier to see how his ideas apply to situations in a non-military context. In chapter eight of his treatise Variations of Tactics, Sun Tzu says:

> In the wise leader's plans, considerations of advantage and of disadvantage will be blended together . . . . If our expectation of advantage be tempered in this way, we may succeed in accomplishing the essential part of our schemes.[252]

Sun Tzu discussed one of the elements of fluidity in this statement by addressing the need to see all the options of a situation and not just planning for the most favorable outcome. This may seem like a simple task, but, as work frequently turns out, it is easier said than done. Scientific studies have shown that people tend to overestimate the success of their plans and minimize their role in any failures.[253] Sun Tzu realized that this type of planning and fluidity needed to be practiced and refined by a military commander so that they could achieve eventual victory.

> The tactical variations appropriate to the nine types of ground, the advantages of close or extended deployment, and the principles of human nature are matters the general must examine with the greatest care . . . Courses of action previously followed and old plans previously executed must be altered.[254]

Sun Tzu extended the concept of fluidity to the specific actions a general must take and adapt to achieve perfect execution. A leader who follows these precepts assumes a winnable position before the fight has even begun but, if there is conflict, he knows all the avenues he must take to achieve victory. Actively addressing the "different types of ground" mentioned by Sun Tzu allows for the fluidity in a plan when the circumstances change. With a simple, yet incredibly adaptive ideology, these teachings influenced leaders during Sun Tzu's time and, when combined with further teaching, today's leaders can still apply them to today's conflicts. Some of that further teaching can be found in the ultimate treatise on leadership strategies, Machiavelli's *The Prince*.

**Renaissance, Enlightenment, and Modern Ideals**

"Thus he must be disposed to change according as the winds of fortune and the alterations of circumstance dictate,"[255] said the oft-quoted Machiavelli in *The Prince*.

During the Renaissance, Machiavelli proposed that a prince (referring to Lorenzo DeMedici, head of the ruling Italian family) should remain fluid to the changes of the world despite having a plan for addressing specific situations. Written in the 16th century—centuries after the golden ages of the Greek and Chinese philosophers—most of Machiavelli's famous leadership treatise addresses the political and military situations that would require decisive action by a ruling king in order to remain in power. A prince in medieval Italy would have to deal with ruling political factions in a splintered Italy, which required various approaches to differing viewpoints. Though a leader may have a generalized strategy on how to rule, in such a muddled political climate, change was always just around the corner.

If a prince remained static in his rule he would likely be overthrown. Machiavelli stated in his chapter on keeping one's word, that to rule effectively one must be disposed to change as circumstances dictate. Machiavelli concludes by urging that "he (The Prince) must stick to the good so long as he can, but—being compelled by necessity—he must be ready to take the way of evil."[256] When necessary to achieve his goals, Machiavelli saw the advantages in a prince's changing his position to achieve better rule.

Throughout *The Prince,* Machiavelli discussed the art of ruling and advocated that a leader should remain fluid in his judgment and actions. Each chapter involves a different set of options to be applied to a new set of circumstances. The ability to remain fluid can be seen as one of the tenets for ruling by one of the world's first modern "political scientists." The ability to remain fluid while following an appropriately detailed and effective plan can mean the difference between a long-standing reign and the quick demise of a leader. Political figures changed frequently during this tumultuous time, but through the principles of the *Prince*, today's leader can take away a strategy that will allow them to remain on top.

Following the Renaissance, Europe experienced the Enlightenment, another revolution of thought similar in scope to the Renaissance. Throughout this period, another wave of thinkers philosophized on the extent of human's knowledge and how we shape our plans and ideas. When discussing the teachings of both John Locke and Rene Descartes, the principles of planning and fluidity are better exemplified and detailed.

An English philosopher, John Locke, believed that knowledge did not come from the mind but rather was based on experiences from the real world. Much like *a priori knowledge*—knowledge used to distinguish two types of propositional knowledge—all knowledge is gained by seeing the changes in the world and interpreting them rather than having a fundamental base of knowledge within the brain. This idea is in stark contrast with the ideas of French philosopher Rene Descartes, who believed that knowledge came from the mind itself (*"cogito ergo sum"*—I think, therefore, I am). For Descartes, man thinks he knows he exists, as opposed to knowing he exists, because he experiences the world around him. As seen from this perspective, strategies are plans that are created from the mind and then implemented to interact with the world.

While the two concepts appear to be in opposition, they are merely two sides of the same coin, foundational thinking of a much larger construct. After witnessing these concepts in action, it is easier to synthesize these theories and make a more practical application to the world rather than a metaphysical concept.

While the knowledge present in the human brain and learned over time can be used to create a plan, an effective incorporation of changes from the surrounding environment is required to put that plan into action. When merged together this knowledge and this thinking allows for the formation of an ingenious plan and the knowledge to remain fluid. While Heraclitus, Socrates, Sun Tzu, Machiavelli, John Locke and Descartes began the discussion of how analytical thinking and exploration of possibilities can be applied to successful implementation, the recognized great thinkers of the last two centuries have taken the views on planning and fluidity and combined them into a cohesive theory that can be applied to practical settings.

Georg Wilhelm Friedrich Hegel was a German philosopher who attempted to create a framework from which ideas would evolve and coalesce into more advanced adaptation. Hegel lived in a post-Kantian era known as "German Idealism" when he proposed that a set of information forms a thesis, which then becomes a basis for understanding.[257] Once a thesis is formed, an anti-thesis is created. The anti-thesis takes the practical opposite of the thesis. After the anti-thesis, there are two competing ideas that are combined to create a synthesis. This new complex idea takes the better qualities from both the thesis and anti-thesis. Thus, presumably, the never-ending cycle of thesis, antithesis and synthesis will allow civilization to evolve over time.

**The way we conceptualize our environment directly shapes the design of our plans. Necessarily, this limitation means we will never fully account for all the variables in any situation, and must be prepared to rapidly adapt our plan to emerging realities.**

For example, during the tumultuous times of the late 18th century, the French commoners became fed up with the depravity of their lives in stark contrast to the grandeur of the lives of their royalty. These commoners revolted, overthrowing the monarchy during the French Revolution. Shortly after the revolution began, however, the leaders began to grow corrupt with their newfound power and began issuing death sentences to anyone opposed to them.

Thus, the Reign of Terror was ushered in, marking the return to oppression of the masses. The revolutionary leaders executed greater and greater numbers of citizens until a political backlash in the arrival of the antithesis: the Thermidorian Reaction, which finally led to a synthesis, a new constitution guaranteeing certain civil rights. The philosophical underpinnings—mentioned so far—combined with the inherent evolutionary disposition toward evolution make it clear that creating a plan while remaining fluid is the optimal way to resolve difficult situations.

Historical backings from some of history's greatest intellects can be systematized into a more cohesive point of view. However, the knowledge of past ideas does not necessarily give someone a concrete application of those ideas. To do so, one must engage and analyze specific examples from history from both a planning and fluidity perspective and attempt to predict potential outcomes.

## Historical Perspectives on Effective Planning

Juxtaposing effective political campaigning with effective economic and military campaigning and similar parallels become apparent in understanding the foundation and structure of productive plans. Looking at the economic stimulus of the U.S.S.R. following World War I as well as the Marshall Plan—which revitalized Western Europe following World War II—more intricate aspects of planning are available for analysis. While proactively addressing a plan will likely yield the ultimate objective, there are generally additional secondary objectives to reach. In a political campaign, the ultimate objective is to win the election; however, in the long term it may be beneficial to simply sway support for future elections or address concerns that did not arise in the present campaign but may crop up in later elections.

Addressing these secondary objectives is much more subtle than the general plan but does require ingenious planning to address them adequately. When achieving the primary plan it is easy to slip into a cadence where the only people being addressed are those who can help achieve an electoral victory. In a political campaign, politicians often address the voters who have the greatest impact on the campaign. If they can sway these voter's minds then they can achieve victory.

However, many times a candidate will shy away from an issue when it appears that failure on the issue is inevitable. The candidate chooses not to address every entangling issue, and therefore the margin of victory for the opponent remains high. If a leader can reduce those numbers across the board, however, they may retain a position for later campaigns. If the candidate can reach out to these voters while continuing to remain faithful to their platform, they can often achieve their secondary objectives. In the examples of Soviet leader Josef Stalin's five-year plans and the Marshall Plan, this aspect fails in one plan while succeeds in another. The United States' Marshall Plan adhered to the fluidity advocated by this maxim. Whereas Stalin remained rigid in the face of change and could not effectively incorporate everyone into the plan.

After the Bolshevik revolution and World War I, the Russian economy in the 1920s was in trouble. Agriculturally and industrially inferior to the rest of Europe, Russia was facing a bleak outlook that would require a drastic makeover. During such grim times any type of economic stimulus plan is generally welcomed with open arms. Enter Joseph Stalin and his five-year plans. Few plans in history are as well known as these were to revitalize the Russian economy and bring Russia into the modern era.

Fearful that the Western countries were attempting an economic overthrow of the Soviet Union, Stalin started his five-year plans to rapidly industrialize the country while collectivizing all the agriculture. Focusing on industry and energy, factories were created to produce steel, iron, heavy equipment, and electricity. To feed the massive influx of workers, all the agriculture was put under state control, and all available grain was allocated for governmental distribution. The plans were set to modernize Russia as quickly as possible with little leeway for anything else; however, progress came at a great cost for the Russian people.

When implementing the economic plan for his country, Stalin failed to see the secondary objectives. Stalin was successful in reaching his primary goal of rapid industrialization, but ultimately the plan failed by not including the very people who were necessary to run the plan. Similar to the previous example of an election, the immediate goal of providing for the Russian people did not foresee the eventual oppression necessary to keep the plan in operation. For Stalin, the future would be paved for Communism with Soviet red dominating the world. By the 1980s, however, Stalin's dream for Communist Russia would fall under the crushing realities of an insufficient economy and an oppressive regime.

If Stalin had been able to see into the future to predict the eventual collapse of the Soviet Union, he might have identified the flaws in his plan and made corrections in anticipation of them. Hindsight is 20/20 and countless leaders would have benefited from a similar crystal ball.

The states of Europe were devastated by the ravages of World War II, but a new conflict began to brew when the Allied forces knew the end of the war was around the corner. Liberating Europe from the west and the south by Allied forces meant that the Russians were liberating Eastern Europe. Stalin was set to establish a sphere of influence in the future Eastern Bloc, creating a buffer between him and the rest of Europe. In contrast, the major European powers like Britain and France were devastated, and a power vacuum had been created that required another country to fill the void in the struggle with Russia. America would eventually come to fill that void, and American policies would be enumerated in the Truman Doctrine. The Marshall Plan (named after George Marshall, Truman's Secretary of State who realized a healthy European economy was vital to America) was presented to Congress to stimulate the economies of Western Europe by packaging aid to any country that needed it.[258] Truman, cleverly, worded his speech to Congress stating:

> It must be the policy of the United States to support free peoples who are resisting attempted subjugation by armed minorities or by outside pressures.[259]

At that time, the aid was going to Greece and Turkey, nations that were battling Communist minorities, and fear of a conversion was eminent; thus, Western Europe was flooded with aid. Approved by Congress, the Marshall Plan became the primary source of aid to Western Europe, providing enough financial assistance to start the rebuilding process. Surprisingly, the plan was offered to every country in Europe, but Russia, suspicious of America's motives, offered its own plan to the Eastern Bloc. Named the Warsaw Plan, it became a symbol for the installation of Russian command economics and forcing Communism on the Eastern European countries. However, the Eastern bloc's economic system relied heavily on support from Russia, whereas the rest of Europe used the assistance from the Marshall Plan as a means to recharge their entire economic systems.

Achieving secondary objectives in a plan is crucial to long-term success. The economic conditions of Western Europe and America, in stark contrast to the systems of the Soviet Union, ultimately led to the deterioration of the U.S.S.R. and the end to the Cold War. The strength of

America's economic objectives, when compared to the Russian system of economic and social intolerance, provides the historical framework to understanding the elements of this maxim. There is a reason why this maxim does not state simply "Make a plan," but rather "Make a plan but remain fluid." The dual objectives of conceptualizing a plan and then remaining flexible and fluid to changes in that plan complement each other to successfully meet one's goals.

**Fluidity to the Modernity**

The objective of remaining fluid at first may appear vague and difficult to pin down. It may be similar to asking a person to be "nice," or to be "smart." How does one achieve the goal of being nice? Do they smile more or give out more compliments? Asking random people on the street to outline their own "how to" list to accomplish this goal and one will likely receive radically different answers. Scientists, however, tackle such soft science questions routinely by applying the tactics of hard science to quantify results and theorize solutions.

The science of organizational psychology has such goals at its heart. Herbert Simon, a 1978 Nobel Prize winning organizational scientist, would likely have looked at the political maneuverings of a Lee Atwater and considered his ability to change his plan to suit that week's agenda to be a master of decision making.[260] During his research, Simon concluded that most people were likely to settle for an acceptable result over an optimal result. Optimal results are those, which achieve maximum utility for a person. Conversely, acceptable results are based on previous experiences and how those situations turned out. People fail to recognize the consequences of their actions and therefore make decisions that "satisfy"—a cross between what it takes to satisfy and accepting just what it takes to suffice.[261]

Optimal results are attained by analyzing all possible alternatives and traversing more than the proverbial "road less traveled." Optimal thinking is the ability to think into the future, analyze possible consequences, and then make not just an acceptable decision, but an optimal one. Author Mohnish Pabrai, a Warren Buffett disciple, argued in his book *Perspectives* that many people invest in Fortune 500 companies because those companies are well known and likely to provide safe returns.[262]

## Maxim 5: Work Your Plan, but Remain Fluid

However, more often than not, these companies have failed to outpace the market by any significant long-term standard. For example, if a person invested $10,000 in the most valuable business on the Fortune 500 when it started in 1987 and then reinvested with the most valuable company until 2002, the person's annualized gain would likely be about 3.3 percent. Over the same period, the S&P (Standard & Poor's) 500 gained an annualized return of 8 percent.[263] When given the facts, most investors would not choose to let their money simply waste away when, with a bit more time and better research, more profitable companies could be identified for optimal returns.

Making the right choice about investments can be difficult for investors who are perpetually worried about their jobs or their day-to-day expenses. If someone's job is to accomplish a task, they must take the time and effort to find the optimal choice, right? Even in issue management, many firms and companies are likely to take the "acceptable" position rather than risk taking the optimal position. It seems that profit—and the growth of it—is tantamount to taking a risk that might grow a business or get a business involved in a new area for potential growth. Winston Churchill once said, "There ought to be ways of reforming a business, other than by merely putting more money into it."[264] However, in most situations the problem is not money, but a conflict of ideas. Micro-targeting and mass citizen involvement campaigns help identify the target audience that is the most affected by a change. Micro-targeting also serves to identify the best options for directly reaching out to those people. It is when people feel personally included in the process of change—and consequently feel as if their issues are personally considered and addressed in some way—that agents for change gain their trust and support. Thus, it is generally best to look for workable alternatives to accomplish an optimal solution than to rigidly charge ahead with only an acceptable plan.

Once a plan has been crafted and implemented, it should be followed up by the identification of well thought out and possible fall back options. The science of decision-making has developed tools to help thinkers identify just which steps to take next. Edward DeBono, perhaps best known as the originator of the term "lateral thinking," uses a tool called "the six thinking hats," which is a technique that helps one look at important decisions from a number of different perspectives. This concept is aimed at pushing the thinker to move outside of previous, habitual ways of thinking.[265] Using different kinds of hats—such as red, white, blue—DeBono emphasizes the different styles of thinking needed to create options to a solution for various business models.

Hypothetically, DeBono's sessions involve a group of business people who have been presented with a problem similar to "How do you start a successful donut cart business in the middle of Times Square?" A person wearing a white hat, for instance, would be asked to come up with ideas involving data, facts, or other necessary information about the problem.[266] Another person, who is wearing a black hat, may present ideas regarding difficulties or potential problems.[267] Each person on the team, wearing a different color hat would explore other areas for potential pitfalls and high notes of the proposed idea. De Bono's thinking tool has been utilized by such corporate giants as American Express, Amgen and Lockheed Martin. All of these companies have learned that remaining open to ideas and strategizing alternative options is a valuable skill for business. Lateral thinking can further be synthesized with another science, game theory, to extend into the area of military maneuvers to help identify successful plans of attack outside of the boardroom and onto the battlefield.

**Panama and the Navy SEALs**

Under the cover of night, the United States Navy SEALs began their approach on an airfield. Fighting had already begun but the darkness surrounding the SEALs provided just enough cover to approach their objective. The opposition general's private plane was at the ready and would have to be disabled to prevent his fleeing the country. Swiftly attacking the airfield, the Navy SEALs were able to destroy the plane and overcome the defending troops. Grounded and unable to flee via the Panama Canal, the general rushed for cover until the fighting subsided. Less than 15 days later, the opposition general surrendered to the U.S. military. This is the narrative of key moments during the United States' Invasion of Panama, codenamed Operation Just Cause, in 1989.[268]

Throughout nearly six American presidential administrations, Panamanian dictator Manuel Noriega had been on the payroll of the United States Central Intelligence Agency. Simultaneously, he was engaged in illegal dealings with Central American drug lords. Although the U.S. government had previously ignored Noriega's covert dealings, relations eventually turned sour.

After the 1989 Panama national election, Noriega refused to accept defeat and considered the election "nullified." Remaining in power by force, he generated contempt among Panamanian citizens and disfavor with President George H.W. Bush, who urged that Noriega step down from his position.

On December 15, 1989, after being threatened by drug charges in U.S. courts, Noriega publicly claimed that a state of war existed between the United States and Panama. The next day, four American servicemen in civilian clothing were stopped at a roadblock near the Panama Defense Forces headquarters. As they allegedly attempted to flee the scene, PDF forces killed one of the passengers—an American Marine.

Quick to respond, President Bush ordered troops to enter Panama and detain Noriega for the drug trafficking indictments levied against him. Within a few hours of the December 20 invasion, Guillermo Endara, the victor of the national election that Noriega had refused to accept, was sworn into power. Two weeks later, Noriega surrendered to American troops. In the time since he was deposed, Panama has held three national presidential elections. Noriega has spent his time imprisoned in America.

The swiftness of victory suggested the military had meticulously planned the attack and knew exactly which objectives to target in order to drive Noriega from his political seat. Military information, such as is found in the Special Forces Operation Manual, is generally suppressed from public dissemination to protect the secrets of the plan and to enhance the overall success of the operations. However, nearly 20 years later, an insight into the workings of the Navy SEALs is now available in its psychological operations (PSYOPS) manual. A look through the manual reveals a number of concepts, which apply to command structure and planning tactics of the Navy SEALs that can be similar to the concepts encompassed by this maxim.

> Themes and PSYOP objectives. The key to centralized planning and decentralized execution of PSYOP is clarity in the statement of objectives and themes. Broad objectives and themes establish the parameters for the development of series that reach foreign TAs (target audiences).[269]

The PSYOPS manual requires clarity in the SEALs' statements while also encouraging the development of broad objectives to reach the overall plan. During the process of subverting a target, for example, the PSYOPS manual refers to a series of options to meet the goal. Commanders who are subordinate to the Combined Joint Task Force (CJTF) are permitted to utilize any of the approved series in order to achieve their specific objectives. CJTFs are also given the option to modify existing series or to develop new series as long as those plans have received approval from the appropriate authority. These instructions give Navy SEALs the ability to change a pre-existing plan when circumstances arise, which require an alternative approach.

Planning is a process. Change is a constant in war planning as assumptions are shown to be false, operations are more successful or less successful, and political events change military objectives. Even as one plan is about to be executed, planners are turning their attention to the next anticipated operation. Flexibility, adaptability, and adjustment are critical to all planning. The importance of adjusting PSYOP plans and series in response to events in the battle space cannot be overemphasized.

> PSYOP planners must, therefore, be agile to be successful in an environment that has simultaneous and competing requirements to plan for an event that is in itself an ongoing process. At any given moment, PSYOP forces may be disseminating messages while military forces are executing a PSYACT (psychological operations actions) in support of PSYOP objectives. At the same time, planners are readying the next action or message and evaluating the effects of the ongoing mission. Managing this dynamic and ongoing series of events is central to creating and adjusting an effective PSYOP plan. Therefore, the need for PSYOP planners to anticipate situations where PSYOP will be crucial to the military operation is essential to success.[270]

A civilian can only imagine the rigors that a Navy SEAL will face when he is behind enemy lines on an active mission. The team would be lost without a comprehensive plan of attack, but what separates the elite forces from the rank and file military is the requirement that SEALs exhibit an ability to think on their feet to improvise a change of course when circumstances dictate. For example, forces on the ground can lose communication with their command during crucial missions. The procedures laid out in the PSYOP Manual give guidance to the leaders of the ground forces so that they can more successfully improvise in a situation. In addition, realistic recreations of those scenarios through mock missions can help further train the leaders to develop and implement the necessary alternatives to the situation, preserving the objective and keeping his soldiers alive.

**The effectiveness of U.S. Navy SEALs derives in part from training that encourages them to adjust to changing circumstances to meet mission objectives.**

The leaders of the troupe adhere to a series of steps to remain fluid in the field: 1) Decide 2) Detect 3) Deliver and 4) Access. Taken directly from the manual—from a report written years after the Panama invasion—this passage sums up how well the procedures were implemented there and the effect they had on future operations:

> Most PSYOP activities and accomplishments in Panama were hardly noticed by either the U.S. public or the general military community. But the special operations community did notice. The lessons learned in Panama were incorporated into standing operating procedures. Where possible, immediate changes were made to capitalize on the PSYOP successes of Operations JUST CAUSE and PROMOTE LIBERTY. This led to improved production, performance, and effect in the next contingency, which took place within 6 months after

the return of the last PSYOP elements from Panama. Operations DESERT SHIELD and DESERT STORM employed PSYOP of an order of magnitude and effectiveness, which many credit to the lessons learned from Panama.[271]

Just as the invasion of Panama led to improved production, performance, and effect for subsequent missions in the 1990s and beyond, the planning of some of our nations most successful (and least successful) military campaigns have also paved the way for subsequent military action. It is likely in an analysis of the games and strategies used in the military that application of successful strategies lies. Game theory can have great application to the political process, as well.

**Game Theory and the Game of Fluidity**

Game theory attempts to identify and quantify the relationship between people and their choices. These choices can range from attacking a renegade dictator to voting for a Republican or Democratic candidate. These decisions do not necessary end with one single choice; there are concepts in game theory that address multitudes of choices and people. An easy introduction to game theory is an analysis of a prisoner forced to decide from among several options with the ultimate aim of getting out of his predicament.

The Prisoner's Dilemma is illustrated by observing two hypothetical prisoners, X and Y. The two are arrested and placed in two different cells. No communication is permitted between X and Y and they are each given a set of choices.

> Choice 1: If both X and Y confess to the crime, they will each serve 2 years in prison. Not a severe punishment for the crime in question. But, if neither confesses, they each will be required to serve 5 years. What is the incentive to confess? Not to confess? The twist occurs when they are each give two additional choices.
> 
> Choice 2: If X confesses while Y remains silent, then X is sentenced to 10 years while the silent partner walks

off scot-free. The reverse is true if Y confesses. This is the Prisoner's Dilemma.[272]

X begins to contemplate, "If I confess I will do the time, but if Y remains silent he goes free while I go to prison. However, if I am silent and Y confesses then I go free, but if Y also remains silent then. . ." and X and Y's thought patterns continue *ad infinitum*.

Obviously, prisoners X and Y feel as though they are in a lose-lose scenario. An innovative game theorist would see it otherwise. Using statistics, the theorist could break down the cost-benefit analysis or utility of the situation. If you ran this scenario through a perpetual loop, the best outcome for both prisoners X and Y is for both to confess, giving each the option for serving the least number of years in jail. Unfortunately, neither X nor Y, nor likely most others in this isolated situation, would be able to trust another with so much at stake. Additionally, many would hold out hope of getting away with it altogether.

In the real world, players are often considering and researching the other side's strategy and attempting to discern the maximum utility. This is known as Cooperative Game theory.[273] In the prisoner's dilemma, X and Y are not privy to each other's decisions (parametric) so they might choose differently if they know what the other player is going to do (non-parametric).

An example of a non-parametric situation can be illustrated through the example of someone pushing a rock down a hill. The rock has no strategy. It must go down the hill. Conversely, if a person were to push another person down a hill, there are variations in the many possibilities that may occur. A thinking human may utilize defensive strategies to fight back, to stop from falling all of the way, or to pull the other person down with him. This part of game theory allows for the human component of thinking on (or off) their feet and changing the scenario along the way as needed.

From an issue management point of view, these game strategies can be integral to a successful plan. For example, an assessment of a particular client's interests can identify several—sometimes even competing interests—at play. The plan to maximum this client's overall interests must address the conflict between these goals and work out the optimal solution. A successful plan will remain fluid enough to allow a client to benefit from parts, while not suffering from others.

Not every situation can be solved with the result allowing everyone to benefit in the end. Sometimes to achieve an optimal situation there are inevitable losses to one of the parties. But the other parties do not always need to lose in a deal when they can be compensated or provided with an alternate set of benefits. In game theory, this concept is known as the *Kaldor-Hicks Efficiency*, which states that one party can compensate another group if there is a negative benefit to them. [274] Again, economists argue the marginal utility of money will cause the rich to take advantage of the poor in this situation. Theoretically, a rich person can compensate another with money costing far less to them than to a poor person. These deficiencies, if they existed, can be solved by using an intermediary partner who is looking for optimal results for all the parties.

Many of the concepts found in game theory play upon the core concepts of this maxim: create a plan, and then remain fluid to change the plan when needed for optimal success. These strategies are clearly seen in the theory's application to winning an actual game. Let us look at the strategic planning involved in a game such as poker to get a better appreciation for planning yet remaining fluid.

**The Flexible World of Competitive Poker**

While admittedly a great amount of luck is involved in a successful game of poker, it also offers great support for the theory that the strategies utilized in the playing of the game—against human opponents, not computers—are the very foundation for human interaction. Competitive poker players use a combination of statistics, psychology, game theory, and more than a substantial dose of instinct to achieve success, not unlike the skills employed by successful business and political leaders. David Moschella, a leading innovator in IT technology, CEO of Fractal Antenna and a writer for *Computer World*, said:

> Industry executives and analysts often mistakenly talk about strategy as if it were some kind of chess match. But in chess, you have just two opponents, each with identical resources, and with luck playing a minimal role. The real world is much more like a poker game, with

multiple players trying to make the best of whatever hand fortune has dealt them. In our industry, Bill Gates owns the table until someone proves otherwise.[275]

The World Series of Poker Main Event, in existence since 1970, features an amalgamation of poker pros and amateurs. The amateurs' dream is in making it to the final table (the final 10 players in the tournament). More often than not, the experienced players make it to the finals by sticking to defensive and aggressive strategies and adapting fluidly to the changing situations.

Poker pros will alter a plan for a particular hand (even to the point of losing) to achieve a greater victory on a hand further into the tournament. Considered one of the greatest poker players of his time, Doyle Brunson has inspired and educated students through his book, *Super System*. He teaches the various strategies, plans and styles that have helped him become a two-time World Series Main Event champion. He stresses the importance of the statistics involved in specific hands, the strategies of other players and the ability to adapt to circumstances quickly.[276] The traits necessary to achieve a high level of poker is remarkably similar to creating a dynamic plan but remaining fluid in its application.

Brunson points out that one of the common mistakes in tournament play is for a player to become aggressive, win as many chips as possible and then quickly exit the tournament. In a tournament of hundreds of people, the key in the beginning is to survive because a player cannot win money in a tournament unless they make it to the "big money." Much like a fluid plan, a poker player starts with a general plan to achieve success. Here the plan is to make the "money" and then hopefully make it to the final table. Next, the strategy to achieve the plan must be implemented in the real game situations. Brunson teaches a player to remain mostly defensive and aggressive, playing only hands that have a high statistical advantage before the community cards (in Texas Hold 'Em) are available to every player. There is a two-fold basis for maintaining this approach at the start: (1) make sure one does not subject himself to low percentages when playing a hand; and if playing a hand, then (2) maximize potential earnings by playing the statistical edge.

Before utilizing a strategy it is imperative to understand all the possible hands and statistics in each situation. If dealt a certain hand before the flop (the three initial community cards) a great player will understand not only the statistical advantages of a poker hand, but also based on how other players bet, the likelihood of which cards they will eventually hold in their hand.

This concept is where game theory comes into play as well as the analogy to fluidity. In poker, the ultimate knowledge is the other player's cards because if they are known, it might not matter what two cards the player has, but rather how they can bet to the other player. Game theory helps to determine the strategies that other players will use and how best to quantify them. Also, similar to the conduct of an issue management campaign, if an executive knows what strategy or plans the opposition will employ, then he can either use the knowledge to sway an issue or counteract the strategy.

**Top poker players have an established plan for winning, based on statistics and odds. But the key to success is reading and adapting to the other players at the table.**

Focusing on the ability to change gears in the middle of a card game is representative of the fluid changes necessary to make successful plans during a campaign. Parallels between secondary objectives and poker are distinctive features of remaining fluid and incorporating changes to capitalize on the long-term plan. Sometimes in poker, there comes a time when a player has to—to paraphrase Kenny Rogers—know when to hold them and likewise, know when to fold them. Poker professional, S.C. Ward says:

> When folding a hand, I never show my cards . . . never give away information but make sure you extract as much information from your opponent's play as possible

so later in the tournament you can use that information to win more money than you lost before.

The principles of betting play another huge part in the statistics and psychology of poker. Conversely they demonstrate how specific issue management techniques can come together to form a more fluid plan. In issue management, many principles like macro-targeting to mass media and cursory exposure are seen as the key methods in creating plans for resolving conflicts. But the precepts of this maxim teach us that to create a successful and fluid plan, it is best to focus on micro-targeting and mass citizen involvement campaigning to resolve issues. A plan that focuses on all the people involved and strategizes to adapt to changing views, situations or regulations, yields the best results. Breaking from the pack and thinking in creative ways takes you far toward these goals.

**Creative Thinking v. Groupthink**

Groupthink, coined by William Whyte in *Fortune Magazine* in 1952 and later in his book *The Organizational Man*,[277] refers to a form of thinking where members of a group attempt to curtail conflict and reach a decision without properly navigating all available options through critical thinking and analysis. Within business and political circles adherence to hierarchical leadership structure allows employees to simply follow the boss and minimize any encounters with other co-workers.

To combat groupthink, leaders must incorporate an environment that is advantageous to fluid thinking. Many of Edward De Bono's exercises can be helpful in these situations but not everyone goes through the thinking hat training or has the time to recreate the activity on the spot. Organizational delegation is the essence in achieving cooperative thinking and avoiding the pitfalls of groupthink.

The actions designed to increase the cooperative work within a group so that the entire plan can remain fluid, is analogous to the physiology of a tree. The trunk and the roots form the foundation of the tree, or the plan. The tree will likely grow upwards and outward by its own natural instinct. However, changes in the supply of sunshine or water will sometimes force the tree to make changes to its original plan so that it can adapt to the changes in resources.

For example, roots will grow around an obstruction in the soil to get to water; branches will slowly grow toward the sun. If the tree were to resist this type of adaption, it would likely languish in its own inactivity. Much like the natural instincts found in nature, humans can successfully adapt to an ever-changing environment. True leaders will anticipate and plan for those changes in developing overall goals.

As a tree grows to new heights, there is a stopping point when the tree reaches the limits of its growth process. Be it a specific part of a DNA strand that informs the tree it cannot expand any farther—or if there is simply not enough resources to continue growing—the tree must stop growing eventually. Similarly, when a plan has been crafted to precise detail and all the possible changes that may occur have been accounted for and alternate strategies formulated, does a planner stop there? Should the designer pat herself on the back for a job well done?

The architect has fashioned an excellent plan, which will accomplish the goals of a client, but there are more clients to satisfy and new projects may require tweaks to the plan, which must be anticipated. Improving on a process has always been the hallmark of human ingenuity but in the modern world it is very difficult to achieve such refinement. Within the business world, the Six Sigma quality improvement methodology, made famous by Motorola, is a process by which an organization assesses when process change is required and how best to identify and implement that change.

**Black Belt Planning**

Six Sigma is methodology for managing a business that focuses on reducing or eliminating the statistical variations within manufacturing processes. Specifically, the process is designed to eliminate defects while focusing on quality outputs for customers.[278] The model involves a measurement-based strategy to reduce defects in manufacturing lines to 3.4 defects per million opportunities. They incorporate the DMAIC system for process improvement (DMAIC is an acronym for Define, Measure, Analyze, Improve, and Control). Process control specialists who have mastered the Six Sigma methodology are called Six Sigma Green Belts, Black Belts (borrowing terms used to describe levels of expertise in the martial arts), or Master Black Belts, depending upon the expertise of the Six Sigma practitioner.

Extensive training and discipline, almost samurai-esque (harkening from the name for an ancient Japanese warrior) in its statistical rigor, enable Black Belts to analyze the situation in a process intensive environment and implement process improvement techniques. Corporations such as GE, Caterpillar, Bank of America, and Amazon.com attest to the value in process improvement activities and attribute thousands, millions, and even billions of dollars in profit to error prevention and cost reduction. In particular, General Electric estimates its monetary benefits for employing Six Sigma Black Belts over the course of five years to be in the billions of dollars.[279] According to the Six Sigma Academy, a Black Belt assigned to a project can save approximately $230,000 per project. With a proven record of accomplishment, the Six Sigma process is known for its innovation and quality control.

The system seeks to take cost-saving projects and quantify them in terms of dollars and cents, thus improving both the processes of the business and the financial bottom line. The modus operandi links all the levels of hierarchy within the company to Six Sigma methods to achieve the highest degree of efficiency. How does a program like Six Sigma achieve this type of success? It employs a systematic plan to go into a company and achieve their directives. Armed with an expertise and a well-crafted plan, the Black Belts systematically approach each avenue of an existing project until they achieve the results desired. Their DMAIC model is supplemented with a similar DMADV (Define, Measure, Analyze, Design, and Verify) model, which is used to create improvements on new projects. Both models allow for an incremental plan, which maps out progress and looks to alternate avenues to attain its objectives.

Businesses that rely on a process improvement methodology such as Six Sigma can expect to see improvements across the board. On the other hand, the inability to recognize the value of such business can lead to stagnation. Likewise, following this maxim goes beyond the initial plan and ensures that every successive project related to the original improvement objectives are created better and require more advanced results. The old saying goes: "If it ain't broke, don't fix it." However, in issue management the solution to one problem may not fit the same problem the next time around. The ever-changing environment in politics, business and the world requires that a manager of his craft must continually improve and narrow any possible deficiencies in his plan.

As Abraham Lincoln was addressing Congress in his annual meeting in 1862, he famously spoke about creating a better system of government when he said:

> Still the question recurs "can we do better?" The dogmas of the quiet past are inadequate to the stormy present. The occasion is piled high with difficulty, and we must rise with the occasion. As our case is new *so must we think anew, and act anew.*[280]

Lincoln knew that the U.S. government needed massive changes to deal with the hardship that the Civil War would inflict. He believed that he must act quickly and decisively if he wanted to achieve his goals. He created an atmosphere of innovation where his cabinet could produce better results compared to a normal bureaucratic assembly.

Wholeheartedly, Lincoln believed in the concept of making better plans and adapting as new situations arose.[281] Remaining fluid with a plan is more than simply changing the plan's designs during the course of the project but also refining and redeveloping the plan after the project has been accomplished. The incorporation of new information learned in the field—combined with the fresh take on the plan after implementation—will lead to new insights that are helpful for future planning.

Charles Darwin likely did not envision the varied applications his theories would have on all the sciences, on business, on leadership, on almost all areas of human interaction. Far from the observation of a particularly useful beak on a particularly unique finch, the theory that characteristics of an organism – successful ones, at least – can change to adapt to new situations in order to survive can be applied to all successful goals. Great leaders of the past, present and future know the value of this strategy and have achieved success in campaigns from the battleground to the boardroom and beyond.

Remaining alert to the changing tides and open to revising plans to meet new challenges head on is the hallmark of successful planning. Lincoln saw the need to be ready with new plans for a new world. Today's leaders of governments and industry will be successful if they do the same.

# Maxim 6
## "Politics Is a Game Best Played On the Ground."

*Because, by being on the spot, one sees trouble at its birth and one can quickly remedy it.*

— **Niccolo Machiavelli, Italian essayist, dramatist, historian, sketch writer, biographer, dialogist, writer of novellas, and poet, (1469–1527), author** *The Prince*

In 2005 I traveled with a team of researchers and environmental experts to Antarctica and bore witness to the palpable effects of a changing climate. From the bow of our steady moving boat, ice-spray kicking up off the sea, I saw the Antarctic shelf looming large on the horizon. It was a sight I'd only seen in movies, and firsthand it was more majestic than I could have imagined. Glaciers jutted into a fierce blue sky as a group of seals lay on its base and cormorants dove down to catch a meal of fish, sending ripples across the placid water.

The serenity of my thoughts was punctured by the captain, who pointed out an iceberg toward the stern. It had broken off from the rest of the Antarctic Peninsula, he told us, and was twice the size of the state of Rhode Island. It is one of several icebergs adrift off the Antarctic Coast, part of a startling phenomenon that is overwhelmingly illustrative of the effects of a changing climate on one of Earth's most pristine, unadulterated environments.

The firsthand observation of this phenomenon provided incontrovertible evidence that climate change is occurring, thus lending credibility to our message in support of a global solution and proving the efficacy of the prefect that Politics is Best Played on the Ground.

— **Thomas S. Mullikin**

## Overview

Seeing is believing. A picture is worth a thousand words. Out of sight, out of mind. Each of these phrases means something slightly different, yet the base of the message is essentially the same; that reality is best discovered through firsthand contact or personal observation rather than through data, reports, or hearsay.

It is beneficial to expound upon what this maxim actually means in terms of its application to issue management. Its scope can be determined primarily through the answers to the following questions: What exactly is meant by the term "politics," when is one "playing" it, and what constitutes "the ground" on which politics is being played?

In an issue management application, the term politics refers to the art of controlling conversation by favorably framing the discourse surrounding a given issue. While the term does not refer specifically to the democratic process of voting or of creating legislation, those facets of politics are inevitably shaped by public dialogue, and therefore exist under a broader definition of politics as an ongoing communal conversation.

The ground refers to the arena in which politics is being played, particularly the community or realm where an issue exists. Often, the ground refers to a specific region or municipality in which we work to extend our message. Being on the ground means interacting with the stakeholders in an issue, witnessing the effects and reactions firsthand, and using the knowledge gained through experience to affect change.

### *Chapter 6 Synopsis*

- Electronic observation can never take the place of being on the scene and having feet on the ground in understanding a location or event.
- Not understanding the terrain has spelled doom for many military endeavors.
- All politics are local.
- Successful politics and issue management require face-to-face communications to understand all viewpoints.

One is engaged in playing politics when he seeks to reach an audience with a specific message. For some, the effort begins and ends with a traditional mass media advertising approach, which blankets the audience with some type of advertisement, whether on television or in other media. As we will discuss later, a truly successful approach to issue management is far more comprehensive than a mass media appeal, and instead employs a tailored, micro-targeted strategy for communicating a message and ensuring its favorable reception.

## Lack of Firsthand Interaction Rendered the U.S. Vulnerable to Attack

There are few contemporary examples as readily known and as illustrative of the importance of politics on the ground as the United States' failures in its counterterrorism efforts against Al-Qaida. Relying heavily on information gathered via satellite, the U.S. did not have human intelligence assets on the ground. According to one counterterrorism official, "[w]e had amazing satellite pictures of them having graduation ceremonies at the camps, but we never had a clue what they planned to do when they left Afghanistan."

In 2004 the 9/11 Commission released a report which gave an account of the circumstances surrounding the events of September 11, 2001 and made recommendations for fortification of intelligence activities as preventative measures against further attacks. The report stressed the need for human intelligence sources, specifically spies who can gather information from within terrorist groups and opposition governments.[282]

In failing to play politics on the ground, the United States' intelligence agencies were aware that terrorist attacks may be imminent but were oblivious to Osama bin Laden's specific plan of action. Thus, unable to protect itself against the unknown, the United States was left vulnerable to the attacks of September 11th, 2001.

Just as satellite pictures alone proved an insufficient means for combating terrorism, an attempt to engage in issue management from afar will not yield favorable results. Campaigns, issue-based or otherwise, are not won through a torrent of advertising. Because all politics is local, Washington, D.C. politicians cannot authentically feel the pulse of the nation, and those who wish to effect change must do so by playing politics on the ground.

In a philosophical application to politics, one of the most well-known proponents of playing politics on the ground was Niccolo Machiavelli, who believed that being on the scene was important because it allowed a knowledge and control that could be neither acquired nor sustained from afar.

With the hopes of being reinstated to his position in the Florentine government, Machiavelli wrote *The Prince*. In this treatise he delineates the method by which a new, non-hereditary prince, specifically Giuliano de'Medici in the context of Florence's political situation, could sustain political power and stability within newly acquired principalities. Medici had recently attained power through force of a coup, and subsequently removed many of the existing government authorities, including Machiavelli himself who was briefly tortured and then exiled.

In *The Prince*, Machiavelli purports that the biggest obstacle to maintaining power is when an acquired province has different language, customs, and laws than those of its conqueror. The most effective way to win over the populace in such an instance is for the ruler to move to the new territory and take up residence there.

> Because, by being on the spot, one sees trouble at its birth and one can quickly remedy it; not being there, one hears about it after it has grown and there is no longer any remedy. Moreover, the province would not be plundered by one's own officers; the subjects would be pleased in having direct recourse to their prince; thus, wishing to be good subjects, they have more reason to love him and, wanting to be otherwise, more reason to fear him. Anyone who might wish to invade that dominion from abroad would be more hesitant; so that, living right there, the prince can only with the greatest of difficulties lose it.[283]

In being "on the ground,'" a prince can stay abreast of slight changes in public opinion, most importantly disfavor or unrest among the population. He can act quickly to remedy problems or rumors that arise and his strength is continually visible to those he has conquered. Also, he is seen as a local, interactive ruler instead of a heavy handed sovereign ruling from afar.

The tactics advocated by Machiavelli are directly relevant and important to issue management today in that, by having feet on the ground one has a direct hand in framing the debate and can immediately adjust to change.

Any objection or opposition can be dealt with efficiently and tactfully, whereas an attempt to mediate from afar may appear intrusive. Also, operating from within a community allows a leader to develop a rapport with the community and to therefore be seen as cooperative rather than domineering or invasive. Playing politics on the ground is necessary to gain control and establish stability in an area.

In the modern information age, politics on the ground may seem to accommodate an outdated mode of thinking. After all, technological developments have enabled us to communicate in increasingly efficient ways and over vast expanses of space. Even the most effective form of mass communication is simply an attempt to replicate the firsthand conveyance of a message from a communicator to intended recipients. As we will explore, these advances in technology are merely supplemental and do not preclude the necessity of playing politics on the ground. A brief timeline of these advances illustrates how politicians have attempted to use new technologies to increase communication with their constituents.

## Developments in Mass Communications: Supplementing not Supplanting a Ground Game

Historically, modern mass communication is often thought of as being born with the invention of Morse code, a system of audible signals of varied lengths and combinations, which allowed messages to be sent faster than land travel for the first time. By 1843, the first telegraph lines were erected to carry a signal from Washington, D.C., to Baltimore, Md., the nascent stages of a technology that would eventually allow messages to be transmitted over any distance.[284] The first message transferred via electric telegraph was interestingly political in nature, announcing the nomination of Henry Clay as presidential candidate for the Whig party at their 1844 national convention.

In 1875 Alexander Graham Bell modified telegraph technology in order to create a working telephone, which he first used to call his assistant in the next room to say "Mr. Watson—come here—I want to see you." Telephones served an increasingly important role in many aspects of American's daily lives, from enabling them to keep in contact with friends and family to stimulating business leads and connections. As a way to reach the average American, telephones became invaluable to political campaigns. A staple of "Get Out the Vote" (GOTV) strategies, phone banks are often used to determine constituents' intent to vote for a specific candidate.

In 1920, the first commercially licensed radio stations began to broadcast to the public using amplitude modulation (AM) and then began using frequency modulation (FM) during the 1930s. On March 12, 1933, President Franklin D. Roosevelt gave the first of his now famous "fireside chats" in which he essentially came into the homes of the American public and made his case directly to them through the radio to counter opposition to his plan for war. By bringing the discussion to this familiar medium, Roosevelt was able to directly address his opponents' points and win over the support of the listening audience. The use of radio allowed FDR to build a personal rapport with his fellow Americans but as was to be seen, television would make even greater strides to that end.

In the United States, the first regularly scheduled broadcasts began in 1939. In 1941, two New York City stations and one in Philadelphia were the first stations to be granted licenses to operate commercially. As the popularity of television sets grew, the stations pumped news and images into an increasing number of households across the nation. Today, every political campaign harnesses television as a medium through which to increase a candidate's presence among the electorate, especially, as we will discuss, in the form of advertisements.

Another monumental advance in communication technology was made in the early nineties, when the Internet began to reach a mainstream audience, allowing for the quick exchange of ideas in an open forum setting, as well as new forms of recreation such as interactive gaming and chatting with people with common interests. In what was then a largely unprecedented tactic at the time, 2004 Democratic presidential candidate Howard Dean harnessed the Internet for his campaigns fundraising efforts and was widely successful at this aspect of the campaign.

Today, the functionality of modern handheld devices such as the Blackberry combine all-in-one Internet, television, and phone capabilities. We can communicate across oceans, send text through time zones, and monitor news and weather from every continent. Politicians can send updates, elicit support, and raise funds, all at great distances from their constituents.

While the technologies allow a virtual interaction to take place between people around the world, none can come close to allowing for the same kind of human interaction available when you meet face to face. There is certain investment you make when you physically come to a place, absorb its sights, sounds, and smells; a certain authenticity in human interaction. Few understand this idea better than those who have engaged in politics or issue management; especially those who misunderstood or even underestimated the importance of the value placed on of personal interaction and were subsequently unsuccessful because of this failing.

**Modern communications technologies should not be ignored. But their role should be to supplement and enhance a campaign on the ground—not replace it.**

Politics, like issue management and even business administration, is not measured just by the success of communication to a broad and undefined universe. Rather, success is measured by persuasively communicating with a well-defined micro-targeted audience of potential voters or key opinion makers. For example, nationally approximately 201 million Americans are eligible to vote, based on 2006 data. The U.S. Census Bureau estimates that of that number of eligible voters only 67.6 percent or 135.8 million were registered to vote in the 2006 off-year elections. Of those registered, only 47.8 percent or 96 million people actually voted.[285]

In American politics there are examples that illustrate the success of playing politics on the ground as well as examples of the failure to do so. As an example of success we will examine Harry Truman's 1948 whistle stop campaign, during which he spoke with residents of towns across the country. In contrast, we will see how incumbent Vice President Richard Nixon failed to engage with his audience and ultimately lost the 1960 presidential election.

**Politics Played on the Ground Yields Historic Results**

During the campaign season for the 1948 presidential election, Republican nominee New York Governor Thomas E. Dewey, was favored to win the election over Democratic incumbent President Harry S. Truman. Prior to his whistle stop campaign Truman's public approval rating, according to a Gallop poll, hovered around 39%.

For an incumbent, this was not a positive political climate in which to gain momentum towards victory. Even more potentially devastating was the fact that the other Democratic candidates were poised to win the votes of previous Truman supporters.

According to pollsters and pundits, a Dewey victory loomed inevitable. This sentiment was so strong among newsmakers that the Chicago Daily Tribune jumped the gun and ran a headline that would soon become one of the most famous mistakes of its kind: Dewey Defeats Truman.[286]

As we now know, Truman was ultimately victorious, having won 49.6% of the popular vote and 303 electoral votes compared to Dewey's 45.1% of popular vote and 189 electoral votes. But how did he do it?

Truman was trailing before he put his boots on the ground and set off on his now well-known "whistle-stop" campaign, mimetic of Franklin D. Roosevelt's previous campaign tactics in which he stopped in towns across the country and gave speeches to crowds from the back of the presidential rail car, The Ferdinand Magellan. Did playing politics on the ground help Truman come from behind to win the election?

Based on their campaign schedules, we know where the candidates made appearances and how many times they stopped in each state. It turns out that Truman made far more stops than his opponents, traveling more than 30,000 miles, visiting 28 states, and stopping 238 times to energize the local population in small towns and big cities alike. In comparison, Dewey visited 22 states and made only 40 stops. Not only did Truman make more stops but his team was more strategic, allocating resources to those states with the closest races or to the states that would eventually yield the biggest prize in electoral votes.

Electoral politics is a context which includes several pieces and parts, many stakeholders, and many centers of energy. In a national election, the candidate must accumulate wins in as many states as possible and in order to be successful statewide, the candidate must fare well in the preponderance of specific communities and precincts. As the examination becomes more surgical, the value of being on the ground is increasingly crucial.

In many states visited, Truman made multiple stops. For example, on September 18 he visited Iowa and over the next several days spoke with people in the towns of Iowa City, Oxford, Grinnell, Des Moines, Dexter, Melcher, and Chariton. Although these towns were small, large crowds were assembled. At the Dexter stop, a crowd of nearly 100,000 gathered to hear what candidate Truman had to say. In comparison, Dewey made only one stop in Iowa. Due largely to these strategic campaign efforts, and despite the fact that Iowa had traditionally voted for Republicans, Truman won the state by three percentage points.

There is evidence of a correlation between campaign stops and votes won. According to an article published by the American Political Science Association, Truman gained .248 percentage points of the vote for every stop he made. In the six states where he stopped 15 or more times, Truman gained an additional 3.7 percentage points. Not only did being on the ground help Truman win more votes than he would have otherwise, it also inversely decreased the votes cast in those precincts for his opponents. For instance in a state visited 15 times by Truman, Wallace's vote dropped .8 percentage points.

On a national level, the whistle stop campaign closed the gap where Truman was lagging behind Dewey, allowing Truman to win several states with close races. He won California, Illinois, and Ohio each by less than one percentage point. Combined, he won these states with 58,584 votes, only .1% of the national electorate. In the states where his campaign stops meant winning a close race, Truman gained 78 Electoral College votes. By targeting states with big electoral prizes and close races the incumbent president was able to divest himself of a poor public approval rating and win the presidency once again.

Analysis of Truman's whistle-stop campaign would be grossly incomplete if discussion ended at the number of stops that were made in each state. Of even greater importance are the messages that Truman delivered at each stop—messages which were tailored to address the specific concerns of those to whom he was speaking. His speeches related the plights of the average working-class Americans in each town to a larger picture, emphasizing the importance of their livelihoods to the future of the country and of the world.

As in issue management, candidates who make local appearances have the chance to deliver their message, usually uncontested by the opposition, in a setting that will bring about extensive local media coverage. After seeing the candidate firsthand, local media coverage reinforces the message, serving to mobilize and persuade the population. Political scientist Thomas M. Holbrook explains Truman's application of politics on the ground strategy in comparison to Dewey's mass media approach:

> In addition, while Truman used his campaign stops to rally the troops and to address issues of local concern, Dewey paid to have his stump speeches broadcast nationwide via radio and newsreels and, therefore, was less likely to tailor his message to local groups and issues.

Truman tailored his message to agricultural and blue collar workers, African-Americans, and minority or disadvantaged groups, all of which he addressed directly through speeches at towns along the route of his whistle-stop campaign. While any speech would serve as an example of this, we will examine Truman's speech from September 18, 1948, in Dexter, Iowa, where, as mentioned previously, a crowd of over 100,000 was gathered.

The speech begins, "I am glad to be here. It does my heart good to see the grain fields of the Nation again."[287] Immediately, Truman has rooted himself in the specific geographic context of his audience. He then acknowledges the fruits of their labor and administers high praise.

"The record-breaking harvests you have been getting in recent years have been a blessing. Millions of people have been saved from starvation by the food you have produced. The whole world has reason to be everlastingly grateful to the farmers of the United States."[288]

In the next paragraph he weaves the farmers' role as producers of food into the cloth of worldwide human interaction, claiming that "the abundant harvests of this country are helping to save the world from Communism," which "thrives on human misery. Your farms," he said, "are a vital element in America's foreign policy."[289] In relating their daily tasks to the stage of world affairs, Truman lent his audience a sense of responsibility and importance and the feeling that they, the citizens of rural Iowa, had a stake in the outcome of the national election as well as in world affairs.

Truman then hinted at how the war and the economy would affect the agricultural industry if managed under Republican rule. He addressed specific concerns, including the storage of excess grain and price supports for corn. He made reference to the devastation of farmers during the Depression, blamed the big business Republicans, and promised that the Democratic Party is on the side of the American worker.

Seconds into Truman's speech and throughout its entirety, it was clear to the audience that the President was not merely delivering a canned response. He had his boots on the ground, he was aware of his audience's specific concerns, and he demonstrated the relevance of those local issues to the national situation. It was not solely Truman's presence in each of these towns that won the people over; it was his interaction through delivery of a tailored message.

Once in office, Truman proposed a package which he termed the "Fair Deal," a set of relief programs whose purpose was to alleviate some of the burdens shouldered by the hard-working Americans with whom he had met and interacted. It was those folks, upon hearing Truman's tailored, hopeful message, who ultimately tipped the balance in his favor during the general election.

Clearly, a sweeping mass media approach would not have been as effective for Truman, nor would it have won him the election. Not only was train transportation efficient and inexpensive, it helped shape public opinion in favor of Truman as a man of the people, an unpretentious guy who cared about issues faced by the vast majority of blue collar and middle class Americans. This perception of Truman as a man willing to get his boots on the ground and talk to America's citizens about issues they deemed important was effective in gaining an advantage over the seemingly pompous Dewey, who was jeeringly said to be "the only man who could strut sitting down."[290]

While the whistle-stop campaign helped shape the public's view of Truman, it also helped shape Truman's view of the public. The President had a genuine concern for the nation's people before his whistle-stop campaign, but over the course of the campaign he met, shook hands, and had conversations with the people he was elected to represent. His one on one interaction with constituents helped him to gain a deeper understanding of how the American people were affected by the policies he enacted and the hardships they bore as a result of those policies. It was an education that he could not have gained without the firsthand experience, without actually being in those places and with the people he sought to lead. For Truman, playing politics on the ground had made all the difference.

**Nixon Fails to Harness the Full Potential of Television as a Medium for Speaking to the People**

Truman's campaign was effective not only because of the message his physical presence sent to the voters whose hands he was shaking in towns across America, but also because of the accessibility he was able to present through his targeted speeches in which he seemed to made the people feel he was speaking *with* them rather than *to* them. Richard Nixon, however, failed to utilize the great power of effectively reaching out to the people.

In 1960, presidential candidates John F. Kennedy and Richard Nixon had a new medium through which to deliver their messages. Just as the FDR's fireside chats brought the voice of the President directly to the people across the radio airwaves, the first televised presidential debates brought the candidates' voices and images right into their living rooms.

The development and popularity of television had exploded after World War II and through the 1940s and 50s, during which time approximately 40 million households purchased a set. By 1960 there was a television in more than 44 million American homes. Television delivered information through sound and images, and changed forever

### Maxim 6: Politics Is a Game Best Played on the Ground

how entertainment and the news of the day were received by the viewer. As Marshall McLuhan observed in his work *Understanding Media*, "The medium is the message."[291]

The advent of television, characterized by McLuhan as a "cool" medium because information received via TV is predominantly visual. The television image did not replicate the face-to-face quality of a campaign stop, but it added increased importance to the visual component of politics. Candidates needed to look good and project a leadership image. In order to gain the support of the people candidates would now need to harness the power of television to speak directly to the voters and deliver a message that gained their confidence.

Throughout the summer and fall of 1960 both Kennedy and Nixon each crisscrossed the country making meet-and-greet campaign stops. However, during this crucial campaign season Richard Nixon suffered a serious knee injury and was forced to suspend his campaign for a two-week convalescence. Meanwhile, Kennedy was touring the country, waving at Americans from the back of a convertible, appearing tanned, high spirited, and accessible to the people he sought to represent. It was his "on the ground" interaction with the people that helped Kennedy craft his message to speak directly to the issues of concern for the American public, and television helped him do that.

Nixon's knee injury and subsequent recovery took a visible toll. In sharp contrast to the healthy and youthful Kennedy, Nixon appeared on the campaign trail visibly thinner and fatigued. Although the men were just four years apart in age, Nixon, especially on television, looked to be much older. By the end of his exhausting campaign Nixon had fulfilled his promise to visit each of the 50 states, but his less than robust physical appearance as he met the voters in each state would fail to win him their support. Nixon's campaign strategy placed a greater importance on the sheer number of stops the candidate should make to large crowds rather than on targeting select local communities with more one on one interaction. This decision would prove decisive in the election.

Near the end of the campaign season, the candidates were slated to appear in the first-ever televised presidential debate. Although Nixon was considered to be a great debater, his appearance on television made him look sickly when juxtaposed on a split screen with his opponent, the slightly younger, more energetic John F. Kennedy. Commentators present at the debates remarked that it seemed as if Nixon treated the television camera as if it were simply a machine present to record a debate between the two candidates. Kennedy, however, seemed to use the camera as a window in to his real audience—the voting public. While Kennedy's tanned face spoke directly to the camera, Nixon, with an unfortunate five o'clock shadow, spoke mostly to his opponent, unsteady as he swayed back and forth at the podium.

The viewing audience, previously accustomed to only being addressed by voices over the radio, could now see the candidates come to life on the small screen. The images presented on television reinforced the message of the candidates' ground campaign strategy—Kennedy was talking with the people, Nixon presenting to the people. For the first time the great majority of American voters were able to view the two presidential candidates. For the first time, a voter could choose a candidate to support based on pure appearances alone. The medium of television became an access point for the American public to interact with these candidates and in this way, the medium became the message. Was there a clear winner in the debates? Depends upon whether the audience listened on the radio or watched on TV:

> In substance, the candidates were much more evenly matched. Indeed, those who heard the first debate on the radio pronounced Nixon the winner. But the 70 million who watched television saw a candidate still sickly and obviously discomforted by Kennedy's smooth delivery and charisma. Those television viewers focused on what they saw, not what they heard. Studies of the audience indicated that, among television viewers, Kennedy was perceived the winner of the first debate by a very large margin.[292]

Playing politics on the ground is not limited to making a physical appearance. As McLuhan noted 40 years ago, television demands interaction. In *Understanding Media*, McLuhan discusses the results of an experiment in which participants were presented with information via print, radio, television, and lecture and tested for comprehension. Surprisingly, radio was by far the most effective medium, followed by television. The reason was not immediately grasped by researchers.

> It was a long time before the obvious reason declared itself, namely that TV is a cool, participant medium. When hotted up by dramatization and stingers, it performs less well because there is less opportunity for participation. . . . TV will not work as background (sound). It engages you. You have to be *with* it.[293]

As was the case with Nixon, a failure to engage with the people will likely render a physical presence to a large group irrelevant. Was Nixon's error simply a failure to engage viewers? What matters most is gaining knowledge about local issues and using that information to help the candidate or issue manager target stakeholder audiences with a powerful message and build rapport with the residents of the targeted group.

Kennedy was successful in building crowd rapport at his personal campaign stops. He could then use the information he gained through interaction with the populace to tailor his message to speak directly to them and to leverage the power of the television cameras at the debates. Kennedy was in a position to influence voters. Politics on the ground means not just being there but learning from congenial interaction with involved stakeholders.

America's third president, Thomas Jefferson, and chief architect of the Declaration of Independence understood well the importance of first-hand knowledge to develop a winnable position in nation building. It is in this vein of thought that Thomas Jefferson made plans for a westward expedition of the North American continent in the early 1800's. He knew that an acquired knowledge of the West through interaction with its native peoples and landscape would give the United States an advantage in commerce. These plans resulted in the well-known Lewis and Clark expedition, a prime example of how the idea of politics on the ground was implemented successfully.

## Lewis and Clark Gain Firsthand Knowledge of Newly Acquired American West

At the time when the Northern American continent was still the property of several different countries, the territory and people west of the Mississippi River were largely unknown to the United States government. The American colonies had gained their independence from

Great Britain less than twenty years before, yet the idea of Manifest Destiny, that American territorial expansion was necessary and inevitable, was already beginning to shape decision making in our nation's capital.

Then Secretary of State Thomas Jefferson was widely thought to be one of the most knowledgeable western geographers and cartographers of the time. He professed interest to develop the West and conducted extensive private research and studies on western-American geography from the library at Monticello, his Virginia residence.[294]

Jefferson understood the importance of playing politics on the ground, that an American presence in the unknown territories and relationship building with the native peoples would give the United States an edge in future commerce there. Soon after American independence, he began to outline plans for a westward expedition that would involve interaction with native peoples and European fur traders, as well as an assessment of the Mississippi River and its branches, with hopes that transport, trade and communication in the west were possible.

What Jefferson intuitively knew about establishing a presence within a community and building a rapport with its inhabitants has since become a pillar of modern marketing strategy, in which a company seeks to infiltrate a host community with its brand and to sustain long term ties, also known as brand loyalty.

In the world of marketing, a host community is defined as any group that shares "essential resources that may be cognitive, emotional or material in nature."[295] Marketing experts know that becoming firmly established within a host community is an important step toward maintaining consumer familiarity and therefore broad loyalty. A community that exists within a physical boundary, as is the case in issue management, shares each of these connections as well as a political structure through which to redress grievances.

In an issue management application, a host community is composed of the people who live in a given geographical region and are commonly affected by a particular issue. Just as Jefferson knew an expedition team would begin to establish a presence in the West, successful issue managers rely on interpersonal communication within a host community to build a foundation for future interactions.

A study by the American Marketing Association, conducted over several years and compiled in 2002, observed the behaviors of consumers in a community based on loyalty to the Jeep Company. The company hosted an event, Camp Jeep, in which novice and veteran Jeep owners came together to try off-roading courses, discuss Jeep ownership experiences, and learn about the newest Jeep products.

Researchers observed and interviewed participants at consecutive events, measuring the sense of community fostered between Jeep owners, and also between participants and the Jeep brand. They discovered that strong bonds were formed in both instances, even when the participants were novice Jeep owners or were initially hesitant about attending the event. The value lay in the actual face to face interaction of participants brought together for a commonly held interest. Authors of the study describe the benefits of personal interaction toward strengthening community ties and loyalty to the Jeep brand.

Compared with the normally diffuse nature of a brand community, the temporary geographic concentrations provide a rich social context for communication. In close proximity, people got to know one another in ways that would be difficult or impossible through electronic or mass media. Face-to-face contact reduces opportunities for personal misrepresentation. They provide more information on which to base judgments about people's credibility, sincerity, and concern.

Overall, data from the study found that relationship-building efforts produced long-term results in terms of increased repurchase rates for the Jeep brand. Events such as Camp Jeep are as effective in an issue management application as they are in a business marketing sense because they create impassioned proponents who are active advocates of a given message. According to the study:

> By proactively providing the context for relationships to develop, marketers can cultivate community in ways that enhance customer loyalty. . . . Community-integrated customers serve as brand missionaries, carrying the marketing message into other communities. . . . Customers who are highly integrated in the brand community are emotionally invested in the welfare of the company and desire to contribute to its success.

For Jefferson, proactively providing a context for relationship building with European fur traders and Native Americans meant sending an expedition team to the West. The importance of this task was such that Jefferson did not give up, despite two failed attempts.

The first attempt took place in 1786, when Jefferson recruited a Connecticut man named John Ledyard to walk across Siberia, into Alaska, and then down to the Mississippi River. While still in Siberia, Ledyard was apprehended by Russian police and exiled. The second attempt at a westward bound expedition was financed by funds raised by Jefferson and the American Philosophical Society. Chosen for the job over Meriwether Lewis, the team was led by a Frenchman, Andre Michaux, who traveled to what is present-day Tennessee before being discovered as a French spy and divested of his duties.

Jefferson was not to be deterred. The potential was too great, and the presence of foreign and native peoples too near, to leave the West unexplored. In his preparations for a third mission, Jefferson played politics on the ground by effectively shaping the dialogue both domestically and with the European governments. At home he appeased the Federalists, who were against western expansion, by classifying the expedition as one purely commercial in nature, stating its goals as the discovery of a Northwest river route to the Chinese market and the ascertainment of potential benefits of trade with Native Americans.

In his request for passports from France, Spain, and England (for all of these preparations were being made prior to the Louisiana Purchase), Jefferson insisted that the presence of American explorers in these regions would be for scientific endeavors, without commerce in mind. Because he was able to frame the discourse on both sides, Jefferson kept the issue from becoming explicitly political and was therefore able to launch what would become an overwhelmingly successful expedition, that of Meriwether Lewis and William Clark.

On January 18, 1803 Jefferson sent a confidential letter to Congress, asking for an appropriation of $2,500 to fund a transcontinental voyage:

> The river Missouri, and Indians inhabiting it, are not as well known as rendered desirable by their connection with the Mississippi, and consequently with us. An intelligent officer, with ten or twelve chosen men . . .

might explore the whole line, even to the Western Ocean.[296]

Upon acquiring funding, President Jefferson wrote an instructional letter to Meriwether Lewis regarding his expectations for a westward expedition. Only months before, the United States of America had acquired 828,000 square miles of territory from France which stretched from the Gulf of Mexico in the south to Canada in the north. It was a huge territorial acquisition, comprising nearly 23% of our current land mass.[297] He directed Lewis to explore and describe the geography of the land in detail, and to make his party acquainted with the native people; specifically with their language, traditions, laws, and customs:

> The commerce which may be carried on with the people inhabiting the line you will pursue, renders a knolege [sic] of those people important. You will therefore endeavour [sic] to make yourself acquainted with as far as a diligent pursuit of your journey shall admit, with the names of the nations & their numbers; the extent & limits of their possessions; their relations with other tribes of nations; their language, traditions, monuments; their ordinary occupations in agriculture, fishing, hunting, war, arts & the implements for these; their food, clothing, & domestic accomodations; [sic] the diseases prevalent among them, & the remedies they use; moral & physical circumstances which distinguish them from the tribes we know; peculiarities in their laws, customs & dispositions; and articles of commerce they may need or furnish & to what extent.
>
> And considering the interest which every nation has in extending & strengthening the authority of reason & justice among the people around them, it will be useful to acquire what knolege [sic] you can of the state of morality, religion, & information among them; as it may better enable those who may endeavor to civilize & instruct them, to adapt their measures to the existing notions & practices of those on whom they are to operate.

These orders are reminiscent of Machiavelli's advice to de'Medici in *The Prince*, that in order to secure power and stability in a newly acquired territory it is best for the ruler to become accustomed to the people's culture through a physical presence. With a strong measure of foresight for future interactions with the West, Jefferson clearly understood the value of putting boots on the ground.

Toward this end, Lewis and Clark led a group of men across the American continent from 1804 to 1806, to the Pacific Ocean and back, documenting their encounters along the way. Many of their diary entries depict the type of relations developed with Native American tribes and European fur traders along the way. In one story, the captains trade their Native American guide's beaded belt for a fur robe intended as a present for President Jefferson.

> [O]ne of the Indians had on a roab [sic] made of 2 Sea Otter Skins the fur of them were more butifull [sic] than any fur I had ever Seen both Capt. Lewis & my Self endeavored to purchase the roab [sic] with differant [sic] articles at length we precured [sic] it for a belt of blue beeds [sic] which the Squar—wife of our interpreter Shabono wore around her waste . . .

An entry from September 26, 1804 describes the appearance of a tribe of Native Americans as the expedition's boat approaches the shoreline, detailing not only their outward appearance but also making observations of their disposition and gender roles.

> Great numbers of men, women, and children on the banks viewing us. These people show great anxiety. They appear sprightly. Generally ill-looking and not well made; their legs and arms small generally; high cheekbones, prominent eyes. They grease and black [paint] themselves with coal when they dress. The distinguished men make use of hawks' feathers [calumet feather adorned with porcupine quills and fastened to the top of the head and falls backward about their heads]... The squaws are cheerful, fine-looking women,

> not handsome; high cheeks; dressed in skins; a petticoat and robe, which folds back over their shoulder, with long wool. Do all their laborious work, and, I may say, perfect slaves to the men, as all squaws of nations much at war, or where the women are more numerous than the men.

As shown in their diary entries, Lewis and Clark's interactions with Western Native Americans began diplomatic relations in the region which set a precedent for further exploration. The same level of personal interaction is important in issue management for the rapport it establishes. Successful issue management produces similar results in that interacting locally and being aware of surroundings results in a stronger relationship to the community in subsequent visits. Later in the same September 26 entry, Clark describes a festival like event in which the native tribe honors the group of explorers in what seems to be an act of making peace.

> On landing, I was received on an elegant painted buffalo robe, and taken to the village by 6 men, and was not permitted to touch the ground until I was put down in the grand council house, on a white dressed robe... A large fire was near, in which provisions were cooking. In the center, about 400 pounds of excellent buffalo beef as a present for us.
>
> An old man rose and spoke, approving what we had done, and informing us of their situation, requesting us to take pity on them and which was answered. The great chief then rose with great state, speaking to the same purpose as far as we could learn, and then, with great solemnity, took up the pipe of peace and, after pointing it to the heavens, the four quarters of the globe and the earth, he made some dissertation [then made a speech], lit it and presented the stem to us to smoke.
>
> The women came forward, highly decorated in their way, with the scalps and trophies of war of their fathers, husbands, brothers, or near connections, and proceeded to dance . . .

The knowledge included in these diary entries and other detailed documentation rendered the expedition a decided success on several fronts. For one, Lewis and Clark returned to the east with extensive knowledge about the vast expanse of land that was now a part of the United States.

Their accurate cartographic information detailed mountain ranges and rivers vastly different from Jefferson's expectations. For instance Nicholas King's map, made directly prior to the expedition, illustrates two mountain ranges in the West thought to be separated by a plateau. The map also incorrectly illustrates branches of the Missouri river. Based on the physical knowledge acquired over the course of the expedition, cartographers were able to create maps of these newly discovered areas and to provide coordinates so that later explorers could reach the same spot.

Along with geographic information, the team also identified and recorded 178 plant species and 128 species and subspecies of animals,[298] recorded vocabulary lists from nearly 50 Native American tribes, and brought back various artifacts. None of these things could have been accomplished if the explorers had not experienced the animals, people, and land of the West firsthand.

**Your decisions must be informed by people with firsthand knowledge of the lay of the land. This not only allows you to accurately assess your strategies, but also gives you the opportunity to build relationships with the target communities.**

The intricacies of the local landscape were determined from a first hand, on the ground perspective. This detailed examination is emblematic of the careful inspection and information gathering that can be collected on the ground during a complex political or issue management campaign.

Just as politics on the ground proved successful in creating a presence and building relationships in the North American west, it successful implementation has been applied repeatedly in military situations. Its importance in warfare focuses mainly on the concept of battlefield terrain, which can set an army at an advantage or disadvantage before fighting commences.

## Military Application of a Ground Game

For centuries, the idea that politics is best played on the ground was employed frequently as a military strategy, examples of which are likely the most illustrative of this maxim because the resulting gains and losses are easily identifiable.

Armies met outdoors and engaged in hand to hand combat; whether organized in lines or engaged in guerilla style warfare, the physical terrain of the land played a central role in the positioning of armies and in many cases, their success in battle. In his work, *On the Theory of War*, Carl von Clausewitz opined that, "Among civilized nations combat uninfluenced by its surroundings and the nature of the ground is hardly conceivable."[299]

Due to the necessity of strategic positioning, surveying battlefield terrain and nearby land formation has always been an important tool when preparing for warfare; in fact, it is one of the earliest strategies to be employed. Viewing or actually traversing the terrain is called "ground truth" and is by far the best method for assessing the lay of the land and for understanding the potential benefits and setbacks to the soldiers. Ground truth in issue management results in first-hand knowledge of an issue through interaction at a local level.

Ancient Chinese military strategist Sun Tzu, author of *The Art of War* recognized the value of assessing a situation first-hand. As a tool for being successful in battle, he had several guidelines for using terrain in order to gain the strategic advantage, for example:

1. We may distinguish six kinds of terrain, to wit: (1) Accessible ground; (2) entangling ground; (3) temporizing ground; (4) narrow passes; (5) precipitous heights; (6) positions at a great distance from the enemy.

2. Ground which can be freely traversed by both sides is called accessible.

3. With regard to ground of this nature, be before the enemy in occupying the raised and sunny spots, and carefully guard your line of supplies. Then you will be able to fight with advantage.

4. Ground which can be abandoned but is hard to re-occupy is called entangling.[300]

Each of Sun Tzu's points regarding physical terrain is analogous to issues management strategies. To his first point, essentially that there are different types of terrain, we must realize that the proverbial battlefield is never uniform, nor should we assume that it is similar to one previously encountered.

For instance, a campaign developed to deal with an environmental issue may encounter distinctly different obstacles than an issue surrounding manufacturing job loss. Each concern is rooted in some degree to intangible notions such as morality or prejudicial underpinnings and will therefore require re-assessment of the social, cultural, and political terrain. While previous campaign tactics can be used as a guide, the reality is that each campaign terrain is different. The same holds true for issue management, which requires feet on the ground assessment of an issue.

Skilled politicians are able to define issues and plot a course for a successful campaign. The best way to do this is by getting boots on the ground and learning the issue from the source. You can chart a campaign's course based on assumptions or third party knowledge of the issue; but the only accurate plan must necessarily include first hand knowledge so that adjustments can be made when necessary.

Each new case requires operation within varying constraints, which depend on both the opposition and the audience. More often than not, one can only fully realize the extent of these constraints by being on the ground, becoming familiar with them, and using the knowledge against the enemy.

On Sun Tzu's second point regarding accessible ground, we must realize that we are sharing the arena in which we are extending our message. In the same way that we have access to a potential electorate or a customer base, so does our opposition.

In light of this understanding we are led to the third point, which states that it is necessary to occupy the ground first, and to guard the line of supplies. In issue management, expediency and first impressions are critical. One must assume a winnable position early, as discussed in chapter one and then act from that position.

Lastly, Sun Tzu warns that abandoned ground is hard to re-occupy. Because it is easier to fight a proactive battle than a reactive one, early seizure is critical. We can see the wisdom of Sun Tzu's military strategies on a conceptual level, but to attain a true sense of their efficacy it is helpful to examine application of these strategies in an actual battle. In the study of battlefield terrain as a variable in military success, the American Civil War provides many useful case studies.

## Civil War Battles Provide Useful Case Studies on Terrain Assessment

Battles of the American Civil War have often been used as case studies with which to educate modern soldiers on the use of terrain. In fact, entire books have been written that are dedicated to the study of how terrain has shaped the outcome of some of the war's biggest battles.

Generals took many factors into account when seeking a piece of ground from which to either attack or defend. The spot they chose would give them a strategic advantage, allowing the men to hold their ground against the enemy. The accurate assessment of terrain was necessary for a successful campaign; to stumble across an uninvestigated piece of land could hinder the soldiers' ability to fight effectively in that their focus may be consumed by the task of maneuvering instead of fighting.

General Robert E. Lee, whose duty as a Captain was to map out terrain in the 1845 war between the United States and Mexico, acquired valuable knowledge of this task which served him well nearly 20 years later in the Civil War.[301] His skill in this area undoubtedly added to his reputation as a venerated general and war hero.

The Battle of Antietam is a significant example in which terrain played a central role in the outcome of a skirmish. The battle was fought among rolling hills, which hid Union and Confederate troops from each other while entrenched but provided no cover for any soldier, on either side, who rose above the hill's crest and became highly visible to the enemy.[302] Therefore, due partially to the lay of the land, it was the bloodiest single-day battle in American history, resulting in roughly 23,000 casualties.[303]

Nearly a year after Antietam, Lee once again attempted to defeat Union troops on their own soil at Gettysburg, Pennsylvania. The battle of Gettysburg, which spanned July 1 to 3, 1863, and engaged 158,300 total Union and Confederate troops, resulted an estimated 51,000 casualties, the largest number in any one battle of the Civil War. Many historians believe that a specific maneuver during this battle was the turning point of the war, sometimes known derisively as the "high water mark" of the Confederacy.

Ordered by General Lee, Pickett's Charge was a failed attack on Union troops. An estimated 12,500 Confederate troops began their fatal march on Union-held Cemetery Ridge, across a mile of open farmland in 87-degree weather, suffering a loss of more than 50 percent of their soldiers. On July 4, when Lee began withdrawing his army toward Williamsport on the Potomac River, his train of wounded stretched more than 14 miles. Many historians believe the Confederates never fully regrouped mentally or physically following this defeat.

The importance of the terrain is obvious to anyone viewing the historic site. Terrain in the town of Gettysburg comprised many ridges and hills to the south. The largest of the hills were Cemetery Hill and Culp's Hill. Cemetery Hill was intersected by the Baltimore Pike and overlooked the main downtown area of Gettysburg from the south at 503 feet (153 m) above sea level and 80 feet (24 m) above the town center. Its crest extended in a southwest-northeast direction for about 700 yards. Culp's Hill was roughly the same height but heavily wooded and laden with large boulders.

Both terrain features played central roles in the Union Army maintaining its strategic advantage. Obstacles on Culp's Hill anchored the Union army's flanks and therefore provided natural protection. Both hills allowed occupation of the Baltimore Pike, which was needed to keep Union troops supplied and to block northern movement of the Confederate Army toward Baltimore or Washington, D.C.

Due to its key role in the outcome of major Civil War battles, and by extension U.S. history, preservation of the topography and landscape of battle sites for the study of future generations has been an important goal of the National Park Service. For instance, the Gettysburg National Military Park recently underwent an extensive series of restorations to return the battleground to its original state. Visitors and history buffs were then able to glean a complete understanding of what the battle was like and of the physical obstacles faced by the soldiers. Even while viewing events from a historical perspective, feet on the ground is still necessary for understanding.

Whether illustrated by the Lewis and Clark expedition's interaction with native peoples or by generals' assessment of terrain prior to a military battle, Playing Politics on the Ground effectively requires a level of interaction that goes beyond mere observation. Firsthand knowledge is important, but it is how that knowledge is used to engage with the community, or engage in battle, that makes Politics on the Ground successful. Failing to apply knowledge effectively is almost as bad as being uninformed.

**Nazi Army Devastated by Ignoring Threat of Russian Winters**

This point is aptly illustrated with the travails of the Nazi army's travails in Russia during World War II. The harsh winters of Russia have long held a reputation for crippling unprepared armies, most notably the powerful military machines of Napoleon and Hitler. As with any far northern territory, one can expect to contend with snow drifts, severe cold, short days, few and poorly maintained roads, and few villages in which to take shelter.

In military terms, these conditions equate to restricted mobility, logistical setbacks, obstructed roadways, and high instances of frostbite. They also require the use of special transport vehicles, adequate footwear for infantry, such as skis or snowshoes, lubricant for weaponry and motors, and portable shelter.

During the first winter of the war, temperatures averaged around -20 degrees Fahrenheit with the record low an immobilizing -63 degrees. The exact temperatures are irrelevant because a soldier can get frostbite anywhere within a range of weather that cold. Blizzards coated the ground with heavy layers of snow measuring between 28-59 inches, which made mobility nearly impossible.[304]

The weather conditions caused an inordinate amount of non-battle related injuries and casualties. Surviving troops resorted to taking clothes from corpses in order to layer and keep warm. By the end of that first winter, the Germans recorded a quarter of a million frostbite cases over 14,000 of which required amputations. On top of frostbite, cases of pneumonia, influenza, and trenchfoot were rampant among the soldiers.[305]

When faced with these unexpected conditions, the Germans found that they were ill equipped in terms of weaponry, transport, and basic supplies. For instance, horses brought from Western Europe were killed by the extreme temperatures. German tanks got stuck in snow due to their "narrow tracks and limited ground clearance."[306] The mechanisms in their rifles froze and cracked.

During one encounter, the Germans found that only one out of five tanks was able to fire. In another incident, the Germans were attacked by Soviets in the middle of the night and found that their machine guns were frozen, and could not return fire. Land mines were inefficient when covered by crushed snow or a crust of ice. Lastly, the motors in vehicles were damaged and ruined.

Having relied on his own, uninformed intuitions, Hitler was blindsided by the harsh reality of Russian winter. His troops were ill prepared for what they found and were therefore defeated. Not only did the Germans lose, but they were wasteful with human lives. Hitler began with the assumption that war would not take long enough to stretch into winter months. He was so sure of an expedient victory that he failed to use foresight, despite the warnings from his generals. His wrong assumption resulted in unpreparedness at the onset of winter, leaving his soldiers ill-suited to the harsh environment.

The parallel to issue management is clear. Acting on assumptions or with a lack of accurate knowledge will very likely be counter productive or even disastrous. If one were to enter a community unprepared, without basic information on social, political and economic demographics, major local issues, local civic and elected leaders, and so on, then being on the ground could easily prove fruitless. The same holds true in business, as success in a new market deals largely on previous study and preparation through observation and interaction with a target audience.

## Corporate Success Involves Politics on the Ground

In the business arena, entrepreneurs know well the importance of playing politics on the ground, especially when it means the difference between success and failure in a new frontier. Here are two examples of how a business based in the United States attempted to expand to an intercontinental market. One company did not follow the politics on the ground strategy and was therefore unsuccessful while the other paid close attention to the cultural terrain of the new market and has experienced unprecedented growth.

Of all the brand names closely associated with American culture, Coca-Cola is probably among the most easily recognizable worldwide. In 2005, the company's Annual Report stated that in addition to its namesake Coke—which accounts for 78 percent of the company's total sales in gallons—it offers almost 400 beverage brands in 312 countries or territories and serves 1.5 billion servings of the 50 billion beverage servings consumed each day across the globe. The 2007 Annual Report breaks down worldwide distribution in gallons as 37 percent of sales in the United States, 43 percent in Mexico, Brazil, Japan and China, and 20 percent other countries worldwide. Coke claims that 94 percent of the world population recognizes the Coke/Coca Cola brand.

With a population of more than one billion citizens and an economy with potential for a steady upswing, the Indian subcontinent was an enticing new market, presumably one in which a Coke expansion would be met with steady growth. Based on the numbers, the company decided to embark on the venture in the late 1990's and launched into its new operations by pumping nearly $800 million into the purchase and renovation of local, pre-existing drink manufacturing plants. They also spent exorbitant amounts on advertising and marketing efforts to get the Coke brand out to consumers.

Despite what appeared to be great potential for success, Coke expansion was not successful in India. In fact, in 2000 the company was forced to cut its losses and write off $400 million worth of assets. While Coke is reluctant to say why the India expansion failed, there are several ways to explain why the beverage giant did not meet corporate expectations. Each of these contributing factors may have been avoided had the company practiced politics on the ground.

For instance, Coke overestimated the allure of an American brand and found that the average consumer was unwilling to pay the high cost of a glass of Coke. With an average annual income of 29,069 rupees or about $670 U.S. dollars,[307] drinking a glass of Coke is as lavish as an American buying an expensive glass of champagne. Had Coke spent more time in the market itself, they may have noticed that an average of 56 gallons of carbonated beverages is consumed by Americans each year, making soft drinks a recreational item in the U.S., not a luxury item as it would be considered in India.

Additionally, Coke's marketing strategy proved ineffective, failing to generate enough sales to break even on the expenditure. There is a strong parallel here to issue management in that traditional, mass-media advertising is expensive and often fails to penetrate the targeted audience, as does micro-targeting techniques that penetrate local communities.

Whereas Coke failed to play politics on the ground, another U.S.-based company has done so effectively. The fast food chain Kentucky Fried Chicken (KFC) has been wildly successful in the Chinese market since 1987 when it opened its first mainland store in Beijing. KFC serves more than 2 million Chinese each day and opens more than 250 new restaurants a year with no sign of slowing down.[308] As a percentage of overall revenue, sales in China constitute approximately 15 percent of "Yum! Brands" profits, the parent company for KFC, Pizza Hut, and Taco Bell.[309]

Much of KFC's success is the result of its attempt to cater to the Chinese palate and to remain sensitive to the local culture. This process is easier because the senior employees are residents of China and are constantly in touch with trends and preferences.[310]

Shanghai KFC vice president Ben Koo aptly described the company's politics on the ground strategy: "We live here, we're Chinese. We see what people prefer."[311]

For instance, KFC changed its chicken burgers from white meat to dark meat and has made other changes to match mainland taste preferences, such as eliminating sides like coleslaw and mashed potatoes. Instead, KFC introduced seasonal vegetables (bamboo shoots in spring; lotus roots in summer), rice pudding, and a soup made of spinach, egg and tomato.³¹² The company has also attempted to suit the lifestyles of China's increasing middle class, opening drive-through restaurants and delivery services for those who wish to eat at home or in front of the television.³¹³

By being on the scene, KFC was able to stay in touch with the preferences and lifestyle choices of its target audience and therefore saw a favorable return on its investment. They were successful where Coca-Cola failed, although both companies faced markets with similar potential in terms of large populations and growing economies. In playing politics on the ground, KFC was able to traverse the cultural terrain and implement changes that not only reached the levels of success in the United States but will likely surpass those levels.

Having seen how politics on the ground has led to success in political, military and business arenas, its application to issue management as the driving prefect for a micro-targeting approach can be explored.

**Micro-Targeting a Defined Universe on the Ground**

Political marketing has been a mainstay of local and national politics for hundreds of years, beginning with the first political endorsements that were printed and distributed in newspapers. Having been funded by specific parties, many 19th century newspapers were blatantly partisan, existing not so much as a tool for reporting news but functioning instead as propaganda machines.

As developments in technology enabled uses of different media for political marketing, politicians adapted their strategies to reach new and varied audiences. For instance, private television ownership in the late 1940s and early 1950s resulted in large, captive audiences who watched the World Series, "I Love Lucy," and the Presidential State of the Union Address, alike. The doors were opened for a brand new advertising venue: commercials.

The first commercial broadcast in the United States aired in New York City prior to a Brooklyn Dodgers baseball game in 1941. The Bulova Watch Company paid $9 for the 20-second spot, which showed the image of a Bulova watch superimposed on a United States map with a voiceover saying, "America runs on Bulova time!"

Since 1952, a few unforgettable political ads have made their way into homes across the country. One of the most controversial was that of incumbent President Lyndon B. Johnson, whose "Daisy Girl" television spot during the 1964 Presidential race versus conservative Republican Barry Goldwater of Arizona generated media controversy. The ad depicted a young girl picking petals from a daisy when suddenly a countdown begins and the image changes to that of a mushroom cloud caused by a nuclear explosion.

The ad exploited voter's fear of Goldwater's hawkish attitude toward use of tactical nuclear weapons in Vietnam, an act many feared would lead to nuclear war with the Soviet Union. Johnson won by a landslide in November, 486 to 52 in electoral votes. Goldwater won his home state of Arizona and playing upon the theme of states' rights, carried five Southern states from the former Confederacy: Louisiana, Mississippi, Alabama, Georgia and South Carolina.

Another memorable ad for its viciousness and alleged play upon racist themes occurred during the 1990 Senatorial election in North Carolina between incumbent conservative Senator Jesse Helms and his

African-American political opponent, former Charlotte mayor Harvey Gantt.

Trailing in the last week of the election, the Helms camp produced the "Hands" ad only the weekend before the election, in which a set of white hands crumple up a job rejection while a voiceover says, "You needed that job and you were the best qualified, but they had to give it to a minority because of a racial quota. Is that really fair?"[314]

This ad linked Gantt to support for affirmative action, an inflammatory issue among white, working-class voters.

Alex Castellanos, a native Cuban, Republican media consultant, and creator of the Hands ad, defends the message as based on a true principle of American democracy: "The message in that spot's very clear and that is nobody should get a job, or be denied a job because of the color of their skin," Castellanos said in an interview with PBS in 2001.[315] "The vast majority of Americans believe that. And if it's wrong for us to discriminate that way it's wrong for our government to discriminate that way."[316]

Dr. Kathleen Hall Jamieson, a professor of communication, rhetorical theory and criticism at the University of Pennsylvania, takes issue with the ad in her book, *Dirty Politics: Deception, Distraction and Democracy*. "The first, when you look frame by frame at the ad, there are frames in the ad in which the hands are crushing the head of one of the candidates. And I reproduce those pictures in *Dirty Politics*," Dr. Jamieson said in an interview with PBS.[317] "Secondly, there's a black mark on the paper. And when you ask Castellanos how did it get there, he says, 'I don't know it's just a piece of paper we picked up.' But there are some people in some focus groups who see that as a black hand holding a black gun."[318]

These advertisements, intended to influence a very specific segment of the population by emphasizing an issue negatively, were highly controversial. They are remembered due to their extremity, and they are the exception. While some countries, such as France, have banned political commercials from television, it would be an unusually odd election, indeed, if a United States politician did not engage in some form of mass media marketing over the course of his campaign.

There are two components to political marketing: advertising, which is easily quantifiable; and public opinion, which is difficult to measure.

First, let's examine the costs and efficacy of both traditional advertising and our approach to issues management.

In general, advertising companies use the following scale for selling ad time: 100 points will translate into one view by the average consumer. So, if a company purchases 600 points, they can estimate that an average viewer will see their ad six times. The majority of political ads go unremembered upon the first or even fifth viewing. In fact, an average viewer must see an ad 10 times in order for the message to take root.

The number of viewers a television ad can potentially reach depends on whether the ad is shown on network television or on cable television, as well as on the size of the media market. Media markets are generally identified by the largest city within its bounds, and can potentially reach the number of people comprised within the city's population. For instance, Charlotte, North Carolina, is currently ranked as the 25th largest television market in the nation with 1,085,640 households owning a television set, 984, 400 of which subscribe to cable.

Newspaper ads can be bought by the page, half page, or quarter page and also have a potential market in terms of circulation numbers, that is, those customers who have subscribed to regularly receive that specific paper. In 2004, Charlotte was the 41st largest newspaper market in the nation. The largest daily newspaper in the area, *The Charlotte Observer*, has a daily circulation rate of 226,082 readers and a Sunday only circulation rate of 278,573 readers.

The cost of traditional advertising via mass media is quite high. In 2008, the National Broadcasting Network sold 30-second ad slots for $3 million during the Super Bowl, which attracted a record number of viewers the previous year.[319]

In the 2008 presidential primary season, Democratic candidate Senator Barak Obama spent $70 million, more than any candidate from either party, on more than 100,000 television advertisements by the beginning of May.[320]

Obviously, these are extreme cases. Nonetheless, they are illustrative of the ballooning costs of mass media when, whether in the commercial or political realm, an entity wishes to reach a large audience and has the necessary funds to do so.

A micro-targeting approach that elicits mass involvement by the local community presents a new and better way to reach an audience, relying neither on negativity nor on a costly barrage of ads. In putting feet on the ground and interacting directly with the people and local leaders: religious, political and civic, there is less need to spend exorbitant amounts on television advertisements and other expensive forms of broadside communications and then hope the important messages will reach the intended viewers.

Instead, it is infinitely more effective to relay the intended message face-to-face, getting it across the first time while also making a personal connection with the various micro-targeted audiences. Through time spent in on a municipal, county or district level, issue managers and members of the communications team come closer to feeling the concerns of average citizens and witnessing the effects of an issue or policy decision firsthand.

**Getting boots on the ground is not only more precise than appeals through mass media, but it will be more cost effective. You can send specific messages to specific constituencies, and build up valuable relationships for substantially less than traditional television or newspaper ads.**

While the ultimate objectives of issue management are closely aligned with those using the traditional mass media approach, to reach an audience with a specific message, micro-targeting is more comprehensive than ad blanketing, and therefore, more effective. Often, the most important component of successful relationship building within a community occurs through one process used to play politics on the ground—town hall meetings.

In the process of preparation for town halls, issue management teams reach out to thousands of local citizens, inviting them to attend and become involved in a public concern. Invitees will receive a mailing, a phone call, a personal introduction, or a combination of the three regarding the issues for discussion and the details surrounding the event. Micro-targeting in this manner can guarantee that recipients of the message number more than the hundreds—or possibly thousands—who actually attend the event. Through the preparation and communications for the town hall, an entire community will be touched by the key messages of the event.

These meetings also are invaluable through the potential for free publicity generated by media attendance. By gathering a group of like-minded citizens and leaders under one roof, there is also the potential to influence the discourse on the issues at stake. An examination of these possible outcomes is worth discussion.

**Leaders and Citizens Together in Accordance**

There is something energizing about a congregation of individuals with a passion for the community who share a desire to become better informed about issues affecting the neighborhood in which they live. The energy and enthusiasm is even more spectacular when those gathered are a mix of citizens, decision makers and local leaders—stakeholders on all fronts participating in an open dialogue about positive change.

As Alexis De Tocqueville observed during his American travels,

> In towns it is impossible to prevent men from assembling, getting excited together and forming sudden passionate resolves. Towns are like great meeting houses with all the inhabitants as members. In them the people wield immense influence over their magistrates and often carry their desires into execution without intermediaries.[321]

Because "all politics are local," the face-to-face interaction that occurs at town hall meetings makes it a priceless venue for at least two reasons. First, citizens are able to voice their opinions on a specific issue, which enables local leaders to discover and better understand their constituents' needs. And second, the event supplies an opportunity for the issue management team to develop a relationship with the community and establish a positive presence through educational discussion of pressing local issues.

## Shaping the News and Earning Media

The traditional approach to political marketing incurs significant costs in repeatedly broadcasting an advertisement in the hopes that the message reaches a certain audience or an intended number of people. Regardless of how much money is spent toward that end, the difficulty and success of penetrating the target audience with a complex message is uncertain at best. In most jurisdictions, commercial messages must be clearly identifiable as a paid advertisement and therefore carry an implicit and detectable bias.

The field operation of an issue management program creates media coverage that occurs in a seemingly organic—or more natural—fashion. Local media outlets, looking for an intriguing local story, cannot afford to overlook a well-organized town hall meeting, because it has become a major part of the community's discourse. It is not necessary to buy time from the local media. A meeting that is open to the public and well attended by local residents creates an event worthy of local news coverage. This type of news coverage is called "earned media." That means the greater the interest generated in the event, the greater the media coverage as a result.

Also, when an issue is presented to the public in a completely different manner as a news event rather than paid advertising, it naturally carries more credibility with viewers and listeners. By working with the local media, granting timely interviews and opportunities for follow up stories, the issues team has a much improved chance of having a positive influence in shaping the way a particular issue is portrayed, including even the vocabulary and the tenor of the message.

## Measuring Success in Terms of Public Opinion

The second component of political marketing is public opinion. Unlike advertising, which has set costs and theoretically a set payoff in terms of viewers reached, the individual opinions are much harder to quantify at any point in the marketing effort. It is generally thought that a correlation exists between advertising and opinion in that, if a person views a given message X amount of times then the greater the likelihood that his opinion will be shaped or swayed. However, the number of times a message must be received to effect a change in a viewer's opinion is unknown. Such an outcome may hinge on multiple subjective factors, such as the message itself and its importance to the individual, who may or may not have previous knowledge of, or opinions about, the issue.

Although it is a difficult task to measure changes in public opinion resulting from political marketing, it is not impossible. One scientific way is to analyze media coverage before and after an event. In parsing the content and presentation of the media before a town hall, there is a basis from which to compare post-event media. Telling signs of changed opinion are upbeat modifications in discourse and tenor and casting of the issue in a more positive light than previous advertisements or news stories were able to accomplish. Scientific probing or surveying can also add greater weight to this analysis.

Success may be measured in favorable changes. For instance, has the issue benefited by any changes in diction or buzzwords commonly used by the media and community to refer to the issue? Has the issue management team positively shaped the discourse or altered the tenor of the message?

Another way of measuring change in public opinion is through the number of event attendees or local residents who respond to the issues by volunteering to work on behalf of an issue. If any of these volunteers are also community leaders, then they are referred to as multipliers because they tend to share key message with their civic groups or religious congregations, thereby increasing exponentially the size of the micro-targeted audience.

Overall, experience has shown micro-targeting to be measurably more comprehensive and multifaceted than the traditional broadside communications methods. Picture a triangle (see figure below) divided into three sections. The small triangle at the top includes leaders and elected officials. The middle section is the process. Third, the bottom section is comprised of the voters.

Traditional issue management techniques target the general population with broad, generic messages and hope that the masses will be influenced to commit to a particular issue or candidate. A one-size-fits-all type of message—a shotgun approach—with no specific targeted groups mainly characterizes this technique.

Micro-targeting sees the challenge as a task in figuring out the obstacles to achieving an objective—elect a candidate, pass a bond referendum, obtain favorable legislation—and identifying the specific groups that must be influenced to achieve the objective.

For example, most presidential races come down to a population of voters split along the lines of 45-45 with 10 percent undecided. It is those 10 percent who will decide the election. The job then becomes a matter of finding issues and solutions that appeal to their daily lives and concerns and communicating the candidate's support for them.

This technique is a rifle approach—a single shot fired at a specific target—as opposed to a large, unfocused blast of birdshot. By microtargeting the ultimate decision-making demographic, messages can be delivered in a precise and surgical "audience-centered" fashion. Microtargeting allows campaign managers to skillfully determine the critical universe and a direct field campaign allows for meaningful one-on-one and small group discourse moving beyond a 15-second sound bite or glitzy print advertisement.

This effective technique applies in virtually every decision-making arena in the world. If a piece of legislation is being proposed in a state general assembly, then the process requires that it first go to a committee for recommendation. On the committee level it becomes a matter of determining what it takes to get a favorable recommendation. If there are 18 members of the committee, then at least ten must be in favor of it and no more than eight opposed.

Discovering where each of the legislators stands and how to approach him or her about supporting the bill or changing their vote is where the experienced political knowledge comes in. It requires an in-depth knowledge of public and private politics of the legislators, past actions, personal idiosyncrasies, even to the level of how they like to be approached initially: is it better in person, by phone, e-mail, private meeting, and so on.

Obviously, most businesses and industries do not have the resources to keep such experienced and knowledgeable personnel on staff and turn to lobbyists and consultants in government, policy, and regulatory affairs. When selecting a representative to go to the state capital, the successful firm looks for experience in working in a particular general assembly and evidence of past success.

Successful management of political, business, military, or issue-based campaigns requires a keen awareness and understanding of the terrain, culture, habits and opinions of the impacted or targeted community. From the directives of Sun Tzu to the legendary chronicles of Lewis and Clarke; from the miscalculations of Germany to the successful application of KFC, it is clear that a surgically applied, well informed ground game is a key factor of success in politics, business and government.

> **Case Studies: Namibia and Antarctica**
>
> Politics is best played on the ground is about firsthand observation; palpable sights, sounds, and smells that allow one to fully understand an issue where it arises and, therefore, to speak knowledgably. With this understanding, traveling to a hard-hit or vulnerable location can prove invaluable in weighing the effects of an issue. Only when you have an intimate knowledge of the environment where an issue has spawned or taken root can you make a realistic plan of action.
>
> Of these locations, Namibia, Africa and the continent of Antarctica provide a stark backdrop of an uninhabited land against which the effects of climate change are pronounced and shocking. As the site for sophisticated research teams and equipment, Antarctica is on the forefront of global climate change research.
>
> In December 2005, I led a group of researchers, environmental experts and policy makers to Antarctica to study the effects of global climate change in the polar region. My team saw firsthand evidence of deterioration of the Antarctic ice shelf; specifically the Larsen B ice shelf, which has visibly deteriorated at a fast clip.
>
> Compared to its size in 1995, only 40 percent of the glacier remains. The massive frozen structure has deteriorated to become a churning sea of water and dangerous ice chunks. Telling evidence was the visible melting, silver rivulets of water that we saw run down the glaciers; ominous little signs of impending deterioration due to worsening conditions. Here we also spoke with the researchers who spend month-long stretches in Antarctica actively researching climate

change and monitoring changing air in the Polar Regions.

In October 2006, I led a team of experts on an expedition to Namibia, Africa. Like Antarctica, Namibia contains large natural areas, unadulterated by direct human impact, that make it easy to observe the effects of a changing climate on the environment. In Antarctica we saw for ourselves and heard from scientist and researchers about the extent of global climate change on the environment.

But in Namibia we saw and spoke with people who inhabit and depend upon the land. These residents' perception of global climate change is rooted in how they are affected firsthand and how their fragile ecosystems have suffered as a result of damage by their developed global neighbors.

Disruption of their fragile Sub-Saharan ecosystems will worsen the impending water scarcity crisis and result in disastrous conditions for health due to lack of clean drinking water, intensified and unpredictable weather events and natural disasters as well as increased flooding and breeding of disease-infected insects such as malaria-carrying mosquitoes.

Attempting to manage an issue from afar is very rarely as effective as doing so at the scene. For instance, the politicians in Washington sit within their air-conditioned chambers and attempt to make positive change, but they are ultimately unsuccessful because many do not realize the scope of the problem outside of their own political discourse. They are removed from the issue itself and therefore do not fully understand its effect on people and communities across the globe.

My team prefers to see firsthand how the issues really affect people. We value observation of quantifiable, demonstrable evidence as a means for increasing our scope of understanding and we use the facts to create a comprehensive plan of action that leads to a mutually beneficial solution.

# Maxim 7

## "Document and demonstrate support to build third-party credibility."

*The trouble was, all people saw on television were a few of my outspoken supporters out front; and they came away thinking that was me.*
 — **George McGovern, Former Senator from South Dakota, 1972 Democratic Candidate for President of the United States**

**Overview**

What McGovern realized, unfortunately too late for his failed campaign to beat Richard Nixon in 1972, was that a candidate for office, like any proponent of a campaign, is more often judged not by the merits of their cause, but by the company they keep. An accomplished leader can embrace and leverage this reality to spur the success of a campaign. Or, he can ignore it and it will ultimately contribute to an eventual failure. Maxim 7: "Document and demonstrate support to build third-party credibility: adheres to the former, proposing an active involvement in identifying the right support necessary to accomplish a specific goal, documenting that support, and then taking this support a step further by enlisting those targeted persons or organizations as supporters in the campaign. The active demonstration of third-party support is what will ultimately promote stakeholder engagement that builds a solid front line for a successful issue management campaign.

Edward Bernays, the self-proclaimed father of public relations, perfected a public relations technique that modern practitioners call the "third-party technique." Merrell Rose, executive vice president of public relations firm Porter/Novelli succinctly describes the technique as "Putting your words in someone else's mouth."[322]

The technique is little more than a more sophisticated form of propaganda. Sheldon Rampton and John Stauber authors of an essay about corporate propaganda and the environmental movement identify four advantages to this technique: acts as camouflage to hide the "profit-driven, self-interest behind a corporate message; encourages conformity to a corporate agenda while feigning independence; weds a corporate agenda to a popular, progressive cause, such as the environment; it drives out factual discourse and replaces it with emotional imagery."[323]

Rampton and Stauber also point out in their essay that corporations and others have discovered the value in hiring so called "experts" to serve as third-party advocates for whatever cause they are sponsoring. There is actually good scientific data to support why this works. A survey by Porter/Novelli found that 89 percent of the survey respondents indicated that "independent experts" were considered a "very or somewhat believable" source of information during a corporate crisis. [324]

My 10 maxims are built upon standards of honest and integrity. Therefore, finding "experts" in pseudo-science or a research organization that happens to spin facts any way you like it not advised. The corporation will be caught. Too many people now wonder about the source of information and can trace tainted research back to the source.

For example, the prestigious *New England Journal of Medicine* has experienced some compromising and embarrassing situations in research findings supported by private interests. In 1986 *The Journal* published the results of one study supporting the use of the antibiotic amoxicillin and rejecting a second study critical of the medication. The two studies were based on the same data, but the scientists involved in the research favorable to the antibiotic received $1.6 million in grants from the drug manufacturer. The scientist who was critical of the drug had rejected funding. Five years later the Journal published the second paper and large-scale testing in children concluded that those who took amoxicillin recovered at a slower rate than those who took no antibiotics at all. [325]

Here is where an earlier maxim becomes important: A political or issue campaign must not only assume the moral high ground but build the campaign upon it. In the next maxim it will become obvious that absolutely factual information—without spin or placement in a phony expert's mouth—is absolutely persuasive and thus, effective. By having a third-party assist you in establishing both, you will have achieved a very strong position, indeed.

# Chapter 7 Synopsis

- Third-party endorsements are significantly more effective and credible than self-endorsement.
- Endorsements from leaders and opinion makers are also an advantage in issue or political management.
- The availability of research data instantly from the Internet requires that those who deliver endorsements be legitimate and above board.
- Opponents who are made stakeholders in an issue through inclusion in the process make highly credible supporters.
- Document support through letters and resolutions by governing bodies and officials as well as various media reports.

**What is third-party credibility?: Aristotle's view**

Just as Socrates exhorted his students employing the Socratic method of inquiry, "Define your terms," a momentary review of the meaning of third-party credibility is in order here. In issue management the speaker's ability to persuade lies in the third-party groups he arranges around him. Third-party credibility is not self-determined like reputation, it is formed by third-party individuals or groups. Self-affirmed facts that emphasize the importance of an issue are inconsequential when presented alone to the public or a decision maker. To persuade these audiences a campaign must have the support from third-party groups. Third-party supporters able to build a credible reputation for a campaign can push the pressure points of decision makers and others and are frequently the most powerful agents of persuasion.

In his treatise *Rhetoric*, Aristotle philosophizes on a speaker's power to persuade. He emphasizes that exact knowledge will not necessarily promote conviction. Conviction, he says, emanates from a speaker's persuasive ability.[326] As we discussed in chapter 3, Aristotle provided three artistic proofs used in rhetoric to engage or persuade an audience: *logos, pathos,* and *ethos* or logical, emotional, and character or credibility driven persuasion.

Aristotle focused on *ethos* as the most effective means for persuasion. He contended that a speaker must exhibit three components of *ethos*—knowledge, goodwill, and virtue—to ascertain credibility. If a speaker demonstrates these components he has an *ethos* that is powerfully persuasive to his audience, according to Aristotle.

James A. Herrick provides an interpretation of Aristotle's *ethos* that affirms its connection to issue management. Herrick defines it as: "the persuasive potential of the speaker's character or credibility."[327] In issue management, a campaign strives to develop an *ethos* to persuade its audience of its credibility by using reputable third-party supporters to fuel this persuasion. When relating Aristotle's philosophy to issue management, the speaker becomes the third-party support and the audience becomes the micro-targeted stakeholders of a campaign. The key to gaining credibility for a campaign relies on identifying the third-party speakers who will construct an *ethos* for the campaign and are consequently powerfully persuasive when attempting to influence decision makers into action. In issue management, it is important that the good words of credible third parties are developed to a stronger and greater level of development to establish the goodwill and virtue that is at the heart of Aristotle's *ethos*.

Ultimately, the end-goal for a campaign is about persuasion. It involves convincing and stimulating an audience—including all stakeholders, such as the public and legislators—to act in support of a particular issue. If persuasion is the ultimate goal, then third-party endorsements, assembled from third-party supporters that add affirmation to a campaign's credibility, is the ammunition a campaign uses to influence an audience. This philosophy can be demonstrated in both modern political, public issues, and business campaigns.

Business and political leaders should first understand the importance of using third-parties to reinforce the validity of an issues campaign. The third parties utilized by these campaigns should consist of objective supporters who bring their own credibility through their unqualified endorsements. Their credibility, hopefully, has been established through their own personal and professional history of past actions that have gained approval and support.

Third-party credibility consists of two primary components: trustworthiness and expertise. The degree to which a public figure or subject matter authority is trustworthy boils down to the degree to which an individual is believable. This fact relies heavily upon the degree of objectivity brought to bear on an issue. The very objective nature of third-party support increases believability more than any self-endorsement or hearty endorsement by a person harboring his own selfish interests. Not only is such third-party believability necessary to increase objective support, it will also assist in creating a winning position because it constructs a campaign permeated by a diverse group of stakeholders.

A self-endorsement, on the other hand, does not involve multifarious groups in a campaign. It does not gather support by including all stakeholders, which may soon open the door to resentment and opposition. Qualified, objective third-parties not only make campaigns more trustworthy, they also augment their endorsements by a significant amount of expertise.

For example, if an automobile salesman touts the economy of a vehicle he is attempting to sell by guaranteeing the car will achieve an average miles per gallon of 35 on the highway, then it is incumbent upon the salesman to document his claims. An obvious way to do this is by producing evidence from an expert source, such as a test lab, that proves his sales point. Without this expert support, he is merely a salesman, and a cautious shopper will be worried that the statement may not be accurate because the salesman is driven by his desire to make a sale. In issue management the trustworthiness and expertise of disinterested, third-party supporters elevate a campaign beyond mere rhetoric to an informed, educated level that addresses the multi-facets of a complex issue. A campaign is more apt to persuade its audience if proposals and supporting arguments go beyond a sales effort, but also incorporate objective—possibly even scientific-based—information and opinions.

Another elementary example of the power of endorsement is in the job applications process. Here is an area in which endorsement from a well-known, respected source can quickly establish a candidate's qualifications for a particular position. Obviously the goal of the job-candidate is to convince a potential employer that she is trustworthy and has an appropriate level of expertise in the required areas. A job applicant's independent claims mean little unless her success in previous jobs can be documented.

The applicant can quickly establish credibility by supplying a list of contacts who can vouch for the applicant's trustworthiness and affirm her positive qualities or accomplishments. Oftentimes a lack of supporting references or some other documentation results in the candidate's elimination from further consideration. Prior work experience or statements from previous employers and associates provide the third-party support necessary for securing gainful employment. Anyone is capable of self-endorsement. The all-important third-party endorsement persuades and convinces.

In a more public forum, an issue management campaign that utilizes support from credible third-parties can properly define their reputation in the public eye, amalgamating all supporters of the campaign and creating an image for the campaign that is powerfully persuasive. In the early stages of an issue management campaign, supporters who can add positive reinforcement to the goals and objectives of a campaign can be more influential that the campaign's policies or actions can. In the initial stages, the campaign may not have had enough time to demonstrate its merits. Thus the third-party supporters can become the face of the cause, giving the campaign familiarity and favorability and eliciting additional support from stakeholders who trust the source of endorsement.

The face of the campaign can come in many diverse forms. For example, endorsement can come from a well-known spokesperson, such as Michael Jordan for Nike. Or, credibility can come from an endorsement from a respected professional group, such as the American Dental Association's endorsement of Crest toothpaste. In an even more powerful example, the American Association of Retired Persons (AARP), made up of 35 million members, can make a significant electoral impact through an endorsement of a presidential candidate. All of the above have the potential to put a face or a name onto a campaign and consequently lend trustworthiness and/or expertise.

However, a campaign need not use a single third party as the face for its campaign—multiple supporters add layers of credibility. The ultimate goal when documenting and demonstrating support is to build a large stakeholder base for the campaign, ultimately amassing so much support from an influential audience that the campaign can influence public perception and affect the choices of decision makers.

## The Components of Building Third-Party Credibility

It is not enough to gain endorsements without the ability to demonstrate and document that support. Three primary steps must be followed to succeed in building credibility: encourage third-party supporters to demonstrate their support, which is then well-documented for the issues campaign. By establishing a base of identified supporters a campaign will have the ammunition to build its credibility with the demonstrated and documented endorsement of a credible third-party source.

The first component a campaign must consider is identifying the appropriate third-party support. Using past political, military, and business examples it has been shown that credible, third-party supporters should genuinely be independent third-parties. They should have no vested interests, such as recipient of research funding or stand to profit financially by putting their stamp of approval on an issue. They should be opinion makers, and if possible, they should consist of not only supporters but also potential adversaries who are brought into the project as stakeholders.

These components ensure that third-party support is honest and legitimate to the point that it will persuade stakeholders and decision makers that they or their constituents have a mutual interest in the campaign's successful outcome. To identify potential third-party supporters with these attributes requires an investigative effort among the mass audience of stakeholders who connect on a familiar level with the community. Once an issue management campaign has completed its investigation among the mass number of stakeholders, the issue manager must complete the process of documenting and demonstrating the newly developed support.

It is essential that the objective, third-party source demonstrate their support for the issue the campaign is advocating. Demonstrating support ensures that the credibility of third-party supporters will extend to the campaign. This usually requires creating an environment in which all stakeholders are engaged in mutually beneficial interactions. Such a mutual partnership enables a campaign to gain from the credibility of its involved, enthusiastic participants.

If the campaign requires re-shaping the opinions of decision makers, then demonstrated and documented support is a powerful tool in making up the minds of decision makers, such as state legislators or county and municipal government. By building third-party support in the early stages of the project, an issue manager is able to prevent future roadblocks because those who could create opposition are part of the solution.

## Identifying the Appropriate Third-Party Supporters

The most important component of third-party credibility is the source of support. This is crucial because the campaign builds its reputation on visible endorsements and support. If persuasion is fueled by credibility as Aristotle proposed, then an issue management campaign must provide its utmost focus on building the required credibility. A blunder or oversight when deciding the source of third-party support can derogate a campaign's credibility. Conversely, a meticulous formation of supporters can build seamless and convincing credibility that lasts for the duration of the campaign.

## The Best Witness Is a Credible Witness

To understand the process for creating effective third-party credibility and support, it may be useful to view the process juxtaposed against a lawyer's use of evidence in the courtroom. Essentially an issue manager is similar to a prosecutor, for example a district attorney, acting on behalf of the state, amassing evidence to sway the opinion of an objective twelve-member jury. The American legal system has at its core the intricate and standardized process for gathering evidence and presenting it in a judicially approved fashion to build credibility in the prosecution's case against a defendant or group of defendants. . In the courtroom, all evidence is subject to challenge. A judge will not allow evidence that our legal system has determined over time tends to be unfair or unnecessarily prejudicial to a defendant's case. Therefore a jury of the defendant's peers considers only evidence that is as relevant as possible to a determination of guilt or innocence.

By the time the jury retires to deliberate on the evidence, they take with them two narratives that have been argued by both sides as to the credibility of the evidence and how the evidence should be viewed in relation to the charges against the defendant. For example, a set of facts may be presented to the jury as proof of a defendant's anger and desire to inflict revenge. The defendant's testimony may indicate, however, that the victim in the case attacked the defendant without just provocation and that the victim was injured by the defendant acting in lawful self-defense.

Resolving the story painted by the evidence in dispute is a task for the jury. Twelve men and women who have heard the evidence in the case must decide what is true and what is false and render their verdict as instructed by the presiding courtroom judge.

Most modern, civilized societies recognize the importance of legal representation in a courtroom matter. The role of the lawyer centers on meticulously amassing enough evidence to make a self-made plea from his client unnecessary. Eighteenth century English writer and essayist, Samuel Johnson, reflected on a lawyer's ability to give credibility to a client's case:

> As it rarely happens that a man is fit to plead his own cause, lawyers are a class of the community, who, by study and experience, have acquired the art and power of arranging evidence, and of applying to the points at issue what the law has settled. A lawyer is to do for his client all that his client might fairly do for himself, if he could."[328]

Johnson's reference to a lawyer's "art and power of arranging evidence" gained from "study and experience" relates directly to issue management. An issue management expert has a similar type of skilled art and power to arrange third-party information in such as way that it gains favorable opinion from all stakeholders. Just as a skilled lawyer can arrange evidence to persuade a judge and/or jury in his client's favor, an issue manager takes a similar approach in gaining the necessary approvals for an issue campaign to succeed.

Johnson's next claim that a lawyer's arranging of evidence does for his client what he is unable to do himself can also be related to issue management. An issue manager of sufficient skill and experience is able to gather third-party support to build the credibility that self-endorsements are wholly lacking. Whether the task is persuading a jury of peers in the courtroom, a decision maker in a state legislature, or voters in an electoral district, all three situations require an expert in communications who is able to shape viewpoints and bring decision makers over to his line of thinking.

**Third-Party Means Just That—Third Party**

Every issue manager must recognize the fact that credible endorsement cannot emanate from the people who have the most to gain. That type of endorsement is viewed as self-serving and may actually damage credibility. A primary stakeholder is a person that is directly involved with the workings of an issue campaign or candidacy. They are required by their direct involvement to support the initiative. This bias severely neutralizes the believability that could potentially be gained from their endorsements. However, secondary stakeholders view a campaign from an autonomous position before deciding if it deserves their endorsement. This independence ensures the honorability of their voluntarily obtained approval.

The danger of self endorsements was acknowledged in written form by one of our country's founding fathers, Benjamin Franklin. Franklin perceived the danger of self-endorsements when creating "The Library Company of Philadelphia" in 1731. In his *Autobiography* he rebuffed the idea of self-endorsing his library project, stating that proposing a project yourself would be seen as an effort to raise yourself above your neighbor and would face objections.

His alternative method of endorsement was to market his library project as a "scheme of friends."[329] Franklin believed that these third-party supporters would effectively promote his project. He recognized that to build credibility for his project he must remain outside the sphere of support. To do this, Franklin appealed to his intellectual group called the "junto" for support of the subscriptions to his library. This "scheme of friends" successfully promoted the project and consequently Franklin formed the first public lending library in the United States of America.

Franklin employed his group of third-party supporters to convince people to take action by subscribing to the library. Franklin declared he had "sacrifice[d] his vanity" in order to accomplish his library campaign's end goal. An issue management campaign must assiduously avoid using primary stakeholders to endorse their platform and sacrifice their own vanity. Franklin's "scheme of friends" takes the form of the third-party supporters in an issue management campaign. Franklin's insistence on third-party support highlights, very early in America's history, that third-party support builds persuasive credibility.

**Franklin recognized that his fledgling library venture would have more success if others spoke on his behalf, rather than relying on self-promotion to convince new people to use the service.**

The 1988 Vice Presidential debates between Republican Dan Quayle and Democrat Lloyd Bentsen provide a more recent example of the adverse effects of a vain self-endorsement. In an October 5, 1988 debate, Quayle was posed a question regarding "what qualifications [he] had to be President" in the event of an emergency.[330] Quayle chose to affirm his experience with an analogy: "I have far more experience than many others that sought the office of vice president of this country. I have as much experience in the Congress as Jack Kennedy did when he sought the presidency."[331]

Quayle's analogy was pure conjecture and Lloyd Bentsen ripped it bare in his response: "Senator, I served with Jack Kennedy, I knew Jack Kennedy, Jack Kennedy was a friend of mine. Senator, you are no Jack Kennedy."[332] Lloyd Bentsen made use of his credible relationship with Kennedy to discredit Quayle's analogy. The point Quayle was trying to interject into the debate was a good one. The 41-year-old Senator from Indiana had to address the anxiety over his age and experience in a debate with the seasoned Bentsen, a 67-year-old three-term Senator from Texas.

But the self-endorsement Quayle maneuvered to prove this point was a mistake, inciting a series of taunting campaign ads by the Democrats. Ironically, the analogy emphasized Bentsen's reputation for having the superior political experience instead of affirming Quayle's political wherewithal. Quayle appeared too vain when making the analogy to JFK and consequently lost significant credibility. In issue management a campaign must be careful not to analogize itself without proper documentation.

Looking at Quayle's blunder and Franklin's success, we can determine that a campaign must utilize credible third-parties instead of self-endorsements to build credibility among the decision makers. A documented endorsement from an independent third-party cannot be subject to the same criticisms and objections as a conceited self-endorsement. An issue management expert recognizes the need to emphasize third party endorsements over self-endorsements.

**Interdependent Support from Independent Third-Parties**

The credible third-party source a campaign utilizes must initially be independent from the campaign itself. However, no stakeholder can ever be completely independent from a campaign. The fact that they are giving their support establishes interdependency. Attracting independent third-parties to support a campaign will promote an interdependent campaign process. Such a process will give a diverse range of groups a stake in the outcome of the issue campaign and added strength to see it through.

In the contemporary business environment, independent third parties are not only beneficial, they are necessary to ensure credibility and transparency. Following the Enron accounting scandal in 2001, the Sarbanes Oxley Act was created in an effort to restore investor confidence in the financial practice and governance of corporations.[333] Section 301 of Sarbanes requires the formation of an "independent and competent" audit committee that hires, sets compensation and supervises the auditor's activities in a company. The formation of this committee increased the transparency of the auditing process by creating an "independent" committee member who was not part of the management team and did not perform any other services for the firm.[334] Although the committee member is originally "independent," they are required to be board members, ensuring their involvement in the company. By hiring an independent third-party audit committee and then giving members a voice in the company, the Sarbanes Oxley Act upholds the credibility of the auditing process. Sarbanes redefines the standards for participation from independent third parties in business accounting and ensures corporate social responsibility in the auditing process.

Sarbanes incorporated independent third-parties into a committee that worked in an interdependent relationship with the community. In issue management, a similar interdependent relationship is necessary between the campaign and its independent third-party supporters. An issue management campaign that involves independent third-party supporters in their effort helps mold a transparent and credible reputation. Having the credibility of these independent stakeholders will give a campaign advantages in proposing legislative action supporting their issue.

Not only is it beneficial for a campaign to include independent third parties when building credibility, it is also the right thing to do. Promoting inclusiveness of third parties expands the scope of the campaign. The increased stakeholder engagement ensures that the campaign's goals are mutually beneficial for all parties. A mutually developed goal has a better chance of being achieved, and it keeps the company in touch with the wants and needs of the community. To achieve such a mutually beneficial goal a campaign must devote attention to the broad range of stakeholders in their audience, supporters and detractors both included.

**Supporters or Detractors Welcome**

The more credibility third parties bring to a campaign, the better chance of success for the initiative in question. Third-party support can range from the most faithful and fitting supporters to the most vehement detractors of a campaign, if an issues manager is able to bring them on board. No matter whether it is a supporter or detractor, campaigns must involve third-party stakeholders in the campaign process, allow them a venue to voice their concerns, and encourage them to feel ownership in the campaign. The campaign, in turn, must incorporate into proposed solutions their viewpoints and concerns. A campaign that manages third-party support as described will have a greatly enhanced chance of success.

When identifying possible third-party support a campaign should begin its search among those groups who will provide expert opinions that have the power to influence decision makers. If the focus is on environmental issues because of the emerging trend of "going green," the support of some credible environmental groups, environmentalists, and politicians who support the environment are necessary. The support and engagement of these groups—leaders in environmentalist opinion-making—will help provide the relevant facts and data to elicit stakeholder buy in. Establishing these facts as a foundation for action attracts ongoing stakeholder support in the future. Once a campaign has secured the backing of qualified, widely recognized experts, communications and public awareness building in the host community become greatly simplified.

Establishing expert support for a campaign is also an effective method to attract those third-parties that would normally oppose efforts for change, even when change means progress. Convincing a stakeholder, whose past record indicates they will oppose your efforts, to endorse the issue management team's objectives requires delicate handling but pays great dividends if successful. Richard Nixon's support of the campaign to open negotiations and trade with Communist China provides an example of an endorsement from such an unlikely source. Nixon was the "last person" Americans expected to endorse diplomatic discussions with Mao Zedong and the People's Republic of China.[335] In his 1960 presidential campaign Nixon affirmed that "until the Chinese Communist Government changes its policies, until it in effect cleanses itself of its present deficiencies, we could under no circumstances agree to its admission to the U.N."[336]

The tough stance Nixon took in his campaign regarding China established the reputation that Nixon was a hardliner against China and Communism. So many were surprised when Nixon announced his intended diplomatic trip to China in July 1971. But the nation's shock was not negative. Because of Nixon's previous hard-nosed policy toward China, Americans generally believed it must be a good thing if Richard Nixon was in favor of it. Nixon was probably the only man credible enough to speak with Mao's Communist government without accusations that he was un-American or becoming "soft" on Communism.[337]

Nixon's support of diplomatic relations with China exemplifies the power that comes from an endorsement by an unlikely source. Adversary support not only establishes a larger third-party support group for an issue campaign, it will help mitigate or even prevent opposition to accepting a previously unpopular issue.

## Adversary Support: Inclusiveness and Involvement

Synthesizing and integrating the support of diverse groups leads to successful campaigns that focus on mutually beneficial goals. The easiest way to promote diversity is to bring an opponent into the fold. Recruiting a critic that will address the objections of the opposing side supplies a campaign the opportunity to work toward a negotiated solution that incorporates multiple needs.

In *Getting to Yes: Negotiating Agreement Without Giving In*, author Roger Fisher advocates the need to incorporate all parties when dealing with a controversial issue. Like Aristotle in *Rhetoric,* his book teaches lessons on how to persuade and compromise to reach a solution. Fisher emphasizes that a speaker must go beyond the provision of facts to develop relationships with those who require a degree of persuasion to reach a different viewpoint. Fisher reveals one of his guidelines for persuasion when he affirms to his reader:

> If you want the other side to accept a disagreeable conclusion, it is crucial that you involve them in the process of reaching that conclusion. In South Africa, white moderates were trying at one point to abolish the discriminatory pass laws. How? By meeting in an all-white parliamentary committee to discuss proposals. Yet, however meritorious those proposals might prove, they would be insufficient, not necessarily because of their substance, but because they would be the product of a process in which no blacks were included.

The involvement of opposition in the process will prevent opponents from completely disregarding a proposal on the table. Fisher's argument affirms that allowing potential adversaries to feel they have a role in the development of a campaign will prevent the malice and resentment that forms when opponents are left out.

The best way to defeat an enemy is to make friends out of them, which was the philosophy 16th U.S. President Abraham Lincoln seemed to practice in his political dealings. Lincoln discovered that to make a friend of an enemy, the adversary must first be brought as close or even closer than ardent supports are allowed. Enemies at a distance remain enemies.

Lack of contact and communication mean there are no opportunities to change opposing opinions or viewpoints. Lincoln's presidency provides the ultimate example for properly engaging adversaries to build third-party credibility. Lincoln's inclusion of a broad base of both supporters and detractors in his 1860 Presidential cabinet allowed him to successfully resolve political differences within the Union during the American Civil War.

The propensity for inclusion that Lincoln maintained in relationships with his administrations cabinet members has a voice in his 1842 address on temperance when he stated "When the conduct of men is designed to be influenced, persuasion, kind, unassuming persuasion, should ever be adopted."[338]

The speech goes further to assert that a person should form a sincere relationship to achieve persuasion, stating that if one attempts to command and control the stakeholders' judgment, this group will close all avenues of influence regardless of the cause.[339] In her book *Team of Rivals*, American Pulitzer Prize winning author and presidential historian Doris Kearns Goodwin reveals how this philosophy materializes in the formation of Lincoln's cabinet. She says that Lincoln formed a sincere relationship with his most ardent political adversaries and as a result was able to persuade them to support his presidential policies. After investigating the tactics Lincoln employed when building his cabinet as Goodwin did, it is obvious that Lincoln's inclusiveness propelled his success. Lincoln provides the successful model for invoking third-party support.

In her book, Goodwin describes how Lincoln attempted to unite former Whig sympathizers, Republicans, and anti-slavery Democrats into a united coalition within in his cabinet. She emphasizes that Lincoln targeted opponents in the Republican Party to create his cabinet instead of forming a cabinet of strictly Republican supporters. This philosophy is evident in his bold action to appoint one of his adversaries William H. Seward, Secretary of State (Whig); another, Salmon P. Chase, Treasury Secretary (Antislavery Democrat), and Edward Bates, Attorney General (Whig). By forming an all and inclusive cabinet that promoted involvement from all members, Lincoln avoided retribution from the differing factions of both parties.

Furthermore, Lincoln demanded that his rival factions work together toward a mutually beneficial eradication of slavery and protection of the

Union. The most important aspect of Lincoln's presidency was not that he merely gave his adversaries a role in government, but that he also drew upon their leadership and experience and involved them in running the country. [340] The best example Goodwin provides for this inclusiveness is Lincoln's call on Seward to revise his inaugural address regarding North-South relations in the tumultuous beginning of his presidency.

**Lincoln was aware that the key opinion makers and leaders for his political opposition had valuable skills and contacts that could be turned to his advantage if he could find a way to reach a position of mutual accommodation with them.**

As Goodwin appropriately describes, Lincoln's March 1860 Inaugural Address had to be meticulously crafted because it came at a pivotal time for North-South relations.[341] The speech could have rendered useless the previous efforts to hold the succession movement at bay if not worded properly towards the South.

As Goodwin relates to the reader, Lincoln not only entrusted Seward with editing his address, but he also took heed of the majority of the Secretary of State's suggestions.[342] Lincoln also took from his adversaries' conciliatory tone toward the South and coupled this with his Republican patriotism to construct an inaugural address that would bide time for the Union to mobilize and prevent immediate secession by the Southern states.[343] Seward's influence on the speech can be seen in its conclusion. Seward prompted a change from the original wording of: "With *you*, and not with *me*, is the solemn question of 'Shall it be peace, or a sword.'"[344] Seward suggested an ending that departed from this firm and patriotic tone:

> We are not we must not be aliens or enemies but fellow countrymen and brethren. Although passion has strained our bonds of affection too hardly they must not,

> I am sure they will not be broken. The mystic chords which proceeding from so many battle fields and so many patriot graves pass through all the hearts and all the hearths in this broad continent of ours will yet again harmonize in their ancient music when breathed upon by the guardian angel of the nation.[345]

Lincoln coupled the conciliatory tone of Seward's suggestion with his patriotism, leading to the renowned ending:

> We are not enemies, but friends. We must not be enemies. Though passion may have strained, it must not break our bonds of affection. The mystic chords of memory, stretching from every battlefield, and patriot grave, to every living heart and hearthstone, all over this broad land, will yet swell the chorus of the Union, when again touched, as surely they will be, by the better angels of our nature.[346]

The "mystic chords of memory" and "angel" references are the most apparent correlations among the two endings. These similarities demonstrate that Lincoln listened to and incorporated Seward's suggestions. As Doris Kearns Goodwin states, Lincoln was able to compose an inaugural address that was forceful yet conciliatory at the same time because of Seward's influence.[347]

Lincoln did not place Seward in his cabinet as a mere figurehead or symbol of alliance. Lincoln included Seward in the process of running the country. The result was the successful leadership and administration of the Union states.

Lincoln's inclusive techniques for building relationships and involving adversary support are a model for issue management campaigns. Lincoln galvanized his supporters behind a campaign to protect the Union and ignored those differences among Republicans, Whigs, and Antislavery Democrats that had polarized the groups previously. He not only brought his adversaries in to provide the façade of a united front, he involved each of these enemies to work together to protect the Union.

Issue management campaigns must borrow from Lincoln's leadership techniques and amalgamate influential third-parties into campaign processes that ensure success. By synthesizing a diverse range of groups in the community to support a specific issue campaign, the issue manager is able to gain the support of influential third-parties. Although incorporating and involving adversaries in a campaign is important, it will provide limited credibility if these endorsers are not influential opinion makers.

**Third-Parties Must Be Opinion Makers**

The unifying characteristic of third-party support is the power to define and shape public opinion. Whether it is a subject matter expert, political or community leader, or a person with charisma and celebrity status, the third-party supporter must have the capability to garner support for the campaign or project. Not attracting the support of the opinion makers can promote assumptions that these groups or individuals—by their silence or non-involvement—do not actually the cause.

For example, a bike ride to support a cure for cancer promoted at a national level might draw questions regarding the legitimacy of the effort if Lance Armstrong (American record-breaking seven-time Tour de France bicycle race winner and cancer survivor) had failed to provide his endorsement. Similarly, a campaign that deals with educational issues will do better if it gains the support of the local superintendent and school board. Identifying and attracting the support of opinion makers will allow a campaign to stimulate broad community support. Decision makers are the ultimate source of third-party support because they have the ability to execute actions on behalf of a campaign. The difference between an opinion maker and a decision maker is the order in which they fall in the mass citizen involvement process.

On a local level, decision makers may be town councilmen, mayors, or county officials. At the state level they include the governor, state representatives and state senators making up the state legislature, and agency heads. At the highest level, they include members of the U.S. House of Representatives and Senate. As you move up the ladder of government, decision makers also become opinion makers that give a campaign the endorsements to approach those at the next rung of the governmental ladder. Opinion makers also include those members of the community that have no government office, but organize, lead, and speak for groups of constituents in these communities.

While opinion makers influence public sentiment, decision makers control government action. For example, U.S. Congressmen have the ability to pass federal legislation and make national policy on issues such as the environment.

## Using Experts to Attract Opinion Maker Support

When a campaign strives to convince public opinion makers in the community to support a specific issue, the campaign must be able to provide credible facts affirmed by experts regarding the issue at hand. The established credibility of an expert supporter gives the campaign the ability to convince opinion makers to get behind an issue. For instance, a statement from a leading biologist stating that a business development will not adversely affect the environment in the community will help convince opinion makers and stakeholders alike that the development does not adversely affect the neighborhoods.

The disparity of information between the expert and a public audience gives the expert the power to influence public opinion. An individual, generally, is discouraged from objecting to what the expert recommends. A member of the community in question may believe that the expert's advice is made in their best interest because of the expert's credibility and objectivity as a scientist. For example, if a dentist informs a patient he needs a root canal, it is not likely that the patient will disagree, especially in the presence of throbbing, unmitigated tooth pain. As an expert in oral health, the dentist's opinion is likely to carry significant weight and credibility. The ability for expert opinion to control public opinion illustrates that an issue management campaign should use facts supplied by legitimate experts to enhance credibility. As mentioned earlier in this chapter, it is counterproductive, however, to use unreliable data as a source of support.

## Stimulating Broad-Based Community Support through Third-Party Opinion Makers

The first step in encouraging action from decision makers is establishing credibility among the decision makers constituent base in the community. Third-party opinion makers in the community can provide a campaign with the powerful stakeholder support it needs to pressure decision makers.

The opinion making power of experts can and should be utilized in issue management campaigns to attract opinion makers to the cause. However, a campaign cannot go to an influential legislator or committee chairman with only expert support. The issue manager must bring forward third-party supporters with opinion making power and leadership capabilities. Having opinion-making power over an audience is the most important component for a third-party supporter. Opinion makers can be experts, leaders of non-governmental organizations like the local Rotary Club or other interest groups, newspapers, editorialists, news stations, newscasters, and religious groups and leaders. The power of these individuals or groups lies in their general hold over an established audience. A campaign must use the support of these third-party opinion makers to help convince the appropriate audience to become engaged even to the point of being active in the campaign.

**The Ability to Influence Decision Makers**

An example of such an opinion maker whose hold over an audience can influence a decision maker is the famed CBS Evening News Anchor Walter Cronkite. President Lyndon B. Johnson's response to Cronkite's statements that the Vietnam War was "a stalemate"[348] emphasizes Cronkite's convincing power. Johnson recognized that Americans trusted Cronkite's claims more than his and that the war effort could not succeed with Cronkite negatively influencing public opinion on the Vietnam War, stating: "If I've lost Cronkite, I've lost America."[349] Cronkite had garnered broad stakeholder support and this support gave his claims credibility.

Walter Cronkite is a contemporary model for Aristotle's persuasive speaker. Cronkite exemplifies the knowledge, goodwill, and credibility that comprise Aristotle's *ethos* in his promise to deliver Americans the news of monumental events in American history with the intent to be "fast, accurate, and unbiased."[350] His accuracy established his knowledge; his impartiality caused Americans to believe he had their goodwill in mind; and the perception that he provided unbiased reporting achieved a virtuous balance between a mere provision of facts and the manipulation of them seen in the media today. The consistent documentation and demonstration of this knowledge, goodwill, and virtue built Walter Cronkite's third-party credibility, or *ethos*. In 2006, Cronkite was still seen as the most credible man in America.[351] Cronkite amassed the support of an entire nation, thus giving him credibility that remains to this day. Cronkite remains the model for a public opinion maker.

**Third-Parties Must Go Beyond Familiarity to Favorability**

The familiarity of Cronkite among the American people contributed to his credibility, but his favorability among this broad audience is what gave him his opinion-making power. To identify the appropriate opinion makers in a community a campaign must find out what is familiar as well as favorable to their targeted audience. An endorsement from third-parties familiar to target audiences provides identifiable support that assists in the management and direction of a campaign. However, garnering supernumerary supporters based on familiarity among an audience has little effect on credibility if these supporters are not viewed in a favorable light as well as familiar.

Many American broadcast networks use a measurement tool called a Q-score to measure qualities of familiarity and favorability. The aforementioned Steven Levitt headlines the company Marketing Evaluations/TVQ Inc. that releases the Q-scores of performers twice a year. The Q-score measures the appeal of various people or things including celebrities, actors, athletes, broadcast programs, and brand and company names. Tom Hanks and Bill Cosby are among those actors with the highest Q-scores.

To determine the score, market research is done by surveying a panel of U.S. consumer households on their awareness and personal opinion of the subject being studied. The Q-score asks people whether they like something and then uses these results to provide a measure of appeal. Analyzing Q-scores can be extremely helpful when looking to identify those celebrities that will generate positive appeal. In Hollywood, analyzing Q-scores provides an accurate estimate how successful an actor has been in connecting with their audience. Because the score relies on favorability more than familiarity, it has the ability to find out what people actually like.

The ability to measure favorability is what separates Levitt's Q-score from other rankings, such as the Nielsen rankings. The Nielsen rankings can be a misleading rating of a show's strength. The show may have high viewer totals because it is the "best of the worst," aired at a certain time or because it is scheduled in between two strong programs that boost its rating. The Nielsen rating only provides information for that specific time, it cannot be generalized to determine a show's potential for success under different criteria. The Q-score goes beyond this limited measure of familiarity to ask why an audience supports a specific person or thing. Understanding this factor may enable an advertiser, public relations firm, network, or broadcaster to micro-target those third-party supporters that have the most potential to help their campaign.[352]

The Q-score not only provides a measure of appeal. It may also yield important conclusions on why or why not the public has given someone a high score.[353] Knowing the psychology of what issues concern or move the public is also important in issue management. This knowledge allows a campaign greater leverage when attempting to influence public opinion formation. To determine the psychology of an audience, issue management campaigns should measure the familiarity and favorability of an issue with its own Q-score. This score could help a campaign identify the opinion makers who are both familiar and favorable to the stakeholder audience. These opinion makers hold the power to sway public confidence and perceptions.

## Why Identify Third-Party Supporters?

The power of stakeholder opinion has grown considerably because of the transparency of modern society. The heightened use of Q-Scores and other public opinion measures affirms the increased power of stakeholder opinion. Third-party support is not only helpful in achieving end goals, it is crucial because of this transparency. The increased need for transparency has required a high level of public participation in efforts affecting the public. This has given various stakeholders among the greater body politic power over the actions of corporations.

When a business endeavors to build a new plant in a community, there are countless permits that must be obtained to begin and complete development. Frequently, these permits have a public participation requirement written into the process of obtaining the permit. The community, therefore, holds immense power over the business' development efforts and can delay development plans for extended periods of time.

To avoid unnecessary public opposition to a business development, the business must help communities better understand critical and complex issues and inform them of the positive intentions of the campaign's efforts before the public hearing takes place regarding the permit. A business must utilize public opinion makers to educate the community on the benefits of the development and establish a positive relationship among the community. If this is done effectively, the impetus for opposition at the public hearings can be reduced significantly and the permit obtaining process becomes easier, saving time and money for the company.

With the tendency of power to polarize stakeholders, issue management campaigns must find the most effective way to control stakeholder opinion. A campaign can only go as far as its third-party support extends. Employing opinion makers to support a campaign will positively influence its reputation among stakeholders. As Aristotle philosophized, developing a positive reputation is the most powerful means for a speaker to persuade an audience to support him.

The influence of stakeholder opinion has increased with contemporary society's transparency, but stakeholder opinion has played a role in reputation from the days of our founding fathers. An example that illustrates the need to shape stakeholder opinion is the "corrupt bargain" of the 1824 Presidential election between John Quincy Adams and Henry Clay.

In the 1824 presidential election the lack of a majority winner in the Electoral College forced the House of Representatives to decide the next president from the top three candidates: Andrew Jackson (99 electoral votes), John Quincy Adams (84), and William H. Crawford (41). With such a disparity between the top two vote getters and Crawford, the House was essentially choosing between John Quincy Adams and Andrew Jackson. The deciding factor became the support of the Western representatives controlled by the fourth-place candidate Henry Clay (37 electoral votes).

The infamous "corrupt bargain" was formed when Clay endorsed Adams for President, thus helping him gain the presidency. Adams subsequently appointed Clay to the Department of State. The Adams-

Clay alliance was doomed to have a bad reputation because of their disregard for stakeholder opinion. Although Adams was able to promote Clay to his department, he was still held accountable for his decision. Jackson would easily win the presidency in 1828. The alliance's poor reputation is evident in its nickname, the "corrupt bargain." This unfortunate nickname could have been avoided if Adams and Clay sought credible third-party support early. This would have given them the credibility needed to dispel the negative rumors regarding the appointment.[354]

**Adams won the presidency, but failed to achieve many of his goals in the face of a hostile Congress. He was easily defeated after one term. Long-term success requires ensuring the stakeholders that matter are invested in your success.**

The corrupt bargain historical example affirms a campaign's need to involve third-party support to dispel negative perceptions. However, a campaign must be meticulous when identifying the third parties. The campaign's credibility can disintegrate with the ill-fortuned support of a non-credible third party.

**Unfavorable Consequences: Poorly Identified Third-Party Support**

As Adams learned to his chagrin, a campaign that fails to pay attention to both the familiarity and favorability of a supporter among the stakeholders will be faced with unfavorable consequences. Although it is true that the higher amount of credible third-party supporters a campaign receives the stronger its reputation, issue management campaigns should be selective when identifying potential supporters and accept only those endorsements that not only cater to popular stakeholder opinion, but also place pressure for action on the appropriate decision makers. An endorsement from a group or individual that will cause an irreparable divide within the ranks of already established supporters—or an endorsement based solely on popularity—must be weeded out in the identification process to prevent disastrous costs for a campaign.

The need to filter inclusion of third parties is can be seen in the example of Vladimir Lenin and the Bolshevik party. After the February Revolution of 1917, Lenin sought to gain broad support to promulgate a one-party state dominated by his Bolshevik Party in the Soviet Union. Lenin and the Bolsheviks consisted of mostly Russian supporters, yet they coveted the support of Georgians, Armenians, Balts, and other members of the Russian empire. To achieve his one-party state Lenin formed an alliance of support with Joseph Stalin. Joseph Stalin was a Georgian, and Lenin felt that he could use his nationality to engage new stakeholders in the empire. Lenin was willing to overlook Stalin's aggressive nature and appointed him General Secretary in 1920, thinking it would lead to a united Bolshevik party. But instead of uniting the party, Stalin exploited his position to ensure his succession to power by eliminating his detractors and replacing them with his supporters. With the death of Lenin in 1923, Russia was thrust into another non-credible government under Joseph Stalin.[355]

Although intended to promote an all-inclusive party, Lenin's appointment of Stalin created a division and allowed corruption to enter the party organization. Lenin was unable to achieve his party-united goal because he did not consider the consequences that would come from Stalin's appointment. In issue management, a campaign should rigorously promote inclusion but not to the point of divisiveness.

## How Do You Identify the Appropriate Third-Party Support?
## Mass Citizen Involvement: A Complex Process

The goal of a broad-based initiative is to connect with a community on an intimate level. This builds knowledge on the issues diverse community groups care about. The intimacy of a broad-based approach allows the campaign to move and influence a community. It is the ultimate method for controlling public opinion. Once a campaign has identified the issues a community cares about, it is able to identify the third-party support that will influence as many stakeholders behind the campaign as possible.

The most important aspect of a mass involvement campaign is its reliance on word-of-mouth interaction. Dr. Roderick Hart, professor of Communication Studies at The University of Texas at Austin, affirms that in Presidential politics, word-of-mouth campaigning still trumps any form of media campaign. He stresses that asking constituents for their votes one-on-one and face-to-face remains the best means to attract voters.[356] Even with the introduction of technological campaign advertisement techniques, Dr. Hart maintains that campaigns should "play politics on the ground" as described in chapter six. Dr. Hart's affirmation stresses that the intimate nature of the word-of-mouth technique provides the utmost credibility for a campaign. Issue management campaigns must practice the word-of-mouth campaign that Dr. Hart praises in order to establish the necessary close-knit relationships in a community.

The credibility that comes with the intimacy of word-of-mouth interaction forces a relationship to develop between all involved parties. A campaign that develops a relationship with the community is better able to determine and quell any negative concerns. These relationships must be established early in a broad-based effort to build a foundation for engaging higher-level decision-makers. A campaign that fails to practice mass citizen involvement early will lack the third-party credibility needed for leveraging support among legislators and other decision makers.

The effort to convince decision-makers to support an issue is called "direct lobbying" and is a step beyond citizen-level campaigning. Direct lobbying seeks to influence decision makers in legislative or executive bodies to support the campaign's objectives. A successful issue management campaign must practice both citizen-level and direct lobbying to be successful. If a campaign approaches a decision maker without adequate third-party credibility as support, the official will have little desire to support the issue. Conversely, if a campaign only raises support within the community and does not communicate the level of support to the decision maker, the campaign is risking failure.

Identifying the third-party support that will build credibility for a campaign is a meticulous process that relies on significant research and extensive legwork within communities and among legislators. Working in the trenches of the community allows a campaign to identify the most credible and important sources of third-party support among the base level of stakeholders. An expert in issue management is needed to effectively allocate efforts to identify key supporters among different audiences and build important relationships among a multitude of groups that will influence the decision making process.

**Documentation and Demonstration**

A leader in issue management can only build third-party credibility by documenting and demonstrating support from third parties that have sufficient expertise and have gained citizens' trust. Documenting and demonstrating support gives a campaign the convincing evidence it needs when meeting with legislators to demonstrate the support for the issue with the voters back home. If a campaign can both document and demonstrate this support, it has accomplished the task of gaining the proper endorsements.

After a campaign has identified the correct third-party support, it must be accurately and completely documented. Documented support is evidence that can be tangibly presented to a decision maker. Think in terms of a student who goes to college for four years, earns a degree but has no diploma or transcript to substantiate degree. The next step after obtaining documentation of an accomplishment is to demonstrate this support. Carrying the analogy further, a college graduate will place information about the college education on a resume to demonstrate the achieved level of education to potential employers. Its value is in its power to substantiate and validate.

By demonstrating support, an individual goes one step further than documented support. When demonstrating support a campaign enlists its supporters and brings them on board to support the issue. A campaign should invest in third-party support to take the campaign beyond documented support and establish a mutually beneficial relationship with supporters. To have the power to persuade a decision maker to act on behalf of an issue a campaign must document and demonstrate support from third parties. These supporters provide the front line for issue management campaigns when attempting to persuade decision makers.

## Documenting Support

How many ever acknowledge support for someone or some thing? This means going to the trouble of writing comments on a piece of paper, such as a feedback form in a restaurant, and dropping it into the provided collection box. Oftentimes this occurs only if a reward of some type, such as a discount coupon, is promised in return. A campaign that brings a comment box overflowing with comments from the community, documenting support for the campaign's issue, will be best equipped to persuade this decision maker to act.

## Documenting Third-Party Credibility: A Credible High Ground

Documenting third-party support positions a campaign atop a credible high ground, a slight variation on the earlier discussed third maxim, "assume the moral high ground." Instead of using morality to gain leverage against an opponent, a campaign assumes the high ground early with the credibility of the third-party supporters. If a campaign documents third-party support it assumes a credible high-ground that opponents must ascend to successfully vituperate against the campaign. A campaign that is proactive in documenting and demonstrating support promptly from third-parties will have this beneficial leverage over any detractors.

Dan Quayle provides an example of the beneficial results stemming from documenting and demonstrating third-party support early. Quayle and his campaign needed to shore up doubts over his military record. His opponents were criticizing him for avoiding service in Vietnam by joining the National Guard. To curb these speculations, immediately following his nomination, Quayle placed printed statements from veterans' groups affirming that it is no disgrace to serve in the National Guardsmen on the seats of the delegates' chairs.[357]

The content of these pamphlets was intended to document credible support for Quayle from third-party veterans groups. By immediately distributing the leaflets among the delegates, Quayle effectively demonstrated support from National Guardsmen. The prompt action taken by Quayle's campaign helped him to quickly regain the high ground. This leverage ensured that Quayle's military credibility was indisputable. By documenting the support of targeted third-party opinion makers and then demonstrating this support among the appropriate stakeholders, Quayle and his campaign defended themselves from even future adversarial attacks. Quayle's effective use of the pamphlets and the timeliness in which they were prepared exemplify the process for defending credibility. Quayle acted quickly and decisively in cutting off the controversy. A Time Magazine article shortly after the Republican convention indicated discussions were ongoing about dropping Quayle from the ticket before he was even nominated. But Quayle and Republicans seized upon the correct strategy as described by Time reporter Walter Shapiro:

> Thursday night, Quayle was nominated by acclamation for Vice President. His acceptance speech was as energetic as it was forgettable. The Bush camp did decide, however, to wrap Quayle in the patriotic bunting of the National Guard. Signs appeared on the convention floor heralding GUARDSMEN FOR BUSH/ QUAYLE. The vice presidential nominee won his loudest ovation when he declared, "I served six years in the National Guard . . . and I'm proud of that." It was textbook conservative confrontational politics: pit the millions of voters who are veterans of the National Guard against a lynch mob from the national media. [358]

**Quayle's team identified the specific opinion makers that would have the most credibility and influence on the immediate issue at hand. Your third-party support must be key influencers who are not only effective, but also relevant.**

An issue campaign can go beyond documenting support to document disapproval in order to protect credibility. There are some instances when a disapproval of support must be documented to prevent negative associations that will hurt credibility. President James Monroe's did just this when Adams and Clay colluded to form the "corrupt bargain." To avoid being identified with such corruption, Monroe documented his lack of support for the bargain in a presidential memoranda dated February 11, 12, and 14 of 1825.[359] This memorandum established Monroe's position and protected his credibility among the public.

A campaign can assume a credible high ground by documenting support or documenting disapproval. Either way, a campaign must embrace the process of documenting a particular position to proactively control the reputation of the campaign. A campaign that proactively seeks to control reputation will be able to form the face of the campaign instead of allowing its detractors to establish its reputation.

**A Medium in Which to Exchange Fire**

With documented third-party support, a campaign has the ammunition with which to "exchange fire when fired upon," as explained in the fourth maxim, to protect its reputation. Using third parties as ammunition deflects the accountability away from the campaign. This allows the campaign to remain atop credible high ground. It also allows identified third parties to assume the front line and suffer the brunt of the attack.

The use of third-parties as a frontline for a political campaign is a fundamental idea of negative political campaigns. By using third-party groups to make detracting statements regarding an opponent, an individual can avoid the accountability that comes with negative advertisement. Employing third-party groups as the front line for an issue management campaign will also decrease accountability while improving credibility.

In the past, presidential candidates would pose direct attacks at each other in television advertisements. President Dwight D. Eisenhower was the first to do so in front of a national TV audience; he personally attacked his future running mate Adlai Stevenson. However there has been a trend moving away from direct personal attacks since; advertisements are now made from third-parties on behalf of the candidate. In 1988, George H.W. Bush used no advertisements that had him directly attacking an opponent; third-party groups were the medium for this negative advertisement instead. The use of third-party groups has shifted accountability from the candidates, offering high reward and low risk for the political campaign.

An issue management campaign should not use third-party support to provide hyperbolic negative advertisements, but they should build credibility by utilizing third-party support to reduce accountability. The credibility that comes with a very low accountability is what provides the allure for negative campaigning; attacks can be made without the fear of retribution and these attacks can give a campaign more credibility in the eyes of a decision maker. An issue management campaign must use third-party supporters as a front line of attack like political campaigns do with negative advertisements.

## More Than a Front Line: Documented Support Influencing Public Opinion

The power that documenting and demonstrating support effectively can have on public opinion is evident in the previously mentioned formation of Abraham Lincoln's 1860 cabinet. Doris Kearns Goodwin expounds on Abraham Lincoln's subtle tactics of documenting support when forming his cabinet. Her primary example of such documented support is a letter Lincoln wrote to Edward Bates upon promising him a position in the cabinet. In the letter, Lincoln responded to Bates request that they publish his appointment to the cabinet in a newspaper. Lincoln suggested that Bates write an editorial in the Missouri Democrat that would declare Bates' cabinet appointment but affirm that the department he would be assigned was still unsettled.[360] Documenting the appointment of Bates procured the support of Bates' Whig followers for Lincoln; not revealing the position prevented malice from forming from other factions of the Republican Party over the degree of importance of appointed positions.[361] By documenting the support, Lincoln maneuvered Bates' Whig followers behind his front line, successfully controlling public opinion to help his endeavor to build a cabinet of adversaries without opposition.

## Documenting and Demonstrating Support in Political Campaigns

The modern political campaign is a pertinent example of a process that documents and demonstrates support to build third-party credibility. Political campaigns must document and demonstrate support from third-party supporters to increase the campaign's credibility. A campaign that can enlist the right third-party supporters to demonstrate support will effectively engage the voters necessary to win an election.

In political campaigns demonstrations of third-party support can come in a variety of forms. One of the more public forms of demonstrated support is interest group support for a campaign. Ronald B. Rapaport affirms the power groups can have in the political process in an article he wrote regarding political endorsements: "Since candidates seek to build momentum early in order to generate credibility and support in the round-robin of caucuses and primaries, groups can be key players."[362] Rapaport's key groups are the interest groups of American politics. His acknowledgement that groups can provide momentum to carry a candidate to victory is apparent in political campaigns; numerous politicians demonstrate support from interest groups to advance the campaign. These interest groups have established followings that they can influence to support the politician; sometimes this increased support can make the difference in an election.

Former President Bill Clinton illustrated the modern politician's propensity for interest group support to build third-party credibility when he termed an endorsement from the Sierra Club as "coveted" in the 1992 presidential campaign.[363] Clinton's record on the environment as Governor of Arkansas was criticized during his presidential campaign; he used the recommendation from the Sierra Club to combat this criticism. The Sierra Club is considered a leader in environmental issues among environmentalists; their motto reads "explore, enjoy, and protect the environment" and they have upwards of 1.3 million members. Clinton correctly identified the Sierra Club as an endorsement that could revitalize his reputation on environmental policy because of their credible objectives and their broad base of support.

Before a speech on his environmental policies in April, Clinton distributed a statement by David Gardiner, the legislative director of the Sierra Club, praising Clinton's energy proposals, demonstrating support from the Sierra Club.³⁶⁴ His demonstration of support successfully engaged the Sierra Club stakeholders behind his environmental agenda. The active demonstration of the Sierra Club support ultimately brought the numerous stakeholders of the Sierra Club behind his environmental agenda. The ability for a campaign to engage enough stakeholders behind the effort is achieved when support from a credible third party group is effectively demonstrated. Just as Clinton used the Sierra Club support as the headline to his environmental agenda, issue management campaigns must use third-party support as the front line for a successful campaign.

The demonstration of third party endorsers as the front-man for a campaign also appears in business. Famous Baseball star Honus Wagner sold his name to J.F. Hillerch & Son Company to use on Louisville Slugger bats in 1905.³⁶⁵ Honus Wagner's immense success hitting a baseball posited him as the most credible source to sell baseball bats. J.F. Hillerch & Son correctly identified him as an important source of third-party support and demonstrated his endorsement by using his name on company bats.

Even experimenting with extremist supporters can have a positive effect for a campaign. Floating extremist supporters as balloons into an audience to gauge public opinion can help a campaign determine the public opinion of a targeted audience. By enlisting a campaign's extremist supporters the campaign is able to gauge public opinion on controversial issues without fearing any unfavorable response from the public; the accountability for the actions falls directly on the third party.

Richard M. Nixon practiced this "floating balloon" technique with his Vice President Spiro Agnew. Agnew was Nixon's "hatchet man", (someone who carries out a hardnosed task);³⁶⁶ he delivered the contradictory speeches vituperating those who were demonstrating against the Vietnam War. His attacks included references to the detractors of Nixon's war policy as "nattering nabobs" and "pusillanimous pussyfooters."³⁶⁷ Because Agnew made these claims, Nixon avoided the accountability that came with them. However, Nixon still benefited from an aggressive denouncement of the war protestors. Although unconventional, Nixon's "hatchet man" injured the war protestors and was an effective means to determine public opinion. By enlisting Spiro Agnew as a supporter, Nixon was able to convince those against Vietnam War protests to become supporters of his presidential policy on the war.

The need to document and demonstrate support in political campaigns to control public opinion exemplifies what it means to document and demonstrate support in issue management. A politician must document third-party support and then demonstrate this support before his opponent's arguments against his campaign gain strength and influence people at the ballot box. In issue management, the best way to prevent opposition at the end stages of a campaign is by documenting and demonstrating support at the citizen-level to begin. Demonstrating a mutually beneficial end goal that leads to identifiable positive results for the primary client and supporters will prevent multiple groups from trying to kill a campaign.

## Documentation in Issue Management

In issue management, there is a diverse range of methods to document third-party support. Some of the more effective means to document support are: a resolution, an op-ed, or a general letter of support form a third-party. The documentation of support provides tangible evidence for the third-party credibility a campaign has received within a community. A campaign can then bring this documented support to help persuade a decision maker to support the cause.

A resolution is one of the more powerful means to document support. A resolution is an official articulation of the opinion of an organization or other group. In issue management, it acknowledges that the third-party group shares the opinion of the campaign supporting an issue. An op-ed article gains its credibility by reaching the broadest range of stakeholders. An article placed in a high volume newspaper public-cation can have a broad range of influence and a decision maker will recognize the power this can have on constituent's opinions. This type of documentation is designed to affirm that an issue is a hot topic among the decision maker's community base. A general letter of support is another type of documented support. It is a tangible form of support that expresses general support of a third party for a campaign.

## Beyond Documentation: Demonstrating Support, an Investment

Documenting support from a credible third-party is a powerful means of persuasion. In issue management, documenting support is the tangible result of identifying credible third-party supporters. Without documentation of the support of credible third-parties, a campaign has no evidence to affirm the third-party credibility they need to be persuasive. However, simply documenting support is not substantial; a campaign must also demonstrate support. Demonstrating support goes beyond documentation and involves these documented supporters in a campaign. Demonstrating involvement of third-party supporters in a campaign will bring along the stakeholders for the third-parties to a campaign. The third-party supporters become the front line of attack for the campaign and stakeholders assume a position behind them in support. The combination of support from opinion makers and stakeholders will provide the strongest front to pressure a decision maker.

Oprah Winfrey provides the perfect example of a third-party opinion maker whose demonstrated support established a front of support that drove a campaign to success. The persuasive power of a demonstration of support or investment by Oprah is best exemplified in her support of Dr. Phil McGraw. Oprah demonstrated support for "Dr. Phil" by having him as a guest on her show in 1998. By inviting him, she demonstrated her support among a national television audience. This gave "Dr. Phil" third-party credibility that helped him galvanize enough stakeholder support to host his own talk show.[368] The success of "Dr. Phil" increased exponentially when Oprah invested support in him.

Oprah has not only helped Dr. Phil build credibility. Her book club's demonstration of support for a book has increased the sales of multiple books. When Oprah endorses a book in her book club a sticker is placed on the edition, demonstrating to the world that she supports reading that book. The book's credibility immediately augments with Oprah's endorsement sticker because her opinion is valued at such a high level by a broad range of American readers. The best example of this was Oprah's endorsement of John Steinbeck's novel *East of Eden*. After Oprah endorsed the novel it spent seven weeks atop the *New York Times Bestseller List*, an unheard of feat for a classic.[369] This success that results from Oprah's demonstration of support is commonly known as the "Oprah Effect." Oprah is the front line of support, but the large number of stakeholders influenced by her opinion is what makes her demonstration of support powerful.

The success that Dr. Phil and Oprah's book club selections have had illustrate the positive effects that can accrue from a mutual investment between a third-party supporter and a primary individual. In issue management, a campaign must promote its third-party supporters to demonstrate their investment in the campaign. Demonstrating support will allow a campaign to benefit from the "Oprah Effect" that has led to the success of Dr. Phil and numerous of books in Oprah's book club by increasing stakeholder support for a campaign.

## What Separates Demonstration from Advertising or Public Relations?

The goal of an issue management campaign is not just to demonstrate the support of the largest number of individuals. These must be targeted individuals who are the opinion makers and leaders who will in turn cause decision makers to act. When attempting to increase stakeholder engagement on an issue management campaign, one cannot merely practice a marketing or publicity campaign. Issue management goes beyond marketing and public relations to establish tangible support from key community members. An issue management campaign documents identifiable support to build stakeholders instead of merely increasing the spotlight on the campaign. The process of documenting support must use marketing tactics to reach a targeted audience, but it doesn't just generate publicity; it must publicize specific support to move people to consider a campaign credible and become engaged stakeholders. .

Demonstrating support is not mutually exclusive to marketing. When demonstrating support a campaign must consider the best mediums for marketing the support. The difference between marketing or public relations campaigns and issue management is that in issue management campaigns marketing is the means to identify support, not the end.

An example of a marketing tactic that went beyond publicity and established a credible reputation is Nike's marketing campaign at the 1989 NBA All-Star Game. Nike donated $1,000 to the Boys Club of

America for inner-city youth programs for every point Michael Jordan scored in the game.[370] Nike chose the Boys Club of America as the target for support because of their established credibility with consumers (in this case, the decision makers). By demonstrating the support of such a credible source to a large population of potential customers, Nike effectively combined marketing with stakeholder engagement to encourage success.

U.S. Senator Joseph McCarthy's unsubstantiated claims that the Department of State had multiple Communists in its ranks illustrate the harmful effects that result when a campaign only relies on marketing or publicity to generate support for a cause.

McCarthy's claims came in a 1950 speech made in Wheeling, West Virginia to a Republican women's group. In the speech, McCarthy argued that the Truman Administration was riddled with communists, and stated that he had a list that named 205 of these communists still working in the State Department. McCarthy's list was unsubstantiated; his claims were based on a 1946 House Committee letter that dealt with a loyalty screening of 3,000 State Department employees. The screening identified 284 cases and 205 of these cases were not discharged. McCarthy inferred from this data that the 205 cases were still working in the State Department and were communists. McCarthy made false inferences from unsubstantiated evidence to fuel his charges.[371]

The allegations gained him immense publicity, but McCarthy never documented or demonstrated support for his claims. McCarthy relied on publicity from Cold War tensions instead of documented and demonstrated support to substantiate his claims. The lack of documented and demonstrated support eventually led to the downfall of his campaign against communist sympathizers in the U.S. McCarthy's credibility waned after he was unable to uncover any specific communists in the government as Chair of the Senate Committee on Government Operations and its Subcommittee on Investigations. McCarthy's fall from credibility hit rock bottom when he was censured by the Senate in 1954.

McCarthy's failure to successfully document support from credible third-parties for his allegations caused his public campaign against communists to dematerialize. Named after his efforts, McCarthyism is defined as "The practice of publicizing accusations of political disloyalty or subversion with insufficient regard to evidence"[372] and refers to a person of limited credibility. Issue management campaigns should avoid any resemblance to McCarthyism. A campaign with "insufficient regard to evidence" of third-party support will merely gain attention for their issue instead of promoting action supporting the cause.

Documenting and demonstrating support has been vital to the success of countless politicians, businesses, and entertainers in America. The public's disenfranchisement in the modern political construct has made third-party demonstration of support necessary to win a campaign. In business, the power of stakeholders has made demonstration of third-party credibility necessary to achieve

## Conclusion

To build third-party credibility a campaign must follow the three-step process of identifying, documenting, and demonstrating support. Although only three steps are involved, this process is complex and is never the same between two different campaign efforts. An issue management expert that can take the soft science of garnering support and make it into a hard science, providing incremental steps to build third-party credibility is necessary for leading a campaign through this process and to a successful end result.

Established third-party credibility—like truth—is absolutely persuasive for an issue management campaign. Nobody can doubt the truth of an endorsement that a campaign has carefully documented and vividly demonstrated to the public. To build third-party credibility, an issue management campaign must focus on presenting the absolute truth to be persuasive. Third-party supporters reveal what the company already supports. In this way, they are the absolute truth when it comes to an issues campaign. Third-party credibility is not formed on the basis of half-truths; it illustrates the true intentions and opinions of the campaign.

# Maxim 8
## "Absolute truth applied absolutely is absolutely persuasive."

A child, however, who had no important job and could only see things as his eyes showed them to him, went up to the carriage.

"The Emperor is naked," he said.

"Fool!" his father reprimanded, running after him. "Don't talk nonsense!" He grabbed his child and took him away. But the boy's remark, which had been heard by the bystanders, was repeated over and over again until everyone cried:

"The boy is right! The Emperor is naked! It's true!"

The Emperor realized that the people were right but could not admit to that. He thought it better to continue the procession under the illusion that anyone who couldn't see his clothes was either stupid or incompetent. And he stood stiffly on his carriage, while behind him a page held his imagery mantle.

— **Hans Christian Andersen, Danish author and poet, most famous for fairy tales, (1805—1875), author "The Emperor's New Clothes."**

## Overview

In the classic children's tale *The Emperor's New Clothes*, a child's casual observation transformed the perception of an entire throng of bystanders. The boy simply stated the absolute truth: "The emperor is naked." He applied his observation absolutely, as his remark "had been heard by the bystanders." The observation spread through the crowd, repeating again and again. The crowd exclaimed "The boy is right! The Emperor is naked!" And thus, the simple statement by a child persuaded absolutely because it was a fact-based truth.

Absolute truths—based in facts and backed by irrefutable data—cannot be counteracted by a glib public relations campaign. So called "spin masters," tricky pollsters, or skilled politicos cannot counter facts applied carefully with doubletalk or euphemisms. As the Emperor in the Hans Christian Andersen story learned, nothing can stop the power of an undeniable fact.

## *Chapter 8 Synopsis*

- An illusion or untruth cannot withstand the probing light of fact.
- The best defense or counterattack to charges by the opposition is the truth.
- Scientific evidence is effective in persuading most people.
- Hiding facts or pretending they do not exist does not make them go away.
- If you tell the truth, you won't be caught in an embarrassing lie.

**What is truth?**

Philosophers have pondered the concept of "truth" since the beginning intellectual inquiry. For philosophers such as Plato, truth is more than just a statement of facts that are left open to a multitude of interpretations. *Plato's Republic*, the philosopher's most well-known work is written in the form of a dialogue in which Plato's mentor, Socrates, is the central character seeking a definition for justice. Truth, which plays a major role in defining justice, is defined by Socrates as something that should be held in high regard—the antithesis of a lie:

> Again, truth should be highly valued; if, as we were saying, a lie is useless to the gods, and useful only as a medicine to men, then the use of such medicines should be restricted to physicians; private individuals have no business with them.[373]

Benjamin Jowett, a translator of *The Republic* states in the introduction to his 19th century translation of this Greek classic, that Plato probably first invented several forms of thought to help arrive at truth that are found in *The Republic*. Among them: the principles of definition; the law of contradiction; the fallacy of arguing in a circle; the distinction between the essence and accidents of a thing or notion, between means and ends, between causes and conditions; also the division of the mind into the rational, concupiscent, and irascible elements, or of pleasures and desires into necessary and unnecessary.[374]

Jowett notes that the greatest of all logical truths—the difference between words and things—which Plato "strenuously insists upon," even though many subsequent writers of philosophy are most apt to lose sight of this truth. And at this stage in the development of philosophy, Plato does not "bind up truth in logical formula—logic is still veiled in metaphysics"—and science that he imagines to "contemplate all truth and all existence is very unlike the doctrine of the syllogism which Aristotle claims to have discovered."[375]

Therefore, the greatest philosopher of ancient Greece associates a kind of sacredness with the pursuit of truth, justice, and virtue. He views the philosopher, the seeker of wisdom, as bound by a scholarly code of honor. Through Socrates he speaks, beginning with a question to his companion in dialogue:

> And if they (philosophers) are to be what we were describing, is there not another quality which they should also possess?
> What quality?
> Truthfulness: they will never intentionally receive into their mind falsehood, which is their detestation, and they will love the truth. . . . And is there anything more akin to wisdom than truth?[376]

Truth for Plato has to be practiced by ethical persons, who seek knowledge, pursue enlightenment, abhor lies, and carry with them the moral shield of right. Only such a well-armed knight is able to ascertain justice in a false world:

And so from every point of view, whether of pleasure, honor, or advantage, the approver of justice is right and speaks the truth, and the disapprover is wrong and false and ignorant.[377]

For issue management purposes, however, truth is more pragmatically related to facts: data collected through analysis of the issue—and of the people affected by it—that can be applied effectively in persuasive arguments that convince absolutely.

Unfortunately, facts can be elusive and, once uncovered, can be wielded by either side of an argument to tip the scales of credibility in one direction or the other. Our eighth maxim, "Absolute Truth, Applied Absolutely, is Absolutely Persuasive," is as much a call to action as it is a warning siren. For, as tempting as it is to craft a set of facts slanted in support of an issue, the same is likely being done on the other side. Successful issue management is the result of building arguments on a foundation of accurate facts at the right time, strong enough to withstand any attacks from critics and without holes allowing for discovery of weaknesses.

**Philosophers' Search For Truth**

A long tradition of philosophers from Plato to modern day has struggled with the notion of truth in many areas of human thought and endeavor. One frequent area for philosophical inquiry is human social structure and government.

Thomas Hobbes, one of the first modern philosophers to develop a detailed theory of social contract, a philosophy acutely influenced by the turbulent 1630s in England, followed by the Civil Wars of 1642 to 1651. Hobbes was controversial during his day because he expressed a preference in his writings for monarch over democracy and a doubt that human beings have the capacity for moral choice.[378]

Hobbes first political science undertaking was *The Elements of Law, Natural and Politic*. The book was circulated privately in 1640, during a time of fiery dispute in Parliament about the extent of the king's sovereignty. Spurred by the controversy, Hobbes relocated to Paris and lived there for eleven years, during which time he published the second version of his work, *De Cive*. The third and final version of Hobbes political science philosophy was published under the name that is widely recognized today: *Leviathan*.

At a broad level, *Leviathan* is about societal structure and the legitimacy of government. One of political philosophy's most well-known quotes comes from *Leviathan*, in which Hobbes describes mankind's interaction in the state of nature. In Chapter XIII, "Of the Natural Condition of Mankind, as concerning their Felicity, and Misery," he describes this interaction as an every-man-for-himself scenario in which life is "solitary, poor, nasty, brutish, and short." In trying to draw conclusions about the role of individuals within a system of government, Hobbes outlines what is known as social contract theory. (For more biographical information about Hobbes and discussion of the social contract theory see chapter 4.)

Briefly, social contract theory states that people give up some of their individual rights to a sovereign state, which in turn provides protection for those individuals. In essence, they trade their natural rights and liberties for civil rights and liberties. The government, as Hobbes viewed it, must be authoritarian; representative government leaves opportunity for leaders to champion specific and competing self-interests. In other words, individuals cannot be trusted to pick leaders who will place the common good and safety over their factious desires.

Hobbes dedicates an entire section of *Leviathan* to the exploration of 'truth' as a part of the social contract, specifically in the context of a religious establishment which exercises a measure of control over society. In Part IV of the book, entitled "Of the Kingdom of Darkness", Hobbes asserts that men are plunged into the darkness of ignorance by relying on the Catholic Church's translation of biblical scripture, and furthermore by following religious doctrines and rituals. He believed that those religious practices arising from the Church's interpretation of scripture are not illuminated by the light of true knowledge; instead, they mask true knowledge.

As evidence of this, Hobbes refers to the trials and tribulations of the Italian astronomer and physicist Galileo Galilei, who faced persecution by the Catholic Church for his assertion that the Earth is not the center of the universe, but instead orbits around the sun. In the following quote from *Leviathan*, Hobbes points out another dispute in which commonly held religious beliefs were pitted against physical and scientific truth—the idea that the Earth was flat. From Chapter XLVI:

> Our own navigations make manifest, and all men learned in human sciences now acknowledge, there are antipodes. . . . Nevertheless, men have been punished for it by authority ecclesiastical. But what reason is there for it? Is it because such opinions are contrary to true religion? That cannot be, if they be true.

Hobbes explains that human exploration of the world proved that the earth has antipodes, points diametrically opposite each other on the globe, but that clergy refuted the idea, decreeing it contrary to true religion. His point is that either the earth is round or the Church is right, both positions cannot claim the basis of truth. Absolute truth will ultimately prevail because there is empirical evidence of its existence. Truth is that which can be seen, felt, or otherwise experienced in some form.

**Claiming the Earth is flat does not make it so.**

**Your positions need to derive from a foundation of truth, or they will inevitably be undone by the discovery of evidence to the contrary.**

John Locke, one of Hobbes' English contemporaries, viewed truth and pursued its conclusions in the context of "inalienable rights," among them "life, liberty and the pursuit of happiness," a familiar phrasing used by American founding father Thomas Jefferson in his writing of the American Revolution's Declaration of Independence. (For more information about Locke, see chapter 4.)

While Locke's contributions to Western knowledge in terms of political philosophy were significant and influential, they do not comprise the whole of his works. Locke was considered to be one of the first British Empiricists. Like Hobbes, he distilled truth from a mixture of experiences and realities. Locke believed that truth could be found through sensory perception and through reason. In his significant work, *An Essay Concerning Human Understanding*, Locke attempts to find the boundaries of human understanding in all modes of thinking, including politics, religion, and self discovery.

He asserts that each individual can use reason and experience to find ultimate truth, the discovery of which was the aim of his life's work. As evidence of that, at the site of his burial place in Essex, England, Locke's epitaph reads, in part: "Bred a scholar, he made his learning subservient only to the cause of truth."

**Truth from a Pragmatic View**

Many philosophers would probably disagree with the notion that truth equates to fact. Actually, truth may be defined in a number of different contexts. For example, truth could be defined simply as honesty. However, this implies that truth should be offered in response to a question or stimulation. It also implies that individuals and organizations must disclose all operational information. Although a certain amount of transparency can reasonably be expected, a significant level of privacy must be allowed to facilitate competition, preserve trade secrets, etc. Furthermore, truth does not depend on the inquisition of others, as it can be offered at any time.

Truth could be defined in another context as common acceptance. But throughout history, man has commonly accepted ideas and opinions that would later prove to be false. Although the public frequently scoffs at its tendency to be fooled into believing untruths, the evidence vividly remains that the public has been fooled repeatedly.

Historically the public has commonly accepted a number of superstitious truths. For example, until Christopher Columbus sailed off into the sunset—and did not actually fall off the edge of the earth—most people believed that the earth was flat, and not a sphere rotating in the universe.

In the Commonwealth of Massachusetts throughout the summer of 1692, 19 men and women were convicted on suspicion of witchcraft and then publicly hanged. Dozens more were questioned and imprisoned, primarily on the unreliable accusations and confused testimony of their neighbors during the Salem witchcraft trials.

And on October 30, 1938, actor Orson Welles' unprecedented CBS radio broadcast of H.G. Wells' classic, *The War of the Worlds*—broadcast as though it were a live report—caused nearly 1.7 million panicked listeners to believe an actual alien attack from Mars was taking place.

At each of these moments in history people believed something to be absolutely true that we now accept to be absolutely false. Though the acceptance of a fact can form one definition of truth, it cannot stand up to the iron-clad truth of an absolute fact.

Finally, truth taken in yet another context could simply depend on some higher power or being. These truths encompass such things as religious beliefs or moral ideals. And the value of these truths should not be ignored. Hopefully, community and civic leaders embrace at least some semblance these truths and incorporate them into their decision making. But this conceptualization of truth can not be given a tangible form. That is, they can not be proved and therefore offer no value in issue management. These truths can not be documented and demonstrated to build third-party support, nor will they offer utility in an exchange of fire when fired upon.

For the purpose of issue management, the absolute truth must be defined by facts, because facts are absolutely convincing and can not be ignored. Unlike theories or mere opinions, facts are "sterile"; they are not tainted by bias and personal agenda. Facts induce objective rather than subjective analysis; they many not provide an explanation as to why a situation is as it is, but they certainly can prove the accuracy of a situation as it appears to be. The objective should thus be to collect as many definite facts as possible to get the message out.

Although this definition of truth offers the most relevance to issue management, it is not without fault. Specifically, questions arise as to what qualifies as a fact, where one finds facts, and how one measures said facts.

To understand what constitutes a fact, it is perhaps better to understand what a fact is not. Facts are not predictive in that they do not express what will happen. Nor are they explicative in that they do not explain what did happen. Rather, facts convey what has happened, what is happening or at a minimum provide descriptive qualities that can not be refuted.

A fact constitutes something concrete—something tangible. Facts are generally associated with numbers, such as statistics, demographics, and other geopolitical data. But facts could also be pictures, sound, and videos. Whether they have been derived from calculated measurements or are simply collected, facts are a recording of objective information that provides a basis for premises, ideas and concepts to grow from.

## Contemporary Conflicts of Truth and Untruths

The 2006 film *Thank You for Smoking* is a good example of the conflict between what constitutes a fact and what does not. The film centers on the exploits of a lobbyist, Nick Naylor, who spins on behalf of cigarette companies while determinedly trying to remain a role model for his son.[379] His adventures highlight many of the underhanded techniques used to manipulate the system, but in the end, the lobbyist wins by presenting the facts within his own framework of understanding—the power of an individual cigarette consumer's freedom of choice. For Nick, the facts are the truth. The causation that gets you there is not.

Nick points out in his soliloquy before Congress that, although it is a recognized fact that cigarette smoking is harmful to your health, Americans routinely make countless other choices which could also be considered "harmful," yet are not regulated. Potentially harmful self acts include consuming dairy products and eating at fast food restaurants. Why then, the lobbyist questions, should the sale of cigarettes be so heavily regulated—with choice taken away from individuals by the government.

The facts represent the raw material with which to derive a truth. The key is to choose the facts that will allow you to deliver the truth you wish to put before the target audience.

**In the movie *Thank You for Smoking*, Naylor does not adhere absurdly to the position that cigarettes are not harmful. Rather, he frames the debate around personal choice. Don't cling stubbornly to losing positions unsupported by facts.**

Where formal language might fail to provide a conceptualization of facts, a colloquialism can address what it fails. A colloquialism consists of language used in common conversation and thus does not appear in formal conversation or writing. The rules of grammar and sentence structure do not inhibit what can be expressed; thus, colloquialisms often explain by analogy rather than by stringing words together to communicate via a cumulative effect.

A colloquialism frequently used to identify fact from fiction is the duck test. The duck test is a well known colloquialism that says "If a bird looks like a duck, swims like a duck and quacks like a duck, then it probably is a duck." Given the struggle to define truth or even fact, the duck test provides one explanation of what it means for something to be considered a fact. Facts can be identified, collected and measured by deploying the duck test. Facts may not swim or quack, but if something looks like a fact, it probably is a fact, and it will be highly persuasive to those exposed to it.

The duck test may not seem like the most formal or elegant way to determine truth or facts, yet it has been successfully used to define other complex concepts. For instance, one would not expect a United States Supreme Court Justice to use the duck test in explaining a legal standard. Yet, in his concurrence in *Jacobellis v. Ohio*, Supreme Court Justice Potter Stewart developed the "I know it when I see it standard" while wrestling with the concept of obscenity.[380] Justice Stewart said, "I shall not today attempt further to define the kinds of material I understand to be embraced within that shorthand description; and perhaps I could never succeed in intelligibly doing so. *But I know it when I see it* (emphasis added), and the motion picture involved in this case is not that."[381]

Politicians also use equivalents to the duck test to get across their point. During the 1988 Vice-Presidential Debate, panelists presented Dan Quayle with questions as to his qualifications for the presidency should something happen to his running mate, George H. W. Bush.[3] Quayle answered by comparing himself to former president John Kennedy, saying that "I have as much experience in the Congress as Jack Kennedy did when he sought the presidency."[3] Seeking to portray Quayle as unqualified, Lloyd Bentsen responded, "Senator, I served with Jack Kennedy: I knew Jack Kennedy; Jack Kennedy was a friend of mine. Senator, you're no Jack Kennedy."[3]

A potential problem with the "duck test," though, is that one might be quick to confuse statistics as definitive support for a particular position. That is, people often become confused as to the difference between correlation and causation. It may seem that the action of one variable produces a reaction in another variable when that is not the case. More often than not, though, the statistical relationship between the two variables exhibits instead only a correlation. A third or perhaps even a series of other variables could in fact be the ultimate form of causation.

**Using Statistics to Distort the Truth: Correlation v. Causation**

As American humorist Mark Twain wrote in his autobiography:

> Figures often beguile me, particularly when I have the arranging of them myself; in which case the remark attributed to Disraeli would often apply with justice and force: "There are three kinds of lies: lies, damned lies and statistics."

One of the most popular methods for determining the truth of a statement is to support it with statistics. Unfortunately, as Twain noted in his autobiography, statistics can be distorted and applied in such a manner to completely confuse an issue. One of the most widely known misuse of statistics occurs when conclusions are drawn from data that does not necessarily support reality. A well-meaning researcher can make outlandish claims that statistical data supports a truth because there is a correlation between two events. However, just because data supports a correlation, it may not necessarily prove a causation.

In 1999, CNN published the results of a study conducted by University of Pennsylvania Medical Center and The Children's Hospital of Philadelphia.[382] In this study of 479 children, a conclusion could be drawn that children sleeping with some form of light on before the age of two years old were much more inclined to develop myopia.

According to the study, of children who slept in darkness before the age of two, only 10 percent developed nearsightedness between the ages of 2 and 16. In contrast, of those who slept in a room with a nightlight, 34 percent developed nearsightedness. Even more telling, 55 percent of those who slept with a room light in the bedroom developed nearsightedness. The article goes on to state that "Taking precautions during infancy, when eyes are developing at a rapid pace, may ward off vision trouble later in life." However, not everyone believed the results demonstrated causation. Foreshadowing the obvious conclusion to this story, many eye specialists found the study to be "premature and incomplete."

A study published almost one year later found the causal link between lighting and myopia to be non-existent.[383] In a study of 1,220 children, researchers found that whether a child slept in the dark, in a room with a nightlight or with a room light—the room lighting bore no relationship to whether or not they would develop nearsightedness.

However, the study did find a link between nearsighted parents and nearsighted children.[384] Genetics do play a role in the potential development of myopia; the study found that nearsighted parents were more likely to leave a light on in their child's room. The study also found that the original researchers employed a biased research pool because the children examined were visiting a sleep clinic. This sample did not accurately represent most children with myopia because they had a higher proportion of nearsightedness than most within their peer group.

The ongoing struggle to identify the difference between what constitutes a fact and what constitutes a conclusion is not limited to obscure scientific studies. These battles often enter into the very controversies that dominate general discourse. Abortion and global climate change, for instance, not only have emotional appeals (morality versus choice; protecting the environment versus protecting commerce), but also ongoing discussions as to the statistics underlying the issues.

Dr. Steven Levitt, co-author of the New York Times bestseller *Freakonomics: A Rogue Economist Explores the Hidden Side of Everything*, and Director of the Becker Center on Chicago Price Theory at the University Of Chicago Department Of Economics, examined abortion via a statistically driven analysis.[385] Specifically, Dr. Levitt cites a causal link between the legalization of abortion in 1973 and the subsequent drop in crime rates in the 1990s.

Dr. Levitt bases his claim on several premises. Teenagers, unmarried women, and poor women are highly likely to exercise a legalized abortion. These groups are also more likely to view a pregnancy as unwanted or untimely. Children born into said conditions are generally exposed to "poorer prenatal care, greater smoking and drinking during pregnancy and lower birth weights." [386] He made an educated assumption that children born into these conditions are more inclined to commit crime.

Dr. Levitt cites three correlations that validate his argument.

> First, the national crime rate peaked in 1991, which would include the years when the first group of legalized abortions would reach the age of 17. Second, the five states in which abortion was legalized before Roe v. Wade demonstrated crime reductions earlier than 1991. Finally, from 1985 to 1997, states with high abortion rates experienced a 30 percent greater decline in crime rates than those in states with lower abortion rates.[387]

The empirical data combined with the initial premise might be quite convincing for some people. However, two Federal Reserve Bank of Boston economists, Christopher L. Foote and Christopher F. Goetz, were not convinced.[388] They cite three problems with Dr. Levitt's study. First, they believe the tests demonstrating cross-state variation in crime rates rather than within-state variation—which represent the majority of tests cited by Dr. Levitt—can be affected by many other factors other than abortion. For example, there are obviously sociological factors isolated to an individual state, as well as differences in state criminal justice systems. For example, the breadth of discretion given to police officers regarding their decisions to arrest can affect the crime rate.

Foote and Goetz recognize the persuasiveness, though, of the tests demonstrating within-state variation. However, due to a computer coding error, a set of regressors—variables used to predict other values—are missing that would have absorbed variations in arrests on the state-year level. Use of an appropriate set of regressors would guarantee that the abortion coefficient was identified using only within-state comparisons.

Furthermore, Foote and Goetz believe only per capita arrest data would indicate whether there is a causal relationship. Nevertheless, Dr. Levitt used total number of arrests as the dependant variable.[389] After adjusting the regressors and switching the dependant variable to a per capita basis, Foote and Goetz re-ran Dr. Levitt's test and concluded that the causal relationship disappeared.

Unlike the preceding study regarding myopia, the story does not end here. In his online blog, Dr. Levitt described the coding error as "personally quite embarrassing."[390] However, he goes on to say that he does not believe the analysis put forth by Foote and Goetz contradicts his earlier findings. It is worth noting, though, that Dr. Levitt also states that his interpretation of the statistics does not give any credence to legalized abortion. Even if an increase in abortions does result in a decrease in crime, this does not automatically make abortions "good" or "just," thereby validating their legalization.[391]

Debate over more pressing societal problems, such as global climate change, are affected by the conclusions—that is, truths—deduced from the mass of environmental data regarding greenhouse gas emissions, ocean temperatures and observable events such as the melting polar cap.

The subject of technical and political debate is now around the question of causation. Did actions by man cause the temperature increases? Many accept some form of causal link, yet question its materiality. Ninety-five percent of greenhouse gas emissions can be attributed to natural water vapor.[392] Only 0.28 percent of greenhouse gas can be linked to manmade sources. Even excluding water vapor, only 5.53 percent of greenhouse gases are manmade. Those who question man's effect on global climate change also point to Earth's history and the cyclical rise and fall of temperatures throughout time.

The extent to which man's 0.28 percent (or 5.53 percent) gas emissions contribute to global climate change is the battle ground for debate. It is a fact that there have been changes in our climate. And it is a fact that that man's emissions have increased over time. But it can not be said with undeniable certainty that man's emissions cause most global climate change we experience today.

That may not be the case, however, as more data is collected and more accurate global scientific models are developed in the near future.

## The Value in Untruths

No matter what definitions are given to truth or descriptions applied to fact, stating that "absolute truth applied absolutely is absolutely persuasive" elicits its own debate. Some philosophers, mythologists, and even psychiatrists would dispute the value of truth in that it implies a lack of value regarding untruth.

Nineteenth century British philosopher John Stuart Mill believed that we place too much value in what we consider the truth to be and do not protect those who offer contrary views. Mill wrote, "If all mankind minus one, were of one opinion, and only one person were of the contrary opinion, mankind would be no more justified in silencing that one person, than he, if he had the power, would be justified in silencing mankind."[393]

To Mill, the threat to freedom of ideas and conjecture no longer stems from a potentially tyrannical government suppressing dialogue, but rather from the majority ignoring or demeaning the opinions of the minority. And this threat is quite grave, as the opinion of the minority, even if it is a single individual and completely untrue, offers at least some social utility.

Mill cites various functions untruths serve in the free market of ideas. First, the alternative theory of truth may in fact be truth. Without at least considering the possibility, a presumption of flawlessness rests with the majority. This presumption would thus remove any inclination to not only validate truths via debate, but more importantly, there would be very little motivation to actively and thoroughly continue to seek the truth.

In the documentary *An Inconvenient Truth,* Al Gore quotes Mark Twain, saying "What gets us into trouble is not what we don't know. It's what we know for sure that just ain't so."[394]

This function of untruth is especially importance in science. A scientist once described the main differences between how scientists see the world as opposed to how the rest of us see the world. He said, "You look at the opposite of truth as an untruth; a scientist looks at the opposite of truth as a new truth." The moral judgment of truth versus untruth is removed from science. It is more a matchup of truth versus ignorance, not lies.

Another function of untruths invokes a discussion of mutual exclusivity. Mill does not view one truth to necessarily be mutually exclusive of another.[395] Each side possesses some form of truth, but not the whole truth. This is similar to the concept of gathering evidence. These truths should be combined, rather than pitted against one another, to yield an even greater truth. Unfortunately, rather than tackle a problem, we often times choose to stake out positions rather than interests, setting aside the broader goal to instead prove that we are correct. By staking out positions rather than focusing on the truth, the opportunity to collaborate—to form a greater truth—is ignored.

Global climate change issues highlight this false dichotomy. An imaginary line of truth and untruth is created. That is, whether one is for or against further regulation. However, this has nothing to do with preserving a healthy ecosystem or a strong economy. These are positions rather than truths.

By collaborating—advancing one truth while accepting another—progress might be made on both extremes. For instance, politicians could instead encourage both the private and public sectors to engage in market-based energy efficiency and conservation efforts as opposed to enacting cumbersome regulations or quasi-regulations. Technology research and development, as well as commercialization of viable alternatives, might be better stimulated by an incentive rather than punitive based tax structure.

The preceding functions both stemmed from the possibility that either the opinions classified as untruths either actually constitute the truth or at least some aspect of the truth. One might be so inclined to assume that utterly false opinions, or complete untruths, do not offer value. However, Mill believes that even ideas that are utterly untrue offer social utility.

For instance, contemplating such untruths, however extreme they might be, forces us to further elucidate our truths. Often we hold beliefs or ideas without ever really understanding why or even how they developed in the first place. However, when someone's truths are challenged they must delve deeper beyond the tertiary levels of their beliefs and completely explore their truths.

**As Mill articulates, examining the arguments that may be made against you will give you a stronger understanding of your own position, and help you rebut allegations that your own position is based on false presumptions.**

It would seem difficult to find a particular person or act responsible for the advent of capitalism. Adam Smith, in writing *The Wealth of Nations*, is reputed to be the "father of economics."[396] However, philosophers such as John Locke touched on the free market years before Adam Smith.[14] Although perhaps more closely associated with political theory, Locke actually argued that property constituted an individual right in his *Second Treatise of Government*.[397]

It was probably Locke's view that the citizenry has the right to overthrow its government that influenced American revolutionists rather than his opinions regarding property rights. The offspring of this revolution and point of civic pride among many Americans was not a free market, but rather the civil liberties and right to elected leadership. Somewhere between the infancy of the country and modern times the application of liberty extended beyond political and religious freedom to our economic infrastructure.

Perhaps the idea of the free market took hold later in the industrial revolution, as the nation shifted from individual subsistence to mutual dependence based on the concepts of economies of scale and comparative advantage. However, the idea gained real traction with the beginning of the Cold War as Americans finally confronted an economic policy contrary to their fundamental beliefs.

Communism presented a perfect foil to capitalism. The former Soviet Union advanced ideals far in contrast to that of the United States, even though the full nature of those ideas had not yet truly been examined.

Communism dismantles the free market and individual property rights in favor of a classless society.

Taking advantage of the platform created by the Cold War and the sudden concern of communism, economists like Milton Friedman pushed the discussion of capitalism. In his book *Capitalism and Freedom*, Friedman intertwined the ideas of political and economic freedom.[398] Friedman subsequently gained even greater notoriety, launching the ten-part television series *Free to Choose* concerning his views on economic freedom.

Even today, in the wake of Soviet collapse, Americans can still find stark contrasts in the communist governments of Cuba and China. These countries engage in such activities as oppression and currency manipulation, which is harshly inconsistent with American free market principles. This provides greater insight into our current economic system and encourages further study into the area.

These untruths not only stimulate further contemplation, but also lend a sense of relevancy to truths. Without them, truths can lurch into a realm of unenthusiastic acceptance, bordering on becoming a sort of dead dogma.[399] The passion behind truth is often fired by a fuse lit by opposition.

Early Christians dealt with far more than endless rounds of theological debates. They faced many forms of persecution from the Roman Empire including arrest, imprisonment, torture, and execution. Yet, in the face of being ostracized and demonized, early followers stood by their convictions. Their religion was not a compartmentalized aspect of their life, but rather had day-to-day relevance and helped define them. Subsequently, Christianity grew rather than wilted. Today, it stands as the largest religion in the world, encompassing a quarter to a third of the world's population.[400] Having moved into a more accepted position worldwide, Christians no longer face mass persecution. However, recognizing the need to challenge their faith continuously, Christians employ other means to remind them of their initial struggles. The Christian cross, for instance, serves as an embodiment of Jesus's crucifixion.

It is important to discuss untruths because an alternative truth may be true or at least partially true. Furthermore, untruths sharpen our understanding for and enhance our appreciation of the truth. But untruths offer other value as well. Fictions may not in and of themselves be true, but they can encapsulate greater truths that speak to us as individuals or society as a whole.

## The Absolute Truths of Fiction and Myth

Joseph Campbell, a scholar of mythology perhaps best known for his Public Broadcasting System television series *The Power of Myth*, believed myths expressed greater truths about mankind. In his book, *The Hero with a Thousand Faces*, Campbell describes what he perceived to be the universal commonalities of all narratives concerning heroes.[401] Essentially the hero follows a fairly stereotypical path on his journey because humanity shares ideas of what it means to be heroic. These truths resonate across borders and throughout time.

Homer's epic poem, *The Odyssey*, recounts the tale of Odysseus' long journey home. Following the end of the Trojan war, Odysseus finds himself far from his home of Ithaca. Suitors raided his family's land in their quest to attain his wife's hand. Aided by the gods, Odysseus begins his journey, along the way sharing his numerous exploits that eventually led him to Calypso, who had trapped him for a great many years. Upon returning, Odysseus thwarts the suitors, killing all those who had harmed his family. His return sparks new life in his father, Laertes, who helps him conclude the battle and bring peace to the area.

According to Campbell, stories like *The Odyssey* follow a simple formula, reflecting both the societal and individual need for heroism. Each shows the challenges a hero must overcome to succeed. Despite their contextual differences of time, place, and culture, they share a common bond—a general conception of truth.

Mythology scholar and psychiatrist Carl Jung's work closely parallels that of Campbell. Jung believed that phenomenon of common ideas and narratives appearing across time and locations resulted from an element of the human psyche.

Jung proposed that three elements composed the human psyche.[402] He referred to one of these elements as the "collective unconscious." The collective unconscious encapsulates the experiences and ideas shared across humankind; it is a sort of shared memory bank for all humans. It could be seen as a common litmus test to evaluate greater truths—a sort of universal "duck test." Or perhaps the collective unconscious creates rather than measures truth—a synthesis of conclusions humans derived over time.

Whichever the case, Jung believed that archetypes composed this collective unconscious.[403] Archetypes encapsulate certain aspects of our personality. Sometimes these aspects can be things we believe constitute "good" and thus identify ourselves with. Others aspects could be considered "bad" and labeled as an opposing force. Archetypes could also represent needs or desires. This could include both the need and desire to be "good" or even "bad." However, it could also be a need to be protected, mentored, or even accepted. We project these archetypes onto other characters, usually mythological or fictional, who reflect certain traits about ourselves.

**Epics, myths, and other fictions capture the imagination of their audiences because the stories are rooted in and depict basic truths about human nature. A narrative that rings true to an audience will be well received.**

These archetypes can be broken into many categories.[404] The "hero" could represent the idealized self; what we hope to be. The "persona" is a sort of false face. Although it is how we wish others to perceive us, it is not our true self. The "shadow" could be considered those aspects of our personality we choose to repress because they are amoral or socially unacceptable. Extending into our needs, the "father" might represent the need to be protected or mentored. A "maiden" might stand for concepts like purity or innocence; a character to be rescued by the hero and thereby fulfills our individual need to be considered "good."

Legends, epic poems, tales, and archetypes all support the notion that untruths can symbolize greater truths. Just as with truths, when shared effectively they can be absolutely persuasive. However, one should not discount the value of short stories such as parables and fables. Although concise, parables and fables do not lack depth, as they can be found within religious scripture and used by parents to instill a sense of universal truths that provide a basic frame work for an accepted code of conduct.

Parables teach some sort of lesson or discourage some form of behavior. The New Testament is littered with parables, as Jesus often used them to convey his message. In the *Gospel of St. Luke*, Jesus offers the story of the good Samaritan. Unlike two Hebrews, the Samaritan took care of man left for half-dead.[405] Jesus concluded by saying, "Which now of these three, thinkest thou, was neighbor unto him that fell among the thieves? . . . Go, and do thou likewise." [406] In the story of the prodigal son, Jesus discusses the importance of forgiveness. After demanding his share of inheritance and leaving his father, a younger son returned broke, requesting only to be a servant.[407] Instead, the father took him in and began a celebration. The older son, who served his father faithfully, became angry, to which his father said, "It was meet that we should make merry, and be glad: for this thy brother was dead, and is alive again; and was lost, and is found."

Meaning can be found beyond the tertiary levels of a parable. Depth resides in simplicity, yielding different layers of meaning. For instance, The story of the good Samaritan might also convey the Christian notion that God loves all of his children and not just those of a particular creed or background. Furthermore, the prodigal son might be an analogy, equating the father to God and the son a sinner. One could thus conclude that the sinner will find salvation not from diligence but rather repentance.

Fables are quite similar to parables except that animals are given human characteristics and serve as the main characters. In *The Boy Who Cried Wolf*, for instance, the boy suffers the fate of being consumed by a wolf because he abuses the trust of others. The moral of the story reads, "Even when liars tell the truth, they are never believed. The liar will lie once, twice, and then perish when he tells the truth." Another well known fable discourages arrogance. In *The Tortoise and The Hare*, a rabbit loses a race to a tortoise after choosing to nap rather than ensure victory. Beyond discouraging arrogance, this story also encourages persistence, as the tortoise won the race despite facing an opponent with greater ability. Finally, it is a warning that no matter how well prepared one is, no victory is assured.

## Fudging Untruths: the Value of Propaganda

Untruths offer some persuasive value, especially if they encapsulate a greater idea. Propaganda lies somewhere between untruth and truth; perhaps true in the facts being offered, yet untrue due to its exaggerated state. Though both untruths and propaganda can persuade, they also are bound to inherent limitations.

Propaganda is a lot like truth in that it is an idea we can conceptualize, but find difficulty verbalizing. In his book, *Propaganda: The Formation of Men's Attitudes*, Jacques Ellul wrote, "Propaganda is a set of methods employed by an organized group that wants to bring about the active or passive participation in its actions of a mass of individuals, psychologically unified through psychological manipulations and incorporated in an organization."[408] The bigger issue in evaluating the utility of propaganda is not so much discerning a definition, but rather dismissing what it is not.

Simply seeing or hearing the word "propaganda" can illicit images of totalitarian governments manipulating their citizens via radio, film, newspapers, and other forms of media. Thus, when we think of propaganda, the natural inclination is to define propaganda as being "bad." Ellul cites two assumptions that obstruct an understanding of propaganda: viewing it as "evil" while associating all propaganda as being "tall stories."[409] Propaganda thus becomes analogous to the phrase "The bigger the lie, the more people will believe it."

We make the mistake of failing to partition the act of disseminating propaganda from its purpose. According to Ellul, "Propaganda as a phenomenon is essentially the same in China or the Soviet Union or the United States or Algeria."[410] There can be no doubt that Nazi propaganda, which led to the Holocaust through its manipulations of Germany citizenry and deception to the outside world, is nothing but evil in its purest form. Nevertheless, it is the context of propaganda, and not the act itself, that defines it.

For example, the Marshall Plan was a form of American propaganda. The Marshall Plan offered aid to suffering countries following World War II. But the plan also spread media material such as American films that highlighted Americans aiding others.[411] Beyond offering a helping hand, this was probably done to win the hearts and minds of these countries. This material served as a means to quell any communist uprising in the face of economic turmoil and thus prevent further expansion on the part of the Soviet Union or its communist allies. This, too, is propaganda; whether or not it is given commendation or condemnation depends on one's beliefs about suppressing communism.

For politicians and business leaders, the truth presents the best means to persuade others. And it might make us feel better to cast propaganda to the side, declaring it to be useless in the face of the facts. However, to believe propaganda is ineffective is to be naïve. According to Ellul, propaganda precipitated Lenin's communist revolution, Hitler's political takeover, and the spread of communism in China.[412]

It is not a question of effectiveness, but rather degree of effectiveness. Although propaganda led to the overthrow of the Russian tsars, Soviet Communism eventually fell under the crushing pressure of the capitalist West. Many Communist sympathizers might still exist in Russia, but the country's economy could be considered, for the most part, a free market. Just as fast as Hitler's Third Reich conquered Europe, Nazism collapsed.

China represents one of communism's last stands. Chinese economic growth could be attributed to government implemented economic reform, decentralizing the command and control aspects and allowing private persons to own property in attempt to slow the depreciation of their governance.

The effectiveness of propaganda depends on time. It at least has short-term value and sometimes can be maintained for a long period. At some point, though, propaganda no longer works due to inherent limitations. "All propaganda evaporates progressively when it ceases. One therefore can not hope to create a final current of opinion or type of man."[413] Another limitation of propaganda goes to its symbiotic nature. Without some form a host, propaganda will illicit no affect. "Certain psychological or sociological conditions must pre-exist for the mechanism to work."[414]

Without an individual or psychological need, propaganda will not penetrate hearts and minds. In a sense, propaganda involves just as much manipulation internal to the individual as it does external manipulation because the person must be receptive to manipulation.

Propaganda also can not circumvent pre-existing attitudes or societal trends and rarely appeals to those "outside" the borders of an entity.[415] Even more so than truth, propaganda requires a inclusiveness and togetherness; a sense of "us" versus "them."

Propaganda bears exorbitant costs in terms of both financing and manpower. It must be continually perpetuated because, as stated above in discussing the relationship between propaganda and time, propaganda will never reach a point of conclusion. "The propagandists work is never done."[416]

For instance, to develop and maintain propaganda, Hitler created an entire division of government. Dr. Joseph Goebbels served as Reich Minister of Public Enlightenment and Propaganda, controlling every aspect of German media. Goebbels crafted themes and messages that corresponded across mediums to coordinate and mobilize German citizenry.

Compare this to modern political campaigns. These campaigns collect over hundreds of millions of dollars, yet their control of the media at best can be considered negligible. To spread propaganda on the same scale as Goebbels, the price would be immeasurable. Furthermore, given the width and depth of information that can be found on the Internet, it would require an even more astonishing level of manpower.

But the most important limitation to propaganda, as well as untruth, is that it wilts in the face of undeniable truth.[417] "Propaganda cannot prevail against facts that are too massive and definitive."[418] For instance, in response to the German's massive defeat at Stalingrad, Goebbels knew it would be futile to spin the incident as some form of success. The undeniable facts forced him to change tracks, shifting the discussion from imminent German success to the heroism of their fallen soldiers.

## The Ultimate Power of Facts

The power of truth stems from its minimal limitations. Truth does not require great effort and expense to perpetuate. Truth is not co-dependant on its audience; it can be persuasive even when there is no physiological or psychological need. Truth does not feel the limitations of time. In fact, it may grow stronger with time. In offering the truth, one need not contemplate the materiality of its content.

Due to its power, truth can pierce through untruths, highlighting absolute offenses while bringing stagnant controversies to an immediate halt.

## Richard Nixon's Smoking Gun

The destruction of political careers often stems from undisputable facts. On November 7, 1972, Richard Nixon concluded a compelling march to victory by being re-elected to the office of President of the United States. Claiming 60.67% of the popular vote, 49 states, and 520 electoral votes, Nixon effectively laid claim to both a mandate to govern as well as his place in history.[419] Just 20 months later, Nixon resigned the presidency of the United States in disgrace because of his involvement in the attempted cover-up of the break-in at the National Democratic Headquarters at the Washington, D.C., Watergate Hotel by Nixon political operatives.[420] What is both highly relevant and quite remarkable about this black mark on American Presidential history is President Nixon's belief that he could completely suppress the truth as well as the immediate repercussions that followed once the "smoking gun" was found.

The effective end of President Nixon's term in office arrived on July 24, 1974, when the Supreme Court unanimously declared that all tapes of White House conversations previously subpoenaed must be released.[421] Ignoring former Republican presidential nominee Barry Goldwater's advice to simply release the tapes months earlier, Nixon "had employed every possible delaying tactic" to keep the tapes out of earshot of the public.[422] Until this point, Nixon had refused to comply with such subpoenas, firing a special prosecutor as part of the "Saturday night massacre," releasing excerpts with significant gaps created by his secretary Rosemary Woods, and finally stubbornly refusing to release any more tapes at all. To Nixon's surprise—likely driven by the same arrogance that prompted him to refuse to turn the tapes over in the first place—his aides and colleagues, after finally listening to one particular tape, viewed it as a "smoking gun."

On August 5, 1974, the administration released this "smoking gun" tape. Until this point, Nixon still enjoyed some support among conservative newspapers and even some members of Congress. It seemed that the Watergate scandal could drag on forever, as the country would have to go through the long process of impeachment hearings. Predictably, however, once the transcript of this factual recording was released, the nation was saved from a drawn out process and a potential stand off between branches of government:

> *Haldeman:* That the way to handle this now is for us to have Walters [CIA deputy director] call Pat Gray [acting director of the FBI] and just say, "Stay the hell out of this . . . we don't want you to go any further on it."
> *President:* How do you call him in, I mean you just, well, we protected Helms from one hell of a lot of things.[423]

This electronically documented interaction, along with other recordings, "confirmed his (Nixon's) participation in obstruction of justice, misuse of federal power, and systematic public deception across the board."[424]

Following the release of the tape and transcript, newspapers called for Nixon's voluntary resignation or forced removal from office. These newspapers included not only those news outlets that could be described as liberal or moderate, but also the conservative editorial boards that previously held steadfast. The only remaining issue to resolve was whether Nixon should resign or whether due process should take its course.[425]

Conservative newspapers were not the only ones to jump ship upon release of the tapes. Every member of the House Judiciary Committee, including 17 Republicans, announced their intention to vote for impeachment.[426] This meant the 10 members who had previously voted against impeachment shifted their vote upon finally hearing the truth. Both the House Republican leader and the Senate Republican Whip agreed with the judiciary committee, and along with Barry Goldwater, called for Nixon to resign.

Most importantly, Nixon lost the support of the American public. A poll conducted by Louis Harris Associates found that 66 percent of Americans supported impeachment.[427] In no presidential election had any candidate ever captured such a high percent of the popular vote.

One might think that politicians would learn some sort of lesson from the mistakes of Richard Nixon. Unfortunately some continue to repeat his errors.

## Facts Highlight another Politician's Monkey Business

Coming off a strong showing in the 1984 Democratic primary against Walter Mondale, polling showed U.S. Senator Gary Hart of Colorado to be the early leader for the Democratic nomination by January of 1987.[428]

However, the 50-year-old Senator never won the nomination. Senator Hart, like Nixon, fell victim to his own hubris. On May 3, 1987, Hart responded to rumors of marital infidelity by challenging the press.[429] Hart said: "Follow me around. I don't care. I'm serious. If anybody wants to put a tail on me, go ahead. They'll be very bored." To the Senator's misfortune, the press responded to the challenge, and on May 4, a 29-year-old model Donna Rice admitted to vacationing with Hart aboard a ship named, of all things, Monkey Business. Weeks after he withdrew, the *National Enquirer* published a photograph of Rice on Hart's lap.[430]

**The truth *will* come out eventually. False indignation and elaborate obfuscation will only make things worse when your opponents bring it to light. Find your moral high ground and be the first to put the matter on the table—on your terms.**

Rather than offer any contrition or apology—or much less an explanation that provided any semblance of truth—Hart lashed out at the media, blaming others, rather than his failure to be forthright, for the downfall of his campaign. A retired politician and former President commended Hart's response to the media, writing that he "handled a very difficult situation uncommonly well."[431]

Who was this politician?

Ironically enough, Richard Nixon.[432]

Nevertheless, politicians are not the only public figures whose careers have been upended by the truth. The truth can illuminate the offense of any public figure, including America's athletic heroes.

## Throwing Vick to the Dogs

As a college football player, Michael Vick, future National Football League Pro-Bowl quarterback and world class athlete, led the Virginia Tech Hokies to a college football championship. His running and passing abilities gained the attention of pro scouts, and the Atlanta Falcons subsequently selected Vick as the first overall pick of the 2001 college draft. By 2005, Vick earned $37.5 million a year and procured sponsorships from Nike, Coca Cola, Kraft, and Rawlings, placing him 33rd on Forbes' top 100 celebrities of 2005.[433]

On December 10, 2007, Vick was sentenced to 23 months in a federal prison.[434] Seven months later, after losing contract money and endorsement deals, Vick filed for bankruptcy.[435] What could possibly bring about such a sudden and tragic end to a promising career? Dogs.

On April 25, 2007, investigators found 66 dogs, along with dog fighting equipment, on Vick's Virginia property.[436] Initially, Vick stated that he did not involve himself in dog fighting and the facts would clear him of any charges.[437] Days later, however, Vick admitted to the act, choosing to plead guilty once it became apparent that he could not evade conviction.[438]

Initially, Vick's main detractors were the People for the Ethical Treatment of Animals (PETA). However, once the facts came out, the chorus of voices calling for his suspension reached a cacophony, and the issue was resolved quickly and swiftly. The National Football League suspended Vick indefinitely, issuing a statement saying, ""We totally condemn the conduct outlined in the charges, which is inconsistent with what Michael Vick previously told both our office and the Falcons."[439] Vick lost his endorsement deals and found himself subject to general public scorn. And in a bittersweet twist of irony, many donated Vick jerseys to an Atlanta Humane Society animal shelter, where they will be used to blanket and clean up after dogs.[440]

Vick was not the first athlete upended by undeniable facts. The steroids saga still raging through Major League Baseball clipped several sluggers on their way to the Hall of Fame.

## Palmeiro Punctured by the Truth

Rafael Palmeiro was enjoying a stellar Major League Baseball career in the summer of 2005. On July 15, Palmeiro became one of only four players in the history of the game to hit 3,000 hits and 500 home runs.[441] Joining such illustrious company would seemingly make Palmeiro an obvious first ballot Hall of Famer when he eventually retired.

And Palmeiro seemingly played the game the right way by avoiding performance enhancing steroids. Facing accusations from former teammate Jose Canseco that he, along with other long-ball hitters such as Mark McGwire, abused steroids, Palmeiro responded unequivocally.[442] In contrast with McGwire, who refused to admit or deny steroid use during Congressional Government Reform Committee panel, Palmeiro told the committee, "I have never used steroids. Period."[443]

In August, Palmeiro tested positive for steroids. As a result, Major League Baseball suspended him for ten days. Palmeiro forfeited $163,934 of his salary.[444] But most importantly, Palmeiro lost his credibility and reputation, as the undeniable facts severely damaged his character.

His manager, Lee Mazzilli, expressed disappointment for his teammates. Congressional members from across the aisles echoed these sentiments, as well as saying that it raised questions as to both Palmeiro's statistics and baseball's integrity as a whole.[445]

Upon his return, the fans demonstrated their discontent, vociferously booing Palmeiro to such an extent that he began using earplugs to drown out the noise. Fan pressure coincided with a dramatic slump in performance, as he only earned two hits in his first 26 at bats after the release of the results.[446]

The harsh emergence of the truth raises serious question as to Palmeiro's admission in the Hall of Fame. On his first ballot appearance, Mark McGwire, who shattered Roger Maris' home run record and hit 583 home runs for his career, garnered only 23.5 percent of the vote. Voters questioned McGwire's record because they assumed he used performance enhancing steroids.[447]

There is no question as to Palmeiro; the truth highlighted an absolute offense, making him even less likely than McGwire to generate enough votes for induction.

Truth has the power to pierce even the corporate veil. Business leaders engaged in improper behavior historically cloak their activities in the shadow of untruth. However, the truth can puncture these untruths as well, shining a light on unethical—as well as illegal—acts and force the guilty parties to answer for them.

## The Meteoric Rise and Fall of Bernie Ebbers

Bernard Ebbers graduated from Mississippi college with a degree in physical education. Investing in a long-distance telephone service company, Ebbers would soon find himself serving as its president as it began to falter in 1985.[448] Despite his lack of business education, Ebbers pursued an acquisition strategy, climaxing with the 1998 purchase of MCI Communications Corporation.[449] In the face of seemingly insurmountable odds, Ebbers and his company, Worldcom, had gone from small time to big time.

Only a few years later, Ebbers found himself on the other end of the stick. In July of 2006, a federal appellate court upheld his conviction, relegating him to 25 years in prison.[450]

A failed merger precipitated Ebber's fall. Anti-trust issues circumvented Worldcom's aggressive growth strategy, preventing a merger with Spring Corporation. At this point, Worldcom's success depended on successful internal management rather than creative deal crafting. Compounding the problem, this obstruction occurred during a communications sector downturn.[451]

Instead of both tackling the problem and being truthful about Worldcom's predicament, the Report of the Special Investigative Committee of the Board of Directors of Worldcom asserts that Ebbers lied to shareholders, board members, and the market by continually projecting revenues that could not allegedly be met. To facilitate this facade, Chief Financial Officer Scott Sullivan manipulated accounting records. According the Report, Sullivan, "Directed the making of accounting entries that had no basis in generally accepted accounting principles in order to create the false appearance that WorldCom had achieved those targets."[452]

Sensing something to be amiss, internal auditor Cynthia Cooper directed her committee to investigate the financial accounting records performed by independent auditing firm Arthur Andersen.[453] Despite being directed to end her investigation, Cooper pressed on, discovering that fees paid to telephone companies had been denoted as capital expenditures rather than expenses. Undertaking such fraudulent accounting practices allowed executives to mask a massive loss instead as an even greater gain.[454]

Despite his best effort, Scott Sullivan could not suppress the facts forever. As a result, the fraud amounted to roughly $11 billion, making it the largest accounting scandal in U.S. history.[455] Eventually a federal court convicted Bernard Ebbers and sentenced him to 25 years in prison.[456] Scott Sullivan pled guilty to charges pertaining to the fraud.[457]

Unfortunately, these were not the only persons affected. Shareholders lost roughly $3 billion. Pension holders like the members of the California public-employees' retirement system lost $580 million. Perhaps worst of all, at least 17,000 employees lost their jobs.[458]

In issue management, the ability of facts to pierce through untruths offers significant value. If one's opposition is foolish enough to base their entire position on untruth, facts provide the perfect offensive tool. "Spinning" can often be contagious, causing those equipped with the truth to engage in behavior that suspends rather than advances their cause. Successful issue management requires one to fight the urge to spin, sticking instead to the difficult truths that dispense with a stagnant problem rather than allowing it to continue to perpetuate.

Fortunately, the power of truth can be useful for other purposes. That is, truth offers more than just an opportunity to disprove an untruth. The facts can just as easily be a defensive tool, dismissing false allegations and resuscitating someone's character that might have otherwise been tarnished. It is one thing to recognize the need to exchange fire when fired upon; it's another to respond with petty name calling or one's own set of unfounded accusations.

When fired upon, the correct response is a proportionate response—an eye for an eye—but it must be a measured, proportionate response grounded in fact. This is extremely important because, although our criminal justice system operates under a presumption of innocence, Americans do not always subscribe to this founding principle of law. Many impaneled jurors continue to view the accused as guilty until absolutely—even beyond the legally required reasonable doubt standard—proven innocent. Worse yet, sometimes the criminal justice system fails to uphold its rigorous standard under the weight of mounting public pressure.

## Truth—A Politician's Best Friend

Truth is not a politician's enemy. If he or she assumes the moral high ground, there is no need to run from the truth. Rather than bringing down their political career or highlighting a scandal, facts can instead be a politician's best friend.

Coming under attacks from rivals, a Congressman or Senator might be inclined to spin or simply not respond. Facing accusations such as "not supporting the troops" or "being a tax and spender" can even elicit angry, embarrassing reactions.

A more effective method involves pointing to unvarnished facts. More than chic commercials or catchphrases, voting records express one's values. Voting records are objective representations of where an officeholder stands on the issues. Tallied votes can not be refuted or ignored because actions speak louder than words, and these actions have been documented by legislative record keepers. Furthermore, news media outlets also possess this documentation as well as issue advocacy groups.

Furthermore, if the rigors of America's criminal justice system break down, the defensive utility of fact is essential to put the system on the right track.

## DNA Truth Is Abolutely Persuasive . . . Most of the Time

DNA evidence offers an objective check on the reasonable doubt standard expected of jurists. Sometimes people fail to uphold this standard either out of a misguided desire to render justice or simply because they do not understand the extent of the threshold.

A factual case study may better illustrate the point. On November 17, 1989, police dogs discovered the body of a 15-year-old girl who, days earlier, had been raped, beaten, and strangled.[459]

The police suspected Jeff Deskovic, a fellow classmate, based on what they deemed to be excessive grief. Deskovic submitted to three polygraphs over a six-hour time period and was interrogated in between each examination. Deskovic eventually confessed and the prosecution proceeded based on this confession in spite of the fact their his DNA test did not correspond with the semen found on the victim's body. The prosecution contended that an unidentified accomplice had committed the sexual assault. Based on a weak theory that the accused killed the victim in a jealous rage involving his accomplice, a jury convicted Deskovic of 1st degree rape and 2nd degree murder.[460]

Prosecutors, police, and jurists ignored facts to this point because it was not conclusive. The criminal justice system failed in that it took on the public's modus operandi—presuming Deskovic's guilt and requiring that he prove himself innocent.

Fortunately, indisputable facts can not be ignored. Over 15 years after his conviction, the Innocence Project, a legal clinic dedicated to freeing the falsely convicted, compared the sample to other samples on file in the New York State DNA databank of convicted felons. Investigators matched the semen to the DNA of a previously convicted murderer. The evidence obligated the district attorney's office to offer an apology and the court freed Deskovic.[461]

The amount of DNA exonerations is quite larger than one might initially assume. Since 1989, DNA technology has cleared 206 people of criminal wrongdoing. This includes 53 falsely convicted of murder.[462] Where the legal system breaks down, facts can salvage a horrific situation because of its indisputable nature.

**Truth: An Absolute Defense to Libel**

Staying within the legal arena, truth also provides an absolute defense to an accusation of libel. This can be especially important to journalists who would otherwise be exposed every time they broke a story which defames individuals. Of course, as previously parsed earlier in the chapter can be quite difficult. American law recognizes this difficulty and makes it more so an issue as to whether the defamatory statements were substantially true, as the defense still holds in the face of "slight inaccuracies of expression."[463] Furthermore, every aspect of a statement does not require proof. Rather, only the "the substance, the gist, the sting, of the matter" must be found to be true.[464]

Sometimes issue management might solely be about a defensive measure. A group may be attacking a company's reputation, placing their profits, as well their very existence, in danger. Facts provide an absolute defense not only in courtrooms, but also boardrooms. In exchanging fire, the correct response in these circumstances is the same: a good, healthy dose of the facts.

The ideas of truth overcoming untruths or providing an absolute defense both inject a negative tone into a discussion of truth. As stated previously, facts are "sterile." Not only does this mean that facts do not possess biased and subjective intent, but also that they can not be defined by their purpose. Facts can be applied to initiate action and to stimulate persons into assuming a certain position. This can be applied from something as simple as a debate between two persons to an overarching marketing campaign from a multi-national corporation.

**Subway's Persuasive Fact-Based Marketing**

Subway restaurants' advertising illustrates persuasive power of truth to sell products. Subway began in 1965 under its original name "Pete's Super Submarines." Since then, Subway has expanded to 29,546 restaurants in 87 countries. Subway is now the largest fast food chain in both the United States and Canada, surpassing such bulwarks as McDonalds and Burger King.[465] And according to *Entrepreneur Magazine*, Subway is the fastest growing global franchise.[466] Subway's rapid expansion has not been driven by traditional fast food imagery. Subway does not push kid's meals, toys, and play places to drive its revenue; they do not have a cast of fictional characters dedicated to promoting Subway.

Instead, their promotions focus on the facts. Subway focuses on things like their eight subs with 6 grams of fat or less, as well as the other health-oriented aspects of their menu.[467] From their television commercials to their in-store signage, Subway seeks to immerse the customer with numbers, relying on the cold, hard facts to drive their business. This contrasts with most other fast-food restaurants, where one probably must ask for a nutritional guide before they will disclose the content of their items.

But perhaps Subway's greatest asset is a real person that starred in their advertising campaign. At age 20, Jared Fogle weighed 425 pounds, consuming roughly 10,000 calories a day. Facing the immediacy to drop weight or face potentially harrowing health consequences, Jared began a diet that came to be known as the "Subway diet." Eating a small turkey and large vegetable submarine sandwich, along with baked potato chips and a diet soda, Jared lost 245 pounds in one year.[468]

Although Subway executives probably felt proud to assist Jared in his weight loss, they did not make the mistake of simply giving themselves a congratulatory pat on the back. Jared, a real person with a true story, became the centerpiece of Subway's marketing campaign, appearing in over 20 commercials.[469] In contrast with his fictional counterparts, Jared's power stems from his true story, which, not only inspires millions of Americans, but also entices customers to partake of Subway's menu each day.

Subway's successful growth follows the basic synopsis of the Maxim. The fast good chain gathered the absolute truth, collecting, documenting and publicizing nutritional data regarding their food products. Subway selectively chose facts that supplemented their expansion goals and marketing message by highlighting their healthiest sandwiches. To complement the data, Subway added a human element to their advertising, the true story of a man who ate their sandwiches every day and achieved massive weight loss.

**Subway seized on a true story to launch one of the more successful advertising campaigns in recent years.**

Subway then applied the absolute truth absolutely, tying the theme of a healthy lifestyle into their products. Their television advertisements applied the selectively chosen facts directly against their competitors, using Jared and his story to hammer home the message. They did not stop by simply placing the facts in media buys, though. Subway napkins, cups, and store décor consistently offers the selected facts as a subtle reminder to return.

Subway found success applying facts as the basis for its marketing campaign, growing into the largest fast food chain in the United States and Canada.

If a multinational corporation can make facts the lynchpin of its successful marketing campaign, the truth must offer value to issue management campaigns as well. There is great value in truth debunking untruths and providing a defense against false allegations, but truth should not be limited solely to these purposes. Facts can complement the entire issue management scheme, from assuming a winnable position to implementation of an idea.

**A Truth Caveat: Use Wisely**

While the power of truth is significantly greater than that of propaganda and/or untruth, it would be unwise to place unconditional faith in its power. Truth has one substantive, as well as one procedural, limitation, both of which must be acknowledged.

For the most part, truth is an asset. It serves as the ideal shield from a public relations or political assault and the perfect weapon for advancement. However, it would be negligent not to respect the downside and even repercussions of the truth. Often times the beauty of the truth derives from its ugliness. It may be a shining light penetrating the hearts and minds of an audience, but it can also just as easily be considered unpleasant or even unwelcome. Thus, the substantive limitations to the power of truth depend on whether an uncomfortable truth is involved.

**Twain's Truths That Ain't So**

Sometimes truth and fact are completely at odds. The era of Jim Crow and segregation following the end of the Civil War represents a clear case in point. While the United States transitioned into a policy of "separate but equal" for freed slaves and their children, this policy effectively ensured that white and black Americans did not eat at the same restaurants or attend the same schools. In theory, the options available to both races were of equal quality. However, in reality whites enjoyed better quality services from the public and private sector.

Louisiana resident Homer Plessy was of mixed racial decent: seven-eighths Caucasian and one-eighth African. Believing that he was entitled to the same rights as any other American citizen of white race, Plessy purchased a ticket for a passenger train and sat in a section designated for white passengers. Refusing to comply with the conductor's instruction that he leave this seating area, police assisted in ejecting Plessy from the seat, as well as jailing him.[470]

By a 7 to 1 vote, the United States Supreme Court effectively rubber stamped the policy of "separate but equal" with their decision in *Plessy v. Ferguson*. The court cited the apparent lack of difference in quality between the two cars. Yet, the court chose to ignore the uncomfortable truth that, in most other circumstances, "separate but equal" consistently dealt blacks a much worse and very much unequal hand.

In his lone dissenting opinion, Justice John Marshall Harlan described what was really happening, candidly writing: "It was said in argument that the statute of Louisiana does not discriminate against either race, but prescribes a rule applicable alike to white and colored citizens. But this argument does not meet the difficulty. Every one knows that the statute in question had its origin in the purpose, not so much to exclude white persons from railroad cars occupied by blacks, as to exclude colored people from coaches occupied by or assigned to white persons."[471]

## The Uncomfortable Truth(s) Concerning Illegal Immigration

Currently, a contentious issue in American political discourse involves illegal immigration. Television personalities such as Lou Dobbs dedicate extensive coverage to the issue while expressing strong opinions that fuel the national debate. On one hand, there are those who advocate open borders, guest worker programs, and the liberalization of immigration policy. These individuals believe that immigrants contribute to the economy by helping offset comparative labor disadvantages, combating inflation, and creating lower costs for many goods and services. Furthermore, they express concern as to what they perceive to be animosity directed toward immigrants.

On the other hand, there are also those who believe illegal immigration to be a national security threat. They claim illegal immigrants create an economic burden through increased taxation and deprive native, unskilled workers of jobs. They seek a wall erected across the southern U.S. border with Mexico and advocate more stringent mechanisms for new immigrants to gain citizenship.

Uncomfortable truths have the potential to bring progress and advancement to a screeching halt. Rather than take an approach that resolves both sides concerns—or at least crafts a workable compromise— illegal immigration remains mired in contentious argument and unresolved because of an inability recognize the truths of both parties in the situation. Whatever the merits of a specific program, it is even more telling that no alternative solution has yet to be seriously contemplated.

Unfortunately, uncomfortable truths can also lead to repercussions quite worse than a standstill. The phrase "shooting the messenger" applies to couriers bearing bad news. In the absence of a party meriting repercussion for the news, the courier is often the recipient of a retaliatory response.

This idea stems from ancient times when messages exchanged between enemy camps were carried by a human messenger. During times of bitter warfare, one side of the warring factions would—in an act of anger and revenge—actually kill the messenger bearing news such as "Surrender or we will annihilate everyone!" In the drama Antigone by ancient Greek playwright Sophocles, he writes: "None love the bringer of unwelcome news."[472]

## Shooting the Messenger of Scientific Fact

Today we commonly accept that the Earth is not the center of the universe. We recognize that the Earth and other planets orbit the sun. This system, in turn, moves around the galaxy. But in the late 1500s and early 1600s, a sun-centered solar system was not accepted fact.[473] The Christian Church in this time period kept with the Biblical tradition that the sun and the planets orbit the Earth and proclaimed this viewpoint to be the only acceptable theory regarding the heavens. Galileo Galilei, though, had very different ideas. Galileo found truth in the teachings of Copernicus that the sun was the center of the solar system. Galileo defended his predecessor in his treatise *Dialogue Concerning the Two Chief World Systems*. In so doing, Galileo was accused of committing an act of rebellion against the church.

In response, the church chose to effectively "shoot the messenger," banning Galileo's book and forcing him into court for defying church doctrine. Finding him guilty, the court sentenced Galileo to life in prison. His sentence commuted to house arrest, Galileo remained under the supervision of Inquisition guards until his death eight years later.[474]

Even today, shooting the messenger may take the form of effectively killing political careers at the voting booth in response to an uncomfortable truth.

Raising taxes is more than a political *faux pas* in politics. After the 1984 Democratic Convention, Walter Mondale learned that being honest about it can be a death wish. In accepting his party's nomination for president, Mondale said ""By the end of my first term, I will reduce the Reagan budget deficit by two-thirds. Let's tell the truth. It must be done, it must be done. Mr. Reagan will raise taxes, and so will I. He won't tell you. I just did."[475] It could be argued that Mondale's approach failed in its delivery more so than its content. However, the result can not. Mondale only carried his home state of Minnesota and the District of Columbia. In total, he won 13 electoral votes and 40.56 percent of the popular vote.[476]

Ultimately, President Reagan also had to increase taxes—as he had been doing nearly every year of his presidency. A year after his massive tax cuts he agreed to a tax increase to reduce the deficit. Fully one-third of the previous year's reductions were restored in the tax hike. Reagan called the three-year $100 billion tax hike, the largest since World War II, a "tax reform" that closed loopholes in the earlier tax cut and therefore did not really amount to a tax increase. As deficits continued to rise, Reagan raised taxes again in 1983 with a gasoline tax and once more in 1984 by $50 billion over three years. In all, Reagan raised taxes four times between 1982 and 1984.[477] The truth is, Reagan raised them every year of his presidency except the first and last.[478]

As in the case of Galileo, whose scientific work is commonly accepted today, more than 359 years after ordering the Italian astronomer to a Roman court, the Church formed a commission to address the injustice. The commission commended Galileo's bravery and apologized for the response to his teachings.[479]

And in the case of Homer Plessy, the United States Supreme Court unanimously struck down the logical fallacy of "separate but equal" with their decision in *Brown v. Board of Education of Topeka*.[480] It took almost 60 years to correct an issue that simply stagnated rather than being correctly resolved because so many refused to acknowledge the truth. Eventually truth won over, and this landmark decision served as an important plank in the newly awakened Civil Rights Movement.

**Hiding Facts Don't Make Them Go Away**

In issue management, one's instinct may be to avoid sharing uncomfortable facts. The short term benefit of avoiding stagnation or "shooting the messenger" might seemingly outweigh the long-term ramifications. But the problem with this line of reasoning is that it fails to account for the information driven world we live in today. Whereas it took the Church and the Supreme Court years to answer for its suppression of uncomfortable truths, it might only be a few hours or days before today's public realizes they have been fed a fabrication rather than the facts, whether they are uncomfortable or not. The Internet has changed our world, allowing almost anyone enough access to confirm the validity of assertion. As a result, the threat of uncomfortable truths, as well as the value in suppressing them, has declined.

While the changes in our world diminish the limitation uncomfortable truths have placed on the power of truth, they also enhance a procedural limitation on truth. The power of truth hinges upon its application, demanding an effective and efficient dissemination of information to all relevant parties, especially for the purposes of issue management.

With the hastening of the modern media cycle, it is no longer sufficient to simply be truthful, especially when fired upon. Blackberry-type devices, blogs, and e-mails have increased the speed of the news cycle we were used to with traditional news mediums or even tabloids. Rather than months or days, the public now expects facts to be dispensed and untruths to be debunked within hours, if not minutes. To effectively respond to the media cycle and especially to exchange fire, absolutely applying the truth, i.e. quickly disseminating information to the correct parties, may now be even important than being absolutely truthful.

**The "Swift Boating" of John Kerry**

The term "swift-boating" entered the political lexicon in reference to personal attacks leveled against a political candidate that undermines a main tenet of the candidate's issue platform.[481] However, to be "swift-boated" successfully depends more upon the reaction of the victim of the attack than upon the aggressor. Understandably, the public's acceptance of the charges is related to how quickly the victim responds or fails to respond. Failure to respond may be viewed as an admission of guilt.

The term itself sprang from the 2004 presidential election, in which Senator John Kerry failed to respond to allegations leveled by the political action committee (PAC) Swift Boat Veterans for Truth. This group of Vietnam War veterans created an advertisement in which they accused the Massachusetts Senator of lying to win the medals awarded for his service during the Vietnam War.[482] A second advertisement produced by the same group then alleged that Kerry described his fellow veterans as "war criminals."[54]

Despite the harsh accusations, Kerry's media consultant Bob Shrum and campaign manager Mary Beth Cahill chose to ignore the attacks.[54] Though Kerry, as well as his running mate John Edwards, were itching to respond, Shrum and Cahill rationalized that to respond would give the ads credibility because the PAC had only purchased a few thousand dollars worth of air time.[54]

Quantifying the effectiveness of an attack based on its initial ad buy costs may have worked in previous elections. However, Shrum and Cahill failed to appreciate the development of the quicker media cycle. Cable news networks continually played the ads as fodder for discussion. And these networks were driven by bloggers across the country, who chose to dignify the attacks whether the Kerry campaign wanted them to or not.[483] The allegations could be analogized to an infectious disease—curable at the outset but quickly becoming organic, undertaking a life of its own.

By the time the Kerry campaign fully appreciated the malignance of the charges, it was probably too late to operate. According to one poll from West Virginia, 65 percent of voters said they had seen the first advertisement. Although highly unlikely that they actually saw the attack ad—given its marginal ad buy—word-of-mouth at least ensured they heard about it. Worse yet, 16 percent who had seen the attack viewed Kerry less favorably.[484]

> **Issue Management Case Study: Landfills and Environmental Justice**
>
> During the late 1980s and early 1990s, I was involved in the spirited debate centered on allegations of environmental racism. This important debate involved allegations that "toxic facilities" were being placed disproportionately in minority communities. These suspicions emerged in the context of a debate concerning a hazardous waste landfill that had been placed in Warren County, North Carolina.

The United Church of Christ, then headed locally by Ben Chavis, a native of Oxford, N.C., who would later become president of the NAACP, asserted that the landfill site had been selected as a result of its racial demography. This assertion and the local activism that resulted started a national debate over the locations of similar toxic facilities. The issue generated Congressional attention to respond to these claims.

The main thesis for these allegations was that toxic facilities were being placed disproportionately in communities of color. This issue was quickly raised in Congress by then United States Senator Al Gore, Senator Carol Moseley Braun and others.

As evidence of this discrimination, legislators sought to prove that within certain geographic areas, corporations were placing their most hazardous facilities and operations in communities of color.

The geographic areas defined in various pieces of legislation were by county, 3-mile radius around the facility or census tract. Citizens alleged that under any of these delineations, discrimination could be proven.

It seems horrific and unbelievable to me that decisions made about placement of these facilities could be made based solely upon the race of the local community. There had been studies conducted around the country examining the placement of various facilities, but no study was conclusive enough to establish the absolute truth of this issue.

To determine the veracity of these allegations, I conducted an exhaustive study of all toxic facilities in one state so that I could speak conclusively to the issue of toxic facilities and their chosen sites (i.e., their proportionality to others and the racial and demographic makeup of an entire universe).

The study considered the placement of the toxic facilities using all three geographic delineations debated in Congress at that time – county, census tract, and three-mile radius. Our study conclusively found that the key factor was socio-economic, likely due to the cost of land. There was no evidence of racial injustice. However, there were two inescapable conclusions:[485]

1. Where the facilities were located, the immediate per capita and family incomes were much lower than the average income of employees at the facility (and, in fact, were much lower than the average income of the state.
2. Where the facilities were located in minority communities, these communities had higher instances of epidemiological/health problems (which were represented state-wide).

Thus, while the study did not support the assertions claimed by opponents of the facilities, it did provide insight as to the reasons for the local hostility. These industries had failed to recognize the underlying concerns of their host communities. This was a conclusion that burdened me for many years and gave me direction and insight for a project I would manage in South Central Los Angeles in the late 1990s (See Case Study of PET project in Chapter 2).

Interestingly, but not surprisingly, the end result of the Environmental Justice debate was to add another layer of bureaucracy to the environmental permitting process, which to date has not appeared to have in any way impacted the very real and underlying concerns of health and economic disparities.

The absolute truth in this matter is that the facilities were not being placed disproportionately in communities of color. As one might expect, they were placed where landfill operators could find the least costly property with sufficient infrastructure.

My study did point up a couple of interesting conclusions, however, which aided a fact-based discussion of this issue and helped illuminate a path to a mutually beneficial resolution for future work. Where

> these facilities were located in communities of color, the local community did not always make significant gains through local employment.
>
> Furthermore, in these local communities, data supported the fact that there was a higher degree of epidemiological problems (which were related to a number of issues consistent with this demographic) and mutual benefits could often be derived from local corporate resources.
>
> As for the policy debate, by reaching down and studying in depth and detail the underlying reasons for concern in these communities and applying the absolute facts absolutely, the results were extremely persuasive in bringing resolution to the issue.

## Informational "Boot Camps" Educate Opinion Makers

One technique to raise awareness and build support for issues is through informational "boot camps." Boot camps are educational events targeted to decision makers, as well as those with direct influence over decision makers. Legislators and members of issue-oriented organizations such as the Chamber of Commerce or union leadership would thus represent the targeted audience. Because of the nature of the event, as well as the target audience, boot camps should be held during the day because information sessions similar to these are not recreational but rather address the core duties and responsibilities of its attendees.

At boot camps, high-level concepts can be conveyed from a presentation of data, charts, and diagrams. By focusing on facts, boot camp sponsors may be able to persuade attendees to take a new viewpoint that is more favorable to the sponsor's own position.

Town hall meetings are similar to boot camps in that they are both educational events. However, the target audience of these meetings is quite different. Fundamentally, though, the goal of a town hall meeting is still the same.

A town hall meeting focuses on the opinion makers, rather than the decision makers, in a community. More often than not, this means that voters, specifically activists in the community, are the target audience.

Instead of holding these events during the day, town halls would ideally occur in the evenings, allowing those who work normal hours to attend. Of course, in a manufacturing-intensive community, these events may not necessarily occur in the evening because many people might have to work at this time.

The point being, sponsors should schedule town halls to elicit as many target audience members as possible. As with boot camps, the facts speak for themselves, eliciting agreement and hopefully action on the part of attendees. Taking the meeting one step further, an additional component of the education process might be to give these opinion makers the contact information available for their representatives or council members so they might act on new conclusions and insights drawn from the facts presented.

From these events, a solution palatable for all parties involved might be developed. More importantly, the company or group attempting to initiate change will involve new stakeholders in their project. Because their success in actions such as obtaining an operating permit or a re-zoning request may affect many different, it is advantageous to involve as many stakeholders as possible.

Creative solutions, such as job training coupled with employment opportunities (see the case study in chapter 2), potentially extending into career advancement spring from absolutely applying the truth. And in doing so, it will enhance the company's chances for obtaining and preserving the operating license.

The value of this approach can not be overstated. Applying the relevant facts to relevant parties yields opportunities to individually persuade rather than assuming an audience is homogenous. Undertaking this method contrasts with the shallower public relations approach because it focuses on expending resources on manpower and community solutions. Public relations and mass messaging may appear to be a seemingly quicker and easier solution. But like many things in life, the quickest and easiest approach does not always equate to the best solution.

## Truth Is the Foundation for Effective Issue Management

Effective issue management does not start by proceeding linearly from one maxim to another. The absolute truth should be applied absolutely at every given opportunity.

From the outset, a winnable position begins by assuming a winning position built on moral high-ground. And there is no better foundation for the moral high-ground than the truth. Documenting and demonstrating support to cultivate third-party credibility bears no value if the documentation has no basis in fact. Finally, planning your work but remaining fluid is accomplished most effectively if truth supported by unchallengeable facts is the lifeblood of the organization.

Using divisive tactics to accomplish a community goal will never fully succeed. Even if one group is able to exercise the power of the majority to overrule the protests of a minority group of stakeholders, the residual enmity can taint community relations for decades. One of the major guiding principles of issue management is to include all stakeholders views and concerns and develop solutions that unite the community or electorate.

American politicians have only recently begun to believe in the power of mass citizen involvement to manage public issues. That is accomplished only by finding common ground and uniting all citizens in a formal compact, or commitment, to accomplish mutual goals that are beneficial to everyone.

# *Maxim 9*
## *"The genius is not in the idea; it is in the implementation of the idea."*

*Genius is the ability to put into effect what is on your mind.*

— **F. Scott Fitzgerald, highly acclaimed American writer, author of *The Great Gatsby*.**

## Overview

After nearly a year of being at war with Great Britain, delegates from the 13 American colonies assembled to discuss a possible separation from the British Crown. In 1776, 56 of the members of the Continental Congress signed the Declaration of Independence. Eloquently worded, the Declaration included several of the democratic ideas that would later be reinforced in the United States Constitution. Aside from the Constitution, it is arguably the most referenced and imitated political document worldwide.

Although a committee of five men participated in editing and adding text to the Declaration, Thomas Jefferson was responsible for creating the original draft and incorporating suggested edits. Both its diction and content are reminiscent of the thoughts and works of European political philosophers; of these, John Locke is often credited as being the major influence.

This supposition arises due to similarities of a specific phrase Jefferson: "life, liberty, and the pursuit of happiness," which is a slight modification of a statement in Locke's work *Two Treatises of Government*. Locke says that a government's purpose is to protect "life, liberty, and estate" and that "no one ought to harm another in his life, health, liberty, or possessions."[486]

*Two Treatises of Government* also contains Locke's social contract theory, which states that people have a "right to revolution." This theory promotes citizens' rights to revolt and to instate a new government if the existing one acts contrary to the will and interests of the people. The idea that individuals have rights that stem from Natural Law, as well as the right to throw off the chains of an unfair government, form the very basis of the Declaration and continue to define our national political identity.

Phrasing similar to that used in our Declaration can be found in the governmental documents of several other countries, including the United Nations Universal Declaration of Human Rights, which states that, "Everyone has the right to life, liberty and security of person."[487] Locke's ideas were implemented in the Declaration of Independence, and in the whole of American government. While the phrase "life, liberty and pursuit of happiness" have come to embody the idea of a democratic government, these ideas were first put into practice in the United States. As an experiment in government, the United States drafted a Constitution that would combine Locke's and other democratic ideals into one system of governance.

## Chapter 9 Synopsis

- Great ideas born of genius are useless if they cannot be implemented.
- One of the great political achievements of the United States is its success in implementing the principles of democracy through a written constitution.
- All technological successes in the United States from the invention of the light bulb to landing on the moon have resulted from implementation of a breakthrough idea.
- Future global challenges, such as world hunger and protecting the environment, will be met and overcome by superior implementation of innovative ideas.

**Democratic Ideals Implemented in the U.S. Constitution**

In May of 1787 some of the most notable figures in our fledgling country convened to consider the Articles of Confederation.[488] A painting entitled Scene at the Signing of the Constitution of the United States shows what this gathering, known as the Philadelphia Convention, may have looked like: a room full of men seated closely together, some standing to make their voices heard or to show support in favor of a proposition, their comments directed toward the front, where George Washington presided at the pulpit.

The Articles was the first attempt at drafting a written constitution and it outlined a workable system of governance for the United States. Soon after meeting, the delegates decided to scrap the Articles and draft an entirely new Constitution. The 55 delegates debated over the provisions of the Articles, each championing the causes of his respective state and working to ensure the most favorable conditions for his own interests while maintaining the overall goal that "the Union shall be perpetual."[489] Tensions ran high as ideologically opposed factions presented plans for proportional representation, slavery, and human rights.

From May until September they hashed out differences, resolving some immediately while agreeing to fix others over time. Even so, no one was fully appeased upon ratification. As Benjamin Franklin explained:

> I confess there are several parts of this Constitution which I do not at present approve, but I am not sure I shall never approve them. . . . I doubt to whether any

other Convention we can obtain, may be able to make a better Constitution. . . . It therefore astonishes me, Sir, to find this system approaching so near to perfection as it does; and I think it will astonish our enemies.[490]

What resulted was a new system of government whose near-perfection is evidenced in its longevity; a product of foresight and structured flexibility that has allowed continued existence and growth of our federal system of government for over 200 years. This bold experiment was successful, not because the ideas were new or unprecedented, but because those ideas, many of which had been tossed around for centuries, were implemented ingeniously.

The ideas for American government came from many sources; from preexisting governments and others from political philosophers. For instance, in the ancient Greek city-state of Athens existed one of the first known democratic models of government. Athenian democracy is best known today as direct democracy, in which people do not elect representatives to act on their behalf, but instead vote directly on legislation.

While Athenian democracy was a step in the right direction in terms of offering a large portion of the population the chance to participate in government, the lack of protection for minorities ruled out exact replication of this model for America's founders. Instead, they took the part of the idea that they believed would work for America. A modern day example of direct democracy exists today in the form of referendums, for which citizens vote directly for or against a specific proposal.

As James Madison explained in *The Federalist Paper #51*, "A dependence on the people is, no doubt, the primary control on the government; but experience has taught mankind the necessity of auxiliary precautions."[491] As such a precaution, the founders drew on the concept of separate branches of government. This idea had existed since 509 B.C.E. in the Roman Republic.

The Constitution of the Roman Republic outlined three branches: a democratic, an aristocratic, and a monarchical or, the legislature, senate, and executive magistrates respectively.[492] In order to minimize absolute power of any one branch over the others, a system of checks and balances was created. Eventually, power-hungry Roman dictators eroded the balance of powers, the validity of the constitution, turning the Roman Republic into the Roman Empire.

Again, in *The Federalist Paper #51*, Madison purports that, "[i]n framing a government which is to be administered by men over men, the great difficulty lies in this: you must first enable the government to control the governed; and in the next place oblige it to control itself." [493] The leaders of the Roman Republic were not obliged to control themselves, so their implementation of a republic failed. The American founders recognized that a balance of power was necessary to ensure that authority and responsibility was shared equally and that one branch could not subvert another.

The idea of separation of powers surfaced again in the 1700s, most importantly in the works of Frenchman Charles de Secondat, often referred to by his title, Baron de Montesquieu. A political philosopher of the time, Montesquieu asserted that a government's structure should protect men from each another through the balance of powers. His works were influential for James Madison as well as other Founding Fathers. Madison evokes Montesquieu's philosophy to explain why the American federal republic is a more effective implementation of democracy than the Roman Republic.

> In a single republic [such as that of Rome], all the power surrendered by the people is submitted to the administration of a single government; and the usurpations are guarded against by a division of the government into distinct and separate departments. In the compound republic of America, the power surrendered by the people is first divided between two distinct governments [on the state as well as the national level], and then the portion allotted to each subdivided among distinct and separate departments. Hence a double security arises to the rights of the people. The different governments will control each other; at the same time that each will be controlled by itself.[494]

The oldest in the world, America's federal constitution was an unprecedented fusion of preexisting philosophies and procedural provisions; but combining these philosophies and procedures was merely the first step to implementation. Part of successful implementation, as we explored in Chapter 5, is being able to 'Plan your work but remain fluid.' As did the Roman Republic, the United States has faced its share of crises and hardships. But unlike Rome, America had the constitutional structure to effectively weather those storms. Let's examine the sustained implementation in the face of challenges to our democratic ideals.

The Presidential elections of 1800 and 1824 presented challenges to the constitutional process for electing a President. The 1800 election led to ratification of the Twelfth Amendment, and in both cases the vote went to the House of Representatives. While the nature of such instances naturally led to strife within and outside the government, the system continued to run as planned, without any forceful coups or unconstitutional alterations.

Another crisis faced in the United States was the Civil War. The Constitution had allowed time to resolve the slavery issue specifically, and generally, the concept of state's rights within the bounds of federalism. Failure to resolve the issue resulted in the outbreak of war between the opposing factions, and the potential destruction of the Union. Even during the war, presidential elections were held and President Lincoln worked to sway momentum by issuing executive orders such as the Emancipation Proclamation. At the war's end, the Thirteenth Amendment to the Constitution officially abolished slavery in every state.

In its nascent stages, and even later with the civil rights and women's suffrage movements, the United States clearly faced obstacles but was ultimately successful in its implementation of the federal system of government. In working through its issues, America has sustained a political system where all citizens are equal, minorities are protected from the majority, and each person has the right to elect the representatives who rule on his behalf.

**Utopias and Communism: Idea Versus Implementation**

We have seen democratic ideas well-implemented in the American context, but democracy is certainly not the only form of government for which attempts at implementation have been made. Two ideas that sound good in theory, but have heretofore not enjoyed substantial or longstanding implementation are the ideas of a utopian society and that of communism.

The idea of a utopia originates in a book of the same name, written by Sir Thomas Moore in 1516. The society portrayed in the book is in all ways perfect. There is tolerance for all religious beliefs, harmony among the citizens, and little need for laws. Peace and accord, not crime and competition, are the prevailing conditions in the community of Utopia.

While Moore's depiction is obviously a fictional idea, several groups have made hopeful attempts at implementation of a utopian society. However, none of these utopian societies could sustain themselves for very long. Common law prevented them from engaging in certain practices, such as polygamy, and other utopian societies were unable to support themselves financially within a capitalist context. The idea of a perfect, harmonized society was great, but implementation was impossible; therefore, the societies continued to fail.

Just as the idea of utopian society could not be sustained, nor could the idea of communism. Communism is a socioeconomic formula for a classless society in which property and means of production are commonly owned; in a sense, it is the opposite of capitalism. Proponents of communism believed that disparities between the rich and the poor would be eradicated if the proletariat working class replaced the ruling, bourgeoisie class.[495] This idea was especially prevalent during the periods of industrial revolution, when the working class grew rapidly to accommodate the burgeoning manufacturing industry and workers were subjected to harsh work environments and few material advantages.

There is a valid argument that communism, in theory, is a practical concept. From a theoretical perspective, it would do the most good for the most people. Common ownership of resources would prevent one segment of the population from controlling the food or property. After all, even in capitalist societies there are government run public services such as transportation and the postal service.

There are a few instances where governments still practice forms of communism today, specifically in China, Cuba and North Korea. However, the implementation of communism in these states has not resulted in peaceful societies devoid of class strata or government. Instead, it has resulted in the rule of resolute and powerful dictators, leaders who used the communist structure to gain absolute control over government and means of production.

## American Inventors Implementing Genius

When Alexis DeTocqueville visited the United States in the 1830s, he made observations about every aspect of society and compiled them into his work *Democracy in America*. In addition to our social, political, religious, and industrial habits, DeTocqueville observed the dogged pursuit of the practical sciences, which drove American productivity and innovation. He said, "In America, the purely practical aspect of science is studied admirably and careful attention is devoted to that theoretical area which is closely related to its application. Americans display, in this respect, an attitude which is always sharp, free, original, and productive."[496] This sharp, original attitude was manifest in America's most prolific men of science, whose inventions, their practical implementation of grand ideas, changed the lives of citizens around the globe.

In the 19th century, while DeTocqueville was writing *Democracy in America*, the United States Patent office was busy issuing record numbers of patents. It was the golden age of invention, and one of the most prolific American inventors was Thomas Alva Edison. Credited with developing incandescent light, the first phonograph, and a way of distributing electrical current, he was a proponent of honing implementation of existing ideas.

**Good ideas are thought of every day. It is the rare individual who acts upon that idea and fulfills the promise of the genius of that idea. As Edison attested, the genius is in the hard work that follows.**

Edison is often credited with saying, "Genius is 2% inspiration and 98% perspiration." If his career is any indication, this is a rule that he followed personally. He held 1,093 U.S. patents and more in Europe, many of which were a product of the work carried out in Menlo Park, the site of the first ever industrial research lab.[497] Edison hired a staff of engineers and researchers who used research done by others as a foundation for their work. They improved the implementation of ideas where previous attempts fell short and produced inventions that were commercially viable, with a focus on mass production. Where Edison's major contributions helped to spur industrialization, another re-nowned 19th century inventor made important contributions to the agricultural sector.

Born of slave parents and living in the Reconstruction South, artist and inventor George Washington Carver had an idea that small-time farmers should live as independently as possible with the resources at their disposal to escape the economic uncertainties of a cash economy. At the time, much of the Southern soil had been divested of its nutrients due to years of cotton planting, and the crop itself had been devastated by the boll weevil parasite.

Carver succeeded in his idea by promoting the growth of peanuts and sweet potatoes as an alternative to cotton and finding profitable uses for this legume. Carver's scientific discoveries included more than 300 different products derived from the peanut, some 100 from sweet potatoes, about 75 from pecans and many more including the agricultural principle of crop rotation. His work with peanuts as a substitute crop resulted in the creation of many peanut-based products that served as a practical substitute for more expensive household chemicals, including cosmetics, dyes, paints, plastics, gasoline and nitroglycerin.[498]

His follow-through resulted in the agricultural education of countless small farmers but it also changed intangible factors. For instance, the high profile achieved by Carver, which included a well received testimony given to the United States Ways and Means Committee of the House of Representatives, helped to erode the stereotype that African-Americans were intellectually inferior to whites and served as a role model of persistence and innovation for all Americans.[499]

Around the same time that Mr. Carver's research led him to discover new uses for peanuts, scientists were focused on implementing scientific ideas which, unlike the inventions of Edison or research of Carver, were intangible and had no readily understood or practical purpose.

## Charles Lindberg's First Transatlantic Flight

It would be difficult to imagine a time when man did not seek to explore the boundaries of his environment, and as a part of that, the desire to join the birds of the air in exploring the limits of the sky. After the Wright brothers soared in their aircraft over sand dunes at North Carolina's outer banks, our dominion of the sky was imminent.

At that point, the idea of flight was still a novelty. The capability existed, and the technology would continue to improve, but practical implications were yet to be identified. In 1927, pilot Charles Lindbergh took the idea of flight to an unprecedented level. Although he was not the first to complete a transatlantic flight, he was the first person to do it alone.

Lindbergh had worked as a mail pilot when, a year before his famous flight, he heard about a contest for a flight between New York and Paris for which, upon successful completion, the pilot would win a prize of $25,000 dollars.[500] Lindbergh readily accepted the challenged and set about supervising construction of his custom-modified plane for which special considerations had been made in terms of weight and fuel capacity. The wings of his plane were extended four feet to help him ascend more quickly.

He also set out with very minimal provisions: four sandwiches, two canteens of water and 451 gallons of gasoline to keep the plane light enough to fly the long distance and be as fuel efficient as possible. Because his view was obstructed by a fuel tank, Lindbergh relied on a periscope to see what was in front of him. At one point, Lindbergh became so weary he almost fell asleep while still in the air. Nevertheless, he decided to press forward rather than returning to land.[501]

By flying across the Atlantic Ocean alone in his plane *The Spirit of St. Louis,* Lindbergh showed that planes were capable of completing a transatlantic flight without stopping. Flight was no longer a novelty but could have utilitarian purposes, such as commercial international travel. He also awakened the American spirit of patriotism and pioneering as no pilot before him had been able to do. The idea of flight had been around for over a decade, but Lindbergh's implementation of that idea created a proud moment in American history.

## Implementation of Atomic Genius

Physics, the study of energy on an atomic scale, was so abstract that top scientists spent their lives seeking ways to test and explain occurrences in this realm. The genius lies in scientists' methods for explaining the unexplainable; that they took complex idea and quantified it through a system of observations and equations, paving the way for a practical implementation. For instance, Albert Einstein's discoveries regarding the atom, as well as the research efforts of several other notable scientists such as Pierre and Marie Curie, laid the scientific foundation for creation of nuclear weapons.

The concept of an atom bomb predated the discovery of the technologies that made it extant. For instance, in 1914 author H.G. Wells describes continuously exploding atom bombs in his novel *The World Set Free*. Although the atom bomb did not turn out as Wells described it in his novel, scientists did use what had been previously discovered about atomic energy to create a powerful weapon.

Implementation of this idea began as experimental research done mostly within university laboratories. Due to the limited human resources, equipment, and financial backing, American efforts toward making nuclear weapons were at risk of being eclipsed by research in other countries. The specific concern was that Nazi Germany would develop the technology to produce weapons that were capable of causing significant damage, especially when placed under the control of their ruthless and opportunistic leader, Adolf Hitler.

The potential nature of atomic bombs, whose powers of destruction were still speculative at the time, could likely be severely destructive if delivered into the wrong hands. As a warning of this, Albert Einstein wrote a letter to President Franklin D. Roosevelt. In that letter, Einstein warned that he had reason to believe that "certain aspects of the situation which has arisen seem to call for watchfulness and if necessary, quick action on the part of the Administration."[502] Subsequently, he proposed a permanent liaison between the Administration and the American scientists who worked with uranium and outlined the tasks that such an official should oversee. Einstein hoped that his suggestions, if followed, would keep the Germans from possession of "extremely powerful bombs."[503]

Several months after receiving Einstein's letter, President Roosevelt decided to create a classified, government-sponsored program for the research and development of nuclear weapons. Thus, scientists and government joined forces to create the Manhattan Project. Established in 1939, the Manhattan Project was fueled by the Administration's belief that America must develop and create an atomic bomb before Nazi Germany, which was suspected of developing its own nuclear armament.

The program, headed by the U.S. Army Corps of Engineers, spawned multiple clandestine research and production sites across the country: in Tennessee, New Mexico, Illinois, Utah, Iowa, Ohio, California, and Washington state. The first nuclear test took place on July 16, 1945, when a bomb was detonated at a site designated Trinity in New Mexico.[504] What came as a surprise to many after the fact was that Germany was actually not as close to developing nuclear weapons as Einstein or Roosevelt believed.

Implementation of the idea of atomic weapons into actual bombs gave the United States a military advantage over any adversary. But the arms race would not be the last time the United States engaged in a competition of technological advancement with another nation. In the 1960s, development of the space program became a matter of national pride, resulting in the devotion of much time and resources to the implementation of the idea of space travel.

## Sputnik!

The period in history known as the Cold War encompassed several unofficial competitions between the United States and the Soviet Union in which each nation "raced" to develop the technologies that would ultimately give one country a military advantage over the other. As a large part of this competition, there was a heavy focus on making scientific advancements toward space travel and exploration. The "Space Race" was analogous to the nuclear arms race of the Cold War. While it played a significant role in igniting nationalist sentiments among the civilian population, the effort was understood within the United States government as a primarily military endeavor.

The launch of the first artificial satellite into outer space occurred on October 4, 1957.[505] Nicknamed "Sputnik," the satellite was of Russian origin and its presence in Earth's orbit was met by many around the world with shock and surprise. "Our movies and television programs in the fifties were full of the idea of going into space. What came as a surprise was that it was the Soviet Union that launched the first satellite," said John Logsdon, Director of the Space Policy Institute at George

Washington University's Elliott School of International Affairs, as he recalled his surprise at the announcement of Sputnik's success.[506]

Although both countries had been engaged in the development of satellites for years, it was the Russians whose implementation made the idea of space travel a palpable reality. For weeks after the launch, citizens who tuned in to short wave radio transmitters could hear Sputnik beeping and clicking.

Russian success was perceived as a failure on behalf of the United States. U.S. Senator Henry Jackson from the state of Washington proclaimed it "a devastating blow to U.S. scientific, industrial and technological prestige." There were also fears about the military capabilities the Soviets had gained through their developments in satellite technology. Senator Mike Mansfield of Montana suggested "a new Manhattan Project" as a means for securing the United States' advantage in intercontinental ballistic missile capabilities. [507]

In 1958, British Labour politician Denis Healey and future Secretary of State for Defense summarizes a fear that resulted as a launch of Sputnik.

> From the military point of view, the sputnik means that Russia has the capacity to produce a missile which is capable of carrying a thermo-nuclear warhead a distance of some five thousand miles in something like twenty minutes, and of guiding that missile with sufficient accuracy to destroy the Capitol building in Washington.[508]

Overall, Russia's early success was the catalyst for a frenetic increase in United States implementation of its resources toward a loftier greater goal of space travel: sending a man to the moon. Our determination is evidenced in part by reports that a larger number of scientists held meetings with President Eisenhower in two weeks than had met with him in the ten months preceding Sputnik's launch. As time would tell, the United States would take the idea of space travel to the next level.

## The Space Race Spawns Large Scale Implementation Attempts

It was Christmas Eve 1968, and excitement for the holidays was compounded by anticipation of an impending broadcast from the crew aboard American space shuttle, Apollo 8. In the United States and abroad, families were gathered, cozy in their living rooms, waiting with bated breath around the flickering blue glow of the television screen.

And then it began; images of the moon and the Earth as seen from space, with a voiceover of the opening lines of the book of Genesis. "In the beginning God created the heaven and the earth." The astronauts took turns reading aloud the story of how God created the air, land, and sea and then looked at what He had done, and called it good. "And from the crew of Apollo 8, we close with good night; good luck, a Merry Christmas, and God bless all of you—all of you on the good Earth."[509]

On that night, a fifth of the world's population was gathered to see those images and hear those words. The broadcast was charged with humanistic, religious, and patriotic emotion: awe at the size of our world in a universal context, pride in the accomplishment of mankind, and wonder in seeing the celestial bodies as perhaps only the God portrayed in Genesis had seen them before. As part of an ongoing space exploration program, the Apollo 8 mission was a culmination of years of preparation, determination, and faith. It was evidence that an idea, no matter how grand or impossible it may seem, can be achieved through ingenious implementation.

Authors and moviemakers of modernity have created masterpieces of speculation regarding human space travel and exploration. For centuries, it was a grand idea and an idea it remained. But the genius was in the implementation, and the implementation began in the early 1960s.

President John F. Kennedy addressed a joint session of congress in 1961 to announce his support for the Apollo program, which officially began America's efforts to put a man on the moon. In his address, Kennedy said:

> First, I believe that this nation should commit itself to achieving the goal, before this decade is out, of landing a man on the Moon and returning him safely to the Earth. No single space project in this period will be more impressive to mankind or more important in the long-

range exploration of space; and none will be so difficult or expensive to accomplish.[510]

A massive undertaking, getting the man to the moon before the Soviet Union would require our nation "to organize and measure the best of our energies and skills." It would not be easy, but hard. In their competition to be the first to land a man on the moon, scientists from both countries worked to develop a space craft that could withstand fast speeds, as well as changes in pressure and temperature, while protecting a living being inside.

They created boosters powerful enough to propel the space craft out of the earth's atmosphere. Then, NASA and the Soviet Union alike sent animals into space: fruit flies, mice, monkeys, cats, and dogs, in order to determine if conditions may be suitable for humans.

On July 20, 1969, Americans Neil Armstrong and Buzz Aldrin were the first men to land on the moon. Although the goal to get a man on the moon was preexisting, the combination of political support, determination, and the hard work and genius of our nation's top scientific minds allowed the United States to pull ahead of the Soviet Union in the space race. What began as a grandiose idea, became a nationally unifying endeavor and one of the most important achievements in the history of mankind.

**In both the space race and the arms race, the United States' success came not from novel ideas, but from superior execution of plans that would accomplish the goals of realizing those ideas.**

The idea was genius because its implementation had benefits that reached far beyond the intended goal. Sending humans into orbit and landing them on the moon resulted in more than answering simple questions of cosmic geography—it fostered the development of technology, which has contributed to the military and civilian sectors, alike.

The satellite technologies that were developed to take images from space not only allowed us to view our Earth in the vast context of space, but were modified and incorporated into our daily lives.

Satellite dishes enable us to watch hundreds of television channels, and to use cell phones to communicate with people on other continents and across our own. In terms of the military and national security, reconnaissance and intelligence missions are exponentially more efficient because of the images captured by powerful satellites.

In both the arms race with Germany and the space race with the Soviet Union, the United States was able to take the common idea and make it a reality, and did so more effectively than anyone else could. Likely these healthy competitions will not be the last. It is not difficult to imagine that the science behind DNA testing, including cloning, stem cell research, et cetera, will become a powerful tool for whichever nation develops the science and implements it in a way that is practical or valuable.

Often it takes a respected leader within a field, such as Einstein in the realm of nuclear physics, to encourage and idea and guide it through to completion. It is true that many successful figures, both past and present, have understood the importance of implementation. In fact, the names of these leaders remain prominent in our collective historical conscious precisely because they were effective implementers of ideas. Due to his many successes in battle, General George S. Patton is one of our nation's most venerated military heroes. His military prowess lay in his ability to form a plan and then execute it in the most efficient way possible, which is especially important in wartime where lives hang in the balance.

**General Patton Hones Execution in the Military Arena**

Patton's ability to understand, plan, and execute military tactics likely began with his early immersion in an atmosphere of veneration for war heroes. He was born into a family with a history steeped in military service, including soldiers who fought in the American Revolution and the American Civil War on behalf of the Confederate Army. Although not a blood relative, John Singleton Mosby was friends with Patton's father and often told stories about his service for the Confederacy. It is rumored that young Patton mistook pictures of Robert E. Lee and Stonewall Jackson as images of God and Jesus, and looked up to them as he knelt to pray. It comes as no surprise that Patton later attended the United States Military Academy, by way of one year at the Virginia Military Institute and worked hard to excel at both the academic and physical challenges presented to him, quickly on his way to becoming a hero in his own right.

As we explored in Chapter 5: Plan Your Work but Remain Fluid, preparation is a key component to successful implementation. Part of Patton's preparation was extensive studying and reading of military logistic and strategy books, ranging from the classical such as Sun Tzu's *The Art of War*, to many contemporary volumes. In his essay, *The Professional Reading of General George S. Patton, Jr.*, author Steve E. Dietrich examines General Patton's library, which is remarkable not only for its vast military resources but for the extensive notes he wrote in the margins. His annotations give us insight as to his thoughts and to how his strategies developed over time.

On the inside front cover of Frederic Natusch Maude's *The Evolution of Modern Strategy*, Patton wrote "to stink (with sweat) not to think – wins." In the margins of another book he wrote "Execution is to plan as 5 is to 1." These notes match part of an entry Patton made into a personal notebook in 1925, which said that "Victory in the next war will depend on Execution not Plans." In making plans for the invasion of Sicily in 1943, he wrote "Some day bemused students will try to see how we came to this decision and credit us with profound thought we never had. The thing as I see it is to get a definite, simple plan quickly, and win by execution and careful detailed study of the tactical operation of lesser units. Execution is the thing, that and leadership."[511] In other words, the legwork behind execution, and not merely a plan itself, is the key to success.

One of Patton's oft repeated mantras was "Do the unexpected." He encountered passages in several other works that advocated a similar message. For instance, Sun Tzu warned that it is better not to repeat successful tactics over and over but instead to modify the tactics each time a new situation is being approached. Similarly, the author of *Infantry in Battle* wrote, "Tactical surprise is usually the reward for the daring, the imaginative, and the ingenious. It will rarely be gained by doing the obvious." In both cases, Patton underlined the passages and summarized them in his own words, "Avoid the obvious. Don't repeat the same method more than twice." In this way, his execution of strategy would contain an element of innovation and surprise.[512]

Patton also focused on more concrete execution strategies. His notes show that he was a proponent of combined arms, meaning the integrated use of several approaches to warfare including infantry, cavalry, and air support. In William Balck's *Development of Tactics*, Patton wrote that the author may have overlooked the efficacy of smaller armies, stating that, "smaller and more proficient armies may be the immediate solution. Not the numbers to be killed but the amount of killing inflicted on the enemy is the index of efficiency." Making notes such as these allowed to him to develop his thoughts by contrasting them with existing military theories and methods for execution.

Patton also developed a high regard for the use of maps, pointing out that the military failures listed in some books may have been as a result of a dearth of maps. In his own execution of strategy, Patton made sure that maps were in the hands of anyone that could benefit from them. For example, in the Battle of the Bulge, Patton distributed 57 tons of maps to his men. Patton was able to improve on existing strategies by implementing them differently than had his predecessors.

In the margins of another book, Patton displayed his conviction for serving hot meals as a method for boosting morale. It seems almost trivial, yet he had witnessed on several occasions that warm food or beverage had an intangible benefit. In a book entitled *The War of the Future*, he added to the author's comments with notes about serving his men hot coffee on at least one occasion, and in another instance "hot turkey sandwiches for dinner" on Christmas day.

**Patton was a firm believer that victory was most often secured by a simple plan with quick, well-implemented execution. Endless discussion and debate will never result in successful completion of your goals.**

We have glimpsed into Patton's psyche by reading the notations in the books of his library, but now let's examine how these notes and observations became part of his strategy for execution in an actual military context. Perhaps the most illustrative battle is one depicted in the movie *Patton*, during a scene in which Patton and three other generals including Eisenhower convened on December 19th, 1944 in the midst of World War II to discuss a decision on how to approach and attack the southern flank of the Bulge. When asked to estimate how soon he could make the attack, General Patton stated that he "could do so with three divisions on the morning of the twenty-third of December." In response, Eisenhower suggested that Patton wait until he had six divisions under his command.

Unsure of how he would amass the three extra divisions, Patton decided that expediency with the existing troops would be the best way to implement the attack strategy. True to the mantra repeated in the margins of several of his books, Patton saw the value in using fewer men and acting early. As a result, the attack was carried out a day ahead of schedule. According to Patton, "I am sure that this early attack was of material assistance in producing our victory." [513]

While the troops under Patton's control were successful, one can only imagine the outcome of if another route had been taken, perhaps by someone with less experience in logistics. As is the case in issues management, an experienced leader is one of the most important tools for successful implementation.

We recall General Patton as an authority in military matters, guiding our nation's troops in World War II through the implementation of strategy and decisiveness. Through his innovation and persistence this war-time icon demonstrated the wisdom of the idea that Genius is in the Implementation, realizing that it is not merely a great idea or strong intellect that defines genius but decisive, yet fluid execution. Just as Patton effectively used this maxim in a military arena, so have contemporary business leaders in their development of strategy for implementing product ideas.

## Business Implementation of Ideas

Walk along the avenues of any major city and invariably you will pass one, and likely several, Starbucks coffee shops. What began as a coffee bean retailer in Pikes Place Market in Seattle, Washington rapidly grew into a worldwide chain, iconic of contemporary culture and a prime example of successful implementation; a business model that turned simple servings of coffee into liquid genius.

Traced back to the eleventh century, the history of coffee beans has reached continents and cultures across the globe. Coffee as a beverage has been enjoyed for centuries, by both peasants and nobilities. Coffeehouses, which serve as a social gathering place, have been used since 15th century in the Middle East.[514] Since neither coffee nor coffee houses are new ideas, it may be a wonder that the Starbucks Company has achieved the level of success it has. Illustrative of this maxim, genius is not in the idea but in the implementation, Starbucks took a common idea and proceeded with a plan for implementation which has made it one of the world's most recognized brands.

In 1971, two teachers and a writer opened the first Starbucks store in Seattle. Hesitant to stray away from its primary focus, the sale of coffee beans and coffee-making equipment, Starbucks did not initially offer beverages to customers. In 1987, the store began selling beverages brewed in-store and expanded to its first locations outside Seattle: Vancouver, British Columbia and Chicago, Illinois. In 1996, Starbucks opened in Tokyo, and then in the United Kingdom in 1998.[515] The chain has continued to expand, with stores in 44 countries worldwide and is opening seven new stores each workday worldwide.[516]

This success can be attributed to the practices of the company's leaders, who have employed innovative practices for sustainable and healthy growth yet, according to chairman and CEO Howard Schultz, have attempted to maintain the culture of a much smaller company. The book *It's Not About the Coffee: Leadership Principles from a Life at Starbucks* presents former Starbucks International President Howard Behar's own set of maxims which center on having a clear path forward, doing what is right, and acknowledging and embracing the value of people at all levels of the company. He knows that the success of any business will be a product of its operation, or in other words, the way the business idea is implemented.

Some of their innovation is shown through product placement decisions, some in the way it treats employees. For instance, Starbucks's joint-venture outlets have allowed them to set up shop in Target stores, Barnes and Noble bookstores, Safeway grocery stores, as well as airports, college campuses, and hospitals. Having stores in these unconventional locations increases visibility of the brand and also breaks down stereotypes of coffeehouses as artsy or exclusive, and instead presents them as a convenient and integral to daily life. The success of the brand has resulted in sales of products other than coffee including mugs, music and flavored ice creams sold in grocery stores, which reinforces Starbucks' as a household name.[517] Consumers no longer think solely of coffee when they see the Starbucks logo.

Not only has Starbucks's marketing of coffee been innovative, but so has its methods for establishing corporate culture, which gives its employees a stake in the success of the company. The employees, which are referred to as partners, receive full health benefits, stock options, and 401k eligibility given they work 20 hours a week for three months. Employees also receive a free pound of coffee each week and a 30% discount on Starbucks' merchandise.

As well as benefits, the company also provides a ladder for upward mobility by allowing employees to complete a Coffee Master course on all aspects of coffee production, tasting, and purchasing. Completion of this course signifies ambition and leadership potential and entitles the employee to wear a black apron that sets him apart from the other partners. It is often a good position from which to move into a managerial position with a store. Due in part to these practices, Fortune magazine ranked Starbucks as the seventh best company to work for in the United States.

Starbucks has created a culture inside and out. The original idea—to sell good coffee—became a lucrative business because of the innovative ways that Starbucks implemented its strategies. Well implemented ideas in the business world often result in large profits, but these are usually contained to a specific company or to a niche within a wider industry. Outside of business, well implemented ideas can affect change far beyond corporate boundaries.

**Well Implemented Ideas Foster Far Reaching Change**

For most Americans sitting at a computer, the world is at their fingertips. They can complete trivial tasks such as buying a movie ticket, booking a flight, checking the weather in town or staying up-to-date on the latest from the world of sport. With the same level of ease they can also access a wealth of valuable information which allows them, among other things, to keep abreast of the latest on climate change legislation, browse through op-ed articles about the housing and energy crises and monitor the state of political situations on other continents. They can access all of this information within minutes and switch back and forth between their Internet's browser windows as often as they like. Moreover, they can do all this from a palm-sized, handheld device while out watching a ballgame or waiting to board a flight.

Though frequently taken for granted, it was not very long ago that today's Internet was unimaginable. Initially, the concept was a very basic one—an idea that computers could connect and share information with each other, specifically concerning the research and development in science, medicine, and military disciplines. Even at its most basic, the idea was visionary. The genius lies in the way that the idea of the Internet was implemented, both in its nascent stages and as it exists now—a tool that Americans have come to rely on daily.

The first proposals for a system of interconnected computers were made in the 1960s, primarily by young men from the Massachusetts Institute of Technology. In 1962, J.C.R. Licklider headed the initial development work as part of the Defense Advanced Research Projects Agency (DARPA). Leonard Kleinrock of MIT and UCLA developed the concept of packet switching, which ultimately enabled data to be transmitted via networks to almost anywhere in the world. Then in 1965, Lawrence Roberts successfully connected a computer in Massachusetts with one in California, using a telephone line to "dial-up" one computer from the other.

This initial trial highlighted the successes and failures of dial-up connections and spawned the evolution of an inchoate Internet. In 1969, under the name ARPANET, the Internet connected computers at four large American universities: UCLA, Stanford Research Institute, UCSB, and the University of Utah. By June of the following year, MIT and Harvard, among others, had joined the online community. [518]

As an ongoing concern during the Cold War period, the threat of nuclear attack loomed unremittingly. Part of the Internet's purpose was to serve as a means of communication, even in the event that one or more of the connected computers were physically destroyed by an attack. At these early stages, the Internet was a tool for scholars, academics, and computer experts. Computers themselves were the size of an entire room and required complex methods of operation that were not readily learned by just anyone. In other words, even though the idea for the Internet had been made a reality, it was so far from user friendly that few imagined it would become a commodity as common as cable television within just a few decades.

A major component of the quick exchange of information over the Internet is e-mail. In 1972, Ray Tomlinson developed e-mail and chose the @ symbol to join the username and address. In the late 1960s, separately from ARPA, libraries began to put their card catalogs online.[519]

As an increasing number of independent organizations made their informational resources available online, the Internet became harder to track and organize. Even while technical commands for using e-mail and the nets became standardized and therefore somewhat simpler, the Internet was still far from being user friendly by today's standards.

The crux of the implementation was the invention of the web browser, which provided a means for user interface and ultimately made it possible for highly interactive sites such as E-bay, Google, and Amazon to become household names. Of the web browsers we know and use today, predominantly Internet Explorer, Safari, or Mozilla Firefox, none was the pioneer for creating a user-friendly interface. Interestingly the first ever web browser, Netscape Navigator, has been all but forgotten. Yet it was the hard work and effective implementation of the ideas by a group of bright young men that launched Netscape in August of 1995.

When Microsoft, which was predominantly focused on personal computers and user-friendly operating systems, got wind of the browser development efforts, they could not fathom the potential of the new technology. A new employee of Microsoft at the time, Sam Jadallah recalled hearing the buzz about Netscape and what it could mean for Microsoft.

> "There was definitely a buzz at Microsoft about the Internet—we were trying to understand why everybody was getting all hyped up. Certainly for us up in the Northwest, we didn't know what to make of it. It seemed pretty cool, pretty exciting, but really what were you going to do with it? How was it going to change your day-to-day work?"[520]

The idea was there but the genius, the implementation, was yet to be seen or understood. The morning after the Netscape Navigator beta version had been released for free on the web, tens of thousands of copies were downloaded to individual computers. When Netscape went public on the stock market, demand for shares was so high that trading did not open for two hours as prices zoomed from $28 dollars a share to $75, finally closing at $58. In February 1996, Netscape Navigator Version 2.0 was released with features that the beta version lacked, including JavaScript which allowed for the use of forms for online shopping and registration. It also enabled anyone with an Internet connection to create their own webpage using one of several easy website creation tools. Within the first year of Netscape's launch, thousands of websites were created. [521]

Today, there are an estimated 1,463,632,361 Internet users worldwide.[522] The rapid communication and ideas, as well as the spread of capitalism and consumerism through a market unrestrained by geographic boundaries, has made the world a much smaller place.

As a tool, the Internet has been used by politicians, businesses, non-profit organizations, and individuals. Fundraising and matchmaking, news and entertainment; there so many uses, all at the click of a mouse, to an extent that was inconceivable just decades ago. Although the idea for the Internet had been around for nearly 50 years, the implementation of Netscape as a medium between the technology and the user was the genius that led to the rapid development of the Internet as an economic, social, and technological giant.

Development of the Internet from its conception as a complex technological idea into a handy user-friendly tool is illustrative of ingenuity, the likes of which changed communication and in fact the very fabric of our society in ways that had scarcely been imagined. Although the Internet resulted in far-reaching benefits, many ideas of a global magnitude can be difficult to implement and therefore fail to create change. As a contrast to the success story of the Internet the chapter will explore the fate of the Kyoto protocol, a good idea which was rendered ineffectual by poor implementation.

**Global Ideas, Personal Implementation**

In 2006, a documentary presented by former United States Vice President Al Gore, *An Inconvenient Truth,* premiered at the Sundance Film Festival and was met with three standing ovations. Afterward, the film opened in New York and Los Angeles, where it was also well received. *An Inconvenient Truth*, which set a record as the highest grossing average for the opening weekend of a documentary, generated $49 million dollars worldwide and, in terms of box office revenue, became the fourth most successful documentary to be released in the United States.[523] For the first time, the public was abuzz with talk of global climate change.

Early in the film Gore says, "I've been trying to tell this story for a long time and I feel as if I've failed to get the message across." The rest of the documentary goes on to show his attempts at getting the idea of climate change across to others, which were met early on with indifference and then later with resistance. As a college student, Gore studied at Harvard University under climate expert Roger Revelle. Deeply affected by his interest in the subject of the effects of humankind's activities on increasing global temperatures, Gore carried his message throughout his political career. During one of his terms in the House of Representatives, Gore held the first congressional hearings on climate change in which scientists and representatives began a discourse on the subject.[524]

Later Senator Gore continued to deliver his message to political audiences, including a conference in 1990 in which he met with legislators from 42 countries to develop the Global Marshall Plan, "under which industrial nations would help less developed countries grow economically while still protecting the environment." In 1992, Gore published *Earth in the Balance*, which includes his Marshall Plan and also touches on other environmental issues. In 1997, he was an advocate for United States ratification of the Kyoto Protocol, an amendment to the United Nations Framework Convention on Climate Change intended to reduce global greenhouse gas emissions.

Unfortunately, the Kyoto Protocol failed to capture some of the largest polluters in the world, such as China and India. Creating such a system may well have led to higher carbon emissions by encouraging industrial sources to move from highly regulated countries like the United States to parts of the world with no enforceable environmental standards.

One argument asserted that Kyoto should set more rigorous standards for emissions reductions. Another group argued that it is unfair or ineffective that Kyoto holds developed countries to a higher standard for reducing greenhouse gas emissions than their less-developed neighbors. Although Gore's efforts up to that point had failed to gain considerable traction, controversy surrounding the Kyoto protocol generated conversation and created significantly more awareness of climate change, despite the fact that the issue had existed for decades. However, the conversation remained among a select segment of the population: forward thinking environmentalists, political activists and government officials.

When *An Inconvenient Truth* premiered nearly a decade after the United States refused to ratify Kyoto, the timing and the medium showed an innovation in implementation that Gore had previously lacked when presenting his message. Whereas discussion surrounding the Kyoto protocol tended to remain at an intellectual level, *An Inconvenient Truth* would be accessible to the public—not only to those who could attend a presentation or who would voluntarily choose to research the issue.

Gore opened the forum to a wider audience through his implementation, which focused less on the framework of government and more on a mass media dissemination of the information in order to encourage personal change. Moreover, the movie was accompanied by a book that compiled much of the slide-show data with additional information as well as a feature on what individuals can do to reduce their personal impact on the environment.

Awareness for the issue has skyrocketed. As a result of increased attention in civilian discourse, commercial, and political responses were launched accordingly to address increased concern from an active and aware population. Today, sales of "green" or earth-friendly products are a common sight on grocery store shelves. Such items include goods made from recycled materials and energy efficient light bulbs and appliances. Many corporations have begun to provide incentives for employees to decrease their carbon footprints by carpooling or using public transit.

Politicians, as part of their platforms, have promised tax credits for environmentally friendly practices such as using solar energy or buying a hybrid vehicle. Legislators already in office have agreed to think outside the box by implementing four-day workweeks and setting personal $CO_2$ rations.

Movements such as the WE campaign, also a brainchild of Al Gore, have begun to garner nationwide support. These and similar programs have created awareness about the Earth's current and future environmental condition. They are the latest evolution of grassroots, unpartisan efforts to address the climate change situation, which had existed previously as a political battle between nations and corporations. Although the climate change issue may be far from resolved, it is clear that the efficacy of Gore's work toward a widespread ground-up awareness campaign has proven to be genius.

**Evolution of the Idea of Surgery**

The popularity of contemporary medical dramas on primetime television illustrates the continued fascination by the populace with the medical profession. While these shows present the most extreme of worst-case scenarios, and though the doctors' fresh hair and makeup cast a shadow of doubt on the overall verisimilitude, viewers are nonetheless captivated by the scientific advancements, extensive training and quick thinking that allow one human being to save the life of another.

Americans accept the glamorization of the surgical profession in the name of entertainment and think nothing of it. Yet few are aware of the period in history when surgery and those who performed it were considered second-rate, and would-be physicians engaged in a barbaric subsidiary of the medical discipline.

Discovery of surgical instruments as artifacts is evidence that surgery was performed in some of civilization's earliest known cultures. These primitive surgeries mainly consisted of circumcision of the foreskin of the penis or the amputation of fingers or limbs. Far simpler than today's surgery, these procedures required little more than a sharp object and minimal skill with which to wield it. The purposes for surgery were utilitarian or religious. For instance, a damaged finger would be amputated to stem the spread of infection, or trepanation, making a hole in the skull, would be performed in order to release spirits believed to cause migraines, epilepsy, and mental disorders.

The original Hippocratic Oath, often recited by modern doctors as a pledge to the ethical practice of medicine, makes a specific distinction between physicians and surgeons: "I will not cut for stone, even for patients in whom the disease is manifest; I will leave this operation to be performed by practitioners, specialists in this art."[525] To "cut for stone" refers to the removal of bladder, kidney, or gall stones. In designating this function to be performed by "specialists," the general physician gives himself the distinction of a comprehensive healer while the surgeon retains the function of an anatomical carpenter.

The idea of surgery, even in terms of helping to remedy or alleviate disease such as gallstones, was still regarded more as grunt work than as a practice requiring dexterity, finesse, and a familiarity with the body's internal systems and functions. To cut the physical body instead of curing it form the inside out seemed like an unsophisticated way of healing or a last resort. An understanding of surgical methods for the medical purposes we recognize today can largely be credited to Greek physician Herophilus, who established an advanced medical school in Alexandria.

Having vivisected nearly 600 live prisoners, Herophilus became familiar with the human body's nervous and reproductive systems.[526] He was one of the first to recognize the brain as central control for the nerves and is credited with discovering ovaries. An understanding of these systems paved the way for future surgeries to be performed as a means for treating specific internal conditions. Although Herophilus had to study on live humans, his innovative views on the nature and necessity of surgery enabled him to gain knowledge in the field of medicine that has been immeasurably beneficial to mankind.

Today, surgery is a main component of treatment in the medical field. Surgeries can be performed anywhere on the body, ranging from methods similar to the early amputation practices to highly complex procedures that require intricate incisions, such as on the heart or the eyes. If the idea of cutting the body had remained as stigmatized as it was in primitive cultures, modern medicine would be unrecognizable. And so, perhaps, would primetime television.

**A Failed Idea Implemented Ingeniously**

Usually, the clarity of hindsight makes it much easier to classify an idea as good or bad. There are ideas that sound wonderful as well as those that sound awful, and the only differentiation between the two is how they are implemented. A failed idea, or an idea for which a practical purpose cannot be imagined, can often be implemented in a way that turns it into a very successful effort. In other words, the genius of the idea is not in the initial concept, but in the success of the idea post-implementation, as it exists in a more tangible form.

Post-It-Notes, the widely popular office product, are illustrative of a seemingly failed idea that was implemented ingeniously. Dr. Spencer Silver, working in the research laboratories at 3M, invented an adhesive in 1968. Described as "inherently tacky elastomeric copolymer microspheres", the adhesive did not bond to the surfaces it touched and was therefore far weaker than any previously developed by the company.[527] Despite attempts to pitch the product over the course of several years, the idea of a weak adhesive did not seem to have a practical purpose and was therefore was not well received by the company's leadership. Silver continued to search for ways to use his "glue."

He did use the adhesive in one invention that was commercially launched: the Post-It Bulletin Board. The background was a picture that resembled a genuine cork board, but the novelty was that it did not require thumb tacks.[528] Memos and flyers could be pressed on, and would remain there until removed. The failure of the product was that dust and dirt also clung to the open plane of adhesive and there was no significant reason why a consumer would prefer to buy the Post-It Bulletin Board as opposed to using cheap and practical thumbtacks on a normal cork board. Poor sales did not stop Silver from continuing to demonstrate his discovery to his colleagues. At one of his seminars, chemical engineer Art Fry, Silver's golfing partner and fellow employee, would learn of the glue and in 1974, he would begin to implement Silver's idea ingeniously.

A member of the choir at his Presbyterian church in Minnesota, Fry used strips of paper to mark the pages in his hymnal book. He grew frustrated at their tendency to flutter out from between the pages, which caused him to lose his place. Fry remembered the adhesive that Silver had demonstrated at his seminar and obtained some from 3M, which he applied to his bookmarks. With some tweaking, he created a bookmark that would remain in place yet that could be removed without causing damage to the pages. Thus, the original Post-It-Notes were born.

But implementation efforts did not end there; they were actually two-fold. Although Fry found a practical application for the adhesive developed by Silver, the public still needed to be convinced of the usefulness of Post-Its. Fry distributed Post-It samples throughout 3M, to secretaries, librarians, and co-workers. When the free samples were used up, many people came back to ask Fry for more. They generated a following within the workplace, but no one was sure if Post-Its would catch on in a wider market. Specifically, would people still want them when they had to pay for them?

Once again, the idea went flat due to failures in implementation; 3M's initial launch of post-it-notes did not generate consumer interest. Fry believed that Post-Its were a great idea and a great product but he was also aware of the need for commercial success. "You can have great ideas, but if you can't sell those ideas, you're dead in the water."[529] He adjusted his sales strategy accordingly.

In 1978, the company distributed free Post-It Note samples to consumers in Boise, Idaho. The new approach to marketing, which they dubbed the 'Boise Blitz', proved successful; 90% of recipients of the sample post-its intended to buy them in the future.[530] In the next two years, Post-Its were available across the United States. Later, they were introduced into the European and Canadian markets.

In 1984, an article in People magazine reported 3M's annual earnings at $45 million dollars. By 1998, Post-It sales generated nearly one billion dollars a year. Post-It Notes and the many varieties and variations are among the top five most popular office products in terms of sales and Silver's adhesive is now used in hundreds of products. Even though the original discovery of weaker glue seemed like a bad or worthless idea, Fry's implementation made it widely successful.

**Assembly Line at McDonalds**

In 1903, Henry Ford's automobile manufacturing company revolutionized mass production by implementing an assembly line process for constructing vehicles. The assembly line allowed for an increased number of cars to be produced in far less time than it would take to assemble each one individually. Increased efficiency in production allowed Ford to sell cars at a more affordable price and as the industry grew, automobiles ceased to be merely recreational vehicles. An increasing number of consumers purchased cars and used them for daily transportation. Though he is often credited with implementing the idea on a larger and more visible scale than ever before, Ford did not invent the concept of assembly line production.

There are a handful of examples of a similar process being employed throughout history. For instance, around 215 B.C.E. the first Chinese emperor ordered a regiment of 8,000 clay soldiers to be constructed. The body parts were formed separately at their respective locations and then brought together for assembly.[531] In the 1500s, the Venetian arsenal was able to produce an entire ship in one day by following an assembly line model.[532] As industrial revolutions swept through the United States and Europe, the systematic handling and assembly of goods became prevalent in all types of manufacturing.

Just as Ford implemented the concept of an assembly line on an unprecedented scale, the idea was implemented ingeniously in a different industry: food service. Ray Kroc, the man recognized for founding the McDonalds fast food chain as we know it today, used the assembly line process to streamline the preparation of food. "I put the hamburger on the assembly line," he'd say.[533]

Kroc believed that assembly line production served as a type of quality control. Serving sizes, as well as processes for cooking, were well regulated. Fries were to be cooked for the same amount of time at each store and burger patties were defined with strict dimensions.[534] The same number of pickles would be placed on every burger. Kroc went so far as to experiment with cooking fries in a self-built laboratory.

**Ray Kroc achieved success by borrowing an old idea and applying it to a new context. Application of an idea is more important than thinking it up in the first place.**

Consistency was a means for establishing a brand. The customer would become familiar with the specific look and taste of McDonald's food. Even if they were traveling across the country, customers who dined at McDonald's along the way could expect the food to look and taste the same as the food at any of the other franchises. Regulation and an assembly line processes made it possible for a high volume of customers to be served in a short amount of time. Eventually the "drive through" would make fast food an even more convenient way to dine.

Kroc took an idea that had already been successful and implemented it in an entirely different venue. The genius of the idea is apparent in success of McDonald's reputation and brand recognition. The "golden arches" symbol is one of the most recognized brand symbols worldwide and national polls have ranked McDonald's french fries as the favorite fast-food french fry in the country. If Kroc had not maintained consistency in the food and processing of McDonald's through the implementation of assembly lines, it would not be the iconic dining venue it is today.

## Underhanded Implementation

When a really good idea is implemented, especially in the realm of inventions and patents, it is not uncommon for a fight for ownership of that idea to ensue. There are at least two instances in the last century in which an idea was implemented by an innovative individual and then mass produced by a corporation. These corporations saw the genius in the implementation and wanted to take the credit and enjoy the success. As a result, a legal battle ensued between the inventor and the business.

In 1953, it was Robert Kearns wedding night and he was celebrating with his wife. While opening a bottle of champagne, the cork popped off and shot directly into his eye.[535] Years later, he was driving through a light rain and the continuous wiper blades began to aggravate his poor vision. Kearns realized that wipers could be mimetic of the human eye; the eyelid, he reasoned, was essentially a wiper for the eye, which closes intermittently.

Kearns built the first prototype for his intermittent windshield wiper system in 1963 from parts he bought at an electronics store. Kearns patented the invention and pitched his idea to large automakers who he thought may wish to use the wiper system on new model vehicles. Ford Motor Company insisted that Kearns explain the technology behind his wiper system. They wanted to know exactly how it worked.

Kearns initially refused to explain the mechanism which he kept sealed in a red box with a label that read "Do Not Open." A Ford executive told Kearns that he was required by law to explain the wipers because they were a safety feature and then he relented. Several months after he revealed the technology behind the wipers, Ford explained that they decided not to use his intermittent wipers, after all. Instead, they claimed to have chosen a similar system that had been developed by their in-house research laboratory.[536]

Kearns was inclined to sue immediately but did not. It was nearly a decade later that Kearns, having disassembled a wiper on one of his sons' cars, discovered that Ford had gone forward with the use of his wiper design. This revelation caused Kearns to have a mental breakdown and to pursue a lengthy and expensive series of lawsuits against Ford and Chrysler. He repeatedly asserted that he would not be happy with winning money, but that it was justice he sought and the ability to control the manufacture and distribution of his own design.

Though Kearns was awarded some settlements, he suffered hardship as a result of the protracted lawsuits, including extreme mental duress and the dissolution of his marriage. Personal life aside, Kearns' idea and implementation of the intermittent windshield wiper were so ingenious that every car made today uses the system.

Also in the late 1960s, a similar legal struggle was underway over patent rights to the portable personal stereo player. Andreas Pavel and his friends often gathered at his home with friends to talk and listen to a variety of music. On several occasions they mused over the potential of being able to take the record player with them anywhere they went, even outdoors. The idea was that music could be portable; that a person on-the-go could carry the music of their choosing along with them.

In 1972, Pavel and his girlfriend tried out the prototype of his new invention, the portable personal stereo player, which he called a stereobelt.[537] They were outdoors, in the mountains in St. Moritz, Switzerland, when the couple listened to the first music over their headphones. Pavel was thrilled with the new ability to carry his music and listen to it anywhere. He took his idea to several audio companies with the hope that one of them would be interested in manufacturing it. One after another, the companies rejected Pavel's idea. He recalls that they ridiculed him: "They all said they didn't think people would be so crazy as to run around with headphones, that this is just a gadget, a useless gadget of a crazy nut."[538]

Although Pavel had filed patents in several countries, including the United States, Italy, Germany, England, and Japan, Sony nonetheless began selling personal portable stereos in 1979. Pavel wanted a royalty fee from sales of Sony's product, which is named the Walkman. The legal battle with the Sony Corporation lasted for over 25 years but the result was positive. Sony finally admitted that Pavel was the father of the Walkman; he could legally take credit for the ingenuity behind inventing headphones and thus implementing his idea of listening to music while on the go.

## Kudzu: Poor Implementation

Anyone who drives down a country road in the Southern United States will inevitably see fences, inclines and old barns that are overgrown with the green, leafy plant known as kudzu. In 1876, kudzu was carried across the ocean, from Japan to America, and introduced at the Philadelphia Centennial Exposition.[539] Kudzu, sometimes also known by other names such as *foot a night vine* and *mile a minute vine*, was touted for its usefulness. It could serve as a forage crop, essentially a food source for grazing animals, or as a purely decorative plant.

In 1935, the United States Soil Conservation Service and the Civilian Conservation Corps persuaded Southern farmers to plant kudzu as a means for stopping soil erosion.[540] It seemed like a good idea, because farmers in the Mid-west were in the midst of the Dust Bowl; a series of devastating dust storms that resulted from poor soil conservation practices.

In addition to its uses on a farm, kudzu can also be used as food for humans. There are many ways to serve the leaves, both raw and cooked, and its purple flowers can be made into a sweet jelly spread. Kudzu also has a host of medicinal benefits and is highly effective at treating migraines.[541] A plant with countless benefits, the introduction and use of kudzu to the United States seemed like a no-brainer.

However, poor implementation turned a good idea and a useful plant into a pesky weed. The climate of the Southern United States was perfect for the plant. The mild winters and hot, humid summers caused the plant to spread like wildfire. It spread outside of the areas where it was intended to grow and overran nearby structures and plants. The roots of the kudzu plant are large, between four and eight inches in diameter and can reach twelve feet below ground. The vines grow a foot a day and 60 feet total during the temperate part of the year.

In order to combat the rampant growth and the consequences of the poor implementation, several methods have been devised. The kudzu can be killed if the crown is cut from the root. If a portion of a root crown remains, the plant can regenerate itself. Herbicides can also be applied and in some cases burning is helpful for removing the leaves so that the vines and roots are more visible for cutting. The U.S. Forest Service has begun to develop a biological control agent to kill and control kudzu.[542] Each of these solutions requires lots of time and energy.

Kudzu is a highly-visible cautionary tale about poor implementation. The planting of kudzu should not have been a free-for all. Botanists should have become familiar with the new species and studied its characteristics before introducing it into a new environment. It should have remained a showpiece at the Philadelphia Centennial Exposition rather than presented as a common plant. Neither caution nor foresight was exercised during implementation and as a result, the spread of kudzu is a nuisance that we must deal with for an indeterminate time.

## Conclusion

As self-help guru and author Barbara Sher said, "Doing is a quantum leap from imagining." Ideas, likely even great ones, occur daily. Ephemeral in nature, these ideas exist solely in the minds of those who have created them and therefore neither deserve nor receive much praise for their ingenuity. It is only through the implementation of a well-developed plan; identifiable goals, fluid execution, and dogged effort, even in the face of unforeseen obstacles, that an idea can become a reality.

In an American context, ingenious implementation of ideas is a defining quality of our government, the first modern democratic model of its kind. It is also characteristic of our citizens, whose individual achievements have advanced their ranks in society while collectively advancing our nation's place on the world stage. Within America and without, the very best ideas are those that were applied innovatively. Be it an old idea revamped or a failed idea resurrected, the genius was in the implementation.

# *Maxim 10*

## *"Politics is like a game of marbles... he who has a bigger pile at the end of the game wins."*

*All political lives, unless they are cut off in midstream at a happy juncture, end in failure, because that is the nature of politics and of human affairs.*

— Brigadier John Enoch Powell, MBE (Most Excellent Order of the British Empire), British politician, linguist, writer, academic, soldier and poet, (1912—1998). Only British soldier during World War II to rise from private to brigadier.

*I'm glad that Governor Romney is happy with his silver, but my experience in politics is there are no bronzes and silvers.*

— Ed Rollins, reaction to a statement by former Massachusetts Governor Mitt Romney, who said he finished with a silver medal in the 2008 Iowa caucuses. Romney later finished second to Arizona Senator John McCain in the New Hampshire primary. Rollins was a political consultant to the 2008 presidential campaign of former Arkansas governor Mike Huckabee.

## Overview

Upon arriving in Keystone, South Dakota, a patriotic traveler is shocked to find that Mount Rushmore has undergone an extensive makeover. The colossal granite monument has been re-outfitted with the heads of William Jennings Bryan, John Breckinridge and Charles C. Pinckney. While the pedestrian American may have heard the names of these men before, he does not readily recall either their countenance or their historical contribution. What the traveler fails to realize is that all three of these men were once prominent American politicians. Bryan, Breckinridge and Pinckney were so distinguished, in fact, that they finished second in the contest for the most coveted political position of all, that of the presidency of the United States of America.

Unfortunately, for these past politicians, they have been overshadowed by the accomplishments of their somewhat more memorable counterparts: Theodore Roosevelt, Abraham Lincoln and Thomas Jefferson, respectively.

Every four years we watch candidates battle it out for a chance to become the next president. Because of the complexity of the political system and the massive amount of votes a candidate needs to advance through the requisite system of presidential preference primaries, it is often the case that all of the top three or four candidates are competent individuals, persons of integrity with a high-level of leadership skills. Perhaps even all of them deserve to be president.

The stark reality, however, is that there is only one desk in the White House Oval Office. And while it may seem like an honor to be considered the second most qualified person in the nation for the position of commander in chief, the aforementioned also-rans would tell you that there is no silver medal in politics. The victors fill the annals of history while the losers fade into relative historical anonymity.

## *Chapter 10 Synopsis*

- By most definitions, politics are all or nothing . . . either you win or you lose. There is no silver medal.
- Even politics can be defined by less than a clear-cut win . . . someone who makes a better showing than expected is said to have achieved a victory or sorts.
- Sometimes victory is denied by the unethical or unpopular actions someone must take in order to win.
- Never use divisive tactics to win . . . uniting tactics work much better and create fewer enemies.

Maxim 10: "Politics is like a game of marbles . . . he who has the most at the end of the game wins" speaks of a fundamental truth about the finality of politics. Either a candidate wins or loses. There is no in between—particularly true if achieving that political victory was the only objective of a long, hard-fought race. The good news is that this isn't necessarily true in all human endeavors.

During this Olympic year, spectators watch athletes mount the winners' podiums to receive one of three medals: bronze, silver or gold. An athlete who finishes third with a bronze has a lot to be proud of: out of all the fine athletes competing internationally, the one who takes the bronze is among the three top contenders in his or her respective sport.

Silver is even better. Nothing to be ashamed of as the second best runner, high jumper, swimmer or whatever in the world. But what about a gold? It says you are the best in the world at that moment in world competition. Mark Spitz won seven gold medals in swimming at the 1972 Olympics in Munich. And in this 2008 Olympic year, along comes Michael Phelps who beats even legendary Spitz with eight gold medals.

Unfortunately, in politics, there's only the gold . . . no silver or bronze. Winning and success are not synonymous. The question for politicians, then, becomes: What does it take to win the most marbles? Is there anything about winning that can be learned from the winners? How far should a candidate be willing to go to win? Is integrity more important than a victory?

The zero-sum nature of the American presidency has a certain semblance to historical military campaigns. This is especially apropos if the two opposing sides are in a fight to the death. Just as an election is either a win or lose situation, in battle the result may be life or death to the loser. For American Lieutenant Colonel George Armstrong Custer, commander of the ill-fated 7th Cavalry massacred by the Cheyenne and Sioux at the 1876 Battle of the Little Big Horn in Montana, winning could have meant the Presidency of the United States or a promotion. Losing, however, meant death to him and 210 soldiers under his command. Defeat also created for Custer a legendary place in the history of the American West.

### Custer's Great Gamble

Custer, a native of Ohio who grew up in Michigan, appeared to have little future in the military after enrolling at West Point. Historians note that at the nation's military academy he "utterly failed to distinguish himself in any positive way. Several days after graduating last in his class, he failed in his duty as officer of the guard to stop a fight between two cadets. He was court-martialed and saved from punishment only by the huge need for officers with the outbreak of the Civil War."[543]

Custer distinguished himself as a war hero in the Civil War. His flashy, aggressive tactics have earned him a reputation as "reckless," but impulsive cavalry charges that saved the day for Union forces in strategically important battle such as Gettysburg. Historian Kennedy Hickman describes Custer's bravery and bold leadership in this battle that turned out to be the turning point of the war.

> As Union troops south of the town were repulsing Longstreet's Assault (Pickett's Charge), Custer was fighting with Brigadier General David Gregg's division against Major General J.E.B. Stuart's Confederate cavalry. Personally leading his regiments into the fray on several occasions, Custer had two horses shot out from under him. The climax of the fight came when Custer led a mounted charge of the 1st Michigan which stopped the Confederate attack. His triumph as Gettysburg marked the high point of his career.[544]

Custer's Indian fighting days proceeded almost as roughly as his days at West Point. He was placed in command of the 7th Cavalry in July of 1866 and become involved in an unsuccessful campaign against the Southern Cheyenne. He was court-martialed in late 1867 for being absent from duty during the campaign and suspended from duty for a year. He appealed to his old Civil War friend, General Phil Sheridan—who agreed with Custer's claim that he was being made the scapegoat of the unsuccessful campaign—and called him back to duty in 1868.[545]

Historians have debated for a century why Custer so recklessly attacked the band of Lakota, Cheyenne, and Arapahoe camped near the Little Big Horn. Some historians cite Custer's tendency to attack when unsure of the appropriate tactics. Others say he was impatient to earn an impressive victory to help him politically.

For decades, some scholars have contended that Custer was hoping to gain military recognition against the Indians and then receive the nomination for president at the 1876 Democratic convention in St. Louis. Others point out that there is no documented evidence that convention delegates were ready to put Custer's name into nomination and that the idea is ludicrous.[546]

Source of the rumor came from reports that Custer told his Arikara scouts that after the campaign he would be their "Great Father" in Washington. Some believe he was referring to an appointment to head the Indian Bureau in Washington, D.C. More than likely, Custer referred to the prospect of a promotion to General had he secured a decisive victory. His hurry to attack also seemed to stem from an urgency to keep the assembled Indians from breaking camp and escaping battle.

Believing there were only 900 to 1,800 warriors in the camp, Custer divided his approximately 650-man force into three separate groups—in addition to Custer's approximately five divisions, a second division was headed by Major Marcus Reno and a third by Captain Frederick Benteen— to attack, encircle and cut off any avenue of escape.[547]

The relatively small, disorganized force expected by Custer in reality were 3,000 strong and armed with the latest Winchester repeating rifles. The soldiers were not as well armed with single-shot carbines that had to be reloaded after a single shot. Thus, the attacking Sioux had superior numbers and fire power. Major Reno's forces were met by a fierce attack, and his group suffered heavy losses. Only the timely arrival of Captain Benteen and his forces reinforced Reno's divisions and saved them from annihilation. Custer's troops, cut off from the others, were wiped out in less than an hour.[548]

## Crossing the Rubicon

Antiquity is replete with incidences in which a commander was faced with a contested course of action to which he would either rise to prominence or fade into relative obscurity. Julius Caesar's decision to cross the river Rubicon in the year 49 B.C.E. provides a brilliant example of this.

By age 50, Caesar had already made a case for himself in the hall of honor of Roman history. The patrician child had grown up to become Pontifex Maximus (the highest Roman priest), had been elected Governor of Hispania Ulterior (Outer Iberia) and as Consul and member of the first triumvirate had conquered Gaul (modern France). The successful general's rise to prominence did not go unnoticed. Fearing that Caesar would echo his predecessor Sulla and lead a dictatorial march on the imperial capital, rival Pompey and the Roman Senate denied him the right to present his candidacy for consulship again and demanded that he return to Rome without his army. Caesar found himself at a difficult crossroads: concede all that he had earned and face uncertain prosecution in Italy or begin another Roman civil war. Suetonius describes the moment of irreversible fate in his *The Twelve Caesars*:

> Then, overtaking his cohorts at the river Rubicon, which was the boundary of his province, [Caesar] paused for a while, and realizing what a step he was taking, he turned to those about him and said: "Even yet we may draw back; but once cross yon little bridge, and the whole issue is with the sword." ... Then Caesar cried: "Take we the course which the signs of the gods and the false dealing of our foes point out. The die is cast," said he.[549]

Although the river Rubicon was only a small tributary leading to the Adriatic Sea, it served a colossal symbolic boundary. Caesar's declaration, "The die is cast," was not a casual pronouncement that he would be visiting Rome but the proclamation of an unwelcomed invasion and the commencement of an epic change, for better or worse.

Suetonius tells of Caesar's campaigns through Gaul, Pontus, Africa and Alexandria. It was on the steps of the Capitol, illuminated by elephants donned with lamps that the general delivered his timeless "Veni, vidi, vici" or "I came, I saw, I conquered."

Before Caesar's fateful rendezvous with Brutus on the steps of the capital, Emperor Caesar was able to make remarkable progress in his five-year rule. The loyal general rewarded his soldier's generously for their efforts and held unprecedented festivities for the people of Rome. Perhaps more lasting, Caesar was able to expand the empire, offering citizenship to former provinces which spread the Latin language and

Roman innovation. Under his direction, the calendar was restructured from 10 to 12 months, one of which would be named "July," honoring Caesar through the variation of his first name, Julius. Caesar was such a consummate administrator that his name became synonymous for future Roman leaders. Over time, Caesar as a ruling title was adapted to other languages to include "Kaiser," in Germany and "Czar," or "Tsar," in Russia.

One must not forget that Caesar's legacy began with the decision to "cross the Rubicon," a term that has become synonymous for embarking on a course of action from which there is no ready escape. It is the proverbial "point of no return." Caesar realized that he would either revolutionize the Roman system or join the long list of Italian intruders that had failed to conquer the Republic.

**Every campaign comes to a moment of decision, where the hard work that has been accomplished results in either success or failure of the objectives. Your Rubicon may be an election, a business contract, or a decision on an air permit.**

Caesar's decision to conquer, lauded as it may be today, was a bold maneuver by any standard. In addition to the newly conquered territories and the considerable resources that went into waging war, Caesar put at risk the greatest asset of all: the life of himself and those of his soldiers.

**Exploring a New World**

Examples of such a resolute decision are rare in history, but the exploration of Mexico led by Hernan Cortes in the 16th century may come close.

Commissioned by the Spanish Empire to explore the Mexican mainland, Hernan Cortes and his roughly six hundred soldiers embarked on an epic exploration in 1519. Cortes was emboldened by a skewed sense of confidence that was not without justification. In just over a quarter century, the Spanish had discovered the Americas, expulsed the Moors from the Iberian Peninsula, and, under Charles V, assumed the direction of the Holy Roman Empire. To acquire the riches of the New World for the Spanish Empire and for himself seemed to be destiny.

Cortes's men, on the other hand, were not as convinced. The prospect of facing an advanced, indigenous civilization for the sake of "Glory, Gold and Gospel," as suggested by historian Winston A. Reynolds, was mitigated by the menace of an unchartered territory rumored to host cannibalistic peoples. Cortes understood the only way to ensure the loyalty of his men was to destroy the only escape route. He proceeded to scuttle his entire naval fleet in order to preclude any possibility of mutiny. Cortes, who was not only a commander but a skilled orator, persuaded his men that the ships were of little service and that the extra materials and manpower (the ship's former soldiers) would be put to better use against the Aztecs:

> As for me, I have chosen my part. I will remain here, while there is one to bear me company. If there be any so craven, as to shrink from sharing the dangers of our glorious enterprise, let them go home, in God's name.... They can tell there, how they have deserted their commander and their comrades, and patiently wait till we return loaded with the spoils of the Aztecs.[550]

Cortes left his men with no option. They would either conquer the massive, advanced Aztec society or die trying. Cortes would either become the epitome of valiant conquistador or would soon be replaced with Spanish reinforcements. The paucity of Aztec peoples as well as the Christian, Spanish-speaking character of what is today Latin America demonstrates the ultimate outcome. Cortes omnipresence in literature, beginning with Golden Age praises and continuing in subsequent movements glorify what the ambitious adventure was able to accomplish.

Before denouncing the campaigns of both Caesar and Cortes as merely reckless, it necessary to understand that both men were led by obligation more than option. Caesar's hostile recall by the Senate left him with no choice but to raise arms, lest he suffer imminent and likely unjust prosecution. As the Consul of Gaul proclaimed, "Even I, Gaius Caesar, after so many great deeds should have been found guilty, if I had not turned to my army for help." Additionally, tribunes who had protested the censure of Caesar were cast out of Rome, giving legitimacy to Caesar's ascension to power.

Cortes was not only driven by the pursuit of glory, god, and gospel but also a serious financial commitment. Records show that approximately half of the cost of the Mexico expedition was funded by Cortes' own estate meaning that a failure to acquire at least a modest amount of New World booty would spell complete bankruptcy for the ambitious adventurer. Cortes's deep involvement in the mission caused a riff between Cortes and Diego Velasquez, then governor of Cuba, who had commissioned the expedition. According to Reynolds, "Shortly before the fleet's departure . . . the governor became suspicious of Cortes spirited-ness and popularity among the men and tried to remove him from command." Instead, Cortes fleet departed against the will of Velasquez, essentially severing all ties with the Spanish Empire. It was unlikely that a defeated deserter like Cortes would have been granted clemency by the rigid Spanish Empire, hence the seemingly desperate action.

One overarching theme that has been presented throughout this book is the advantages of the inclusive over the exclusive. Generally that precept has been used to describe the incorporation of a variety of stakeholders so that none felt they were marginalized. The idea of inclusiveness can also be ascribed to wins. Unlike conventional election campaigns that see only one winner or military campaigns in which there are only the conquerors and the conquered, a successful issue management campaign will avail itself a spectrum of potentially beneficial outcomes. Rather than crossing the Rubicon and embarking on a no holds barred campaign, the "invasion" becomes more of a calculated advance. Instead of destroying the escape route in order to ensure resolution, metaphorical ships are docked in ports where there are multiple exits.

An all out loss is unacceptable in issue management. The introductory chapter "Assume a winnable position" suggested the factors that go in to determining whether a win is possible or not. "Assuming a winnable position" means just that, striving for success but not being foolhardy with ambitions. The worst thing that a campaign can do is have an obvious failure. Whether it is a candidate that loses in an election or a resolution that does not pass a vote, the stigma that results from an apparent loss will terminate the short-term campaign and stifle the long term process.

That complete failures should be unbearable is not merely the result of pride. Though a loss is humiliating to the individual or individuals involved, the residing impact lies on the stakeholders who associate a loss with an inferior position. Furthermore, because most election cycles occur on a set timetable, a failed campaign must wait until the next cycle to present itself. A bill that dies in the legislative process, for example, cannot be reintroduced until the next congress has been instated.

There must be a way to promote an issue that does not put a campaign at risk of losing everything. Legendary Prussian military strategist Carl von Clausewitz echoed the words of the great Napoleon Bonaparte when he suggested that a commander is always peace loving and would prefer to take over a country unopposed. At first glance, this idea appears to contradict the traditional understanding of military campaigns wherein bellicose generals exert great force to bully their opposition into submission. The primary objective of a commander, clarifies Clausewitz, is not to decimate our adversaries but to disarm them. Aggression, therefore, should be used only as a last resort.

Winston Churchill echoed this sentiment in his book on World War I, *The World Crisis*. According to Churchill: "The greater the general, the more he contributes in maneuver, the less in slaughter. . . . There is required for the composition of the great commander not only massive common sense and reasoning power, not only imagination, but also an element of legerdemain, an original and sinister touch, which leaves the enemy puzzled as well as beaten . . . the object of all is to find easier ways, other than sheer slaughter, of achieving the main purpose."

To the extent that politics is much more civil than war, Churchill added "Politics are almost as exciting as war and quite as dangerous. In war you can only be killed once, but in politics many times." Issue management, though generally less savage than conventional warfare, often parallels the strategies employed by military men like Clausewitz, Bonaparte, and Churchill. Obstacles are generally manifested in the form of public opposition and the legislative bodies acting on behalf of their constituents. Rather than adopt traditional positions which attempt to resolve the conflict through the use of corporate clout, an issue management campaign is much more likely to achieve sustainable results if it is able to eliminate the resistance of the stakeholders. Having accomplished this end, there is no reason to believe that elected officials will not champion a particular cause.

Unlike the previous ultimatums, it is unlikely that a business will ever be guaranteed impunity or doomed to failure based on singular issue but that is not to suggest that their interests cannot be seriously compromised. Not all wins in an issue management campaign are uniform. Successful legislation may increase profitability by increasing competitiveness, reducing obstacles, or monitoring free and fair practices. Likewise, the ability to prevent harmful legislation can reduce the impediments of a functioning business practice.

Wins need not always be tangible. Often support from local officials comes in the form of written or spoken support. Though this does not translate to immediate benefits for the business, it is a win because it means that the business can count on the backing of important decision makers in future negotiations. Rather than oral commitments, non-binding resolutions have the ability to document and demonstrate support without making the decision makers feel that they have assumed an irrecoverable position. This does not mean flippant sponsorship but having some levity may make the decision makers feel more comfortable.

Public participation is another form of a win. Because legislators are elected by the people, a significant demonstration of support is likely to influence their position on an issue.

Assuming a winnable position certainly values ambition but realizes the risk in Cortes's destruction of the ships. Unlike the above ultimatums in which there is a clear winner and loser, the nature of an issue management campaign is often much more subtle. It is unlikely that a business will ever be guaranteed impunity or doomed to failure based on singular issue but that is not to suggest that their interests cannot be seriously compromised. Successful legislation may increase profitability by increasing competitiveness, reducing obstacles, or monitoring free and fair practices. Likewise, the ability to prevent harmful legislation can reduce the impediments of a functioning business practice.

The post modern adage suggests that the journey is just as valuable as the destination. In issue management, though the formation process is important, it is ultimately the outcome that matters. In American football, a team does not score any points by merely advancing down the field but must cross the goal line. While garnering support in an issue management campaign is critical, the accumulation of marbles does not matter until the final tally has been made. Knowing where the goal line is. Have you reached it? Chapter 2, "Set task and goals that lead to identifiable progress" suggested the importance of establishing and adhering to a meticulous timeline. Chapter 5, "Plan your work but remain fluid" reinforced the necessity of a blueprint but discussed the possibility of adapting to meet the circumstances. As a campaign reaches the final threshold, it is important to assess the progress to date and determine how close a victory is. In NFL football, the goal line is made distinguishable by fluorescent pylons; in issue management, however, the goal line may not be so readily apparent. The decisive moment in an issue management campaign involves the powerful transition from subjective support to objective gains. Because the consequences of such an action are so grave, the timing of this decision must be made with expert calculation.

The key to this approach is an understanding of the impact that campaigning has had on the constituents and how ambitious a proposal can be. Though a campaign is commenced with extensive foresight, it is often impossible to predict what the value of win is until the process comes to a conclusion. If enough support has been gained then a bill or resolution might be received unconditionally. If, however, there is reason to believe that the win faces serious obstacles, the objective may have to be tailored to accomplish the best result possible. This does not translate to a concession so much as maximizing the utility of a contested campaign. Persistence is certainly a value to be employed in an issue management campaign but this must not be confused for obstinacy. The previous chapter discussed how the true success of a campaign was the transition from idea to implementation. While it is great to have an ideal objective in mind, it is necessary to realize that a win is always contingent upon the support of the stakeholders. British Prime Minister Winston Churchill was quoted as saying that he liked to address perfection by its other name: paralysis. If a campaign cannot achieve the ideal 5% tax break it is looking for, it may have to settle for 3 or 4%, admirable gains in their own right.

One very important distinction from the above historical campaigns in that in issue management, the outcome should only be considered a win if everyone involved can consider themselves a winner. Whereas Caesar's rival Pompey was decapitated and Montezuma was pummeled with stones before dying at the hands of the Spanish, a contemporary issue management campaign stands to gain little from decimating its opponents. Creating a favorable situation for only the business may cause a riff with the opposition that could hinder future negotiations. For this reason it is important that a win be assessed not solely from the perspective of the campaign itself but from that of the stakeholders as well. If the stakeholders, those who are affected, feel that the business has in fact engaged them in the process and worked towards a mutually beneficial scenario, the outcome is much more likely to be sustained. By making the stakeholders feel that their interests have been sufficiently addressed, the affected communities are then likely to view the campaign with amity and work towards common goals in the future.

**The Marbles Analogy**

Until this point, the components of an issue management campaign have been presented rather piecemeal. In order to demonstrate how previous tools and methods come together, the entire political process can be compared to the game of marbles. In the game of marbles, the players use a shooter marble to knock the smaller marbles out of a ring. At the end of the game, whoever has the most marbles is declared the winner.

If the game of marbles is an extended metaphor for a contended issue management campaign, the stakeholders represent the marbles that both sides are vying for. With the help of the opinion makers, analogous to the shooters, the opponents attempt to accumulate the most marbles into their purse. If sufficient stakeholder support has been gathered, an issue management campaign should have little difficult in obtaining their objective. The marbles are analogous to stakeholders. A stakeholder is an individual or individuals whose interests are potentially compromised by a pending policy. Because legislators are accountable to their constituents, the best way to gain leverage over them is to have the stakeholders on your side. It is not necessary to draw a parallel between every single marble and every interest group because these groups often differ depending on the particular situation. It is important, however, to understand that potential support is not uniform in character and can often be compartmentalized based on interests.

The distinction should be made between stakeholders and voters. Of course within America's democratic system of government, there is no question that all votes are equally important. However, there may be certain interest groups—collectively based on demographics, values, income levels, political power and so on—that could disproportionately impact a decision. If the installation of a new plant has environmental repercussions, for example, it is possible that an environmental lobby will present a more challenging obstacle than a less organized, less politically experienced and mobilized issue group. Therefore, the most valuable marbles generally become the interest groups that represent the most vocal and politically powerful opposition. What is important is that the game is not strictly quantitative but also has a qualitative aspect to it, depending upon the number of marbles held by the various categories of stakeholders.

**The maxims outlined in this treatise provide the techniques with which to accumulate the necessary support for every campaign in which you engage.**

As in the game of marbles, larger, heavier "shooters" are used to propel the marbles out of the ring. Extending the metaphor to an issue management campaign, the shooters are represented by the local leadership and opinion makers, who are generally the particularly influential members of the community. Opinion makers usually assume these roles because they have a strong leadership presence and are regarded as capable of molding and shaping popular opinion. Whether their influence is either subtle or overt, members of the community turn to opinion makers for a carefully measured opinion of current events. Having the involvement and support of these community leaders is essential to the success of a political or issue campaign. Based simply on the fact that certain individuals are able to influence popular opinion, they probably possess a sophisticated, in-depth understanding of influences on community thought—such as past history, prejudices, ethnic concerns—and are able to diffuse a complex message through a specific paradigm.

## What Is a Win and Does It Always Equate to Success?

A successful implementation of a winnable position greatly improves the chances of a victory in politics or issue management. In politics, most frequently there is only one winnable position . . . a clear-cut electoral victory and control of the elected office. That said, not all triumphs in an issues management campaign are so clear cut. Unlike election campaigns in which there is a clear winner and loser, the nature of an issue management campaign is often much more subtle. Victory may come in increments. For example, to obtain state legislative action on a matter, the first victory may be in getting a bill introduced in the house or senate. Another victory comes when it receives favorable review and recommenddation in legislative committee. Other victories occur as the bill winds its way through the legislative process—success in keeping the proposed legislation alive; success in preventing revisions that thwart part of the objectives of the legislation; success in getting support from a majority of house or senate members; and so on as the bill slowly makes its way toward becoming law.

While it is unlikely that a business will ever be guaranteed success or doomed to failure based on a singular issue. That is not to suggest, however, that the specific interests of a business cannot be advanced by appropriate governmental action. For example, successful legislation can enhance profitability by increasing competitiveness, reducing regulatory obstacles or monitoring free and fair practices. Likewise, the ability to positively influence—or in a best-case scenario prevent—burdensome legislation can reduce the impediments to a functioning business practice.

This is where proactive measures utilizing the best resources available can improve the destiny of a business organization even when the chances of total success are minimal to none. For example, both public and private concern about global changes in the Earth's climate will most likely result in both state and federal legislation at some point. While there are many factors beyond the control of a corporation, that is not to say that a large corporate citizen cannot at least influence what will happen. Legislators must be informed about the effects of legislation on the ability of the company to make a profit, which in turn affects the fate of employees and their families. While a win may be defined by some businesses and industries as stopping pending legislation, that is often impossible. As discussed in chapter 1, in order to win, one must first choose a winnable position.

## Achieving a Victory Following a Loss

Al Gore narrowly lost the 2000 race for President. Gore won the popular vote, but lost the Electoral College by only five votes (271-266). In early 2001, if anyone was talking about Gore it was most certainly related to his failed presidential bid. Rather than brood on what was so nearly a victory, however, Gore decided to continue on his goal of becoming an instrumental leader in environmental consciousness, an issue that had been incorporated into Gore's political platform since early in his Tennessee days. With his political days behind him, Gore was now able to focus solely on global climate change.

Gore began advocating the impact of climate change through a series of lectures, the product of which was a documentary titled *An Inconvenient Truth*. The film was eventually awarded the 2007 Oscar for Best Documentary Feature and the accompanying non-fiction book reached #1 on the New York Times non-fiction list.

Gore along with Rajendra K. Pachauri of the Intergovernmental Panel on Climate Change were awarded the Nobel Peace Prize in 2007 "for their efforts to build up and disseminate greater knowledge about man-made climate change, and to lay the foundations for the measures that are needed to counteract such change." Perhaps the most coveted humanitarian recognition in the world, the presentation of the Nobel Prize in Oslo solidified Gore's critical role in the search for a more sustainable environmental policy.

If the motivation for being president was to provide integral leadership on vital issue, Gore managed to accomplish the task without ever being elected. Gore was able to convert a perceived failure into an overwhelming success and his contribution to the American public (and the global public) has been profound.

Few 20th century politicians have earned the renown of former British Prime Minister Winston Churchill. A man who held every major cabinet position but one and earned a Nobel Prize for Literature for his account of the Second World War, it is not an exaggeration to suggest that Churchill was the consummate politician. Though he is today revered as one of the principle figures in halting the Nazi advancement and preserving freedom and democracy in the West, his legacy was not always so certain.

Churchill had only recently been appointed Prime Minister when the situation for the Allied Forces began to look dire. The Dunkirk evacuation saw hundreds of thousands of British and French troops fleeing continental Europe in a desperate effort to avoid a German slaughter. There was much talk that Hitler would take Paris and with the aid of the Italians offer peace terms. It was in a meeting on the aforementioned challenges that Churchill took a definitive stance that would dictate the course of the war. Hugh Dalton, minister for economic warfare, recorded in his notes of the meeting Churchill's declaration to fight on:

> "And I am convinced," [Churchill] concluded, "that every man of you would rise up and tear me down from my place if I were for one moment to contemplate parley or surrender. If this long island story of ours is to end at last, let it end only when each one of us lies choking in his own blood upon the ground."

Echoing Cortes' steadfast resolve, Churchill determined to stay and fight the Nazis at all costs. The idea of sending the British fleet, vulnerable children, or even precious art to the relative security of North America was vehemently denounced as "defeatist." According to historian and Churchill biographer Steven F. Hayward, "Any discussing of transferring the fleet, [Churchill] wrote, 'is bound to weaken confidence here at the moment when all must brace themselves for supreme struggle.'" Later, even under the direst circumstances, Churchill held his ground, suggesting "None must go. We are going to defeat them."

That an issue management campaign should draw a parallel to three ultimatums may seem paradoxical at first glance. The entire book to this point has demonstrated the advantages of compromise in achieving objectives. Previous chapters provided tools and methods that would reduce opposition, not create conflict. Even the chapter on "Exchange Fire" was only meant to demonstrate the use of retaliation as a means of maintaining a reputation—it was not a figurative call to arms. How, then, does one reconcile the idea that a campaign is either pass or fail?

The book *has* concentrated on mutually beneficial scenarios. In issue management there is great value in garnering the support of the people but that is not the target purpose. While the previous chapters provide objectives that are gratifying in and of themselves, one must concede that the aim of a campaign is to achieve a particular end to which there is no consolation prize. And while previous chapters had soft or gradient outcomes in which the success of a campaign could be measured along a spectrum, ultimately, a political campaign allows for no second place. It is with an understanding of this conclusive nature of politics that the introductory ultimatums begin to unfold as remarkable analogies to a convincing campaign.

The expression "Crossing the Rubicon" has become synonymous for embarking on a course of action from which there is no ready escape—it is the proverbial "point of no return." Caesar realized that he would either revolutionize the Roman system or join the long list of Italian intruders that had failed to conquer the republic. Cortes, likewise, knew that following a vigorous confrontation with the Aztec he would either "dine to the sound of trumpets, or perish on the gallows."[551] Churchill's situation was more defensive but one must recognize that the Prime Minister had the chance to flee and fight another day or stay and suffer the unyielding German barrage.

When candidates decide to embark on an issue management campaign, they must realize the formidable task that is ahead of them. The introductory chapter "Assume a Winnable" position demonstrated how campaigns are based on a precise calculation of the chances of winning—it did not suggest that they would be easy. The term *ultimatum* means a final, uncompromising demand or set of terms issued by a party to a dispute, the rejection of which may lead to a severance of relations. Could this not also serve as the conditions of a highly contested political campaign? There is certainly no compromise in politics and the severance of relations may be the interim period in which a candidate returns to his constituency, revamping his image for the next election cycle. The Mount Rushmore scenario at the beginning of this chapter shows that political campaigns are particularly difficult because there is only one individual elected per seat. To make this more concrete, a candidate who gets 40% of the total vote does not get to propose four out of ten bills or to serve a proportional amount of time in office but returns to his constituency an ordinary citizen.

## Maxim 10: Politics Is Like a Game of Marbles

If the idea of a political ultimatum sounds daunting, perhaps it is because the observer is approaching the campaign from a macroscopic level. Certainly the aforementioned commanders did not summarize their campaigns as "Defeat Rome," Defeat Mexico," and "Defeat Fascism," respectively, but operated on a much more microscopic scale. Every battle, every allegiance, every opportunity was distinguished as a singular event that was part of a greater cause. Douglas L. Davis of *Anthropological Quarterly* assessed the "on-the-ground" factors that gave the Spanish an advantage over the Aztec suggesting that that "The variability of unit and unit size was adaptive in the sense that a commander could adjust the organization of his command to the needs of the moment." In this sense, a campaign is similar to a mosaic: seemingly whole when viewed from a distance but actually composed of differing individual components. Prime Minister Churchill understood the necessity of addressing major issues on a minute level when he wrote "An efficient and successful administration manifests itself equally in great as well as small measures." Again, this concept is best illustrated through a presidential campaign.

The number of eligible voters refers to the number of American citizens who are above age 18 (with a few exceptions). In the 2004 presidential election, this figure was 200,000,000, a number that may be daunting at first glance. The next important figure is the number of registered voters. Though voter registration has been on the rise in recent years, the unfortunate realty of civics is that not everyone who can vote does. In 2004, only 120 million were registered to vote. Of these registered voters, only a fraction generally show up to the polls—80 million in 2004. Finally, a candidate may consider (not assume) that a large portion of the voters are necessarily going to vote along party lines. By taking the middle 20% of the previous statistic, it is possible to see how a presidential campaign becomes more manageable—only 16 million of the original 200 million. When the elections are held on a state or local level, that number becomes much smaller.

An understanding of the diametrically opposed outcomes of a political campaign and a deduction of what it takes to win are not always a product of intuition but rely greatly on experiential knowledge. Caesar's nine year campaign against the Gallic people gave him confidence in his troops and his tactics. His political savvy taught Caesar the importance of lobbying for the support of the tribunes who had been dejected by the

Senate and represented the public opinion. While Cortes' study of the wars with Italy and the conquest of the Moors coupled with an unyielding faith granted him confidence, perhaps it was his first hand experience were the most useful. According to J. H. Elliott, in his *The Mental World of Hernan Cortes*:

> There is in Cortes' correspondence a constant insistence on the importance of *experiencia*—that personal and individual knowledge of men and of things which an increasing number of early sixteenth-century Spaniards were coming to regard as superior to the knowledge derived from traditional authority.

Churchill's extensive administrate career, including his roles as President of the Board of Trade, Home Secretary and Chancellor of the Exchequer followed a youth that had been spent fighting in the Boer War and exploring extensively the English colony of Sudan. The purpose of citing the credentials of these commanders is to suggest that vigorous political campaigns should not be left to novices. There is great encouragement the Prime Minister's advice to "Always look for opportunities to advance bold new initiatives" but before embarking on a campaign that could potentially lead to absolute failure, a sufficient repertoire of personal experience is certainly a valuable asset.

This entire book has provided examples of both successful and failed issue management campaigns. The historical anecdotes, philosophical concepts, and case studies allow the reader to learn the lessons of campaigns past without having to relive the experience. In this way it is possible to appreciate the "do's and don'ts" of issue management vicariously. If one has executed effectively the tools and methods outlined in previous chapters, there should be no reason to balk at the challenge of an intimidating campaign. The thesis of this book, in fact, is that a comprehensive understanding of historical experiences combined with a proper effectuation of the recommended tactics and strategies will be sufficient to lead an effective campaign. This must not be approached casually, however, as there is much to be lost from missteps and miscalculations.

Caesar left the recently conquered and probably still volatile province of Gaul in order to lead multiple legions into battle against his rival Pompey. In addition to the hundreds of troops fostered by the Spanish Empire, historians suggest that Cortes poured his entire personal estate into the Mexico expedition. Churchill's valiant stance put at risk the safety of thousands of innocent British citizens, not to mention all of the trappings of British progress and prosperity. What has perhaps been alluded to but not made perfectly clear is that these three courageous commanders stood to lose the most costly asset of all: their lives.

Though the loser in a political campaign does not face the same perilous fate as the aforementioned commanders, due to the level of investment in a campaign, there is little margin for miscalculation. Talk may be cheap but politics are not. Certainly one would not advise cutting corners on the expenses of a campaign but, at the same time, there should be a concern that the considerable time and energy required for a campaign are put to good use. Spending millions on a campaign that reels in some 30% or 40% of the vote, while it may subtly affect the opposition's platform, is largely wasted if the desired official is not put into office. On the contrary, a carefully calculated campaign, though it may require considerable investment, stands to gain everything. Those who survive the rigorous election process are able to represent their constituency, propose public policy, and serve as a model citizen in the way the manner they believe to be the most effective, without directly competing with the opposition.

In addition to understanding of the make or break nature of campaigns and the considerable investment required to launch them, the effect of a steadfast resolve is crucial to the approach. Though legend may portray Julius Caesar as a fearless leader, history proves that there was much deliberation about his choice to cross the Rubicon. Likewise, to observe Cortes' decision to burn his ships as a reckless maneuver that precluded any opportunity of escape is to miss the point. What this anecdote emphasizes is that reluctance or the failure to commit one hundred percent is tantamount to desertion. A favorite adage of Cortes was that "necessity sharpens a man's wits." Like the parable of the tortoise and the hare, a belief that a campaign is destined to succeed may lead to the detrimental attributes of indifference and carelessness. Understanding that politics is a process with two diametrically opposed outcomes is as invigorating as it is intimidating. Coupled with a precise calculation of the situation, the knowledge that comes from experience, and effective investment, an internal decision to succeed can act as a self-fulfilling prophecy.

Churchill echoes the determination of Cortes but provides the perspective of a defensive position. Like an incumbent politician defending his seat against a viable challenger, Churchill understood the implications of not conceding anything. Every precinct, every voting group, every single vote must be retained if one hopes to achieve the "critical mass" needed to win an election. As soon as the candidate suggests that a few votes are expendable, he begins a vicious downward cycle. A successful politician will not let the idea of an imminent challenge translate into a feeling of diffidence. Morale must be resolute, never waning; even in dire conditions, it must be prevalent.

**Losing the Battle**

Perhaps there is no adage more overused than that of losing the battle and winning the war. The age old consolation to defeat suggests that an intermediary obstacle may not necessarily spell ultimate failure so long as the consummate effort results in a victory. At the risk of averring this cliché, it should be recognized that political campaigns are prolonged and few, if any, are flawless.

The previous subchapter provided three historical figures faced with dire ultimatums: to achieve victory or die trying. The legacies left by Julius Caesar, Hernan Cortes and Winston Churchill may suggest that each of these men led a flawless existence. A further investigation of history, however, provides that these men faced their own trials and travails in route to greatness. There is great solace in recognizing that these three immortals faced their share of struggles but there is even greater wisdom to be gained from understanding their reaction to adversity.

When we left off, Julius Caesar had decided to pursue Pompey from the north. Caesar stormed through Umbria, Picenum, and Etruria (Northern Italy) and forced his rival consul to cross the Adriatic. He then changed courses and confronted Pompey's leaderless men in Spain. Caesar eventually made his way to Alexandria—only to find out that Pompey had been slain—and it was here that he helped resolve the dispute between Ptolemy and the legendary Cleopatra before returning to

Rome to consolidate his power. The historian Suetonius lauds Caesar's accomplishments but recognizes that even Julius was human:

> Personally he always fought with the utmost success, and the issue was never even in doubt save twice: once at Dyrrachium, where he was put to flight, and said of Pompey, who failed to follow up his success, that he did not know how to use a victory; again in Spain, in the final struggle, when, believing the battle lost, he actually thought of suicide.[552]

Despite Caesar's broad success, he was not without fault. Defeats in Dyrrachium (modern Albania) and Spain proved that even the great Caesar was human. Suetonius suggests that many great lieutenants were lost in the fighting as well including Gaius Curio in Africa, Gaius Antonius in Illycium and Gnaeus Domitius Calvinus in Pontus. If this history of Cesarean warriors appears to be exhaustive, at least it serves to indicate that Caesar's en-route-losses may have been more common than traditionally believed.

Even the mythical Hernan Cortes was not without fault. Fellow conquistador and historian Bernal Diaz de Castillo recounts the Spanish departure of Tlacopan with great sobriety. After much deliberation, the Spanish decided to leave the capital of Tenochtitlan via a tortuous series of causeways because they were not the most logical route of escape and for this reason were less likely to be guarded. Though the actual date is debated (late June or early July 1520), the escape was carried out during the evening to further prevent detection. Cortes had the foresight to construct a portable bridge manned by a team of soldiers which would solve the problem of the gaps in the causeway. Some of the Spanish, mostly the former soldiers of Cortes' foe Narvaez, fled the capital of Tenochtitlan laden with precious metals and jewelry— a decision that would later prove very costly.

Much to their surprise, the stealthy Spanish exodus was detected and a ferocious battle erupted. Historian William H. Prescott describes the engagement in vivid detail, alluding to the "torrent of missiles," the "shouts of vengeance . . . mingled with groans of agony," and desperate soldiers trampling on "the weak and the wounded, heedless whether it were friend or foe."[553] To make matters worse, the portable bridge became lodged in one of the crevices and the men had to fight their way through standing water.

The result was a massacre in which hundreds of Spaniards and thousands of their indigenous allies were killed. Conservative estimates put the Spanish number at 150 while others exceed 400. There is little disagreement that the number of indigenous allies lost reached into the thousands. No one left the confrontation uninjured and many of Cortes' most valiant men were lost.

Prescott gives reason to believe that Cortes took the debacle deeply to heart: "Though accustomed to control his emotions, or, at least, to conceal them, the sight was too much for him. He covered his face with his hands, and the tears, which trickled down, revealed too plainly the anguish of his soul." The catastrophe is now commonly recognized as "la noche triste (the melancholy night)" because the legend is that upon reaching the relative security of Tlacopan, Cortes sat down on the roots of a kapok tree and began to weep.

**Even Churchill Suffers a Military Defeat**

One could discuss the Allied losses in War World II in order to demonstrate the adversity incurred by Winston Churchill but it may be more insightful to look at the Prime Minister's World War I experience. The consummate administrator, Churchill was appointed the position of the First Lord of Admiralty during the First World War where he was charged with leading the failed Dardanelles initiative.

The Dardanelles is the narrowest point on the Bosporus Strait (located in modern day Turkey) which connects the Black Sea and the Aegean Sea. The logic behind invading the Dardanelles was that if the Allies were able to execute an offensive here and weaken or defeat Turkey, they might relieve some of the pressure on Russia in the Eastern front and garner support from unaffiliated Balkan countries. The idea of an amphibious assault including the support of the 29th infantry division wavered back and forth but eventually the occupation was strictly maritime and the time of its commencement.

The inability of the Allies to supplement sufficient infantry allowed the Turkish to reinforce troops and what resulted was a lengthy standoff in which over a quarter million Allied troops perished in just eight months of battle. In addition to the grief caused by the loss of lives, there was much belief that the valuable resources that could have been used elsewhere were squandered. The always erudite Churchill described the static nature of the situation: "The Dardanelles has run on like a Greek tragedy." Unfortunately, however, he was unable to talk his way out of his culpability in the affair and as a result was held as a scapegoat for the Dardanelles and dismissed from his position.

**Issue Management and Military Struggles Are Similar**

Previous maxims demonstrate how it is possible to break a campaign up into stages that allow for diagnosable progress. When those objectives are not met—that is, when the proverbial battle appears lost—it has been suggested how the plan might be altered. One way is by dividing a campaign into a series of individual "battles" that make the process more digestible. Politics is not a bare bones science. The tendons linking these individual battles can be as important as the confrontations themselves. The importance here is continuance and perseverance.

Caesar's accusation that "Pompey . . . did not know how to use a victory" suggests that battles are not isolated incidences. In fact, the result of the battle is often only as important as the follow through. While Pompey's campaign was inhibited by his inability to utilize the inertia of a successful battle, Caesar was endowed with great resolve that allowed him to learn lessons from his failure to strengthen his campaign. Certainly the battle of Dyrrachium was important to the seizure of Rome, but Caesar realized that it was not the ultimate objective and that its loss could be reconciled if the next battle were a success.

Political battles are comparable to the changing tides of public perception. Polling shows that popular support can waver greatly between two candidates. Favorability of a candidate is likely to change from week to week but candidates cannot rest on their laurels and take victories for granted. The popularity contest matters only on one day: Election Day. Until that point, victories must be aggressively pursued to ensure the continuance of success. A successful campaign must not let down its guard when things seem to be going its way but follow the issue until all of the ballots have been counted. Likewise, a campaign that is trailing must have the resolve to persevere despite the greatest consternation.

The Spanish inability to reposition the portable bridge they had constructed in the causeways surrounding Tenochtitlan serves as an illustrative metaphor for the necessity to remain fluid in our campaigns. Cortes and his men had gaps in their plan, which they believed they could fill with ingenuity. It was not until that fateful July night that Cortes and his men realized the shortcomings of their planning and faced their fate. The skillful commander had recognized that there would be crevices in the causeway but assumed that his adjustment would be adequate to solve the problem. He did not foresee that the wooden bridge would become lodged in the stone and lead to a massacre. The altercation itself was ferocious but Cortes was miraculously able to survive to fight another day.

When political bridges become stuck and the grace of a campaign is forestalled, it may become necessary to fight through the masses. Just as the covert, unhindered getaway that Cortes would have liked to enjoy was ruined by Aztec sentinels, a political campaign may be stifled and the candidate may be left with an undesirable alternative. There may never be the occasion in which a campaign has to resort to the use of swords but there are instances in which civics can become less than civil. The chapter "Exchange Fire When Fired Upon" demonstrated the necessity of confronting slander in order to restore reputation but this in only one of the many darker sides of politics. When these instances occur, the best attributes that a politician can possess are endurance and versatility.

The annals of history prove that Churchill's Dardanelles debacle was not sufficient to end his political career forever. That was certainly not apparent at the time however. Steven F. Hayward writes that upon being ousted from admiralty in 1915, Churchill summed up his sentiments as "I am finished." Within the political circles of London, the incident was frequently referred to as "Churchill's folly." Churchill, however, knew that he could either give up his political aspirations or learn from the disaster. The tenacious Prime Minister once quipped "success is going from failure to failure without loss of enthusiasm."[554] None would like to suffer defeat but one must admit that there is some truth to the aphorism that "that which does not kill you only makes you stronger."

How often does an unlikely candidate come from the shadows to become the frontrunner in an election? On the other hand, how often do the "obvious" candidates incur insurmountable obstacles on the campaign trail that lead to the waning of their influence. Because political campaigns are often complex and prolonged, a less than ideal start, when managed correctly, can be transformed into a victory. If the dejected First Lord of Admiralty can rise to become the principle protector of freedom and democracy in the West, there is reason to believe that some losses are not permanent. Certainly—this does not mean that the candidate should give up at the first misstep.

**Political Pride Goes Before the Fall**

The second lesson to be learned from these lost battles is that there is much peril in pride when it comes to politics. History provides that Caesar did not succumb to the temptation of suicide following his rout in Spain. How different might history have been had Caesar believed that defeat was more than he could take and as a result taken his own life. The already volatile state of Rome would likely have erupted into total chaos and the advancements of Imperial Rome may never have occurred.

Who is to blame for the assumption that Caesar executed his campaign without obstacle if not the general himself? It was from the steps of the Capitol illuminated by forty elephants bearing lamps that Caesar summarized his experience with the now timeless "Vini, vidi, vici." Perhaps the Latin *labori* should be added to this statement so that the proclamation reads "I came, I saw, *I suffered*, and then I conquered." There is a prejudice in history to remember the legendary figures in a generous light, often shedding some of their shortcomings. Even the most cursory overview of a political campaign could never be summarized as "I came, I saw, I conquered," without accounting for the necessary obstacles that are to be incurred.

Even the mythical Cortes was not without his sensitivity. Is it strange that a man who had proven himself so bold would cry over the loss of his soldiers? Cortes was certainly courageous, he had proven himself a brilliant commander, but one should not forget that he too was human. Rather than be stunned at the loss of a few hundred men after the Aztec capital had been sacked, history students should be more appalled at the seemingly flawless progress that Cortes had made up to the altercation leaving Tenochtitlan. Not only had he been able to make allegiances with indigenous tribes and Montezuma, he had won an overmatched contest against a Spanish general Narvaez who was sent to recall him. More than a disappointment, it would seem that the conquistador's inability to leave Tenochtitlan was more of a reality check than a defeat.

Often an intermediary loss or setback can serve as a proverbial slap in the face. A smooth sailing campaign has the capacity to distort the reality of the competitiveness of the process. Cortes was able to use psychosocial factors like the myth of Quetzalcoatl to advance on the heart of the Aztec Empire with relative impunity until the fateful "noche triste." Perhaps it was necessary to confront adversity before Cortes was able to assess the true gravity of his situation. Ideally, adversity would never be encountered in a political campaign but, unfortunately, the process is rarely ideal. The best alternative is to view obstacles as surmountable and valuable lessons that can be used toward future endeavors.

Winston Churchill's administrative career spanned nearly half a century and saw remarkable ups and downs. As late as 1937 Churchill wrote an essay chronicling a legacy of mistakes which he titled "A Second Chance." He also wrote "I do not seek to tread again the toilsome and dangerous path. Not even an opportunity of making a different set of mistakes and experiencing a different set of adventures would lure me." This is only three years before Churchill rose to power and rescued the British from the grip of the Germans.

Churchill's ironic fatalism suggests that previous shortcomings do not necessarily dictate the future. Following the Dardanelles incident, the Allies were able to rally and win World War I. As per the career of one Winston Leonard Spencer Churchill, the First Lord of Admiralty who was "finished" continued to serve in various and sundry positions in the British government until being appointed Prime Minister in 1940 and leading the British and the Allied powers to a victory against the forces of tyranny once again. One of Churchill's celebrated maxims was that "nations which went down fighting rose again but those which surrendered tamely were finished."[555] There is certainly something to be said about humble determination over pride.

The reason, one might argue, that these commanders incurred intermediary setbacks is that they assumed the risks that naturally accompany any contested campaign. Any ambitious pursuit necessarily involves the possibility of failure but that is no reason to not accept the challenge. Plutarch's account of Caesar's crossing of the Rubicon suggests much more internal strife preceding the epic decision than that of Suetonius. Caesar approached the symbolic barrier and "Then, halting in his course, he communed with himself a long time in silence as his resolution wavered back and forth, and his purpose then suffered change after change." Certainly the accomplished general knew there was no guarantee that he would succeed but the risk was worth taking.

Perhaps no situation was as precarious as that of Cortes. Cortes could not have believed that even with his faith and confidence in his soldiers that he would override the immense Aztec Empire with perfect impunity. The strength of the Spanish Empire, however, was based on a propensity to take chances. One must remember that it was Ferdinand and Isabel who commissioned a sailor named Christopher Columbus to sail into the Atlantic abyss in search of a shorter route to India. The process of colonization would certainly have been more prolonged if Europeans hesitated every time there was a threat of indigenous reaction. In the case of Churchill, the PM learned many important lessons from his failure at the Dardanelles. One observance was that progress was stifled by an administration that was unable to execute decisively. Churchill suggested that:

> It is not right to condemn operations of war simply because they involve risk and uncertainty. Some operations of war can and ought to be made certainties. Others belong to the class where one can only balance the chances, and action must proceed on a preponderance of favorable chances.[556]

Perhaps the reader raises an eyebrow at the idea of "the preponderance of favorable chances." What Churchill probably means by this is that in war, like in politics, it is impossible to guarantee victory. Instead, the best thing that a campaign can do is to align all of the necessary tools and proceed with conviction. In another speech characteristic of Churchill's skepticism, the Prime Minister suggests that the likes to address perfection by its true name: perfection. Too often candidates search for the perfect solution when an adequate one will do.

**The Triumph**

A reader might contest that all of the examples chosen represent victorious campaigns and this is no coincidence. As the introductory scenario suggested, it is the conquerors that make history while the conquered fade into relative obscurity. Countless generals did not survive to tell their version (or did not have a story worth telling) at the hands of the chosen commanders. For this reason their account cannot be analyzed, nor should it. Politics is no different. Asking the random American to name a handful of former presidents will yield much better results then asking them to recount the same number of runner-ups.

It is not necessary to depict an extensive history of the accolades of Caesar, Cortes, and Churchill in order to understand the impact of their campaigns. From the beginning, all men knew that they were either going to achieve remarkable success or perish. As this chapter has demonstrated, their campaigns were calculated, courageous, and persistent. They were able to use tools analogous to those illustrated in previous chapter and in doing so achieved legendary fame. It is not, however, the fame that we are concerned with but the ability to achieve the aforementioned objectives. Before Caesar's fateful rendezvous with Brutus in the Senate Forum, the general was able to make remarkable progress in his five-year rule. Suetonius tells of Caesar's campaigns through Gaul, Pontus, Africa and Alexandria.

Triumph in issue management comes in various forms: a successful vote in a legislative committee or subcommittee; a larger number of votes with a candidate or on a ballot initiative; or a broader public awareness and participation with an issue. Just as with Caesar, Cortes, Churchill and many others, understanding the ultimate goal is imperative to achieving the ultimate victory.

# *Image Credits*

**Page**

7- "Great Wall." K. Tuck *at* http://www.sxc.hu.

16- "Network." Rodolfo Clix.

18- "Make a Deal 2." Sanja Gjenero.

24- "President Ronald Reagan." U.S. State Department.

38- "President Richard Nixon." U.S. Library of Congress.

52- "Demonstration in Washington, D.C. Justice Dept. Bobby Kennedy speaking to crowd." U.S. Library of Congress.

54- "Maslow's Hierarchy of Needs." J. Finkelstein.

57- "Zimbabwe." Office of U.S. Global AIDS Coordinator and the Bureau of Public Affairs, U.S. State Department.

64- "Ian Smith's Rhodesian front reached a settlement to allow a power sharing government with Robert Mugabe." New York State Education Department, Global History and Geography Online Resource Guide.

71- "Wooden Cross." Andrea Kratzenberg.

78- "Mongolia." U.S. State Department.

81- "Genghis Khan." Unknown artist.

85- "Peter the Great." *The New Student's Reference Work.*

88- "President Franklin Roosevelt." U.S. Department of Energy, Office of History & Heritage Resources

91- "Rene Descartes." U.S. Library of Congress.

98- "USA Puzzle." Creative Draw.

103- "Survey Results." Sanja Gjenero.

110- "Target." Eliseeva Ekaterina.

125- "Thorvaldsen Cicero." Louis le Grand.

131- "Busto di Aristotele conservato a Palazzo Altaemps, Roma." Giovanni Dall'Orto.

144- "Profile of Adam Smith." Cadell and Davies (1811), John Horsburgh (1828), or R.C. Bell (1872).

147- "Assorted capsules and tablets." Brian Hoskins.

157- "Decalogue Parchment." Jekuthiel Sofer.

*Image Credits*

159- "Illustration for Edgar Allan Poe's story 'The Cask of Amontillado'" Harry Clarke.

163- "Leviathan." U.S. Library of Congress.

171- "Gandhi Allahabad 1931." Yann Forget.

181- "Nuclear Blast at Bikini Atoll, 1954." U.S. National Park Service.

184- "Munich Agreement." Imperial War Museum, image no. D 2239.

198- "Mission Control celebrates successful splashdown of Apollo 13." NASA.

202- "dna 1." Svilen Mushkatov.

206- "Alessandro Magno." Giovanni Dall'Orto.

215- "Glacial Rapids." Gavin Mills.

220- "The Thinker, by Auguste Rodin, at the California Palace of the Legion of Honor." Andrew McMillan.

229- "US Navy SEALs Insignia." Darz Mol.

234- "Poker Chips and Cards." Lance Palmer.

245- "Satellite Antennae." Serge Timakov.

260- "Lewis and Clark on the Lower Columbia." Charles Marion Russell.

270- "Daisy Girl." CONELRAD.

273- "Boots 5." Carlos Paes.

291- "Portrait of Benjamin Franklin." U.S. Library of Congress.

297- "Abraham Lincoln." D. Van Nostrand.

305- "John Quincy Adams." U.S. Library of Congress.

310- "Official Photo of Fmr. Vice President Dan Quayle (1989-93)." Biographical Directory of the U.S. Congress.

326- "Mappa Mundi." in Jean Mansel La Fleur des Histoires. Valenciennes, 1459-1463, manoscritto, penna, inchiostro e colori su pergamena.

330- "one too many." Sanja Gjenero.

337- "John Stuart Mill."

340- "Icon Greek Mythology Odysseus Mast." Marie-Lan Nguyen.

347- "Senator Gary Hart." U.S. Congress.

355- "Baguette 3." Ove Tøpfer.

*Image Credits*

369- "Scene at the Signing of the Constitution of the United States." Howard Chandler Christy.

374- "Edison and Phonograph." Levin C. Handy, U.S. Library of Congress.

381- "11-40-5886." NASA.

384- "George S. Patton." U.S. Library of Congress.

397- "McDonald's." Alex Ling.

409- "Büste des Gaius Iulius Caesar." Archäologischen Nationalmuseum, Napoli.

416- "Marbles." Malgorzata Replinska.

*Image Credits*

# References

[1] Shirer, William L. <u>The Rise and Fall of the Third Reich: A History of Nazi Germany</u>. The Ballentine Publishing Group, 1960.

[2] "The Invasion of Russia June 22, 1941 - December 1941." <u>The World War II Multimedia Database.</u> MFA Productions LLC. 17 July 2008 <http://worldwar2database.com/html/barbarossa.htm>.

[3] "The Soviet Union and the Eastern Front." <u>United States Holocaust Memorial Museum</u>. 17 July 2008. <http://www.ushmm.org/wlc/article.php?lang=en&ModuleId=10005507>.

[4] *Id.*

[5] *Id.*

[6] *Id.*

[7] Applebome, Peter. "Busing Is Abandoned Even in Charlotte." <u>New York Times</u>. (15 Apr. 1992). 15 Aug. 2008 <http://query.nytimes.com/gst/fullpage.html?res=9E0CE0DB1139F936A25757C0A964958260>.

[8] *Id.*

[9] Rawls, John. <u>A Theory of Justice</u>. United States: Harvard University press, 1999.

[10] "The Difference Principle." <u>Political Philosophy</u>. 2 Jan. 2009 <http://www.politicalphilosophy.info/differenceprinciple.html>

[11] Freeman, Samuel. <u>Rawls</u>. New York: Routledge, 2007.

[12] Rawls, *supra* n. 9.

[13] "A Theory of Justice." <u>Wikipedia</u>. Aug. 22 2008.

[14] Anderson, Martin. "The Reagan Boom—Greatest Ever." <u>New York Times</u>. 17 Jan. 1990.

[15] "What is Reaganomics and Did It Outlive the Reagan Administration." The Hauenstein Center for Presidential Studies. 25 July 2008. <http://www.gvsu.edu/hauenstein/index.cfm?id=602EE20B-05B8-8A4D-90F298E71E800588>.

[16] "How Quickly We Forget – Economic Successes During the Reagen Administration – Column." <u>National Review</u>. 1 Aug. 1994.

[17] "Presidential Elections, 1789–2004." <u>Infoplease</u>. 25 Jul. 2008 <http://www.infoplease.com/ipa/A0781450.html>.

18 Mandell, Michael J. "Reagan's Economic Legacy," BusinessWeek Online. (28 July 2008). June 10, 2004 <http://www.businessweek.com/bwdaily/dnflash/jun2004/nf20040610_9541_db038.htm>.

19 *Id.*

20 *Id.*

21 Locke, John. "Of Political Power." Second Treatise on Civil Government. 1690. Liberty Online! 15 Aug. 2008 <http://libertyonline.hypermall.com/Locke/second/second-1.html>.

22 "For Whom Would Jesus Vote." Christianity Today. (1 Nov. 2004). 15 Aug. 2008 <http://www.christianitytoday.com/ct/2004/november/16.32.html>.

23 "Atheists Group's Head Resigns After 26 Years." New York Times. (20 Apr. 1986). 28 July 2008 <http://query.nytimes.com/gst/fullpage.html?res=9A0DE0DC1131F933A15757C0A960948260>.

24 Blanton, Dana. "More Believe in God than Heaven." FoxNews.com. (18 June 2004). 21 July 2008 <http://www.foxnews.com/story/0,2933,99945,00.html>.

25 "Poll: Religious Devotion High in U.S." USA Today. (6 June 2005), 21 July 2008 <http://www.usatoday.com/news/nation/2005-06-06-religion-poll_x.htm>.

26 *Id.*

27 Kohut, Andrew, et al. The Diminishing Divide Religion's Changing Role in American Politics. Brookings Institution Press, 2000. 195.

28 *Id.* at 4-5.

29 "Romans 8:31." The New Testament. Nashville, TN: Holman Bible Publishers, 1998. 290.

30 "Richard Milhous Nixon Quotes." QuotesHead.com. 21 July 2008 <http://www.quoteshead.com/quotes/8/richard-milhous-nixon-quotes.html>

31 Black, Earl and Merle Black. The Rise of Southern Republicans. The Belknap Press of Harvard University Press, 2002. 2.

32 *Id.* 3.

33 *Id.*

34 Frederickson, Kari. "Strom Thurmond's Mixed Record." George Mason University's History News Network. 17 Dec. 2002.

35 Truman, Harry S. Special Message to the Congress on Civil Rights. 2 Feb. 1948.

36 *Id.*
37 *Id.*
38 Boyd, James. "Nixon's Southern Strategy: It's All in the Charts." New York Times. 17 May 1970.
39 *Id.*
40 *Id.*
41 Stout, David. "Harry Dent, an Architect of Nixon 'Southern Strategy', Dies at 77." New York Times. (2 Oct 2007). 14 Aug. 2008 <http://www.nytimes.com/2007/10/02/us/02dent.html>.
42 *Id.*
43 *Id.*
44 Raspberry, William. "Reagan's Race Legacy." Washington Post. 14 June 2004.
45 CAFE Overview: Frequently Asked Questions. National Traffic Highway Transportation Safety Administration. 29 July 2008 <http://www.nhtsa.dot.gov/CARS/rules/CAFE/overview.htm>.
46 "HR 6124, Second Farm Bill 2007." Key Votes 110th Congress. "Project VoteSmart." 29 July 2008 <http://www.votesmart.org/issue_keyvote_detail.php?cs_id=20022&can_id=50722>.
47 The Blue Dog Coalition. United States House of Representatives. 29 July 2008 <http://www.house.gov/ross/BlueDogs/>.
48 "A Brief History of the Iowa Caucus." Dayton Daily News. (30 Dec. 2007). 12 Aug. 2008. <http://www.daytondailynews.com/n/content/oh/story/news/local/2007/12/30/ddn123007iowahistory.html>.
49 About the Iowa Caucuses. Iowa 2008 Caucus Project. 12 Aug. 2008 <http://www.iowacaucus.org/iacaucus.html>.
50 Benenson, Bob. "A History of Presidential Primaries: 1988." Congressional Quarterly Politics. (26 Dec. 2007). 14 Aug. 2008. <http://jjb.yuku.com/topic/215542/t/History-of-presidential-primaries.html>.
51 Dowd, Ann Reilly. "No Longer the Solid South." Fortune Magazine. (14 Mar. 14, 1988). 14 Aug. 2008 <http://money.cnn.com/magazines/fortune/fortune_archive/1988/03/14/70305/index.htm>.
52 Benenson *supra* n.50.
53 *Id.*

54 "1988: Thank You New Hampshire." Union Leader Manchester, N.H. (1 Nov. 2004). 14 Aug. 2008. <http://www.unionleader.com/article.aspx?articleId=79cd006a-04a7-4520-a2f4-e702dcd3af89>.
55 Oreskes, Michael. "After Super Tuesday; Turnout in South Seen as Boon for the G.O.P." New York Times. (10 Mar. 1988). 14 Aug. 2008 <http://query.nytimes.com/gst/fullpage.html?res=940DE2DC1E3CF933A25750C0A96E948260>.
56 Helling, Dave. "Super Tuesday Might Be Super Confusing." McClatchy Washington Bureau. (21 Jan. 2008). 14 Aug. 2008 <http://www.mcclatchydc.com/227/v-print/story/25010.html>.
57 "Super Tuesday, 1988." MacNeil Lehrer News Hour. PBS. 9 Mar. 1988. 14 Aug. 2008 <http://www.pbs.org/newshour/retro/super_tuesday_88.html>.
58 Benenson *supra* n.50.
59 Berke, Richard L. "Jackson's Triumph in South Carolina Illustrates Dramatic Change Since Vote in '84." New York Times. (14 Mar. 1988). 14 Aug. 2008 <http://query.nytimes.com/gst/fullpage.html?res=940DEED7103DF937A25750C0A96E948260>.
60 Surratt, Clark. "Gore's S.C. Delegates Stand Firm." The State. 22 Apr. 1988. Metro/Region, page 4A.
61 Corn. United States Grains Council 14 Aug. 2008. <http://www.grains.org/corn>.
62 Rohter, Larry. "Obama Camp Closely Linked with Ethanol." New York Times. (23 June 2008). 14 Aug. 2008. <http://www.nytimes.com/2008/06/23/us/politics/23ethanol.html?_r=1&oref=slogin>.
63 *Id.*
64 *Id.*
65 *Id.*
66 Brief History of the 1968 Democratic Convention. CNN-Time. 12 Aug. 2008 <http://www.cnn.com/ALLPOLITICS/1996/conventions/chicago/facts/chicago68/index.shtml>.
67 Eisele, Al. "New Hampshire 1968: A Primary That Really Mattered." HuffingtonPost. (3 Mar. 2008). 13 Aug. 2008. <http://www.huffingtonpost.com/al-eisele/new-hampshire-1968-a-pri_b_89707.html>.
68 *Id.*

# References

[69] Zoroya, Greg. "Return of U.S. War Dead Kept Solemn, Secret." USAToday. (13 Dec. 2003). 13 Aug. 2008 <http://www.usatoday.com/news/nation/2003-12-31-casket-usat_x.htm>.

[70] Brown, Drew. "Troop death rate highest since Vietnam War." Knight-Ridder Newspapers. (17 Apr. 2004). 13 Aug. 2008 <http://media.www.thetraveleronline.com/media/storage/paper688/news/2004/04/19/News/Troop.Death.Rate.Highest.Since.Vietnam.War-663723.shtml >.

[71] *Id.*

[72] Gallop, Alec, et al. The Gallop Poll: Public Opinion 2005. Rowman & Littlefield, 2006. 240.

[73] Axelrod, Alan and Charles Phillips. What Every American Should Know About American History: 225 Events That Shaped the Nation. Adams Media, 2007. 314.

[74] Maisel, Louis Sandy and Mark D. Brewer. Parties and Elections in America: The Electoral Process. Rowman & Littlefield, 2007. 274.

[75] *Id.*

[76] Palermo, Joseph A. "Here's What RFK Did in California in 1968." HuffingtonPost. (10 Jan. 2008) 13 Aug. 2008. <http://www.huffingtonpost.com/joseph-a-palermo/heres-what-rfk-did-in-ca_b_80931.html>.

[77] "United States Presidential Election 1968." Wikipedia. 13 Aug. 2008 <http://en.wikipedia.org/wiki/United_States_presidential_election,_1968>.

[78] Johnson, Haynes. "1968 Democratic Convention: The Bosses Strike Back." Smithsonian Magazine. (Aug. 2008). 13 Aug. 2008 <http://www.smithsonianmag.com/history-archaeology/1968-democratic-convention.html>.

[79] *Id.*

[80] Yepsen, David. "Caucus history: An Early Test of Strength." Des Moines Register. 12 Aug. 2008. <http://www.desmoinesregister.com/apps/pbcs.dll/article?AID=/99999999/NEWS09/41208005>.

[81] *Id.*

[82] Benenson, Bob. "A History of U.S. Presidential Primaries: 1968-72." CQ Today Online News. (26 Dec. 2007). 12 Aug. 2008. <http://www.cqpolitics.com/wmspage.cfm?parm1=5&docID=news-000002649447#>.

83 Maslow, Abraham H. "A Theory of Human Motivation" <u>Psychological Review</u> 50 (1943): 370-96.

84 "ZIMBABWE: Wives playing seductress for food." <u>IRIN</u>. (30 July 2008). 5 Aug. 2008. <http://www.irinnews.org/Report.aspx?ReportId=79529>.

85 *Id.*

86 "Economy." <u>Profile: Republic of Zimbabwe</u>. July 2008. United States Department of State, Bureau of African Affairs. 5 Aug. 2008. <http://www.state.gov/r/pa/ei/bgn/5479.htm>.

87 "Zimbabwe Knocks 10 Zeros Off Hyperinflated Currency." <u>Newsday</u>. (30 July 2008). 5 Aug. 2008. <http://www.newsday.com/news/nationworld/wire/sns-ap-zimbabwe-currency,0,3501546.story>

88 "Zimbabwe." <u>CIA The World Fact Book.</u> July 2008. The United States Central Intelligence Agency. 5 Aug. 2008 <https://www.cia.gov/library/publications/the-world-factbook/geos/zi.html>.

89 Sheeran, Josette. Statement to U.S. House of Representatives Committee on the Budget. 30 July 2008. 7.

90 "People." <u>Profile: Republic of Zimbabwe</u>. July 2008. United States Department of State, Bureau of African Affairs. 5 Aug. 2008. <http://www.state.gov/r/pa/ei/bgn/5479.htm>.

91 *Id.*

92 "Rank Order - HIV/AIDS – people living with HIV/AIDS." <u>CIA The World Fact Book.</u> 2005. The United States Central Intelligence Agency. 4 Aug. 2008 <https://www.cia.gov/library/publications/the-world-factbook/rankorder/2156rank.html>.

93 <u>World Health Statistics 2008</u>. World Health Organization. 39-45. 6 Aug. 2008 <http://www.who.int/whosis/whostat/2008/en/index.html>.

94 United States Department of State *supra* n.90.

95 *Id.*

96 *Id.*

97 *Id.*

98 <u>Winds of Change: The End of Colonialism in Africa</u>." PBS. 25 Aug. 2003. 5 Aug. 2008 <http://pressroom.opb.org/programs/windofchange>.

[99] Dixon, Robyn. "Ian Smith, 88, last white leader of Rhodesia." Los Angles Times. (21 Nov. 2007). 5 Aug. 2008 <http://articles.latimes.com/2007/nov/21/local/me-smith21>.

[100] "Smith Keeps Power in Rhodesia." BBC. (13 Aug. 1977). 5 Aug. 2008 <http://news.bbc.co.uk/onthisday/hi/dates/stories/august/31/newsid_2510000/2510755.stm>.

[101] "Exiled Mugabe Returns to Rhodesia." BBC. (27 Jan. 1980). 4 Aug. 2008. <http://news.bbc.co.uk/onthisday/hi/dates/stories/january/27/newsid_2506000/2506219.stm>.

[102] "1983: Nkoma Flees Zimbabwe 'Death Threats.'" BBC. (13 Mar. 1983). 5 Aug. 2008. <http://news.bbc.co.uk/onthisday/hi/dates/stories/march/13/newsid_2543000/2543101.stm>

[103] Talbot, Stephen. "From Liberator to Tyrant: Recollections of Robert Mugabe." PBS. (27 June 2006). 5 Aug. 2008. <http://www.pbs.org/frontlineworld/stories/zimbabwe504/profile.html>.

[104] "Zimbabwe Crisis: The Battle For Land—The Bush War." BBC News Online. (8 Aug. 2002). 5 Aug. 2008 <http://news.bbc.co.uk/2/hi/africa/594522.stm>

[105] "Who Owns the Land." BBC World News Edition. (8 Aug. 2002). 5 Aug. 2008. <http://news.bbc.co.uk/2/hi/africa/594522.stm>

[106] Talbot *supra* n.103.

[107] *Id.*

[108] *Id.*

[109] *Id.*

[110] *Id.*

[111] Wines, Michael. "Zimbabwe Takes Harsh Steps to Counter Unrest." New York Times. (2 June 2005). 6 Aug. 2008. <http://www.nytimes.com/2005/06/02/international/africa/02zimbabwe.html?>.

[112] *Id.*

[113] "Country Profile: Zimbabwe." BBC News. (22 July 2008). 4 Aug. 2008 <http://news.bbc.co.uk/2/hi/africa/country_profiles/1064589.stm>.

[114] Talbot *supra* n.103..

[115] Riechmann, Deb. "Bush Expands Sanctions against Zimbabwe," New York Sun. (25 July 2008). 6 Aug. 2008 <http://www.nysun.com/foreign/us-strengthening-zimbabwe-sanctions/82648/>.

[116] *Id.*

117 *Id.*

118 Keyes, Charley. "Bush Calls for More Pressure on Zimbabwe." CNN. (15 July 2008). 6 Aug. 2008. <http://www.cnn.com/2008/WORLD/africa/07/15/bush.zimbabwe/>.

119 *Id.*

120 "Galatians 2:1 – 21." New English Translation Bible. The Biblical Studies Foundation. 7 Aug. 2008. <http://www.bible.org/netbible/acts.htm>.

121 Top Ten Organized Religions of the World. Infoplease Almanac. 7 Aug. 2008 <http://www.infoplease.com/ipa/A0904108.html>.

122 Hulme, David. "Paul and Paula: Interview with Paula Fredriksen." Special Report: Before Christianity—A First Century Perspective. (Fall 2005). Vision.org. 8 Aug. 2008 <http://www.vision.org/visionmedia/article.aspx?id=265>.

123 *Id.*

124 *Id.*

125 *Id.*

126 "Acts 8:1-3." New English Translation Bible. The Biblical Studies Foundation. 8 Aug. 2008. <http://www.bible.org/netbible/ acts.htm>..

127 White, L. Michael. "Paul in Corinth." From Jesus to Christ: The First Christians, Paul's Mission and Letters. Apr. 1998. Frontline. 8 Aug. 2008 <http://www.pbs.org/wgbh/pages/frontline/shows/religion/first/missions.html>.

128 L.Michael White, "Controversy: Do you have to become a Jew to follow Jesus?" From Jesus to Christ: The First Christians, Paul's Mission and Letters. Apr. 1998. Frontline. 8 Aug. 2008 <http://www.pbs.org/wgbh/pages/frontline/shows/religion/first/missions.html>.

129 *Id.*

130 *Id..*

131 Bowker, John, et al. "The Jerusalem Council." The Complete Bible Handbook. London: DK Publishing Inc., 1998. 394-95.

132 *Id.*

133 "Apostolic Beheading; the Death of Paul." Glimpses of Christian History. 29 June 2001. Gospel.com. 11 Aug. 2008 <http://chi.gospelcom.net/DAILYF/2001/06/daily-06-29-2001.shtml>.

134 White *supra* n.127.

135 *Id.*

136 Johnson, Barton Warren. "Introduction to First Corinthians." The People's New Testament. St. Louis: Christian Publishing Company, 1891. 11 Aug. 2008 <http://www.ccel.org/ccel/johnson_bw/pnt.pnt0700.html>.

137 Id.

138 White *supra* n.127.

139 Ratchnevsky, Paul. Genghis Khan: His Life and Legacy. Oxford: Blackwell Publishers, 1993.

140 Grousset, Rene. The Conquerer of the World: The Life of Chingis-khan. New York: Viking P, 1944.

141 Corvisier, Andre. A Dictionary of Military History and the Art of War. Blackwell, 1994.

142 Smitha, Frank E. "Genghis Khan and the Mongols." Macrohistory and World Report. 2000. 16 July 2008 <http://www.fsmitha.com/h3/h11mon.htm>.

143 Michael C. Paul, "The Military Revolution in Russia 1550–1682", The Journal of Military History 68. 1 (Jan. 2004). 31.

144 "Peter the Great (Peter I)." History of St. Petersburg. 16 July 2008 <http://saint-petersburg.com>.

145 Abbott, Jacob. "Peter the Great: Conclusion of the Tour." The Baldwin Project. 16 July 2008 <http://www.mainlesson.com/display.php?author=abbott&book=peter&story=tour>.

146 "Peter the Great (Peter I)" *supra* n.144.

147 Anisimov, Evgenii V. The Reforms of Peter the Great : Progress Through Coercion in Russia. Trans. John T. Alexander. Danbury: M. E. Sharpe Incorporated, 1993.

148 Hughes, Lindsey. Peter the Great : A Biography. New York: Yale UP, 2004.

149 "Encyclopaedia of St. Petersburg." Population. 17 July 2008. <http://www.encspb.ru/en/index.php?level=1&kod=2803920836>.

150 Manza, Jeff. "Political Sociological Models of the U.S. New Deal." Annual Review of Sociology 26 (2000): 297-322.

151 Smith, Jean Edward. FDR. New York: Random House, 2007.

152 "C-SPAN Survey of Presidential Leadership, Performance within Context of Times." American Presidents: Life Portraits. 1999. 20 July 2008 <http://http://www.americanpresidents.org/survey/historians/performance.asp>.

[153] Clarke, Desmond M. Descartes : A Biography. New York: Cambridge UP, 2006.
[154] Finkel, B. F. "Biography: René Descartes." The American Mathematical Monthly 5 (1898): 191-95.
[155] Comte, Auguste. Course of Positive Philosophy. 1830. Lectures on Modern European Intellectual History. 10 Mar. 2008. 20 July 2008. <www.historyguide.org/intellect/comte_cpp.html>.
[156] *Id.*
[157] Randi, James. James Randi Educational Foundation. 18 July 2008 <http://www.randi.org/>.
[158] "LabWrite Glossary." 2004. North Carolina State University.
[159] Rohr, Janelle, ed. Science and Religion : Opposing Viewpoints. New York: Greenhaven P, Incorporated, 1988.
[160] Einstein, Albert. Albert Einstein- Autobiographical Notes. Ed. Phillip. A. Schilpp. Open Court Publishing Co., 1979. 8–9.
[161] The Nobel Prize in Physics 1921. Nobel Foundation. 18 July 2008 <http://nobelprize.org/nobel_prizes/physics/laureates/1921/>.
[162] Hawking, Stephen. The Universe in a Nutshell. 1st ed. Bantam Books, 2001. 31.
[163] Pickering, Mary. Auguste Comte: An Intellectual Biography, Volume I. Cambridge University Press, 1993. 566.
[164] "Diagnostic and Statistical Manual of Mental Disorders, Fourth Edition (DSM-IV)." AllPsych Online. 15 May 2004. AllPsych. 18 July 2008 <http://allpsych.com/disorders/dsm.html>.
[165] Manza, Jeff. "Political Sociological Models of the U.S. New Deal." Annual Review of Sociology 26 (2000): 297-322.
[166] Berndtson, Erkki. Behavioralism: Origins of the Concept. Department of Political Science, University of Helsinki Finland. 1997. <http://www.valt.helsinki.fi/vol/tutkimus/julkaisut/verkko/behavior.htm>.
[167] Manza *supra* n.165.
[168] "Behavioralism." Encyclopedia Britannica. 2009. Encyclopedia Britannica Online. 21 July 2008 <http://www.britannica.com/EBchecked/topic/1084717/behavioralism>.
[169] Turner, Jonathan. The Structure of Sociological Theory. Wadsworth Publishing Co., 1990. 354.

[170] The First Political Poll. 18 June 2002. Franklin & Marshall College Center for Politics and Public Affairs. 18 July 2008 <http://www.fandm.edu/x3905.xml>.

[171] Id.

[172] Squire, Peverill. "Why the 1936 Literary Digest Poll Failed." The Public Opinion Quarterly 52 (1988): 125-133.

[173] "George Gallup and the Scientific Opinion Poll." The First Measured Century. PBS. 24 July 2008. <http://www.pbs.org/fmc/segments/progseg7.htm>.

[174] George Gallup, 1901-1984. The Gallup Organization. 8 Aug. 2008 <http://www.gallup.com/corporate/21364/george-gallup-19011984.aspx>.

[175] Id.

[176] "Before & After." TIME (6 Mar. 1950). 7 Aug. 2008. <http://www.time.com/time/magazine/article/0,9171,858648-2,00.html>.

[177] About Gallup. The Gallup Organization. 8 Aug. 2008. <http://www.gallup.com/corporate/115/About-Gallup.aspx>

[178] Trochim, William. "Nonprobability Sampling." Research Methods Knowledge Base. 20 Oct. 2006. Web Center for Social Research Methods. 8 Aug. 2008. <http://www.socialresearchmethods.net/kb/sampnon.php>.

[179] Mokrzycki, Mike, and Trevor Tompson. "Cell-Phone-Only Crowd May Alter Polling." CBSNews.com. (16 May 2006). 18 July 2008. <http://www.cbsnews.com/stories/2006/05/16/ap/politics/maind8hkkfj81.shtml>.

[180] Id.

[181] Story, Louise. "Facebook is Marketing Your Brand Preferences (with Your Permission)." New York Times. (7 Nov. 2007). 18 July 2008. <http://www.nytimes.com/2007/11/07/technology/07adco.html?_r=2&oref=slogin&oref=slogin>.

[182] Kleinfield, N. R. "Targeting the Grocery Shopper." New York Times. 26 May 1991.

[183] Stephen R. Covey. The Seven Habits of Highly Effective People. New York: Free Press, 1989.

[184] Tzu, Sun. The Art of War. Transl. Lionel Giles. Forgotten Books, 2007. 21.

185 "Moral High Ground." <u>International Online Training Program On Intractable Conflict</u>. 1998. Conflict Research Consortium, University of Colorado. 29 Aug. 2008 <http://www.colorado.edu/conflict/peace/treatment/moralhg.htm>.

186 *Id.*

187 Lavine, Thelma.Z. <u>From Socrates to Sartre: The Philosophic Quest</u>. Bantam, 1985. 180.

188 Clinton, William Jefferson. Speech to 2008 National Democratic Convention. 27 Aug. 2008. 28 Aug. 2008 <http://www.huffingtonpost.com/2008/08/27/bill-clinton-democratic-c_n_121941.html>.

189 Machiavelli, Niccolo. <u>The Prince</u>. Transl. Daniel Donno. New York: Bantam Books, 2003. 95.

190 *Id.* at 62.

191 Plato. <u>Plato's Republic</u>. Trans. Benjamin Jowett. Project Gutenberg, 2008. <http://www.gutenberg.org/files/150/150.txt>.

192 Lewis, C. S. <u>Mere Christianity: A Revised and Amplified Edition, with a New Introduction, of the Three Books, Broadcast Talks, Christian Behaviour, and Beyond Personality</u>. Harper Collins, 2001. 4.

193 Smith, Adam. <u>An Inquiry Into the Nature and Causes of the Wealth of Nations: With a Commentary</u>. Plain Label Books, 1835. 10.

194 Smith, Adam. <u>The Theory of Moral Sentiments</u>. H.G. Bohn, 1853. 3.

195 *Id.*

196 "Scottish Philosophy in the 18th Century." <u>Stanford Encyclopedia of Philosophy</u>. 6 July 2005. Metaphysics Research Lab Stanford University. 8 Aug. 2008 <http://plato.stanford.edu/entries/scottish-18th/>.

197 "Analysis: Case Study—The Johnson & Johnson Tylenol Crisis." <u>Crisis Communication Strategies</u>. Department of Defense Joint Course in Communication. 29 Aug. 2008 <http://www.ou.edu/deptcomm/dodjcc/groups/02C2/Johnson%20&%20Johnson.htm>.

198 *Id.*

199 Rehak, Judith. "Tylenol Made a Hero of Johnson & Johnson: The Recall That Started Them All." <u>International Herald Tribune</u>. (23 Mar. 2002). 29 Aug. 2008 <http://www.iht.com/articles/2002/03/23/mjj_ed3_.php>.

200 Fon, Vincy and Francesco Parisi. "Revenge and Retaliation." <u>The Law and Economics of Irrational Behavior</u>. Eds. Francesco Parisi and Vernon

# References

Smith. Stanford, California: Stanford University Press, 2005. 141-168. 142.

[201] *Id.* 148.

[202] Malik, Muhammad Farooq-I-Azam. <u>English Translation of the Meaning of Al-Qur'an: The Guidance for Mankind</u>. Igram Press, 1997.

[203] Fon and Parisi *supra* n.200 at 148.

[204] Rousseau, Jean-Jaques. <u>The Social Contract, & Discourses</u>. Trans. G.D.H. Cole. London: J.M. Dent & Sons, Ltd., 1920. 15.

[205] *Id.* at 14.

[206] Thoreau, Henry David, et al. "Civil Disobedience," <u>The Writings of Henry David Thoreau</u>. Boston and New York: Houghton Mifflin Co., 1906. 356-387. 360.

[207] *Id.* at 371.

[208] Brogan, Hugh. <u>Longman History of the United States</u>. London and New York: Longman, 1985. 656.

[209] Tzu *supra* n.184 at 26.

[210] Mill, John Stuart. <u>On Liberty</u>. London and New York: Longmans, Green, and Co., 1921. 10.

[211] *Id.*

[212] Fon and Parisi *supra* n.200 at 143-44.

[213] Locke, John. <u>Second Treatise of Government</u>. Ed. C.B. Macpherson. United States of America: Hackett Publishing Co., 1980. xi-xii.

[214] Clausewitz, Carl von. <u>On War</u>. Transl. Michael Howard and Peter Paret. United States: Oxford University Press, Inc., 2007. 167.

[215] Tzu *supra* n.184 at 27.

[216] Clausewitz *supra* n.214 at 161.

[217] *Id.* at 167.

[218] *West Virginia State Board of Education v. Barnette*, 319 U.S. 624 (1943).

[219] Ducat, Stephen J. <u>The Wimp Factor</u>. Boston: Beacon Press, 2004. 89.

[220] Rosenthal, Andrew. "Bush Weak on Law, Dukakis Asserts." <u>New York Times</u>. 24 Aug. 1988.

[221] Alterman, Eric. "G.O.P. Chairman Lee Atwater: Playing Hardball." <u>New York Times</u>. (30 Apr. 1989) 2 Sept. 2008. <http://query.nytimes.com/gst/fullpage.html?res=950DE0D6173BF933A05757C0A96F948260&scp=1&sq=Atwater%20hardball%201989&st=cse>.

222 Brady, John. "I'm Still Lee Atwater." <u>Washington Post</u>. (1 Dec. 1996). 2 Sept. 2008 <http://www.washingtonpost.com/wp-srv/style/longterm/books/bckgrnd/atwater.htm>.
223 Alterman *supra* n.221.
224 *Id.*
225 Cass, Stephen. "Apollo 13 We Have a Solution." <u>IEEE Spectrum</u>. (13 Apr. 2005). 2 Sept. 2008 <http://www.spectrum.ieee.org/apr05/2697>.
226 *Id.*
227 *Id.*
228 *Id.*
229 *Id.*
230 Nixon, Richard M. Remarks on Presenting the Presidential Medal of Freedom to Apollo 13 Mission Operations Team in Houston (Apr. 18, 1970).
231 "Charles Darwin." <u>Explore Galapagos</u>. Galapagos Conservation Trust. 10 Sept. 2008 <http://www.gct.org/darwin.html>.
232 *Id.*
233 Watson, J.D. and F.H.C. Crick. "A Structure for Deoxyribose Nucleic Acid." <u>Nature</u> 171 (25 Apr. 1953). 737-38.
234 Lewis, Ricki and Bernard Possidente. "A Short History of Genetics and Genomics." <u>Celebrating 50 Years of DNA</u>. Cold Spring Harbor Laboratory. 8 Sept. 2008 <http://www.dna50.com/main.htm>.
235 Watson and Crick, *supra* n.233.
236 "Basic Genetics." <u>Building Biotechnology: The Definitive Biotechnology Industry Primer</u>. 1999. DNApatent.com. 12 Sept. 2008 <http://www.dnapatent.com/science/index.html>.
237 Lincoln, Abraham. "Letter to Horace Greeley." (22 Aug. 1862). <u>Collected Works of Abraham Lincoln, Volume 5</u>. University of Michigan Digital Library Text Editions. 389-90. <http://quod.lib.umich.edu/cgi/t/text/text-idx?q1=greeley;rgn=div1;c=lincoln;view=text;type=simple;cc=lincoln;subview=detail;sort=occur;idno=lincoln5;node=lincoln5%3A848>.
238 Lincoln, Abraham. Remarks at Second Inauguration. Mar. 4, 1865.
239 Berrigan, Joseph. "Siege of Tyre and Gaza." <u>Ancient Mesopotamia</u>. 18 Sept. 2008. <http://joseph_berrigan.tripod.com/ancientbabylon/id34.html>.

240 Churchill, Winston. <u>The Second World War, Volume II: Their Finest Hour</u>. United States of America: Houghton Mifflin Harcourt, 1985. 291.
241 Shirer *supra* n.1 at 1020.
242 *Id*. at 1025.
243 Hitler, Adolph. <u>Mein Kampf</u>. Trans. Ralph Manheim. Houghton Mifflin, 1998.
244 Cherkasov, Vitaly. "Stalin Was Preoccupied With the Role of the U.S.S.R. in the War: Victim or the Aggressor?" <u>Pravda</u>. (17 June 2002). 3 Sept. 2008 <http://english.pravda.ru/main/2002/06/17/30506.html>.
245 Shirer *supra* n.1 at 1088.
246 Bedin, David. "Theater of Operations." <u>D-Day</u>. 6 June, 2004. Sept. 3, 2008. >http://www.history-online.com/DDay/en/Theater.aspx>
247 Hammond, William M. <u>Normandy: The U.S. Army Campaigns of World War II</u>. United States Army Center of Military History, 1995. 3 Sept. 2008 <http://www.history.army.mil/brochures/normandy/nor-pam.htm>.
248 *Id*.
249 *Id*.
250 Kidder, David and Noah Oppenheim. <u>The Intellectual Devotional: Revive your Mind, Complete your education, and Roam Confidently with the Cultured Class</u>. New York: Rodale, 2006. 6.
251 Tzu *supra* n.184.
252 *Id*. at 26-27.
253 Levinthal, Daniel, A. and James G. March. "The Myopia of Learning." <u>Strategic Management Journal</u> 14 (1993): 95-112.
254 Tzu, Sun. <u>The Art of War</u>. Trans. Samuel B. Griffith. Oxford University Press: 1988. 133.
255 Machiavelli *supra* n.189 at 69.
256 *Id*.
257 Kidder and Oppenheim *supra* n.250 at 258.
258 Brogan, Hugh. <u>The Penguin History of the USA</u>. New York: Penguin Books, 1999. 592.
259 *Id*.
260 <u>Nobel Lectures, Economic Sciences 1969-1980</u>. Ed. Assar Lindbeck. World Scientific Publishing Co., 1992.

[261] Simon, Herbert A., et al. "Report on Research Briefing Panel on Decision Making and Problem Solving." <u>Research Briefings 1986</u>. Washington, D.C.: National Academy Press, 1986.
[262] Pabrai, Mohnish. <u>Mosaic: Perspectives on Investing</u>. Grammer Buff, Inc., 2004.
[263] *Id.* at 34.
[264] Hayward, Steven. <u>Churchill on Leadership: Executive success in the face of adversity</u>. New York: Gramercy Books, 1998. 48.
[265] de Bono, Edward. "Lateral Thinking." Lecture at Union Building,. Bristol University. 13 Oct. 1979. 9 Sept. 2008 <http://www.schumacher.org.uk/transcrips/schumlec-79_Bris_Lateral Thinking_EdwardDeBono.pdf>.
[266] <u>Six Thinking Hats</u>. de Bono Consulting. 9 Sept. 2008 <http://www.debonoconsulting.com/images/six-hats-brochure.pdf >.
[267] *Id.*
[268] Phillips, R. Cody. <u>Operation Just Cause: The Incursion into Panama</u>. United States Army Center of Military History, 2004. <http://www.history.army.mil/brochures/Just%20Cause/JustCause.htm#StratSet>.
[269] Department of the Army. <u>Psychological Operations, FM 3-05.30, MRCP 3-40.6.</u> Washington, D.C.: Headquarters, Department of the Army, Apr. 15, 2005. 1-8.
[270] *Id.* at 5-1.
[271] *Id.*
[272] Kuhn, Steven. "Prisoner's Dilemma." <u>Stanford Encyclopedia of Philosophy</u>. 22 Oct. 2007 . Metaphysics Research Lab Stanford University. 9 Sept. 2008 <http://plato.stanford.edu/entries/prisoner-dilemma/>.
[273] Fonseca, Gonçalo L. "Game Theory." <u>The History of Economic Thought</u>. The New School for Social Research. 9 Sept. 2008. <http://cepa.newschool.edu/het/schools/game.htm>.
[274] Markovits, Richard S. <u>Truth Or Economics: On the Definition, Prediction, and Relevance of Economic Efficiency</u>. Yale University Press, 2008. 51.
[275] Moschella, David. "Column: Each Round of Poker Could Be Bill Gates' Last." <u>Computerworld</u>. (18 Sept. 1999). 10 Sept. 2008. <http://www.computerworld.com.au/index.php/id;313050019>.

[276] Brunson, Doyle. Super System: A Course in Power Poker. New York: B & G Publishing, 2002. 28.
[277] Whyte, William. The Organization Man. New York: Doubleday, 1956.
[278] What Is Six Sigma? The Six Sigma Group. 8 Sept. 2008 <http://www.onesixsigma.com/thesixsigmagroup/What-is-Six-Sigma-18102006>.
[279] Six Sigma: What Is Six Sigma? iSixSigma. 8 Sept. 2008 <http://www.isixsigma.com/sixsigma/six_sigma.asp>.
[280] Phillips, Donald T. Lincoln on Leadership. New York: Warner Books, 1992.
[281] Id. at 137.
[282] National Commission on Terrorist Attacks Upon the United States. The 9/11 Commission Report. 22 July 2004. 415.
[283] Bondanella, Peter and Mark Musa, eds. The Portable Machiavelli. Penguin, 1979.
[284] Bellis, Mary. "The Beginning of Electronic Communications." The History of the Electric Telegraph and Telegraph: The Beginning of Electronic Communications. About.Com. 21 Sept. 2008 <http://inventors.about.com/od/tstartinventions/a/telegraph.htm>.
[285] U.S. Census Bureau. Voting and Registration in the Election of November 2006. Washington D.C.: U.S. Department of Commerce, June 2008. 2, tbl. 1. <http://www.census.gov/prod/2008pubs/p20-557.pdf>.
[286] 1948 Truman-Dewey Election. 2004. Eagleton Institute of Politics. Rutgers, the State University of New Jersey. 23 Sept. 2008. <http://www.eagleton.rutgers.edu/e-gov/e-politicalarchive-1948election.htm>.
[287] Truman, Harry S. Address at Dexter, Iowa, on the Occasion of the National Plowing Match. 18 Sept. 1948.
[288] Id.
[289] Id.
[290] Tim Jones, "Dewey Defeats Truman." Chicago Tribune (3 Nov. 1948). 23 Sept. 2008 <http://www.chicagotribune.com/news/local/chi-chicagodays-deweydefeats-story,0,5072116.story>.
[291] McLuhan, Marshall. Understanding Media: The Extensions of Man. New York: McGraw-Hill, 1964.
[292] Allen, Erika Tyner. The Kennedy-Nixon Presidential Debates, 1960. The Museum of Broadcast Communications. 16 Sept. 2008

<http://www.museum.tv/archives/etv/K/htmlK/kennedy-nixon/kennedy-nixon.htm>.

293 McLuhan *supra* n.291 at 271.

294 "Introduction." Exploring the West From Monticello: A Perspective in Maps from Columbus to Lewis and Clark. 29 Apr. 2008. University of Virginia Library. 22 Sept. 2008 <www.lib.virginia.edu/small/exhibits/lewis_clark/exploring/intro.html>.

295 McAlexander, James, et al. "Building Brand Community." Journal of Marketing 66 (2002): 38-54. 38.

296 Jefferson, Thomas. United States. Cong. Transcript: Jefferson's Secret Message to Congress. 18 Jan. 1803. 29 Apr. 2008 <http://www.loc.gov/exhibits/lewisandclark/transcript56.html>.

297 United States Bureau of Land Management. "Land Resources and Information." Public Land Statistics 2006. Apr. 2008. 29 Apr. 2008 <http://www.blm.gov/pgdata/etc/medialib/blm/wo/Business_and_Fiscal_Resources/2006_pls.Par.21111.File.dat/Part_1A.pdf>.

298 "Lewis and Clark Expedition." Encarta. MSN Encarta. 29 Apr. 2008 <http://encarta.msn.com/encyclopedia_761569929/lewis_and_clark_expedition.html>.

299 von Clausewitz *supra* n.214 at 92.

300 Tzu *supra* n.184 at 34.

301 Brasington, Jr., Larry. "Robert E. Lee: Beloved General of the South." From Revolution to Reconstruction . . . and What Happened Afterwards. 5 May 2003. University of Groningen. 7 May 2008. <http://odur.let.rug.nl/~usa/B/relee/relee.htm>.

302 "Wednesday, September 17, 1862 - the Impact of Terrain." The American Civil War: Battle of Antietam / Sharpsburg. Oct 2003. BrothersWar.com. 7 May 2008 <http://www.brotherswar.com/Antietam-13.htm>.

303 National Park Service. "Antietam." CWSAC Battle Summaries. American Battlefield Protection Program. 21 Aug. 2008. <http://www.nps.gov/history/hps/abpp/battles/md003.htm>.

304 Chew, Allen F. "Fighting the Russians in Winter: Three Case Studies." Leavenworth Papers 5. Fort Leavenworth, Kansas: Combat Studies Institute, U.S. Army Command and General Staff College, 1981. 15 May 2008 <http://www-cgsc.army.mil/carl/resources/csi/Chew/CHEW.asp>.

305 *Id.*
306 *Id.*
307 Pradesh, Andhra. "Average Annual Income of Citizen Goes Up in State." The Hindu. (20 Feb. 2007). 22 Aug. 2008. <http://www.hindu.com/2007/02/20/stories/2007022011440400.htm>.
308 Adler, Carlye. "Colonel Sanders' March on China." Time (17 Nov. 2003). 3 Oct. 2008 <http://www.time.com/time/magazine/article/0,9171,501031124-543845,00.html>
309 *Id.*
310 *Id.*
311 *Id.*
312 *Id.*
313 *Id.*
314 Cooper, Christopher and Gibbs Knotts. "Political Ads are Still Important to Democracy." Asheville Citizen-Times. 4 May 2008.
315 "Historical Timeline." The 30-Second Candidate. Wisconsin PBS. 22 Aug. 2008 <http://www.pbs.org/30secondcandidate/timeline/years/1990_c.html>.
316 *Id.*
317 *Id.*
318 *Id.*
319 Futterman, Matthew and Suzanne Vranica. "NBC Super Bowl Ads to Cost $3 Million." Wall Street Journal. 6 May 2008. 8 May 2008 <http://online.wsj.com/public/article/SB121004269277469845.html?mod=blog>.
320 Cooper and Knotts *supra* n.314.
321 de Tocqueville, Alexis. Democracy in America. Transl. George Lawrence. Ed. J.P. Mayer. HarperCollins, 2000. 279.
322 Rampton, Sheldon and John Stauber. "Silencing Spring: Corporate Propaganda and the Takeover of the Environmental Movement." Reclaiming the Environmental Debate: The Politics of Health in a Toxic Culture. Ed. Richard Hofrichter. Cambridge, MA: MIT Press, 2000. 158-59.
323 *Id.* at 159.
324 *Id.* at 159-160.
325 *Id.* at 160.

326 Herrick, James A. The History and Theory of Rhetoric. Arizona: Gorsuch Scarisbrick, 1997. 79.

327 Id. at 88.

328 Boswell, James. The Life of Samuel Johnson, LL.D. Including a Journal of a Tour to Hebrides. Ed. John Wilson Croker. New York: George Dearborn, 1835. 328.

329 Franklin, Benjamin. The Autobiography of Benjamin Franklin. New York: Dover Publications, 1996. 61.

330 Woolley, John and Gerhard Peters. "Bentsen-Quayle Vice Presidential Debate." The American Presidency Project. 20 July 2008 <http://www.presidency.ucsb.edu/showdebate.php?debateid=26>.

331 Id.

332 The Bentsen- Quayle Vice Presidential Debate. 5 Oct. 1988. Commission on Presidential Debates. 11 July 2008 <http://www.debates.org/pages/trans88c.html>.

333 "Brief Summary of Sarbanes Oxley Act of 2002." 11 July 2008. Ohio Cooperative Development Center. <http://ocdc.osu.edu/pdf/sarbanes.pdf>.

334 Id.

335 Overholt, William H. "President Nixon's Trip to China and Its Consequences." Asian Survey 7.7 (1973): 707-721.

336 Bostdorff, Denise M. "The Evolution of a Diplomatic Surprise: Richard M. Nixon's Rhetoric on China, 1952- July 15, 1971." Rhetoric & Public Affairs 5.1 (2002): 31-56.

337 Greenstein, Fred I. The Presidential Difference: Leadership Style from FDR to Clinton. New York: Simon and Schuster, 2000. 102.

338 "Abraham Lincoln and Public Opinion." Abraham Lincoln's Classroom. The Lincoln Institute. 11 July 2008 <http://www.abrahamlincolnsclassroom.org/Library/newsletter.asp?ID=124&CRLI=172>.

339 Id.

340 Goodwin, Doris Kearns. Team of Rivals: The Political Genius of Abraham Lincoln. New York: Simon & Schuster, 2005. 280.

341 Id. at 324.

342 Id. at 324-25.

343 Id. at 325.

344 Id. at 326.

# References

345 *Id.*
346 *Id.*
347 *Id.*
348 Auster, Albert. Cronkite, Walter. The Museum of Broadcast Communications. 30 July 2008 <http://www.museum.tv/archives/etv/C/htmlC/cronkitewal/cronkitewal.htm>.
349 Clark, Leslie. "Walter Cronkite." American Masters. PBS. 2006. 11 July 2008 <http://www.pbs.org/wnet/americanmasters/episodes/walter-cronkite/about-walter-cronkite/561/>.
350 Auster *supra* n.348.
351 Levitt, Steven D. "The Most Trusted Man in America (and an apology)." New York Times. (4 Nov. 2006). 30 July 2008 <http://freakonomics.blogs.nytimes.com/ 2006/11/04/the-most-trusted-man-in-america-and-an-apology/>
352 Marketing Evaluations Inc. TVQ vs. Nielsen: How Are They Different. The Q Scores Company. 2 Aug. 2008 <http://www.qscores.com/ContentPages/11/Site11/TVQ%20vs.%20Nielsen.doc.>.
353 Lowry, Brian. "Q Marks Spot in the Hunt for What Sells." Los Angeles Times. (12 Sept. 2001). 2 Aug. 2008 <http://articles.latimes.com/2001/sep/12/entertainment/ca-44798.
354 Brown, Everett S. "The Presidential Election of 1824-1825." Political Science Quarterly 40.3 (Sept. 1925): 384-403.
355 Streissguth, Thomas. Soviet Leaders: From Lenin to Gorbachev. Oliver Press: Minneapolis, 1992. 51-55.
356 Griffith, Vivé. "The Influence of Media in Presidential Politics." Think Democracy. 3 May 2004. The University of Texas at Austin. 11 July 2008 <http://www.utexas.edu/features/archive/2004/election_media.html>.
357 Wills, Gary. "The Power Populist." Time. (21 Nov., 1988). 11 July 2008 <http:// www.time.com/time/magazine/article/0,9171,968978-6,00.html>.
358 Shapiro, Walter. "The Republicans: The Quayle Quagmire." Time. 28 Aug. 1988). 25 Aug. 2008 <http://www.time.com/time/magazine/article/0,9171,968278,00.html>.
359 Lathrop, Barnes F. "Monroe on the Adams-Clay 'Bargain.'" The American Historical Review 42.2. (Jan. 1937): 273-276.
360 Lincoln, Abraham. "Letter to Edward Bates, December 18, 1860." The Complete Works of Abraham Lincoln 6. Ed. John G. Nicolay, New York:

Francis D. Tandy Company, 1894. 11 July 2008 <http://lincoln.lib.niu.edu/file.php?file=Nh662z.html>.

[361] Goodwin *supra* n.340.

[362] Rapoport, Ronald B., et al. "Do Endorsements Matter? Group Influence in the 1984 Democratic Caucuses." <u>American Political Science Review</u> 85.1 (1991): 193-203.

[363] "The 1992 Campaign: On the Trail; 'Coveted Endorsement' in a Verdant Setting." <u>New York Times</u>. (Sept. 5, 1992). 11 July 2008 <http://query.nytimes.com/gst/fullpage.html?res=9E0CEFDA143AF93 6A3575AC0A964958260#.>

[364] Ifill, Gwen. "The 1992 Campaign: Environment; Clinton Links Ecology with Jobs." <u>New York Times</u>. (23 Apr. 1992). 11 July 2008 <http://query.nytimes.com/gst/fullpage.html?res=9E0CEED7143CF930 A15757C0A964958260>

[365] Combs, James E. <u>Polpop: Politics and Popular Culture in America</u>. Popular Press: 1984. 67.

[366] Clines, Francis X. "Spiro T. Agnew: Point Man for Nixon who resigned Vice Presidency, Dies at 77." <u>New York Times</u>. (19 Sept. 1996). 11 July 2008 <http://query.nytimes.com/gst/fullpage.html?res= 9F0CE5DA1F3AF93AA2575AC0A960958260>.

[367] *Id*.

[368] "Dr. Phil McGraw, Biography (1950-)." <u>Bio. True Story</u>. 2004. A&E Television Networks. 13 Aug. 2008 <http://www.biography.com/search/article.do?id=9542524.>

[369] Wyatt, Edward. "Tolstoy's Translators Experience Oprah's Effect." <u>New York Times</u>. (7 June 2004). 13 Aug. 2008 <http://query.nytimes.com/gst/fullpage.html?res=9F07E6D81131F934 A35755C0A9629C8B63>.

[370] <u>Corporate Global Citizenship: Doing Business in the Public Eye</u>. Eds. Noel M. Tichy, et al. San Francisco: The New Lexington Press, 1997.

[371] Oshinsky, David. "McCarthy, Joseph." Feb. 2000. <u>American National Biography Online</u>. American Council of Learned Societies. Oxford University Press. 15 July 2008 <http://www.anb.org/articles/07/07-00188.html>.

[372] "McCarthyism." <u>The American Heritage Dictionary</u>. New York: Bartleby.com, 2000. <http://www.bartleby.com/61/>

[373] Plato *supra* n.191.

374 *Id.* at 2.
375 *Id.* at 203.
376 *Id.*
377 *Id.* at 327.
378 Kaplan, Robert D. Warrior Politics: Why Leadership Demands a Pagan Ethos. New York: Vintage Books, 2002. 79.
379 Thank You For Smoking. Dir. Jason Reitman. Perf. Aaron Eckhart, Maria Bello, Adam Brody, Sam Elliott, Katie Holmes, Rob Lowe, William H. Macy, and Robert Duvall. FOX, 2006.
380 Jacobellis v. Ohio, 378 U.S. 184 (1964).
381 Levitt, Steven and John J. Donohue III. "The Impact of Legalized Abortion on Crime." Quarterly Journal of Economics 116.2 (2001): 379-420.
382 Etheridge, Pat. "Nightlight May Lead to Nearsightedness." CNN. (19 May 1999). 4 Aug. 2008 <http://www.cnn.com/HEALTH/9905/12/children.lights/index.html>.
383 Wagner, Holly. "Night Lights Don't Lead to Nearsightedness, Study Suggests." Ohio State University Research News. (9 Mar. 2000). 4 Aug. 2008 <http://researchnews.osu.edu/archive/nitelite.htm>.
384 Etheridge *supra* n.382.
385 Levitt and Donohue *supra* n.381.
386 *Id.*
387 *Id.*
388 Foote, Christopher L. and Christopher F. Goetz. "Impact of Legalized Abortion on Crime: Comment." Quarterly Journal of Economics 123.1 (Feb. 2008).
389 *Id.*
390 Levitt, Steven D. "Everything in Freakonomics is Wrong!" New York Times. (28 Nov. 2005). 4 Aug. 2008 <http://freakonomics.blogs.nytimes.com/2005/11/28/everything-in-freakonomics-is-wrong/>.
391 Levitt and Donohue *supra* n.381.
392 Hieb, Monte. "Water Vapor Rules the Greenhouse System." Global Warming: A Closer Look at the Numbers. (10 Jan. 2003). 4 Aug. 2008 <http://www.geocraft.com/WVFossils/greenhouse_data.html>.
393 Mill *supra* n.210.

394 Gore, Al. An Inconvenient Truth: The Planetary Emergency of Global Warming and What We Can Do About It. Emmaus, Pa.: Rodale Books: 2006. 20-21.

395 Mill *supra* n.210.

396 Mattick, Paul. "Who Is the Real Adam Smith?" New York Times. 8 July 2001.

397 Locke, John. Second Treatise on Civil Government. 1690. Liberty Online! 15 Aug. 2008 <http://libertyonline.hypermall.com/Locke/second/second-treatise-on-govt.html>.

398 Friedman, Milton. Capitalism and Freedom. University of Chicago Press, 1962.

399 Mill *supra* n.210.

400 Hinnells, John R. The Routledge Companion to the Study of Religion. Routledge: New York, 2005.

401 Campbell, Joseph. The Hero with a Thousand Faces. New World Library, 2008.

402 Boeree, C. George. "Carl Jung." Personality Theories. 2006. Psychology Department, Shippensburg University. 4 Aug. 2008 <http://webspace.ship.edu/cgboer/jung.html>.

403 *Id.*

404 *Id.*

405 Episcopal Church Joint Commission on Marginal Readings in the Bible. The Holy Bible, Containing the Old and New Testaments. Thomas Nelson & Sons, 1903. (Luke 10:30-37) 74.

406 *Id.* at (Luke 10: 36-37) 74.

407 *Id.* at (Luke 15: 11-32) 81-82.

408 Jacques Ellul, Propaganda: The Formation of Men's Attitudes. New York: Random House Inc., 1965.

409 *Id.*

410 *Id.*

411 *Id.*

412 *Id.*

413 *Id.*

414 *Id.*

415 *Id.*

416 *Id.*

417 *Id.*

418 *Id.*
419 Leip, David. <u>Atlas of U.S. Presidential Elections</u>. 24 Jan 1999. 4 Aug. 2008 <http://uselectionatlas.org/RESULTS/index.html>.
420 Olson, Keith W. <u>Watergate: The Presidential Scandal That Shook America</u>. Lawrence, Kansas: University Press of Kansas, 2003.
421 *Id.*
422 *Id.*
423 *Id.*
424 *Id.*
425 *Id.*
426 *Id.*
427 *Id.*
428 Dionne, Jr., E.J. "Poll Gives Hart and Bush Clear Leads for Nominations." <u>New York Times</u>. (25 Jan 1987).
429 Dionne, Jr., E.J. "The Elusive Front-Runner Gary Hart." <u>New York Times</u>. (3 May 1987).
430 Polman, Dick. "Those Aren't Rumors." <u>Smithsonian Magazine</u>. (11 April 2008). 4 Aug 2008 <http://www.smithsonianmag.com/people-places/presence-200804.html?c=y&page=4>.
431 "Nixon, Dixon and Hart." <u>New York Times.</u> (16 July 1987). 10 Sept. 2008 <http://query.nytimes.com/gst/fullpage.html?res=9B0DEFD91331F935A25754C0A961948260>.
432 *Id.*
433 Miller, Matthew, ed. "Special Report: The Celebrity 100." <u>Forbes</u>. (11 June 2008). 4 Aug. 2008. <http://www.forbes.com/lists/2005/53/20CG.html>.
434 "Vick Sentenced to 23 Months for Dog Fighting." <u>CNN</u>. (10 Dec. 2007). 4 Aug 2008 <http://www.cnn.com/2007/US/law/12/10/vick.sentenced/index.html#cnnSTCText>.
435 Ledbetter, D. Orlando and Steve Wyche. "Vick Files for Bankruptcy Protection." <u>Atlanta Journal Constitution</u>. (July 8, 2008). 4 Aug 2008 <http://www.ajc.com/news/content/sports/falcons/stories/2008/07/08/vick_0709.html>.
436 "Vick Faces Prison Time after Agreeing to Plead Guilty." <u>ESPN.com</u>. (21 Aug. 2007). 4 Aug. 2008. <http://sports.espn.go.com/nfl/news/story?id=2983121>.
437 *Id.*

438 *Id.*
439 *Id.*
440 *Id.*
441 "Palmeiro Docked 10 days for Steroids." ESPN.com. (2 Aug. 2005). 4 Aug. 2008 <http://sports.espn.go.com/mlb/news/story?id=2121659>.
442 *Id.*
443 *Id.*
444 *Id.*
445 *Id.*
446 *Id.*
447 Associated Press. "McGwire Denied Hall; Gwynn, Ripken Get In." MSNBC.com. (10 Jan. 2007). 4 Aug 2008 <http://nbcsports.msnbc.com/id/16541906/site/21683474/>
448 Elstrom, Peter. "The New World Order." BusinessWeek. (13 Oct. 1997). 8 Aug. 2008. <http://www.businessweek.com/1997/41/b3548001.htm>.
449 Beresford, Dennis R., et al. Report of Investigation by The Special Investigative Committee of the Board of Directors of WorldCom, Inc. Securities and Exchange Commission, 31 Mar. 2003. 4 Aug. 2008 <http://www.sec.gov/Archives/edgar/data/723527/000093176303001862/dex991.htm>.
450 "Appeals Court Upholds Ebbers Conviction." USA Today. (28 July 2006). 4 Aug 2008 <http://www.usatoday.com/money/industries/technology/2006-07-28-ebbers_x.htm?csp=34>.
451 Beresford, et al. *supra* n.449.
452 *Id.*
453 Ripley, Amanda. "The Night Detective." Time. (30 Dec. 2002). 4 Aug. 2008 <http://www.time.com/time/magazine/article/0,9171,1003990,00.htm>.
454 *Id.*
455 "Ebbers Indicted, Ex-CFO Pleads Guilty." CNN. (2 Mar. 2004). 4 Aug 2008 <http://money.cnn.com/2004/03/02/technology/ebbers/>.
456 USA Today *supra* n.450.
457 CNN *supra* n.455.
458 Ripley *supra* n.453.

# References

459 "Jeff Deskovic." <u>Innocence Project</u>. Benjamin N. Cardozo School of Law at Yeshiva University. 11 Sept. 2008 <http://innocenceproject.org/Content/44.php>.

460 *Id.*

461 *Id.*

462 Santos, Fernanda. "Vindicated by DNA, but a Lost Man on the Outside." <u>New York Times</u>. (25 Nov. 2007) 4 Aug. 2008 <http://www.nytimes.com/2007/11/25/us/25jeffrey.html?pagewanted=1&_r=1&hp>

463 <u>Lathan v. Journal Co.</u>, 30 Wis.2d 146, 158, 140 N.W.2d 417, 423 (Wis. 1966).

464 <u>Gomba v. McLaughlin,</u> 180 Colo. 232, 236, 504 P.2d 337, 339 (Colo. 1972).

465 <u>Subway Chain Facts</u>. Feb. 2006. Subway. 8 Aug. 2008 <http://www.subway.com/Subwayroot/AboutSubway/SubwayPressKit.aspx>.

466 "2008 Global Franchise Rankings." <u>Entrepreneur Magazine</u>. 5 Jan. 2009 <http://www.entrepreneur.com/franchises/rankings/globalfranchises-115388/2008,-1.html>.

467 "Subway Chain Facts," *supra* n.465.

468 "The Subway Diet; Jared Fogle Becomes A Celebrity By Losing Weight." <u>CBS News</u>. (3 Sept. 2004) 4 Aug. 2008 <http://www.cbsnews.com/stories/2004/03/02/48hours/main603484.shtml>.

469 *Id.*

470 <u>Plessy v. Ferguson</u>, 163 U.S. 537 (1896).

471 *Id.*

472 Sophocles. "Antigone." <u>The Seven Plays in English Verse</u>. Trans. Lewis Campbell. Project Gutenberg, 2004. 11 Sept. 2008 <http://www.gutenberg.org/files/14484/14484-8.txt>.

473 Kidder, David S. and Noah D. Oppenheim. <u>The Intellectual Devotional: Revive Your Mind, Complete Your Education, and Roam Confidently with the Cultured Class.</u> New York: Rodale Inc., 2006.

474 *Id.*

475 Mondale, Walter. Democratic Nomination for President Acceptance Speech. Democratic National Convention. Moscone Center, San Francisco, CA. 19 July 1984.

476 Leip *supra* n.419.
477 Green, Joshua. "Reagan's Liberal Legacy: What the new literature on the Gipper won't tell you." <u>Washington Monthly</u>. (Jan./Feb. 2003). 11 Sept. 2008 <http://www.washingtonmonthly.com/features/2001/0301.green.html>.
478 Drum, Kevin. "Tax Cuts and Deficits." <u>Washington Monthly</u>. (16 Dec. 2004). 11 Sept. 2008 <http://www.washingtonmonthly.com/archives/individual/2004_12/005340.php>
479 Kidder and Oppenheim *supra* n.473.
480 <u>Brown v. Bd. of Educ.</u>, 347 U.S. 483 (1954).
481 Zernike, Kate. "Veterans Long to Reclaim the Name 'Swift Boat'." <u>New York Times</u>. (30 June 2008). 8 Aug. 2008 <http://www.nytimes.com/2008/06/30/us/politics/30swift.html?>.
482 Thomas, Evan. "The Vets Attack." <u>Newsweek</u>. (15 Nov. 2004). 8 Aug. 2008 <http://www.newsweek.com/id/55728>.
483 *Id.*
484 *Id.*
485 Mullikin, Thomas S. and Nancy S. Smith. "Community Participation in Environmental Protection," <u>UCLA Journal of Environmental Law and Policy</u> 21 (2002/2003): 75-95.
486 Locke, John and Quentin Skinner. <u>Locke: Two Treatises of Government</u>. Ed. Peter Laslett. New York: Cambridge UP, 1988.
487 <u>The Universal Declaration of Human Rights</u>. 10 Dec. 1948. 8 Aug. 2008 <http://un.org/Overview/rights.html>.
488 "Constitution of the United States." <u>The Charters of Freedom: A New World Is at Hand</u>. U.S. National Archives and Records Administration. 8 Aug. 2008 <http://www.archives.gov/exhibits/charters/constitution.html>.
489 The Articles of Confederation and Perpetual Union, Art. XIII.
490 "Editor's Table." <u>Harper's New Monthly Magazine</u> XXV. New York: Harper's Magazine Co., 1862. 118.
491 Madison, James. "The Federalist Paper #51," <u>The Federalist Papers</u>. New York: Penguin Books, Limited, 1987.
492 <u>The Roman Republican Constitution</u>. Classics Department, University of Texas at Austin. 18 Aug. 2008 <http://www.utexas.edu/depts/classics/documents/RepGov.html>.
493 Madison *supra* n.491.

References

494 *Id.*
495 "Communism." <u>All About Philosophy</u>. 18 Aug. 2008 <http://www.allaboutphilosophy.org/communism.htm>.
496 de Tocqueville *supra* n.321.
497 Beals, Gerald. "Be Enlightened." <u>Thomas Alva Edison</u>. 1999. Brockton Historical Society. 24 July 2008. <http://www.thomasedison.com/enlightened.html>.
498 Bellis, Mary. "George Washington Carver." <u>Inventors</u>. About.com. 24 July 2008 <http://inventors.about.com/library/weekly/aa041897.htm>.
499 Mackintosh, Barry. "George Washington Carver: The Making of a Myth." <u>The Journal of Southern History</u> 2 (1976): 507-28.
500 "The Flight." <u>Charles Lindbergh: An American Aviator</u>. Spirit of St. Louis 2 Project. <http://charleslindbergh.com/history/paris.asp>.
501 "The Plane." <u>Charles Lindbergh: An American Aviator</u>. Spirit of St. Louis 2 Project. <http://charleslindbergh.com/history/paris.asp>.
502 Einstein, Albert. "First Letter to President Franklin Delano Roosevelt." 2 Aug. 1939.
503 *Id.*
504 "The Trinity Test." <u>The Manhattan Project: An Interactive History</u>. Office of History & Heritage Resources, U.S. Department of Energy. 18 Aug. 2008 <http://www.cfo.doe.gov/me70/manhattan/trinity.htm>.
505 Garber, Steve, ed. <u>Sputnik and the Dawn of the Space Age</u>. 10 Oct. 2007. National Aeronautics and Space Administration. 18 Aug. 2008 <http://history.nasa.gov/sputnik/>.
506 Launius, Roger D., et al., eds. <u>Reconsidering Sputnik : Forty Years since the Soviet Satellite</u>. New York: Routledge, 2000.
507 Eberhart, Johnathan. "The Day the Sky Was Opened." <u>Science News</u> 122 (1982): 220-21.
508 Healey, Denis. "The Sputnik and Western Defence." <u>International Affairs</u> 34.2. (1958): 145-56.
509 Williams, David R. <u>The Apollo 8 Christmas Eve Broadcast</u>. 25 Sept. 2007. National Aeronautics and Space Administration. 18 Aug. 2008 <http://nssdc.gsfc.nasa.gov/planetary/lunar/apollo8_xmas.html>.
510 Kennedy, John F. "The Decision to Go to the Moon." Speech Before a Joint Session of Congress. 25 May 1961.
511 Dietrich, Steve E. "The Professional Reading of General George S. Patton, Jr." <u>The Journal of Military History</u> 53 (1989): 387-418.

512 Id.
513 Patton, George S., and Rick Atkinson. War As I Knew It. Boston: Houghton Mifflin Company, 1995.
514 Belachew, Mekete. "Coffee." Encyclopaedia Aethiopica. Ed. Siegbert von Uhlig. Weissbaden: Horrowitz, 2003. 763.
515 "Company Timeline." Feb. 2008. Starbucks Coffee Company. 16 Aug. 2008 <http://www.starbucks.com/aboutus/company_timeline.pdf>.
516 "Company Fact Sheet." Feb. 2008. Starbucks Coffee Company. 16 Aug. 2008 <http://www.starbucks.com/aboutus/Company_Factsheet.pdf>.
517 Moskowitz, Milton and Robert Levering. "100 Best Companies to Work for In 2008." Fortune. (4 Feb. 2008). 16 Aug. 2008 <http://money.cnn.com/magazines/fortune/bestcompanies/2008/>.
518 Howe, Walt. A Brief History of the Internet. 16 Jan. 2007. Walt Howe's Internet Learning Center. 16 Aug. 2008 <http://www.walthowe.com/navnet/history.html>.
519 Id.
520 Lashinsky, Adam. "Remembering Netscape: The Birth Of The Web." Fortune. 25 July 2005.
521 Id.
522 "World Internet Users and Population Stats." Internet Usage Statistics: The Internet Big Picture. 2008. Internet World Stats, Miniwatts Marketing Group. 18 Aug. 2008 <http://www.internetworldstats.com/stats.htm>.
523 "An Inconvenient Truth." Box Office Mojo. Internet Movie Database. 18 Aug. 2008. <http://www.boxofficemojo.com/movies/?id=inconvenienttruth.htm>.
524 Aldred, Jessica. "Timeline: Al Gore: The Life and Career of Al Gore." The Guardian. (12 Oct. 2007). 18 Aug. 2008 http://www.guardian.co.uk/environment/2007/oct/12/climatechange1>.
525 Hippocrates. "The Hippocratic Oath." Greek Medicine. Trans. North, Michael. 2002. History of Medicine Division, U.S. National Library of Medicine. 16 Aug. 2008 <http://www.nlm.nih.gov/hmd/greek/greek_oath.html>.
526 Acar, Feridun, et al. "Herophilus of Chalcedon: A Pioneer in Neuroscience." Congress of Neurological Surgeons 56 (2005): 861-67.

References 469

527 Beato, Greg. "Twenty-Five Years of Post-it Notes." The Rake. (24 Mar. 2005). 23 Aug. 2008 <http://www.secretsofthecity.com/magazine/reporting/features/twenty-five-years-post-it-notes-0>.

528 Id.

529 Id.

530 Id.

531 Portal, Jane and Qingdao Dan. The First Emperor: China's Terracotta Arm. British Museum Press, 2007. 170

532 "Mass production." NationMaster Encyclopedia. 28 Aug. 2008 <http://www.nationmaster.com/encyclopedia/mass-production>.

533 Gross, Daniel. Forbes Greatest Business Stories of All Time. New York: Wiley, 1997.

534 Id.

535 "Robert Kearns, Inventor of Intermittent Windshield Wipers and Battled Car Companies, Dies at 77." The Auto Channel. (25 Feb. 2005). 28 Aug. 2008 <http://www.theautochannel.com/news/2005/02/25/005398.html>.

536 Id.

537 Rohter, Larry. "An Unlikely Trendsetter Made Earphones a Way of Life." New York Times. 17 Dec. 2005.

538 Id.

539 O'Meara, Donna. "Kudzu." Faces: People, Places, and Cultures. (1 Apr. 2007): 6-7.

540 Id.

541 Balch, Phyllis A. Prescription for Herbal Healing : The Most Comprehensive A-Z Reference to Hundreds of Common Disorders. New York: Avery, 2002.

542 Britton, Kerry O., et al. "Kudzu." Biological Control of Invasive Plants in the Eastern United States. USDA Forest Service, 2002. 28 Aug. 2008 <http://www.invasive.org/eastern/biocontrol/25kudzu.html>.

543 "George Armstrong Custer." New Perspectives on The West. PBS. 2001. 28 Aug. 2008 <http://www.pbs.org/weta/thewest/people/a_c/custer.htm>.

544 Hickman, Kennedy. "Indian Wars: Lieutenant-Colonel George A. Custer." Military History. About.com. 28 Aug. 2008 <http://militaryhistory.about.com/od/1800sarmybiographies/p/custer.htm>.

545 PBS *supra* n.543.

546 Welch, James, et al. Killing Custer: The Battle of Little Bighorn and the Fate of the Plains Indians. W. W. Norton & Company, 2007. 302.

547 Hickman *supra* n.544.

548 *Id.*

549 Suetonius. Suetonius. Transl. John Carew Rofle. London: W. Heinemann, 1914. 45.

550 Prescott, William H. History of the Conquest of Mexico. Philadelphia: David McKay, 1892. 339.

551 Elliott, J.H. Spain and Its World: 1500-1700 . Yale University Press, 1990. 34.

552 Suetonius *supra* n.549 at 51.

553 Prescott, William H. History of the Conquest of Mexico. Philadelphia: David McKay, 1892. 596.

554 Hayward *supra* n.264. at 29.

555 *Id.* at 147.

556 Churchill, Randolph S. and Martin Gilbert. Winston S. Churchill vol. 3. Boston: Houghton Mifflin, 1966. 262.

# About the Author

As a senior environmental attorney with the Charlotte law firm of Moore & Van Allen, Tom Mullikin leads the firm's Government, Policy and Regulatory Affairs Team. His practice focuses on corporate compliance, regulatory relations and legislative representation. Tom's career spans more than twenty years and includes key legislative staff roles, direct legislative advocacy, extensive environmental legal representation and management of environmental and energy issue campaigns for industry.

Tom works with clients to address the practical social, political, and environmental impacts of climate change. He has been recognized as a Distinguished Lecturer on climate change at the Illinois' Governors State University and at Loyola University New Orleans, and presented in the University of the Ozarks Distinguished Speaker Series. He has spoken on the intersection of the economy and our environmental challenges at international conferences in Australia, Russia, and the Czech Republic, and across the United States in conjunction with industry associations and state and regional chambers of commerce.

In 2005, Tom led a team of researchers and environmental experts on an Antarctica expedition studying the effects of climate change on the polar regions. He told the story of this expedition in a video documentary, *Climate Change: Global Problems, Global Solutions*, which received widespread acclaim in both business and environmental circles, and was broadcast on New Hampshire Public Television, with a Boston-area viewership of more than 2.4 million households. He has led subsequent expeditions to the Namib Desert of Africa, the Amazon River Basin of

Peru, and the Great Barrier Reef of Australia to highlight the global effects of climate change.

Tom is the author of *Global Solutions: Demanding Total Accountability for Climate Change* and *Truck Stop Politics: Understanding the Emerging Force of Working Class America*. He has been widely published in both legal and mainstream periodicals, including *UCLA Journal of Environmental Law and Policy*, *Georgetown International Environmental Law Review*, *Campaigns and Elections Magazine*, *South Carolina Jurisprudence*, *Navigating the Government Contracts Process*, and *Vital Speeches of the Day*. Further, he has been quoted for his experience in both the law and the environment by *Los Angeles Times*, *Newsday*, *Associated Press*, *St. Petersburg (Fla.) Times*, *Charlotte Observer*, *Richmond Times Dispatch*, *Roanoke-Chowan News-Herald*, *Duluth News Tribune*, *Hibbing Daily Tribune*, *Wichita Eagle*, *Business North*, *Business News Publishing Co.*, *Rocky Mountain News*, *Salt Lake Tribune*, *Post and Courier*, *Hamilton Spectator*, *Natural Awakenings Charlotte*, and *Huntinamibia*.

Tom previously served as Chief Counsel and Vice President for Public Affairs to the largest environmental services company in the world. He has served on state legislative and congressional staff, and as an advisor and campaign manager to senior members of Congress and U.S. Presidential candidates from both the Republican and Democratic parties.

Tom formerly served with the United States Army Judge Advocate General Corps, USAR, where he served as the Assistant Staff Judge Advocate for the 360th Civil Affairs Brigade (Airborne), United States Army Civil Affairs and Psychological Operations, United States Army Special Operations Command. For his service, he was awarded, among other honors, the Meritorious Service Medal, Army Achievement Medal, and Global War on Terror Service Medal. He has also received the Order of the Palmetto, the highest civilian honor bestowed by the State of South Carolina.

www.mvalaw.com<br>www.mullikinsmaxims.com